ESSAYS ON MUSIC
IN THE BYZANTINE WORLD

ESSAYS ON MUSIC
IN THE
BYZANTINE WORLD

OLIVER STRUNK

Princeton University

FOREWORD BY KENNETH LEVY

W · W · NORTON & COMPANY · INC · *New York*

Library of Congress Cataloging in Publication Data
Strunk, William Oliver, 1901–
    Essays on music in the Byzantine world.
    Includes bibliography and index.
    1. Music, Byzantine—Addresses, essays, lectures.
2. Church music—Orthodox Eastern Church. 3. Paleography,
Musical. I. Title.
ML188.S87   783'.026'19   74-23928
ISBN 0-393-02183-1

FIRST EDITION

All Rights Reserved

Published simultaneously in Canada
by George J. McLeod Limited, Toronto

This book was designed by Andrea Clark.
The type is Garamond and Aeterna.
The book was manufactured by Haddon Craftsmen.

Printed in the United States of America

1 2 3 4 5 6 7 8 9 0

*To my colleagues past and present,
and to all my students.*

CONTENTS

FOREWORD

TWO recent essays have put into words some special qualities of
mind and spirit that distinguish the career of Oliver Strunk. In
Harold Powers's "Scholar and Teacher," prefacing the collection
of essays by colleagues offered to him in 1968, and in Lewis Lockwood's Foreword to the first volume of the present edition of his
collected papers, the figure of the man and the profile of the mind
emerge with genial clarity. The contents of the first volume in
themselves form a substantial portrait, for they display some of the
astonishing versatility and the high scholarly and musical competence that have put Strunk in a class by himself among musician-
scholars of his generation. The wide range of subjects—from the
late Middle Ages through the northern Renaissance, Palestrina,
and the works of Haydn and Verdi—cannot fail to impress. Yet
what surprises and delights the reader most is the sharpness of focus
and freshness of imagination. With a few neat intuitions and a few
deft touches Strunk always gets to the heart of a matter.

In this second volume of the collected papers the scope is quite
different though the total effect is no less compelling. The field of
inquiry shifts to what may strike the casual reader as narrow and
specialized—medieval liturgical chant, in particular the chant and
liturgy of the Eastern Orthodox church. In place of the broad
canvas and virtuoso display of varied interests found in the first
volume, there is the concentration on an austere and unspectacular
body of music that has little in common with the conventional
musical styles of the Western world. These studies in Eastern chant,
however, are the one large and unified body of work that Strunk

has produced. Representing a sustained creative endeavor that covers nearly forty years, they illumine, as nothing else can, the developing qualities of Strunk's mind, the remarkable perseverance and powers of penetration combined in him. If Volume I shows a wide-ranging brilliance, it also shows a characteristic impatience with a field once it has been fairly mastered. Volume II offers instead the core of a life's work—the one subject that captured Strunk's imagination and held it over a long period of time. To fathom the craft and intellectual artistry of this extraordinary scholar one must turn to the field that he himself has preferred.

The question will arise: Why does a scholar whose mind and ear rank with the best ever drawn into historical musicology put the major portion of his efforts into an area that on its surface seems so narrow, that offers no scope for his manifest powers with conventional musical styles, and that provides so little outlet for communication with large numbers of students and colleagues? Why does the bulk of a life's work go into this one recondite specialty? Those who know Strunk at all know that such questions are not readily put to him. And such answers as are ventured here are perhaps at odds with those he himself would give. Factors of personal taste must be involved. The eastern Mediterranean and its past still exercise fascination enough to fuel many a lifetime's endeavor. The spirit of the church and a penchant for ancient ceremonial still fuel many others. There is another personal factor—a distaste for subjects where unrefined speculation is in oversupply. Strunk's leanings are to uncluttered fields where vision can range and exciting new shapes can be discerned. He knows the crowded fields. They are handled as masterfully in the earlier volume of essays as are the less crowded ones in this volume.

Yet this explanation is not enough. Something more must urge the rejection of Western common practice as the principal field of inquiry. There are, at bottom, just two tests for the worthiness of a musicological undertaking: (1) that it be concerned with first-class music; and (2) that it be concerned with a first-class problem. Byzantine chant amply meets both tests. What Eastern church music offers a scholar of expansive capacities, beyond its exotic appeals, is a sophisticated challenge of monumental proportions. It represents a thousand years' growth of styles—a luxuriant accretion

of musical practices that flourished over vast areas of the Middle
East and that survive now in an imposing bulk of some five thousand noted manuscripts. The chants are transmitted in notations
that must be prudently converted into modern notations in order
for the underlying structures to emerge. Linked with the music are
the large sister worlds of liturgy, theology, history, literature, and
the fine arts of late antiquity and the Eastern empire, each with its
highly professional scholarly tradition. All of this touches on many
Eastern languages and peoples beyond the Greeks. Byzantine
waves also wash on Western shores, leaving traces in the musical
rites of pre-Carolingian Spain, Rome, and Ravenna; marking fundamentally the chant recensions of the Franks; and lingering finally
in pockets of the later south Italian rites.

As for the music itself, what warrant is there for describing it
as first-class? If this volume has a prime lesson, it is the unique-
ness of Byzantine chant among bodies of liturgical chant in the
rigor of its organization—in the systematic treatment of the
eight modes, the characterization of individual modes, the deli-
cately worked accommodations between psalm cadences and
hymn openings, the fine distinctions maintained between styles.
Byzantine composition is an exercise of craft that regularly
touches the level of high art in the subtlety of its centonate
procedures, the responsiveness of musical fabric to text prosody,
the sense of style intimately tied to elegant details. None of this
is surprising. All that is best of late ancient and early medieval
culture is epitomized at Byzantium. The chants represent the
same high ideals as do the mosaics of Karieh Djami, the minia-
tures of the Menologion of Basil II, or the dome of Hagia
Sophia. Between the fourth and ninth centuries, the music of
Byzantium is the pace setter for musical styles in Western Chris-
tendom. It is the model when the West goes about ordering its
"Gregorian" chants in the later eighth century. Even when the
Byzantine political decline sets in with the thirteenth century
the musical styles are embarking on fresh explorations that carry
them forward as living art into the eighteenth century. This is a
late flowering denied the monodic styles in the West.

Thus our questions return. Does one have in Byzantine chant a
first-class problem and first-class music? Or, better yet, can a concern for first-class musical scholarship be incompatible with a con-

cern for these artfully structured and culturally powerful styles? In short, can a challenge like this one be ignored?

Students occasionally observe that Professor Strunk's literary presentations are uncommonly compressed, sometimes making for slow comprehension even after repeated readings. One has only to sample a few sentences in this book to see that Strunk's prose style is of a wholly different order than the general run in professional journals. Its difficulties, however, lie rather in the habits of readers than in any obscurities of the style itself. There are really two issues here—one, the style; the other, the preparation asked of the reader by an out-of-the-way subject matter. Concerning the style, Strunk's presentations are invariably models of clarity and economy. He has a lively distaste for discussions that straddle issues and stir theories about without a solid result in sight. And he has no use for prose that is wordy, or laden with conditionals, or that makes its points with rhetoric instead of reasoned sequence. Strunk writes a lean prose muscled with cogent fact and salted with applications of the *mot juste*. Partly masking the taughtness of logic, data, and word, however, is an extraordinary flair for the graceful turn of phrase. The casual elegance of this language sometimes catches a reader unawares. Carried along on its flow, one may not notice that the clockwork-tight content is slipping by. The arguments here are precise and subtle. Their illuminations must be savored at tempo andante, never allegro or presto.

Now must these papers be read only after a large store of outside fact and concept has been laid up? For articles on medieval music this is too often the case. For these, the answer is no. The field of Christian chant and liturgy has a large and precise technical vocabulary. Yet it is a matter of obvious pride with Strunk to include within each article all of the special information needed by the novice. There is some natural continuity between articles—one that reflects the widening of Strunk's grasp and the growth of the field itself. This is particularly noticeable here, with the articles collected in the order of composition. In each there is the overriding concern for getting matters straight—not just straight in themselves, but for the reader as well. No factual or logical steps are missing. The deft explanation is always at hand to render the exercise complete. Yet, again, these are not materials for speed reading.

They have to be taken with the sustained awareness that every word counts.

What this book offers, then, is witness of an extraordinary scholar's ability to penetrate time and again, and in a manner that radiates effortlessness, to the heart of complex and provocative musical matters. Strunk has the legendary "nose" for the essential. Coupled with the clarity of mind and resourcefulness of imagination that this betokens are his gifts for elegant and compelling presentation. With him, intellectual control and verbal style are essentially one. Those who on occasion receive his incisive, stylish letters on professional or scientific matters know that his masterful co-ordination of language and subject matter has for decades been attained simply by dictating to a secretary. The grand lines of an article's structure as well as the details of literary composition are settled in his mind before they go down on paper. The first draft is by and large the final draft. Such facility is granted only to a happy few.

The polished essays in this book, while they may on their face address the musicologist, Byzantinist, or humanist, are in the larger sense an invitation to anyone who relishes superior intellectual fare. The subjects are not everyday but the treatments are self-explaining, and a newcomer can pick up any article with confidence that full understanding is possible if it is read at a pace appropriate to the care lavished on it by its author. The rewards for such industry are considerable. There are too few worthy occasions to exercise the mind. There are too few examples of first-class subjects treated in a first-class way for anyone to ignore the rich satisfactions gained from an exposure to examples like these.

KENNETH LEVY

Princeton, New Jersey
May, 1974

PREFACE

SHORTLY after I began teaching at Princeton in the fall of 1937, I received a call from my colleague Albert M. Friend, Jr., Marquand Professor of Art and Archaeology, later director of the Dumbarton Oaks Center for Byzantine Studies in Washington. Through his younger associate, Professor Kurt Weitzmann, Friend had secured from Mount Athos complete photographs of an illustrated Byzantine choir book, and of this he was planning an edition in facsimile. The primary interest of the manuscript was art historical; the quality and quantity of its illustrations made it a unique document. Yet it was only incidentally a picture book; its actual purpose was practical—to provide the members of a medieval Byzantine choir with the texts and melodies they would need from day to day in their celebration of the Office. With this in mind Professor Friend invited me to collaborate with him, and although it meant taking on a task for which I was almost totally unprepared, I rashly accepted.

It has seemed to me that I could not introduce this volume more fittingly than by invoking the names of Professors Friend and Weitzmann, the men who first aroused my interest in Byzantium and helped me to realize the enormous possibilities of Byzantine music as a field of study. Without their encouragement I might never have begun; without the force of their example I would surely not have persevered. Music historians have much to learn from art historians, I have found. With Friend and Weitzmann at my side I soon came to realize that, in early Christian music as in early Christian art, one must begin in the East, above all in the

Greek-speaking East, if one's aim is full understanding of the music or the art of the medieval West. And if this preface and the essays that follow it serve their purpose, the reader will come to share that realization with me together with the further realization that Byzantine music is in itself a subject worth studying, with an importance and a fascination of its own.

The prevailing political climate did not favor our enterprise. Sealed off from Europe by the war, I lacked the resources I needed to make comparisons. Of the hundreds of extant manuscripts with which our photographs might have been compared, not one was held in the United States, although one had been published in facsimile in 1935 and although single folios from a few others were available, chiefly in paleographic albums. That was all, and, as I reluctantly concluded, it was not enough. In wartime one must make do with what one has. The larger project was accordingly laid to one side in favor of lesser ones to which the resources at hand lent themselves more readily. And when the war ended and I could again visit libraries abroad, one absorbing new problem after another challenged my attention and the original plan was, for the moment, lost from sight.

In my paper for the Oxford congress I have spoken of the year 1950 as constituting a sort of turning point for research in Byzantine music. What was true of the research as a whole was also true of my own involvement in it. Until 1950 I had been obliged to work almost entirely from facsimiles and a limited stock of photographs; now I could at last begin to build up a familiarity with the principal sources at firsthand. Thanks to the extraordinary kindness of Father Lorenzo Tardo of Grottaferrata and to the warm welcome extended to me by his younger disciple, Father Bartolomeo Di Salvo, I could spend part of the summer of 1950 in the library of the Badia greca in the Alban hills, and between 1951 and 1958, with help from my university and from the John Simon Guggenheim Foundation, I could also visit Messina, Mount Athos, Athens, Patmos, and Mount Sinai. In the meantime the American expeditions to Jerusalmen and Sinai had placed microfilms of more than 1,750 Greek manuscripts at the disposal of interested scholars; more recently a similar project, initiated by the Institute for Patristic Studies in Salonica, has begun microfilming the manuscripts of the Athos monasteries. Never again will students of Byzantine chant be forced to contend with difficulties of the sort that confronted me in those early years or that had confronted my older fellow workers from the very beginning.

In principle, the essays in this volume are printed in the order in which they were written. Yet no reader need begin at the beginning, and those to whom the whole subject is entirely new will probably do best to begin with the longer essay placed arbitrarily at the end although it was actually written before the essays for Bari and Bucharest—the broad summary written for K. G. Fellerer's *Geschichte der katholischen Kirchenmusik,* the original English text of which is here substituted for the German translation published by the Bärenreiter-Verlag. Addressed primarily to readers interested in the music of the Western rites, this essay assumes only that such a reader may be tempted to dip into an account of parallel developments in the Eastern empire provided it is written in language that he can understand. Chiefly because it is a summary, but also because it is accompanied by an extensive bibliography, I have printed it out of order, making it an exception to my general rule.

A further exception, this time to another general rule of mine, is the essay with which the volume opens. Its argument is not easily followed, and as originally printed it was made still less so by my vain attempt to solve the typographical problem in which I had involved myself. Reluctant as I am to tamper with a text already in print, I have, in this instance, allowed myself to insert an additional paragraph which, without affecting the substance of the argument in any way, permits a drastic simplification of the typography, making the essay distinctly easier to read. At bottom, "The Tonal System of Byzantine Music" is an outgrowth of my unwillingness to accept as axiomatic a set of widely accepted assumptions without knowing why I was justified in doing so. The essay seeks to answer that question, and in its day it may have served a useful purpose. But since the demonstrations by Wellesz and Handschin that certain Byzantine melodies, their texts translated into Latin, are transmitted in diastematic Western neumes, the question no longer calls for an answer. Like Rosetta stones, the antiphons "O quando in cruce" and "Veterem hominem" answer it for us, and the reader will discover that in my essay for Fellerer I have been able to dispose of it quite simply.

The three essays that follow "The Tonal System" were also written before I could begin working with manuscripts in Europe. This is already sufficiently evident in "Intonations and Signatures of the Byzantine Modes"; it becomes still more so in my little contributions to the symposium at the Temple Emanu-El and to the International Congress for Sacred Music in Rome. Byzantine psalmody and the classification and development of the early Byzantine notations are problems that cannot be presented profitably until the essential sources have been identified and studied; since 1950 these problems have never ceased to concern me, but it was years before I could confidently return to either one. Even so, the two little papers touch on ideas that I was later to develop, and without specifically locating them they at least refer to two of the key sources—Iviron 985, which I knew at the time only from the description in the Lambros catalogue, and the Carbone Menaia, a few thought-provoking photographs from which had been published without comment by Fathers Petrescu and Tardo.

At this point I can perhaps afford to abandon my running commentary, for insofar as the remainder of the volume is concerned the commentary is, as a rule, built in. Inevitably I have found myself obliged to return again and again to certain basic topics, and when a correction or an amplification of an earlier essay seemed called for, I have usually made it in a later one. Further correction or amplification here would be inappropriate.

Until now, only a very few of these essays have been published in the United States. Not previously published anywhere in any form is the essay on the music of the kontakion; previously published only in a fourteen-line abstract is the one dealing with the Italo-Greek tradition. Previously published only in Italian translation are the essays commenting on a passage from the papal encyclical "Musicae sacrae disciplina" and on the edition of the Oktoechos brought out by Father Lorenzo Tardo. Like the essay for Fellerer, the appraisal of the two choir books at the Chilandari monastery has previously been published only in German translation; for this I have preferred to print the original English text of the abbreviated version from which the translation was made, and I am printing it exactly as I read it in Bratislava in early August, 1964, at a symposium on the beginnings of Slavic music. Not included here is the essay "A Cypriot in Venice," already reprinted in my

Essays on Music in the Western World. Also not included are two longer contributions of mine to the series Monumenta musicae byzantinae, useful only when accompanied by the hundreds of plates to which they refer—the introductions to the *Specimina Notationum Antiquiorum* and to the edition in facsimile of the Triodion Vatopedi 1488, prepared in collaboration with Enrica Follieri.

If the reader follows my earlier suggestion and begins with the essay for Fellerer, he will find that from time to time I have drawn attention to the dependence of Western liturgical music and practice on the liturgical music and practice of the East and to the many ways in which the two phenomena resemble one another. Thus what is relatively familiar becomes a point of departure for what is less so, an entering wedge opening up territory the reader has still to explore. Here and there, as in the close parallelism of the Greek and Latin orders of Mass or in the virtual identity of the two responsorial practices, the dependence is perhaps deceptive and more probably to be understood as an indication of common origin. In other instances—for example, in those involving bilingual singing or in the rites formerly celebrated at the Lateran during Easter Week—the Greek language is joined with the Latin in order to typify symbolically the ecumenical universality of the Christian faith. With the same purpose in mind the Eastern church still reads the Easter gospel in as many languages as can be managed, just as in the Western world, at the dedication of a church, rubrics once prescribed that the officiating bishop should trace with his staff, in sand strewn upon the pavement, the Greek and Latin alphabets intersecting in the form of a cross, or again as the Ordines Romani, in setting forth the rite of baptism, once called for the singing of the creed in Greek and Latin by an acolyte. But where the Latin rites have translated, paraphrased, or imitated Greek texts that are neither scriptural, as with the Alleluia verses, nor doctrinal, as with the creed, the case is entirely different. How frequently this has happened we have barely begun to learn, yet even the few instances touched on in the essays that follow can teach us that the Western world was sufficiently familiar with Byzantine ecclesiastical poetry to admire and seek to recapture its formal symmetry, its eloquence, and its vivid imagery. So far as we can at present determine, this sort of indebtedness seldom extended to Byzantine melody, but even

here there were exceptions and they were doubtless more numerous than we think.

At the same time there are differences as well as resemblances,
and in defining a less familiar phenomenon in terms of a more
familiar related one, they too will need to be considered. To begin
with the canonical hours, the correspondence of this cycle in the
several Latin rites to the Greek cycles is minimal and largely
confined to the most venerable elements. Utterly different from
any Western distribution of the psalter are the Byzantine distribu-
tions, whether monastic and Palestinian, or "ecclesiastical" and
Constantinopolitan. In the West the antiphons attach themselves
mainly to the psalms of the cursus; in Byzantium, just the other
way, the troparia are sung with the Ordinary psalms of the Orthros
and Vespers or with Ordinary or Proper verses while the psalms
of the monastic cursus have only Alleluia refrains. In the West it
is the music of the Mass that is the richest and most highly developed; in Byzantium it is the music of the Office. Peculiarly Byzantine is the tendency to rely on oral tradition where the melodies
affected were held to be generally known.

Thus West illumines East, and East illumines West. Indeed, the
reader will find that certain basic phenomena in the music of the
medieval West cannot really be understood at all without some
familiarity with the comparable phenomena in the East. The meaning of the eight-mode system, the normalizing of syllabic and melismatic psalmody, the technique of centonization—these things reveal themselves more readily or are more readily studied in the
music of Byzantium than in that of the Western world. To say that
the study of Byzantine chant is the best and simplest preparation
for the study of the chants of the Latin rites is a paradox, a seeming
absurdity that is literally true.

In the course of my more than thirty-five-year involvement with
the study of Byzantine music I have been assisted in any number
of ways by any number of generous people. I am grateful to them
all, and in the essays that follow I have thanked a good many of
them individually, some of them repeatedly. Here I can mention
only a very few—Professor Ernest W. Saunders of the Garrett
Biblical Institute; the Abbé Marcel Richard of the Centre national
de la recherche scientifique, now retired; Professor Linos Politis of
Salonica; Mr. Georgios Kournoutos, the former curator of manu-

scripts at the National Library in Athens; Professor Nikolai Uspensky of the Leningrad Theological Academy and Seminary; and
the librarians of the many monasteries whose hospitality I have
been fortunate enough to enjoy, in particular Father Panteleimon,
the librarian of the Great Laura at the time of my visits there in
1953 and 1955, and Father Marco Petta, the librarian of the Badia
greca di Grottaferrata.

More than to anyone else, however, I am indebted—and deeply
indebted—to those distinguished scholars, my immediate pre-
decessors, to whose earlier writings I owe my first introduction to
the study of Byzantine music and with whom it was later my privilege to collaborate. Thanks to these men and to the solid foundations they laid down, I need not apologize for this volume's many
omissions or for its lack of continuity. They are deliberate. To the
heroic achievements of H. J. W. Tillyard and Father Lorenzo Tardo
I have paid tribute in two of the essays that follow. From Carsten
Høeg, founder of the Monumenta musicae byzantinae, I have perhaps learned most of all, although in 1958 the state of his health
prevented our meeting as often as I should have liked during the
months I spent in Copenhagen at his invitation. He was kindness
itself, a born teacher from whom one could learn even when one
disagreed, original, independent, quick to question received opinion, one who thought things through, self-confident but with confidence also in those whom he admired. And to Egon Wellesz we
owe an immense debt. The first to recognize and state the case for
the study of Byzantine chant as a field of music-historical research,
the one musicologist on Monumenta's original board of editors,
Wellesz was in the strictest sense of the word a founder. His death
in Oxford on November 9, 1974, marked the end of an era.

Nothing can be more heart-warming to a man who has spent a
good many years in teaching than to follow or look back upon the
brilliant careers of the talented younger men whom it has been his
good fortune to have as students. He doubts, of course, that he
really taught them anything, but he is naturally gratified when he
discovers that they believe he did and that they insist upon saying
so. While disclaiming any responsibility for the far too generous
things they have said, I have concluded that I ought to allow Lewis
Lockwood and Kenneth Levy to say what they pleased in their
forewords, for I am deeply grateful to them both for all that they

have done for my two volumes. And with editorial work on this second volume in the final stages, when failing eyesight made it impossible for me to do anything further for it, two capable colleagues from the University of Rome came providentially to my rescue—Ariella Lanfranchi, of the Istituto di Storia della Musica, and Enrica Follieri, of the Istituto di Filologia Classica. To them, for their readiness to help and for their devoted application to the task they had taken in hand, my warmest thanks. Acknowledgment is due also to Norton's music editor, Claire Brook, for the careful attention she has given to an assignment that has involved a great deal of transatlantic correspondence, for her interest, her patience, and her resourcefulness.

OLIVER STRUNK

Rome, Italy
April, 1976

ESSAYS ON MUSIC
IN THE BYZANTINE WORLD

THE TONAL SYSTEM OF BYZANTINE MUSIC[†]

T HE present studies offer the results of preliminary investigations undertaken in connection with a projected edition, in facsimile, of an illustrated MS from Mount Athos, the early 13th-century Sticherarion Koutloumousi 412, to be published within the next year or two by the Princeton University Press under the editorship of Professor A. M. Friend, Jr., of the Department of Art and Archeology, Princeton University, with the collaboration of the author. The first of the three studies deals with the tonal system underlying the medieval Byzantine chant and attempts to show—on the basis of literary and musical evidence, and without resort to analogy—that this system is a wholly diatonic one, its central octave lying between D and d; the second will deal with the Byzantine formulas of intonation and the modal signatures, the third with the psalm-tones of the Eastern Church.

The conclusions reached in this first study are in themselves not new. They have indeed been widely accepted from the first. Yet it must be said that the arguments brought forward in their support by Riemann, Thibaut, Fleischer, Tillyard, Wellesz, and Gombosi have not entirely dispelled the last remaining doubt and are perhaps in part responsible for the skepticism with which the subject as a whole is often still regarded.[1]

†From *The Musical Quarterly*, XXVIII (1942), 190–204; read at a meeting of the Greater New York Chapter of the American Musicological Society on May 17, 1940. Reprinted with permission of G. Schirmer, Inc.
    [1]See, for example, A. J. Swan, "The Znammeny Chant of the Russian Church,"

This study, then, is a reopening of the question. If its conclusions are old, its basis, at least, is new. It makes no attempt to reconcile the modal systems of medieval and ancient Greek music. For the old hypotheses—that the Byzantine chant is diatonic and that the tone D is the point of departure for its modal system—it substitutes two simple propositions regarding the tetrachord and the tritone. Aside from this, it attempts to settle the question of chromatic alteration and to show the reasonableness of certain observed procedures not previously understood.

As set forth by the author or authors of our principal literary source, the Papadike,[2] the theoretical starting-tones of the four authentic modes form an ascending series,[3] the theoretical starting-tone of Mode II lying one step above that of Mode I, the theoretical starting-tone of Mode III lying one step above that of Mode II, the theoretical starting-tone of Mode IV lying one step above that of Mode III. On ascending a step further, the theoretical starting-tone of Mode I recurs and a new ascending series begins. Four steps below the theoretical starting-tone of any authentic mode lies that of its plagal. As set forth in the Papadike, these tones form a descending series, the theoretical starting-tone of Mode III Plagal lying one step below that of Mode IV, the theoretical starting-tone of Mode II Plagal lying one step below that of Mode III, the theoretical starting-tone of Mode I Plagal lying one step below that of Mode II. On descending a step further, the theoretical starting-tone of Mode IV Plagal recurs and a new descending series begins.[4] These relationships, it may be added, are not only fully and

in *The Musical Quarterly*, XXVI (1940), 233–234, where it is held that the nature of the Byzantine chant has still to be "definitely established" and that "time and further exploration have yet to vindicate" the findings of Wellesz and Tillyard.

[2]Among the published texts, only Codex Barberini, Gr. 300 (Lorenzo Tardo, *L'antica melurgia bizantina* [Grottaferrata, 1938], pp. 151–163) and Codex Chrysander (Oskar Fleischer, *Neumen-Studien*, III [Berlin, 1904], 37–38) contain full statements of the Byzantine theory of the modes. Codex Barberini gives the better text; Codex Chrysander has, here and there, a helpful amplification.

[3]This first requirement alone is enough to invalidate the elaborate construction of Petrescu *(Les idiomèles et le canon de l'office de Noël,* [Paris, 1932], pp. 15–22), according to which, to put it bluntly, Mode I is a D mode, Mode II a C mode, Mode III a transposed A mode, Mode IV a transposed G mode, while Mode III Plagal is made a low G mode with B as "intense" final.

[4]In conclusion, Codex Chrysander adds this comment: "So it is, even if you descend a hundred steps or ascend again as many more."

clearly set forth in the text of the Papadike; they are also graphically represented, usually in the form of a tree or wheel.[5]

To the eight starting-tones and their recurrences at the fourth step above or below correspond the basic signatures of the eight modes, the Greek letter-numerals α, β, γ, and δ, conventionalized and combined with certain step signs, representing the theoretical starting-tones of the four authentic modes, the same letter-numerals, with the qualifying prefix $\pi\lambda$, again combined with certain step signs, representing those of the plagal.[6] For teaching purposes, these basic signatures are used as a sort of alphabetical (or, strictly speaking, numerical) notation, authentic signatures representing ascending progressions, plagal signatures descending ones.

As implied by the foregoing, the tonal system of Byzantine music centers in a series of eight pitches arrived at by combining disjunctly two similar tetrachords. As an ascending series, these eight pitches are written:

as a descending one:

In each of the eight modes the basic signature remains invariable, consisting always of the same conventionalized letter-numeral combined with the same step signs. Here we are concerned only with the basic signatures; this being the case, it will make for easier reading and vastly simplify the typography if, in what follows, we eliminate the step signs entirely and substitute for the conventionalized letter-numerals the familiar ones of the standard Greek alphabet.

The precise nature of the steps within the two series, ascending and descending, remains for the present unknown; for all that we can learn from the Papadike, the step α to β may be a whole tone, a half tone, or some other larger or smaller interval. All we know is that the sum total of the seven steps (the interval from α of the lower tetrachord to δ of the upper, or from $\pi\lambda$ δ of the upper to $\pi\lambda$ α of the lower) is an octave.[7] If we may assume, however, that

[5]See, for examples, Tardo, *op. cit.,* pp. 258–260.

[6]Mode III Plagal is represented by an abbreviation of the word $\beta\alpha\rho\acute{\upsilon}\varsigma$ (low), combined as usual with a step sign.

[7]On descending seven steps from α, runs a comment of the Codex Chrysander, one finds $\pi\lambda$ α which, as a result of having sounded the seven steps one after another ($\H{0}\varsigma$ $\dot{\alpha}\pi\grave{o}$ $\kappa\tau\acute{\upsilon}\pi\sigma\upsilon$ $\delta\iota\grave{\alpha}$ $\tau\grave{\eta}\nu$ $\dot{\epsilon}\pi\tau\alpha\varphi\omega\nu\acute{\iota}\alpha\nu$), is the same as α.

the interval α to δ is a perfect fourth—a reasonable assumption, to say the least, for a tetrachordal system based on any other interval is virtually inconceivable[8]—the interval δ to α, as the difference between an octave and two fourths, becomes a whole tone and the remaining intervals fall readily into line.

Provided it be based on the perfect fourth, a tetrachordal system involves perfect fifths between the corresponding pitches of adjacent disjunct tetrachords, perfect fourths between the pitches of adjacent conjunct ones, these intervals remaining constant no matter what the division and internal structure of the tetrachord itself may be. Conversely, a system of disjunct tetrachords produces unequal fourths, a system of conjunct tetrachords unequal fifths; or, to put it differently, the fourth is the critical interval in a disjunct system, the fifth in a conjunct one.

Applying these general truths to the central octave of the Byzantine tonal system, we may conclude that, provided the interval α to δ be a perfect fourth, all four intervals of the type α to α will be perfect fifths. Aside from this, we may conclude that the succession of fourths β to α, γ to β, and δ to γ will present some irregularity. If the division of the tetrachord be diatonic, two of these intervals will be perfect fourths while a third will be a tritone; if the division be chromatic, two intervals will be tritones while a third will be an interval consisting of a whole tone plus two half tones (equals major third); if the division be enharmonic, two intervals will be of the type augmented fourth plus quarter-tone while a third will be an interval consisting of a whole tone plus two quarter-tones (equals minor third). As

---

[8]If we assume an augmented fourth, the interval δ to α disappears altogether, leaving the tetrachords conjunctly combined; if we assume a diminished fourth, the interval δ to α becomes the equivalent of a major third, the division of the tetrachords a chromatic or enharmonic one, leaving us with octaves of the general type:

½	½	1	2	½	½	1
¼	¼	1½	2	¼	¼	1½

The result is a shift of interest, as it were, from the two tetrachords to the single connecting interval; to recognize the absurdities to which this leads, one need only construct the octave species. A further diminution of the interval between the "standing tones" only heightens the absurdity.

before, these intervals will remain constant no matter what the internal structure of the tetrachord may be.

Now we should be able to assume that in vocal music the more complex fourths occurring in the several genera will be in principle avoided as direct leaps. If this be granted, it follows that, in a system of disjunct tetrachords, the division of the tetrachordal unit will be reflected in the rejection of one or more of the possible fourth leaps and in the acceptance of others. Where several leaps are rejected, the division will remain in doubt; where only one is rejected, we shall have no choice but to infer a diatonic division, and in such a case the internal structure of the tetrachordal unit will be easy to determine, for the rejected fourth will obviously mark the position of the half-tone.

Turning now to the Byzantine melodies themselves, we find the fourths α to δ, β to α, and δ to γ in regular and constant use—for the most part in characteristic, recurrent situations, the fourth γ to β deliberately avoided, its rare occurrences far too infrequent to justify a further reservation.[9] We can only infer a diatonic division of the basic tetrachord, and, since the rejected fourth lies between the third step of the lower tetrachord and the second step of the upper, the internal structure of the tetrachordal unit is obviously whole tone, half-tone, whole tone. The central octave of the Byzantine tonal system has then the relative pitches of our white-

---

[9]In the 86 "November Hymns," as transcribed by Tillyard for the Monumenta Musicae Byzantinae, Transcripta, 2 (Copenhagen, 1938), the fourth occurs as a direct leap well over 600 times. Of these leaps, nearly 300 represent the interval δ to γ, more than 200 the interval α to δ, nearly 200 the interval β to α. The leap γ to β occurs only in Mode I, authentic and plagal, and is found three times in all —once in Hymn 31, line 9, once in Hymn 40, line 5, and once in Hymn 81, line 5. In all three cases the situation is the same—a medial cadence in Mode III is approached by way of the figure $\delta\gamma\beta$. The progression obviously calls for the flat which Tillyard supplies and is doubtless to be understood as a transposition of the extremely common pattern $\alpha\delta\gamma$, properly of Mode II, authentic and plagal, as seen in Hymn 7, line 5, Hymn 9, line 3, and elsewhere.

It goes without saying that there are among the more than 3,000 melodies of the Sticherarion and Heirmologion many other examples of the tritone as a direct leap, and that some of these may very well occur in situations other than the one just described. A considerable number prove, however, to be mere text variants to which no real importance need be attached; for examples, see the musical illustration published at the end of this study, variants 1 and 2.

In the figures just given for the November Hymns are included not only those leaps which lie within the central octave but also those involving one or more tones which lie beyond it, above or below.

key scale D to d. The actual substitution of these absolute pitches in transcription yields a result virtually free from accidentals, lying for the most part well within the range of the average voice. We need no longer hesitate to make it.

Ex. 1

The demonstration just offered involves at least one important corollary which, for systematic reasons, might well be touched on here. If, in Byzantine melody, the fourth γ to β is deliberately rejected as a direct leap, but as deliberately accepted as an indirect one (accepted, that is, when altered by the interpolation of δ or α or both), it should follow that the leap is regarded as objectionable only in its direct form. Where the interval is "saved" by the interpolation of one or both of the included pitches, there is no need or warrant for a supplied accidental. Wellesz[10] takes the opposite view, supplying an accidental, not only in the exceptional situation where the tritone is taken directly, but also in the normal one where it is taken indirectly and in the progression a b-natural a, which, to him, "suggests" the substitution of a b-flat a. To take this position is to apply to Eastern melody a rule formulated in the West, the absolute validity of which, even for the Gregorian chant, is, to say the least, open to question.[11]

Having gone this far, we could complete our construction by extending the central octave above and below, did we not find ourselves confronted by the essential paradox in the Byzantine theory of the modes—its insistence on the recurrence of the modes both at the fifth and at the octave. Whether we continue with disjunct tetrachords or, abandoning them, put conjunct ones in their place, we shall be running counter to one or other of these requirements. The theorists do not help us to resolve

---

[10]Monumenta Musicae Byzantinae, Transcripta, 1 (Copenhagen, 1936), p. xxx.
[11]The chromatic implications of the Phthorai, or "modulants," will be discussed in a second study, in connection with the Byzantine system of modes, intonations, and signatures.

this contradiction; to do so we must turn again to the melodies themselves.

Using these, the procedures to be followed in carrying out the upward extension of the system can with some difficulty be pieced together, above all, from the medial signatures (modal signatures occurring as guides within the melodies themselves, usually at important medial cadences). For the most part, these signatures will fall within the central octave, telling us nothing that we do not already know. But in melodies of Mode IV—a mode lying so high that it has usually been shifted to the fifth below in published transcriptions—they will mark pitches belonging to the highest tetrachord sufficiently often to enable us to draw a conclusion regarding its arrangement. On examining a representative group of these melodies we find:

1. that d (or, in transposition, G) is marked, not only by δ, but also by α and πλα;
2. that e (or, in transposition, a) is marked, not only by α, but also by β;
3. that c (or, in transposition, F) is sometimes marked by a medial signature representing the mediant in Mode II and having, then, the force of δ.[12]

[12]In November Hymn 85, to take a specific example, the Trinity College and Grottaferrata MSS insert the signature πλ α to represent d (or, in transposition, G) after line 8 (see Tillyard's note); Koutloumousi 412 (f. 57ᵛ) agrees. In view of this agreement, one can scarcely call the signature "wrong" (as Tillyard does in commenting on a similar use of it in Hymn 29, line 14), or question it (as he does in commenting on its use in Hymn 57, line 7); to explain its occurrence in Hymn 85 as "looking forward to the next progression" carries little weight, particularly in view of the signatures after line 11, where Trinity College has πλ α, Grottaferrata α, and Koutloumousi 412 δ, all three signatures representing the same pitch as after line 8. In line 13, to represent c (or, in transposition, F), Grottaferrata has the signature calling, in Mode II, for the mediant, G; Koutloumousi 412 agrees. Aside from this, Koutloumousi 412 writes, after line 9, πλ α to represent d (or G) and in line 12, before ὕπερ ἡμῶν, α to represent e (or a).

Similarly, in Hymn 84, an example in Mode III, to represent c, the Grottaferrata MS writes the signature used later in Hymn 85, line 13 (using it, then, with the force it may have in Mode IV); Koutloumousi 412 (f, 57) has the signature Nana, having the force of γ.

In Mode IV, moreover, the signatures α and πλ α serve, not only to mark the pitch, but also to introduce transpositions, to the octave above (or to the fourth above) of familiar opening patterns belonging to Mode I Plagal. There can then be no question of their correctness or of their implications.

What could point more clearly to a conjunct upward extension of the central octave than these identifications of γ with δ, of δ with α, and of α with β? Their implication is unmistakable. Yet our conclusion need not rest on this alone.

Byzantine melody, the reader may be reminded, is a sort of mosaic in which conventional melodic formulas are combined, now in one order, now in another, producing designs which, despite their general similarity, are never twice the same.[13] These conventional melodic formulas are of two sorts. On the one hand are what we may call the patterns. Roughly comparable to the single phrases of the Gregorian "typical melody," these are ideal melodic forms; their actual shape, as a function of the momentary text, varies from use to use. On the other hand are the ornaments and melismas. Roughly comparable to the composite neumes and "wandering melismas" of the Gregorian chant, these are set figures; as pure vocalizations they tolerate no essential change. The patterns are restricted in principle to a single mode or pair of modes and are thus a significant factor in modal individualization. The ornaments and melismas, though for the most part free from this restriction, tend nevertheless to attach themselves to fixed points within the tonal system.[14] Not every ornament or melisma exhibits this tendency in the same degree. To consider only the simplest figures, the Kylisma is available as from D, E, F, and G; the Thematismos eso as from D, F, and G, but not as from E; the Thes-kai-apothes as from D and E, but not as from F and G; the Thematismos exo as from G only.[15]

Ex. 2

[13]The stylistic situation has been admirably defined by Wellesz, most recently in the introduction to his transcriptions of the Hymns for September, pp. xxiv–xxv, xxx–xxxii; see also his essay, "Are the Foundations of Our Musico-Historical Training Sound?" *The Musical Quarterly*, XI (1925), 476–477, and A. J. Swan, *op. cit.*, 241.

[14]This basic principle, which bears in an important way not only on the general question of Byzantine melody but also on the special problem of the early Byzantine notation, was first stated, if somewhat tentatively, by Tillyard in the *Annual of the British School at Athens*, XXXI (1930–31), 120.

[15]For these formulas in general, see Tillyard, *Handbook of the Middle Byzantine Notation* (Copenhagen, 1935), pp. 26–28; for the Kylisma, Wellesz, *op. cit.*, pp. xxii–xxiii; for the Thematismoi, Tardo, *op. cit.*, p. 298, note.

In the marked tendency of certain ornaments and melismas to recur always as from the same tetrachord-step, we have a second means of determining the arrangement of our highest tetrachord. A number of these restricted figures are shown in the example that follows, first as used in the central octave, then as used in its upward extension.[16]

Ex. 3

[16]Quotations from melodies in Mode IV have been left untransposed; the names given to the various figures are taken from the "Lehrgedicht" of the fourteenth-century teacher Joannes Koukouzeles (published in facsimile by Gerbert, *De cantu et musica sacra* [St. Blasien, 1774], II, pl. viii—still the best edition, Fleischer, *op. cit.*, III, pls. 27–33, Tardo, *op. cit.*, pp. 179–182). Where folio-numbers are cited in this example, the reference is to Koutloumousi 412.

In each case, the recurrences of the restricted figure are at the fifth and octave, pointing as before to a conjunct upward extension.

The same inference can be drawn from the situation, in the highest tetrachord, of those patterns which occur both in the central octave and in its upward extension. Such a pattern, properly of Modes I and I Plagal, is shown in the example that follows, first in its normal position, then as borrowed by Mode IV.[17]

Ex. 4

Here again the recurrence is at the octave, the upward extension a conjunct one.

[17]Quotations from melodies in Mode IV have again been left untransposed.

Approaching the problem from three different angles, we have arrived, each time, at the same result. There should be no room for further question.

We have still to determine what procedure is to govern the downward extension of the central octave. Here the situation is less clear. A Byzantine melody seldom descends below C, almost never below A; medial signatures and transpositions of restricted figures and patterns occur infrequently and tell us little. Inasmuch, however, as the highest tetrachord is conjunct, it is only reasonable to infer that the lowest is of the same order. This inference is strengthened by the passage previously quoted from Codex Chrysander,[18] a statement of the identity of the octave in terms of a descending progression. Aside from this, a disjunct downward extension would leave us with the virtually superfluous tone G_1. In any case, the matter is of little consequence, for, apart from the tone C, the lowest tetrachord is usually avoided, the low A being virtually restricted in practice to a single opening pattern of Mode I Plagal.[19]

Adding, as uppermost limit of the system, the tone a^1, we can now express our completed construction in terms of the staff:

Ex. 5

With very few exceptions, the melodies of the medieval Byzantine collection lie wholly within this two-octave system.[20] Thus the

[18]Note 7, above.

[19]For an example, see Wellesz, *op. cit.*, Hymn 47; to illustrate this opening, which has a special intonation and a special signature, the MSS Leningrad 711 (J. B. Thibaut, *Monuments de la notation ekphonétique et hagiopolite* [St. Petersburg, 1913], pl. 27) and Vaticanus, Gr. 791 (Tardo, *op. cit.*, p. 177) cite the Sticheron Σημερον ανετειλεν (Koutloumousi 412, f. 128).

[20]I have found low G_1 only in the important and thoroughly unusual Φεροντες τα παροντα γενναιως (Koutloumousi 412, f. 118ᵛ), where it occurs as a result of what we should call a modulation to the subdominant. High b^1 may be seen in a very few melodies belonging to Mode IV (for example, in September Hymn 93 and in November Hymns 68 and 73)—always as highest tone of the ornamental Thematismos eso. What appear to be irregular uses of this tone in September Hymn 32 and in the "Morning Hymn" in Mode IV published by Tillyard in the *Annual of the British School at Athens*, XXX (1928–30), 101–102, are due to poor readings

working range of this music barely exceeds that of the Gregorian chant, and there would seem to be no good reason for evading, through transpositions to the fifth below, the writing of an occasional high note in Mode IV. Everyone understands that, in unaccompanied vocal music, the actual pitch taken in performance is dictated, not by what is written, but by the singers' convenience. Aside from this, the systematic transposition of Mode IV destroys the inner logic of the melodies themselves, bringing this mode at one level when it is primary, at another when it is reached through modal modulation, and involving transpositions of the other modes when they follow a primary Mode IV.[21]

Exceptionally one finds a melody which, after modulating to what we should call the dominant or subdominant, continues for some time—perhaps to the very end—in the new key.[22] Where such a modulation is to the dominant, the octave a to a[1] will be treated as central and the key-signature one sharp will be obligatory; where it is to the subdominant, the central octave will lie between G and g, requiring the key-signature one flat.[23]

---

of the Vienna and Trinity College MSS.

[21]Where such a transposition is made, it is in effect a transposition of the system and ought of course to be indicated by a key-signature, not by a series of supplied b-flats. Wellesz and Tillyard, in their transposed transcriptions from Mode IV, waver between b and b-flat, supplying the accidental primarily to avoid the continual tritones resulting from the transposition of the fourth leap F—b. But, as we have seen, the implications of the medial signatures and of the restricted figures and patterns make the systematic use of b-flat obligatory if the system is shifted.

[22]Tillyard's suggestion (op. cit., pp. 95 and 137) that these shifts to the dominant may be due to errors of the archetype in the round notation, errors which arose in a perfectly natural way in translating the melodies from the early Byzantine notation, is an attractive one. At the same time, no instance of any emendation of such a shift has come to light thus far, a perhaps significant circumstance in view of the frequency of emendations of other kinds.

[23]November Hymns 56 and 75, in Mode II, are cases in point. In Hymn 56 it is, as Tillyard says, quite possible that the whole passage from the middle of line 15 to the end of the hymn may be a fifth too high. As it stands, however, it represents, not an upward extension of Mode II, but an out-and-out change of key. The cadences at the end of line 15 and at the end of the hymn are cadences on the dominant, not as dominant, but as tonic. Aside from this, the conventional melisma on καὶ in line 16, one of the two forms of the figure later called Ouranisma, is taken elsewhere from b-natural only, filling out a major third (see Hymn 66, line 10, where it is combined, as in Hymn 56, with the figure called Thematismos eso, Hymn 3, line 12, Hymn 32, line 11, Hymn 74, line 15). Its transposition to the fifth above would seem to call for f-sharp. As to the medial signatures of the Grottaferrata MS, α for e after line 16 is confirmed by Koutloumousi 412 (f. 50),

Perhaps the most striking example of this procedure is the Doxastikon Θεαρχιω νευματι (for the Festival of the Assumption, Koutloumousi 412, f. 161ᵛ), printed in full as a supplement to this study. Beginning in Mode I, this melody runs through the eight modes in order (Mode I, Mode I Plagal, Mode II, Mode II Plagal, and so on), ending with a single phrase in the mode with which it began. The section in Mode III Plagal stands in a transposition to the dominant; Mode IV, which follows, is again in the original key; on reaching Mode IV Plagal the modulation is to the subdominant, in which key the melody ends. It may be added that this same series of modulations is exactly duplicated in a second melody running through the eight modes in order, the Sticheron Σημερον η ανοσιουργοτροπος (for the Festival of the Beheading of St. John, Koutloumousi 412, f. 168ᵛ). Thus the one example confirms the other, and the possibility of a misunderstanding would appear to be ruled out.[24]

---

which has at this point the equivalent signature Nenano. In Tillyard's view, the melody "goes against" these signatures. But, provided one takes a different view of their implications, it is also possible to say that it agrees with them.

In Hymn 75, in what is essentially the same situation, Tillyard assumes an error of the archetype and, from line 3 on, transposes to the fifth below. This brings the conventional melisma at the beginning of line 3 (a form of the figure later called Chairetismos) in its normal position. But the ending of line 2 suggests that the change of key called for by the MSS is really intended, for, just as the Chairetismos from G is regularly prepared by the figure E F D (see Hymn 11, lines 8 and 9, Hymn 66, lines 7 and 8, Hymn 74, lines 10 and 11, 14 and 15), the figure b c a should prepare a transposed Chairetismos from d. The hypothetical error of the archetype cannot possibly have occurred before this point; to place it later would serve no purpose, for the change of key would still remain to be accounted for. Here, then, we have again a melody involving a change of key; eliminating the transposition from line 3 on, the implications of the medial signatures are altered, the b-naturals of the published transcription become f-sharps, and the melody ends, as in Hymn 56, on the dominant as tonic.

Still another melody of this exceptional type, also in Mode II, is the "Hymn for Thursday in Holy Week" which Tillyard has published in facsimile and transcription (after a MS belonging to Mr. Joseph Bliss) in the *Annual of the British School at Athens,* XXXVI (1935–36), 134–135, pl. 20. This example, too complex for discussion here, involves not only a change of key and an extended exploitation of the new tonality (the implications of the medial signatures altered), but also, in line 16, a return to the original key and a cadence on the dominant as dominant.

A modulation to the subdominant may be seen in the "Morning Hymn" in Mode III Plagal published by Tillyard in the *Annual of the British School at Athens,* XXXI (1930–31), 126–128; the change of key begins at line 9; the melody ends on the subdominant as tonic.

[24]My attention was drawn to these melodies by Tardo's remarks on "canti

At this point, we shall do well to summarize the conclusions reached thus far Provided our preliminary assumptions be granted:

1. the tonal system of the medieval Byzantine chant is a wholly diatonic one, its central octave having the internal structure of our diatonic octave D to d;

2. as a matter of convenience and with a view to simplifying transcription from Byzantine neumes to staff-notation, these two octaves are best equated;

3. excepting in melodies involving changes of key and in transcriptions arbitrarily transposed, key-signatures and supplied accidentals are inadmissible;

4. to avoid obscuring its relation to the other modes, Mode IV is best left untransposed.[25]

---

politonali," *op. cit.*, p. 321. For a translation of Θεαρχίω νεύματι see Isabel Florence Hapgood, *Service Book of the Holy Orthodox-Catholic Apostolic (Greco-Russian) Church* (Boston, 1906), p. 264.

[25]This paper was already in proof when Professor A. J. Swan brought to my attention the publication of Tillyard's *The Hymns of the Octoechus, Part I* (Monumenta musicae byzantinae, Transcripta, 3 (Copenhagen, 1940), and kindly arranged to have the Swarthmore College copy of this volume sent to me for study. The 145 transcriptions there offered, evenly distributed among the eight modes, afford striking confirmation of our earlier findings regarding the tritone leap, all occurrences of this progression (and there are only a very few of them) falling under one or other of the types described in Note 9 above. As regards the transposition of Mode IV, it is now clear that this has been done primarily with a view to bringing the melodies of this mode out on G; where this procedure would lead to an ending on C (as in Antiphons 1, 2, and 3, i–ii) the melodies are left untransposed. Tillyard's suggestion that "the singer knew by experience which note to take" (i.e., whether or not to transpose) does not seem to me wholly plausible. Ought we not rather to conclude that, just as the authentic modes I, II, and III have two finals, one identical with the final of the corresponding plagal mode, the other a fifth higher, so Mode IV authentic may end either on G or on d, the cadence at the fifth above being in this case the preferred one?

The Doxastikon Θεαρχιω νευματι

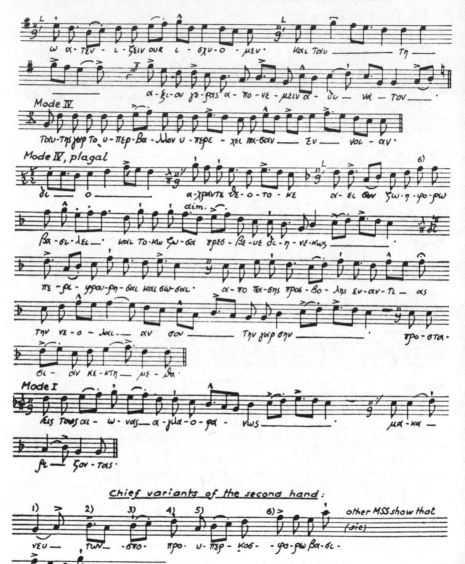

INTONATIONS AND SIGNATURES OF THE BYZANTINE MODES[†]

T HAT there is a connection of some sort between the intonation-formulas and the signatures of the Byzantine modes was suggested some years ago by Tillyard.[1] It is the aim of this study to demonstrate that such a connection exists in fact, to clarify its precise nature, and to explore the further evident connection between the formulas and the signatures of the modes on the one hand and the opening patterns of the melodies themselves on the other.

In view of the recent publication by *The Musical Quarterly* of Dr. Eric Werner's conjectural explanation of the linguistic origin and meaning of the Byzantine modal formulas,[2] I can afford to pass over, for the time being, the problem of the mysterious syllables to which these intonations are sung. I shall likewise pass over, as being for the moment of distinctly secondary interest, the further problem of the discrepancies, musical and textual, between the

---

[†]From *The Musical Quarterly*, XXXI (1945), 339–355; read at a meeting of the Greater New York Chapter of the American Musicological Society, October 23, 1944. Reprinted with permission of G. Schirmer, Inc.

[1]"We now suggest that in these invocations is to be found one clue to the mystery of the varied signatures of the eight modes; that, as the singer's art in the thirteenth and fourteenth centuries made a diversity of formulae possible, the signatures indicated the general nature of the introductory flourish." "Signatures and Cadences of the Byzantine Modes," *Annual of the British School at Athens*, XXVI (1923–25), 78–87.

[2]"The Psalmodic Formula *Neannoe* and Its Origin," *The Musical Quarterly*, XXVIII (1942), 93–99.

Eastern and Western traditions for the intonation of the modes. For the present I need only say that the Byzantine modal formula (ἤχημα, ἐνήχημα, ἀπήχημα) is a diminutive vocalization designed to introduce (or to prepare) the singing of a chant in some one of the eight modes and that there are in principle eight such formulas, one for each mode. Authentic formulas descend from a, b, c, and d and remain for the most part within the range of a fifth; plagal formulas ascend from D, E, F, and G and remain for the most part within the range of a fourth. On the musical side these formulas are subject to a certain amount of variation—various endings are used, and the bare outlines of the more-or-less standard tone-successions are sometimes considerably elaborated; the syllables remain constant, in the classical Byzantine practice, and are as follows:

Mode I	Ananéanes	Mode I Plagal	Anéanes
Mode II	Néanes	Mode II Plagal	Néanes
Mode III	Anéanes	Mode III Plagal	Ánes
Mode IV	Hágia	Mode IV Plagal	Nehágie[3]

As explained in our first study, the Byzantine modal signature (μαρτυρία) is a conventionalized letter-numeral combined with characters borrowed from the musical notation; it is designed to indicate to the singer the modality of the melody to follow and, at the same time, the precise step of the system ("starting-tone") from which the initial tone ("initial") of that melody is to be reckoned. Here too we find a certain amount of variety—a given letter-numeral is combined, now with one cluster of neumes, now with another. One of Tillyard's principal contributions to the advancement of our understanding of Byzantine music was his empirical demonstration[4] that these various forms of a given signature are

---

[3]If these syllables, as here given, depart in certain respects from those given by Wellesz in his *Byzantinische Musik* (Breslau, 1927), p. 47, this is because the later teaching of the Papadike, followed by Wellesz, is not wholly in agreement with the thirteenth-century practice, on which we have based our enumeration. Tillyard (*Handbook of the Middle Byzantine Musical Notation* [Copenhagen, 1935], p. 31) has brought together intonation formulas "typical of the many varieties found in the MSS." But even here the syllables for Mode I are given incorrectly as Ananes.

[4]In the study cited in note 1 and, in a more elaborate form, in his paper on "The Stichera Anastasima in Byzantine Hymnody," *Byzantinische Zeitschrift*, XXXI (1931), 13–20, and his *Handbook*, pp. 32–35.

not used indiscriminately, as was once supposed, but actually represent different "starting-tones" within a single mode. This important discovery, confirmed since its first announcement by hundreds of practical tests, opened the entire contents of the Byzantine service-books to transcription, reducing the more involved plagal melodies to the same basis as the simpler authentic ones and making possible the comparative study of the modes. Why the signatures mean what they do[5] and what the practical necessity is for so elaborate a system[6] it fails to tell us. It was primarily with a view to answering these two questions that we returned to the problem.

One striking characteristic of the Eastern service-book is that each melody—indeed, each text intended for singing—is headed by some indication of its mode. In Byzantine service-books intended for the choir this indication may be a formula, preceded by the simple letter-numeral of the mode; more usually it is a signature; occasionally a formula and a signature are combined, the one above the other, or the one to the left, the other to the right. It appears, then, that the two devices may have a single function. This being the case, we might assume that formula and signature are interchangeable; seeing that each is subject to some variation, we might go on to search, within a given mode, for evidences of correspondence between specific variants of the one and the other; and finding these, we might then, as a final step, attempt to determine the reason for these variants, the principle that governs their employment. But it so happens that the problem can be approached more simply, for the theoretical manuals of the medieval Byzantine chant give us the key to its solution in their practical illustrations of the formulas and their use.

Under the heading Ἀρχὴ τῶν κατ' ἤχων ἠχημάτων ("The Beginning of the Formulas in the Order of the Modal Cycle"),

---

[5]Even in Tillyard's latest publication, *The Hymns of the Octoechus, Part I* (Copenhagen, 1940), it is emphasized (p. xx) that the meaning of the Byzantine modal signatures has been discovered only "by trial."

[6]In Mode II Plagal, for example, what practical necessity is there for a special signature indicating G as "starting-tone" when G, as the initial tone of a melody in this mode, can as easily be represented by the musical signs for the ascending third? And what practical necessity is there, in this same mode, for two distinct signatures indicating D as "starting-tone" when one of them is used only with the initial C, the other only with the initial G, while D as initial is found only in conjunction with the F signature?

practical illustrations of this sort are contained in nearly every one of the available texts of the so-called Papadike, specifically in texts published by Gerbert (G),[7] Fleischer (F),[8] Thibaut (Th),[9] and Tardo (Ta 1 and 2),[10] and in unpublished texts contained in MSS belonging to the Koutloumousi Monastery on Mount Athos (K),[11] the Bibliothèque Nationale in Paris (P 1 and 2),[12] and the libraries of Columbia University (C)[13] and the University of Messina (M).[14] Each mode is illustrated by at least one example, usually by three or four, sometimes by as many as six. In each example an intonation-formula introduces the opening phrase of a melody belonging to the standard repertory. This is drawn regularly from the Sticherarion, usually from the music for an important festival; as a rule, one such phrase under each mode will come from the cycle of the eleven Heothina, or "Morning Hymns."[15] Where a single mode is illustrated by several examples, the formula normally takes different endings and introduces opening phrases representative of sharply differentiated melodic patterns. Collating our various texts, we find a certain degree of unanimity—Th and K, for instance, contain the same examples in the same order, and we have Flei-

[7]MS S. Blasianus; the illustrations in facsimile: *De cantu et musica sacra* (St. Blasien, 1774), II, pls. viii, 8–11.

[8]"Codex Chrysander"; transcription and facsimile: *Neumen-Studien,* III (Berlin, 1904), pp. 3–7 at end, pls. 20–23.

[9]Petropolitanus gr. 711; facsimile: *Monuments de la notation ekphonétique et hagiopolite de l'église grecque* (St. Petersburg, 1913), pls. xxvii–xxviii.

[10]Barberinus gr. 300 and Vaticanus gr. 791; facsimiles; *L'antica melurgia bizantina* (Grottaferrata, 1938), pp. 156–157 and 176–178.

[11]Codex 447, described by S. P. Lambros, *Catalogue of the Greek MSS on Mount Athos* (Cambridge, 1895), I, 316 (*3520); a few photographs from this MS, including its illustrations for Modes I to IV, were available to me among materials collected by the Athos-Princeton Expedition of 1936.

[12]Ancien fonds gr. 2541 and Suppl. gr. 1171, described by Amédée Gastoué, *Introduction à la paléographie musicale byzantine* (Paris, 1907), pp. 87 (No. 41) and 93 (No. 78); photostats of these two texts were generously placed at my disposal by Mr. Frederick Yeiser, of Cincinnati.

[13]Plimpton 5, described by De Ricci and Wilson, "Census," II (1755) (see also S. A. Ives in *Speculum,* XVII [1942], 34); this MS, which has lost its illustrations for Modes I and II, was brought to my attention by Dr. Erich Hertzmann, of Columbia University.

[14]S. Salvatore 154; this text is not now accessible in its entirety, but Fleischer assures us (*op. cit.,* 24, 36, 49) that it includes illustrations and that these agree in the main with those of his principal MS, the "Codex Chrysander."

[15]Published in full by Tillyard in the *Annual of the British School at Athens,* XXX (1928–30), 86–108, and XXXI (1930–31), 115–147.

scher's assurance[16] that F and M are in substantial agreement; G, Ta 1, P 1, and C supply a few additional examples, with many confirmations of those already seen; Ta 2 and P 2 are almost wholly independent. In all, we have in these ten texts nearly seventy examples, illustrating every ending and most of the openings used in actual practice.

To give the reader a more precise idea of the nature and implications of these examples, I am inserting at this point a composite illustration, embracing all examples given in the manuals for Mode IV Plagal, the mode affording the most varied—and, at the same time, clearest—picture of the workings of the Byzantine intonation-system. In assembling this illustration I have taken two liberties: for each of the opening phrases cited by the manuals I have supplied the modal signature with which it is associated in Koutloumousi 412, the Sticherarion on which these studies are based;[17] then, for the actual readings of the intonations and opening phrases as given in the manuals, I have substituted the readings of these same intonations and opening phrases as given in Koutloumousi 412[18]—partly because the occurrence of several of these examples in more than one source suggests the adoption of a normalized text, partly with a view to simplifying the discussion by eliminating textual features not characteristic of the classical practice. This substitution involves little more than the suppression of an occasional rhythmic or dynamic nuance. And for our present purposes, it is not in their readings, but in their choice of examples and in

---

[16]*Op. cit.*, III, 49.

[17]Koutloumousi 412 (briefly referred to in our first study) gives what is clearly the most correct and most authentic text of the Sticherarion now available, virtually free from errors, easily read, and superior in every respect to the Vienna MS published in facsimile as Vol. 1 of the Monumenta. Unfortunately, this text is no longer complete. The month of September and a considerable section of the Triodion are wanting and have been partially restored by relatively modern hands; the last two weeks of the Pentekostarion and all but a few folios of the Oktoechos have wholly disappeared. Where an opening phrase cited by the manuals is not contained in Koutloumousi 412, or is given there without signature, or with a signature no longer legible, I have used the signature regularly associated in the MS with other opening phrases of the same type.

[18]For opening phrases from the month of September and from the Oktoechos I have followed the readings adopted by Wellesz and Tillyard in their published transcriptions; for opening phrases from the Heothina (not contained in Koutloumousi 412) I have used an excellent sixteenth-century fragment at the Library of Congress (MS M 2156.XVI.M1).

the evident importance they attach to a proper relationship between intonation and opening pattern that the usefulness of the manuals lies.

Ex. 1

These twelve examples illustrate six variants of a single modal formula, differing from one another only in their endings, the difference beginning in each case with the final syllable of the standard text. To indicate the nature of the connection between formula and signature I need only repeat these variants in the original notation. It will be seen that the musical signs representing

the various endings of the formula[19] agree exactly with those added to the letter-numeral of the mode in the corresponding variants of the signature. To put it differently, the Byzantine modal signature is simply an abbreviation. Its letter-numeral stands for the body of a formula—since this is regularly the same, the singer may safely be left to supply it; its added neumes give the required ending—since this varies from case to case, it must be written out in full. If this be true, not only of Mode IV Plagal, but also of the remaining modes, our first question will have been answered. The connection between the formulas and the signatures will have been established and defined; it will be clear why the signatures mean what they do. To answer our second question—to explain the esthetic, if not practical necessity for this elaborate system and to establish and define the connection between the formulas or signatures and the opening phrases of our illustration, we shall need to consider, one by one, the examples cited.

[19]In the example above I have used colons to separate these from the body of the formula.

To begin with, the manuals give three examples (Ex. I, 1–3) showing various uses of what we may call the basic formula of the mode. In the first of these, this basic formula is shown in connection with one of the Heothina, or "Morning Hymns," of the Emperor Leo. The opening phrase is not elsewhere used and the melody has doubtless been included here as important and well-known and as a means of establishing continuity;[20] the Heothina, while making some use of conventional figures, are essentially "original melodies." In the second example, from P 2, the formula is shown in connection with a Troparion of the Christmas Hours,[21] again an important and well-known melody with an "original" opening. The last of the three examples is more instructive—its opening phrase belongs to a familiar type.[22] In all, Koutloumousi 412 contains 14 melodies beginning in this fashion;[23] these are regularly prepared by the basic formula or its abbreviation. One function of this basic formula, then, is the preparation of "original" openings with the initial G; another is the preparation of the opening pattern represented by Ἐν εὐσή-μῳ. It is also used in connection with other opening patterns, among them the following, represented in Koutloumousi 412 by 5, 23, 26, 5, and 5 examples.[24] (See p. 27.)

In Mode IV Plagal, as in the other modes, the basic formula is the one associated with the greatest number of opening patterns.

---

[20]It will be recalled that one example under each mode is usually an Heothinon.

[21]In P 2 the full text of this opening phrase is Τάδε λέγει ἰωσὴφ πρὸς τὴν παρθένον; with other texts the melody recurs among the Troparia of the Epiphany and Good Friday Hours.

[22]For the melody in full, see September Hymn 39; for other examples of this opening pattern, September Hymns 10 and 107 and November Hymn 71.

[23]The reader will bear in mind that, as explained in note 17, the text of Koutloumousi 412 is no longer complete. The Vienna MS published in facsimile as Vol. 1 of the Monumenta is said to contain 1,404 melodies and has lost 4; Koutloumousi 412 has only 1,088.

[24]Δεῦτε ἅπαντες is September Hymn 40; for other examples of these opening patterns see (1) September Hymns 25 and 70 (a single melody); (2) September Hymn 71 and November Hymns 34 and 80; (3) September Hymn 85, November Hymn 63, and Anastasima Anatolika 1, 2, 7, 9, and 10, these last examples in *The Hymns of the Octoechus, Part I,* under Mode IV Plagal; (4) Anastasimon Anatolikon 8, or, for the same opening in Mode III Authentic, Anastasima Anatolika 10 and 11. The opening pattern represented by Μεσούσης τῆς ἑορτῆς (5) is properly of Mode II Authentic; for examples see September Hymns 13 and 104, November Hymns 18 and 76, and Anastasimon Anatolikon 7.

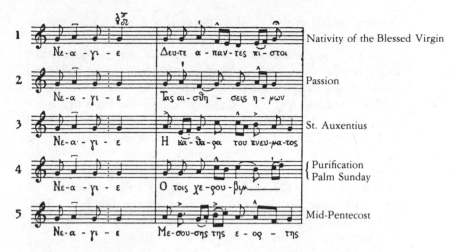

Since its use is general rather than specific, it was evidently thought unnecessary to illustrate it in detail.

As their fourth example (Ex. I, 4) the manuals show the use of the ending G-E-F in connection with the opening phrase of a Troparion of the Epiphany Hours.[25] Koutloumousi 412 contains 13 melodies beginning in this fashion (the first word commonly Σήμερον or Κύριε); these are regularly prepared as the example indicates[26]—the ending G-E-F has indeed no other use. This restricted association is the more striking in that the tone-succession (G)-E-F-D-G plays a similar role in other modes. In Mode II Plagal, for instance, the basic formula, ending on E, has as one use the preparation of the opening pattern E-F-D-G;[27] in Mode II Authentic this same pattern is prepared by a special formula, ending on G and used only in this connection;[28] in Mode II Plagal, again, the ending E-F prepares the

[25]In the manuals, the full text of this opening phrase is Σήμερον τῶν ὑδάτων ἁγιάζεται; with the text Σήμερον τοῦ ναοῦ τὸ καταπέτασμα the melody recurs among the Passion Troparia and (with a florid opening) among the Troparia of the Good Friday Hours.

[26]In all cases, then, where the preliminary indication can be read, it is either the formula with the expected ending, or a florid version of the formula, again with the expected ending, or the corresponding signature.

[27]As in September Hymn 65 and Anastasima Anatolika 8 and 9.

[28]As in September Hymns 27, 29, 44, and 103, November Hymn 54, and Anastasimon Anatolikon 1.

opening D-G,[29] as above, while the ending E-F-D is used only in connection with an initial G.[30] I mention this simply to suggest that, in some cases, associations of this kind may prove stronger than modal ones and that when an opening pattern is shared by several modes it may carry its regular preparation with it.

The formula of Mode IV Plagal has two distinct and important endings on a, the one preparing an initial D, the other an initial E. For one of these the manuals give three examples, for the other, two (Ex. I, 5-9). The opening pattern represented by Πιστούμενος, Ὑπόδεξαι, and Τῆς νίκης shows considerable variation, although D is always the initial.[31] Koutloumousi 412 has 15 melodies with openings of this general type, regularly prepared as the examples indicate. Similar openings from D, used in connection with this same ending, are the following:[32]

Epiphany Hours

Maundy Thursday

As to the opening pattern represented by Παντοκράτωρ κύριε and Ὁ δαβίδ,[33] this shows little variation. The Koutloumousi MS has 12 melodies with openings of this type; as usual, these are regularly prepared as the examples indicate—the ending has no other use.

[29]As in September Hymn 66, November Hymns 33 and 58, and Anastasimon Anatolikon 10.

[30]As in September Hymn 34.

[31]Τῆς νίκης is September Hymn 73; for other examples see September Hymn 96, November Hymn 86, and, in The Hymns of the Octoechus, Part I, under Mode IV Plagal, the Alphabetikon Χριστὸν δοξολογήσωμεν and the Theotokion Ἀνύμφευτεπαρθένε.

[32]The melody of the Troparion Ὡς ἄνθρωπος recurs among the Troparia of the Good Friday Hours with the text Ὡς πρόβατον; Μηδεὶς ὦ πιστοί has a parallel in November Hymn 78.

[33]Παντοκράτωρ κύριε is published by Tillyard in Byzantinische Zeitschrift, XX (1911), 482–484, and, with the Latin text Omnipotens Domine, in The Musical Quarterly, XXIII (1937), 207; Ὁ δαβίδ is November Hymn 72; for other examples of this opening pattern see September Hymn 86 and Anastasima Anatolika 3 and 6.

Thus far, we have seen in Mode IV Plagal two groups of melodies with D as initial tone and two variants of the formula with a as final tone. We have also seen that the distinctions between these two groups and these two endings are rigidly maintained—no melody of the Σήμερον group is associated with an a-ending, no melody of the Πιστούμενος-Ὑπόδεξαι-Τῆς νίκης group is associated with the F-ending, in no case is the one form of the a-ending confused with or substituted for the other. Even at this stage of the discussion it should be very clear that the primary function of the Byzantine formula of intonation is one of melodic preparation or transition and that this preparatory or transitional procedure is governed by rules which, though complex, are consistent and intelligible.

In further confirmation of this view it may be added that neither one of the two a-endings just discussed is ever used to prepare an initial a. For such an opening the regular preparation is the basic formula. Where an a-ending is used in this connection it takes a third form, not shown in the manuals and restricted, in Koutloumousi 412, to this single function.[34] I can give only three examples:

As a preparation for the two melismatic openings Σήμερον[35] and Ἐπιστάς this portamento-like ending seems appropriate and effective; its use in connection with the opening Τὴν πονηράν—a member of the Ἡ καθαρά group already shown in

---

[34]Vienna theol. gr. 181 sometimes uses it in connection with melodies of the Πιστούμενος-Ὑπόδεξαι-Τῆς νίκης group, as in September Hymns 73 (Τῆς νίκης) and 96 and the Theotokion Ἀνύμφευτε παρθένε.

[35]This is the florid opening referred to in Note 25 above. The preliminary indications are no longer distinct; the melody reads in any case from a and can scarcely have been otherwise prepared.

connection with the basic formula[36]—is the one instance of an inconsistent preparation that I have found in Koutloumousi 412 among the 185 melodies of the mode.

For the intonation of melodies with the initials c, d, and e, the formula of Mode IV Plagal takes a c-ending and the syllables Naná are added to the standard text. The manuals give two examples (Ex. I, 10 and 11), showing this ending in connection with opening phrases of a single type, properly of Mode IV Authentic.[37] The c-ending, however, is by no means restricted to this one function—not only is it used in connection with other openings borrowed from Mode IV Authentic and in connection with "original" openings with the initial c, it may also prepare openings reminiscent of Mode III Authentic, which has c as the initial tone of its formula of intonation and as its principal starting-tone. This explains why, in the later practice, the c-ending with the syllables Naná first alternates with and finally supersedes the earlier formula of Mode III with the syllables Anéanes. Where an opening reminiscent of Mode III has the initial b, as in Βλέπε τὴν ἐλισάβετ (Ex. I, 12), the starting-tone may be either c, as is the invariable practice of Koutloumousi 412 and the Vienna MS, or d, as shown in Tardo's second text (Ta 2), from which our example is drawn. A comparison of this opening with another of the same general type will indicate what has prompted the choice of d as alternate starting-tone.

Nativity of St. John the Baptist

Holy Maccabees

Where the pattern represented by Βλέπε τὴν ἐλισάβετ has a preparatory syllable, as in Οἱ ἅγιοι μακκαβαῖοι, this is regularly sung to a sharply accented d; where such a syllable is wanting, the

---

[36]P. 28 above.

[37]Δόξα σοι is Anastasimon Anatolikon 4; for another example in Mode IV Plagal see November Hymn 48. November Hymn 29 will illustrate the use of this pattern in Mode IV Authentic.

preparatory d with its sharp accent is simply transferred to the formula of intonation. In all, Koutloumousi 412 has in Mode IV Plagal 31 melodies which read from c—5 of these are of the type Δόξα σοι–Σέλας φαεινότατον, 7 of the type Βλέπε τὴν ἐλισάβετ–Οἱ ἅγιοι μακκαβαῖοι.

In a study primarily concerned with the formulas and signatures of the Byzantine modes and only incidentally with the problem of the opening pattern, there cannot be room for examples enough to show the precise degree of stability which such a pattern exhibits or the precise point at which variation ends and differentiation begins. But even so, the examples of the manuals will already have suggested that the most stable and characteristic elements involved are dynamic and rhythmic ones. For instance, in the two opening phrases just cited in connection with the c-ending in Mode IV Plagal (Ex. I, 10 and 11), the exact correspondence is accentual, not melodic.[38] Further correspondences of this sort will be found among the opening phrases enumerated in our references to the September and November Hymns and to the Oktoechos. Non-essential melodic variation is wholly normal; an essential variation in nuance is nearly always due to an inferior reading. Thus, for the opening phrases of September Hymn 10 and November Hymn 29, the readings of Koutloumousi 412 are preferable to those of the Vienna MS used by Wellesz and Tillyard; for the opening phrase Πιστούμενος, cited in our illustration (Ex. I, 5) after Koutloumousi 412, the Vienna MS gives the better text.

In the course of our discussion of Mode IV Plagal and its intonation we have dealt with every ending and every opening pattern in common use and in so doing have reduced the openings of something like seventy per cent of the melodies of this mode, as contained in Koutloumousi 412, to eleven distinct and characteristic types. Given a melody of this mode, we can safely predict its preparation; given an intonation of this mode, we can in most cases safely predict that the opening to follow will conform to a specific type or to some one of several specific types; given a thematic list of the melodies of this mode, we have only to arrange the incipits

[38]For Δόξα σοι our illustration gives the reading of Vienna theol. gr. 181; the uniform reading of the manuals (G, Th, and C) is e d d a b a G.

according to their intonations or signatures to obtain a rough classification.

I have purposely treated this one mode in considerable detail in order to establish once and for all the nature and meaning of the connection between the formula or signature and the opening pattern. To deal in the same fashion with each of the remaining modes would lead too far and could serve only to confirm conclusions already sufficiently obvious. But I have still to establish that the signatures of the remaining modes, like those of Mode IV Plagal, may also be explained as abbreviated intonations. A simple correlation of these signatures and the intonations for which they stand will show that this is true.[39]

[39]For purposes of comparison and to permit a comprehensive view of the whole, I have included in this correlation the signatures and intonations of Mode IV Plagal, already shown on p. 24. Without discussing the use of each individual signature I may say that: (1) Mode I D¹, rarely used, prepares an initial C; (2) Mode II a² is used only once—before Τῆς ἀμωμήτου πίστεως (St. Julianus)—and is perhaps to be understood as a mere variant of Mode II a¹; (3) as indicated in Note 28 above, Mode II *G has its own intonation and is used only in connection with openings of the type Εἰς τὰ ὑπερκόσμια σκηνώματα (St. Demetrius)—Τὴν τῶν ἀποστόλων ἀκρότητα (September Hymn 103); (4) Mode I Plagal D¹, like Mode I D¹, is rarely used and then only to prepare an initial C; (5) Mode I Plagal E is used only in connection with openings of the types Σήμερον ἀνέτειλεν (St. Theodore the General), as in September Hymn 47 and the Alphabetikon Ξένη σοῦ ἡ σταύρωσις, and Κύριε, as in Anastasima Anatolika 1, 2, and 11 (Tillyard's numbering); (6) Mode I Plagal F is used only in connection with the Troparion Δεῦτε χριστοφόροι λαοὶ κατίδωμεν (Christmas and Good Friday); (7) Mode II Plagal D¹ prepares an initial C; (8) as indicated in Note 30, Mode II Plagal D² prepares an initial G; (9) as indicated in Note 29, Mode II Plagal F prepares an initial D; (10) Mode III Plagal D is rarely used.

In every instance the musical signs added to the letter-numerals of the signatures agree exactly with the endings of the intonations to which they correspond.[40] This being the case, the connection between signature and intonation must be considered established and defined. It is now clear why each signature means what it does.

---

[40]The one exception is Mode II *G. This has the signature of Mode II G, which represents another approach to the same starting-tone. The difficulty, of course, is that the ending *G, beginning as it does from E rather than from G as do the other endings of this mode, cannot be abbreviated without ambiguity.

It is now clear why in certain modes the first sign added to the letter-numeral is the Double Apostrophus (prolonged descending second) while in others it is the Ison over Diple (prolonged unison) or Oligon over Diple (prolonged ascending second). The choice of sign is always determined by the relation of the last tone of the unwritten body of the formula to the first tone of the ending. In other words, the sign is always precisely what it would be if the intonation were written out in full. This disposes of Tillyard's thesis that in the signature of Mode I the sign above the letter-numeral is not the Double Apostrophus, but rather a relic of the small semicircle used in earlier MSS to imply that a letter has a numerical value.[41] Again, it is now clear why in certain modes the first tone of the ending is the "mediant" and not the expected "tonic." We need no longer ask why the signature reads from the "mediant" in Mode II or in Mode III; the question now is why the body of the intonation has so restricted an ambitus in these two modes, a question that may be answered provisionally by saying that it is perhaps because the tritone is involved, perhaps also—although this amounts to very much the same thing—because the fifth-leaps E to b and F to c are not characteristic of the classical practice. The transcriber can now dispense with tables of signatures and need no longer be at a loss on encountering a previously unrecorded signature for the first time. Provided he knows the formulas of intonation and understands the principle according to which they are abbreviated in the MSS, he will be prepared to deal with any signature he may meet.[42]

As to the formulas themselves, the reader can easily satisfy himself that there is nothing particularly memorable or characteristic about them. Except for the arrangement of the whole and half tones, the basic formulas of Modes I and IV Authentic and of Modes I and II Plagal are virtually the same; Modes II Authentic and III Plagal operate with only three tones, Mode IV Plagal with

---

[41] *Handbook,* p. 32; objections to this thesis have already been voiced by Høeg, *Hirmologium Athoum* (Copenhagen, 1938), p. 16.

[42] It goes without saying that each MS has its own usage in this respect. The intonations and signatures in the correlation above represent the usage of Koutloumousi 412, a MS exhibiting unusual consistency and discrimination in these matters. In comparison with the usage of this MS, that of Vienna theol. gr. 181 seems almost haphazard, the signatures given being often inappropriate, improperly formed, or incorrect.

only two. Thus the formulas can scarcely have been intended primarily for use in teaching—as *"Memorierformeln,"* or summaries of the more usual progressions of the single modes—and while it cannot be denied that some of them have left their mark on Byzantine melody, the view that they are modal archetypes or *"Ur-Melodien"* presents insurmountable difficulties. But once they are regarded as formulas of preparation or transition they are seen to be admirably suited to their purpose. The reader should bear in mind that the melodies of the Byzantine Sticherarion and Heirmologion åre choral melodies, that Byzantine practice does not provide for the division of the choral melody into a solo opening and a choral continuation, and that the singing of the Byzantine Sticheron, Heirmos, or Troparion is usually preceded by the choral recitation of a verse στίχος taken from a Psalm or from a Canticle. Where such a verse precedes, the formula of intonation, sung by a solo singer, the Canonarch or Protopsaltes, serves as a link connecting the verse with the chant that follows; where no such verse precedes, as is the case with the Processional Stichera, for example, it serves as a preparation and as an announcement of the mode. This last applies also to the formula which precedes the verse itself.

The reader may already have anticipated the conclusion implicit in this line of argument and will perhaps have asked himself whether the Byzantine formula of intonation, with its various endings, is not somehow comparable to the Gregorian "Seculorum Amen" or psalmodic difference. Here is what Peter Wagner has to say about the *differentiae:*[43]

> The technic of the difference has its origins in the old practice of repeating the antiphon after each verse of the psalm and aims to give the psalm-tone an ending that will enable the whole choir to attack the beginning of the following antiphon without difficulty. Thus the difference connects the psalm-tone, or rather its dominant, with the beginning of the antiphon in a way that it is practically convenient and melodically coherent. . . . In Mode I, the differences of the psalm-tone consist essentially in nothing more than varied treatments of the last two syllables, "Amen." For this very reason their number seems extraordinarily high. It is striking that several of them have the same final tone. One asks oneself why there should be two differences with the final G and as many as three concluding with the progression G-a. . . . But there

[43] *Gregorianische Formenlehre* (Leipzig, 1921), pp. 129–134.

is nothing arbitrary or accidental about this choice. Its economy becomes apparent the moment one compares with the differences the beginnings of the antiphons corresponding to them. . . . Invariably, the connection of the antiphon with the psalm-verse takes place smoothly, without hitch or melodic harshness. Each characteristic beginning calls forth its difference.

To be sure, the function of the Gregorian difference is purely transitional while that of the Byzantine formula of intonation may be either transitional or preparatory; again, the Gregorian difference stands before the recapitulation of an antiphon and is thus, strictly speaking, not transitional but retransitional. Even so, many of Wagner's observations will recall observations made earlier in the course of our own discussion, and by changing only a very few words, much that he says could be applied with equal justice to our own topic. The correspondence of the one device to the other is so close that it places their essential identity beyond question. A similar correspondence can be seen between the Gregorian "Tonarius," in which the openings of the antiphons are arranged, mode by mode, according to the differences with which they are associated in practice, and the practical illustrations of the formulas and their use, as found in the Byzantine manuals. But what is most important, both bodies of chant, Eastern and Western, are now seen to be governed by a single law of style—the law of melodic adjustment, the law requiring that, when two melodies stand in immediate succession, the first must be accommodated to the second by means of an appropriate treatment of its ending.[44]

[44]Peter Wagner's *"Anpassungsgesetz"; op. cit.*, pp. 78–79 and elsewhere.

A FIRST LOOK AT
BYZANTINE PSALMODY[†]

THE psalmodic recitation-system of the Greek Orthodox Church in Early Christian and Medieval times has not until now been studied at all, and the very existence of such a system is not yet by any means a generally accepted historical fact. For the present I cannot aim to do more than ask the reader to take the existence of the system for granted in order that I may give him some idea of how it works. This paper is in effect an *ad interim* report on studies with which I am still occupied. I base it primarily on MSS containing complete services, in each of the eight modes, for the Saturday evening and Sunday morning offices. While I believe that the melodies given in these MSS preserve the essential features of a practice dating from earliest Christian times, I cannot prove that any of them are older than the fourteenth century. This may seem strange, but it will seem only natural if it is assumed that the early church at first committed to writing only what was relatively new, relatively complex, and relatively difficult to sing from memory, and that the older, simpler music, consisting largely of modal formulas and model melodies, was left to oral tradition until the imminent collapse of that tradition made its recording imperative. The earliest dated example that I know is an Athos MS from the

†From *Bulletin of the American Musicological Society,* II/13 (1948), 19–21; read at a symposium on ancient Hebrew and early Christian melody at the Temple Emanu-El, New York, on March 24, 1946, under the title "Byzantine Psalmody and Its Possible Connection with Hebraic Cantillation." Reprinted with permission of the American Musicological Society.

year 1425; with the sixteenth and seventeenth centuries such MSS became extremely common.

Reduced to its essentials, the Byzantine psalm-tone is simply a melodic formula for the recitation of a verse or half-verse from the Psalter, an elaborated monotone with two principal inflections—an intonation and a cadence. These two inflections give to the individual psalm-tone whatever character it has, for the recitation proper, although always elaborated, remains relatively neutral. When such a formula is used for the recitation of a particular verse or half-verse from the Psalter it must adapt itself to the specific requirements of its text. Two factors will control this adaptation—accent and syllable-count. Accent will be the determining factor for the intonation and the recitation proper; the distribution of the textual accents within the particular verse or half-verse may effect an expansion or contraction of the initial motive of intonation and will govern the elaboration of the reciting-tone. Syllable-count will be the determining factor for the cadence; regardless of their accentuation, the final syllables of the particular verse or half-verse will be mechanically applied to the tones and tone-groups of the cadential part of the formula. Less importance will be attached to the recitation proper than to the cadence, and the dividing line between reciting-tone and cadence will be clearly drawn. All this applies with equal force to the psalm-tones of the Gregorian chant, for the recitation systems of the Christian East and West are in principle the same. Where they differ, they differ in detail. To some extent they differ in their intonations and in their cadences, here and there they differ in their choice of a reciting-note, they differ also in that the Byzantine psalm-tones successfully resisted the process of stylization that reduced the Gregorian formulas to formulas in the most literal sense of the word. Finally and most important, they differ in that the Byzantine psalm-tone is as a rule designed for the recitation of the half-verse. The parallel structure of the poetic line is thus exactly reflected in its musical setting, and the Latin distinction between a medial and a final cadence no longer applies.

Is there a significant connection between the Hebraic and Byzantine traditions for the musical recitation of the Psalms? Has not Idelsohn already shown that such a connection exists for the Hebraic and Gregorian traditions? The recitation-systems of the Christian East and West are in principle the same. In so far, then, as

Idelsohn's "parallels" argue the existence of the one connection, they also argue the existence of the other. I ought now to ask which of the two connections is the more significant, or to put it differently, which of the two great Early Christian traditions is the more likely to have made direct borrowings from the Hebrew? Peter Wagner has suggested an answer that is at once simple and striking. Throughout its history, the Greek Orthodox Church has recited the Psalter in the version of the Septuagint, a version made in Hellenic Alexandria by and for the Jews of the Dispersion in the third and second centuries before the beginning of the Christian era. Was this Greek Psalter ever publicly recited in the synagogues of Alexandria, Antioch, and Ephesus by the Jews themselves? Opinions differ. But even if it was never publicly recited, even if it remained strictly a book for private use, the argument still carries a certain weight. The Septuagint would seem to me to be the strongest link we may expect to find. Its use by the Greek Church should point to two conclusions: (1) the Byzantine tradition for the musical recitation of the Psalms may actually date from pre-Christian times and represent a direct survival of the practice of the Synagogue itself; (2) if this be granted, the Byzantine tradition becomes the central tradition in Early Christian music, the tradition by means of which Jewish elements are transmitted to the Christian churches further West and further East.

THE CLASSIFICATION AND DEVELOPMENT OF THE EARLY BYZANTINE NOTATIONS†

I F we may compare our modern musical notation to a system of numerals, that is, to a system logical in its arrangement, universally intelligible (or capable of being so), and potentially applicable to any situation or problem, no matter how novel or how complex; then the several neumatic notations of Early Christian Music may be compared to systems of letters. Just as an alphabet is at best a random accumulation of seemingly arbitrary symbols that has grown up in connection with the development of a particular *language* and that is imperfectly suited to *other* languages, even after more or less drastic modification; so a neumatic notation, likewise a random accumulation of seemingly arbitrary symbols, grows up in connection with the development of a particular *melodic idiom* and under the influence of the *inflections and phonetics* of a particular language—it too is imperfectly suited, even after more or less drastic modification, to *other* melodic idioms and to the inflections and phonetics of *other* languages.

Thus, on comparing the neumatic notations of the Greek East and Latin West, we may expect to find about the same amount of common practice that we find when we compare these musical traditions themselves. Like the two chants, Greek and Latin, the two methods of writing have a common origin. They have also in

†From *Atti del Congresso Internazionale di Musica Sacra,* ed. Igino Anglès (Tournai, 1952), pp. 111–113; read in Rome at a meeting of the congress, late May, 1950. Reprinted with permission of Desclée & Cie.

common a few basic signs, chiefly accentual, and they share certain typical procedures, for example, the duplication of a few of the basic neumes for purposes of emphasis or intensification and the formation of composite signs from simple ones. Aside from this, one may at least put forward the hypothesis that the two notations were introduced at about the same time and for precisely the same reason: that in the East as in the West the rapid growth of the repertory during the seventh and eighth centuries meant for music the end of oral tradition and the beginning of a written record, however imperfect and ambiguous it may have been. Observing, then, that both notations underwent radical modification later on, one may also suppose that the reason for this was in either case the same: that by the beginning of the eleventh century, when the West adopted the staff, or by the year 1175, or thereabouts, when the East adopted the so-called "round" notation, the imminent collapse of the pure tradition—a tradition that had ceased to grow and hence to live—forced on either chant the introduction of a more precise method of writing. Finally, to round out the parallel, we may draw an analogy between the rise of polyphony on the one hand and the rise of the kalophonic chant on the other, stylistic innovations that were decisive in that they destroyed the last vestiges of the pure tradition, leaving at best the possibility of a renewal or an archeological restoration.

In the last analysis, however, these and other speculations concerning the relationships and parallels between the two notations will not lead us very far. To approach more nearly to the heart of the problem we shall need to consider, not similarities, but differences. In the West one was satisfied with a relatively small number of radical signs (virga, punctum, strophicus, oriscus, quilisma); from these five radicals one developed the remaining neumes by modification (liquescence) and by a synthetic process whose possibilities were almost unlimited. The radicals appear to have been wholly accentual or, what amounts to the same thing, cheironomic; letters of the alphabet were employed only as auxiliaries; one made no use whatever of the stenographic principle, whereby whole ornamental groups or conventional melismas might be represented by a single symbol. In the East the situation was altogether different. Here one began with a somewhat larger number of radicals or simple signs—just how many remains to be determined—and, while one made some use of duplication and synthesis, the tendency was to introduce new signs rather than to form combinations from those already at hand. Among the oldest signs are several that appear to be wholly arbitrary; one is already a letter of the Greek alphabet, the letter theta; as to the stenographic principle, this played at first a most important, indeed decisive role.

If we ask, now, what changes took place during the first stages in the development of the Byzantine notation, that is, from about the year 900 to about the year 1200, we shall not find that our question has been at all satisfactorily answered. From the first, dynamic and rhythmic distinctions, together with other refinements affecting the style of performance, were indicated as fully, or nearly as fully, as in the later practice of the thirteenth and fourteenth centuries; the melodic contours were clearly delineated; the principal changes, accordingly, were changes in the direction of a more precise distinction between the step and the leap and between the syllabic and the neumatic. This much is generally understood. Then it is a well-established fact that in the very earliest MSS many syllables are not provided with signs at all and that the practice of giving each syllable its sign or signs marks the beginning of a second stage. Formerly much was made of a change in the character of the musical script; the earlier notation was called "linear" and described as made up of strokes and dots, as opposed to the later "round" notation, with its broader, less angular forms. Today, however, one is less inclined to consider this change a significant one, for it appears unlikely that it is related in any way to the changes that took place in the notation itself.

Thus far we have been on familiar ground. Of the various changes that have been reviewed, the most useful, clearly, is that from the stage in which certain syllables were left unprovided for to that in which there was musical notation throughout. Using this change as a criterion, one can readily separate the early from the late; in some instances, one can even distinguish, within a single MS, an earlier layer and a later one. To simplify the discussion to follow, I shall suggest that the notation before this change be called the "interrupted" notation, or the notation "in detached phrases," and that the later stages of the Paleobyzantine notation be called "continuous."

Just as the change from the "interrupted" notation to the "continuous" enables us to segregate our earliest documents from those that followed, so a quite different sort of change, which seems to have taken place about the year 1100, will enable us to segregate our latest Paleobyzantine documents from those that preceded them. This change is one affecting the character of the modal signature, a change from the indication of mode by means of a simple letter-numeral to the use of the modal signature proper, which combines a letter-numeral with characters borrowed from the musical notation itself. Here again we have a useful distinction. The modal signatures of the later "round" notation have already been studied in great detail; the investigation of their first development during the final stage of the Paleobyzantine notation we have still before us.

I shall not tire you by speaking at any length of those other aspects of the development whose investigation appears also to promise significant findings. It should be enough, I think, to enumerate them briefly. Most important, perhaps, is the gradual change in the meaning and function of the stenographic signs, which begin as representations of ornamental groups and conventional melismas but which end as mere auxiliaries, accompanying melodic progressions written out in full. Then I might mention, as scarcely less important, the gradual introduction and change in meaning of the four signs later associated with the leaps of the ascending and descending third and fifth. Finally I should draw attention to the gradual change in the writing of certain synthetic signs, which in their earliest form are seen at once as composite characters made up of simple elements but which in their later form become conventionalized and undergo a change in meaning.

In this rapid and somewhat sketchy survey I have aimed above all to indicate those lines of investigation which seem to me to be the most promising and to raise those questions which seem to me to be the most urgent. I hope also to have made it clear that what has been accomplished thus far is only a beginning. It may well be that this great Congress, in bringing together a representative group of those most actively concerned with the scientific investigation and practical performance of the two sister chants and in providing opportunities for an exchange of views and opinions, may make this Holy Year a significant turning-point for musicology. Speaking for those primarily occupied with Byzantine music, I think that I may say that we are still far from having reached the point attained years ago by our fellow students of the Western chant. From them, particularly from the meticulous scholarship and exemplary method of the Benedictine editors of the latest volumes of the *Paléographie musicale,* we have much to learn. They have shown us the way: it remains for us to follow it.

S. SALVATORE DI MESSINA AND THE MUSICAL TRADITION OF MAGNA GRAECIA †

S. SALVATORE *in Lingua Phari,* the latest and the most powerful of the Greek monasteries of Norman Sicily, was destined from the outset to play a dominant role in shaping the musical tradition of Magna Graecia. Like Grottaferrata, it had begun as a spiritual outpost of Rossano, for it was to this influential center of Basilian monasticism in Calabria that both monasteries owed their foundation. But if S. Salvatore had looked at first to Rossano and the Patirion, the authority vested in its archimandrite by the charter of Roger II soon made it an influential center in its own right. Its library, transferred to the University of Messina on the suppression of the monastery in 1866, ranks immediately after that at Grottaferrata among the Greek monastic libraries of the West. In 1904, with the publication of the third volume of Oskar Fleischer's *Neumenstudien,* largely based upon a manuscript from this collection,[1] the library was brought to the attention of musical scholarship, and in 1937 Ottavío Tiby published in the *Accademie e biblioteche d'Italia* a general survey of its musical materials.[2]

Desirable as it would surely be to have a fresh and more detailed study of these materials, one that would relate them to the Italo-Greek tradition in general and that would also attempt to trace those manuscripts from S. Salvatore that have found their way into

---

†Written for the Ninth International Congress of Byzantine Studies (Salonika, April 1953); hitherto published only in abstract.

[1] S. Salvatore 154.

[2] "I Codici musicali italo-greci di Messina," XI (1937), 65–78.

other libraries, the present paper has a much more modest aim. It restricts itself to a small group of related manuscripts, written at S. Salvatore in the thirteenth and fourteenth centuries. Two of these are still preserved at Messina, a third is at Grottaferrata, a fourth is in Rome at the Biblioteca Vaticana. Their common characteristic, apart from their place of origin and their melodic tradition, is that they constitute the only known examples of a unique and highly original type, uniting in one volume the contents of two books originally kept separate—the Psaltikon and the Asmatikon.

The terms *Psaltikon* and *Asmatikon* are commonly treated either as wholly synonymous and interchangeable or as vague, colorless, and without precise meaning. Yet they refer in fact to two distinctly different compilations, each with a function, a content, and a style of its own. They differ also in the little they have in common, for even where their texts agree, their melodies do not. Each follows its own rule and arrives at its own result. The distinction, as I see it, may be summed up briefly by saying that the Psaltikon is a soloist's book, containing nothing beyond what the soloist sings, while the Asmatikon is a choir book, restricted to chants and parts of chants that are sung by the choir or by several soloists in unison. Thus the two books are mutually exclusive, but at the same time complementary, for each is essential to the proper conduct of the musical part of the service.

That the distinction is substantially as just described and that the two compilations are in fact intended to supplement one another becomes immediately evident when one compares their contents. Thus the Great Troparia of the Christmas and Epiphany Vigila[3] are divided between the two books, with the Asmatikon containing the freely composed refrains, as sung by the choir, and the Psaltikon the psalmodic verses, as sung by a soloist. The graduals (προκείμενα), too, are analogously divided: the Psaltikon gives the first half of the refrain, together with the verses; the Asmatikon has only the full refrain with which the choir responds to the soloist's final verse.[4] For the communions (κοινωνικά) and the ordinary chants of the liturgy one turns to the Asmati-

---

[3] Λαθὼν ἐτέχθης, Ἀνέτειλας Χριστέ, Ἐπεφάνης ἐν τῷ κόσμῳ, and Ἁμαρτωλοῖς καὶ τελώναις.

[4] The Psaltikon contains the graduals of the liturgy and the Great Graduals of Vespers, the Asmatikon the daily graduals only.

kon,[5] while the Psaltikon contains the Alleluia verses and kontakia. The responds (ὑπακοαί) are found in either book, many of them with two more or less independent settings, one in the style of the Asmatikon, the other in that of the Psaltikon (as we know, such chants were sometimes performed by one singer, at other times by more than one).[6]

Before turning to those manuscripts from S. Salvatore that consolidate the two books, making one volume of them, I ought perhaps to give some account of such copies of the separate books as I have thus far been able to study and collate. As a separate book, I know the Psaltikon from four copies:

Grottaferrata, Γ.γ.iii;[7]
Vaticanus graecus 345;[8]
Paris, Bibliothèque Nationale, Ancien fonds grec 397;[9]
Sinai 1280.[10]

All four appear to be derived from a single archetype—in principle they contain the same pieces; they contain them in the same order (and it is in part an arbitrary one); they belong to the same melodic tradition; and, what is most conclusive, they agree in the occasional "second versions" that they provide for single phrases.[11] In no case

[5]There are, however, two communions τοῦ ψαλτικοῦ—settings of Ποτήριον σωτηρίου (Mode II Plagal) and Σῶμα Χριστοῦ.

[6]The responds with two settings, one τοῦ ἀσματικοῦ, the other τοῦ ψαλτικοῦ, are those of the eight modes and the following Great Responds: Εἰς δρόσον (Forefathers), "Αγγελος παίδων (Fathers), Μετὰ κλάδων (Palm Sunday), Προλαβοῦσαι (Easter), Ποῖα φυλακή (Peter and Paul), and Μακαρίζομέν σε (Festivals of the Virgin).

[7]A. Rocchi, Codices cryptenses (Grottaferrata, 1883), pp. 434–435; L. Tardo, L'Antica melurgia bizantina (Grottaferrata, 1938), pl. xxvii.

[8]R. Devreese, Codices vaticani graeci, II (Rome, 1937), 21–23.

[9]A. Gastoué, Catalogue des MSS de musique byzantine (Paris, 1907), p. 85; J. D. Petrescu, Condacul nasterii domnului 'Η παρθένος σήμερον (Bucharest, 1940), pp. 62–63.

[10]V. N. Beneševič, Catalogus codicum manuscriptorum graecorum qui in monasterio Sanctae Catharinae in Monte Sina asservantur III, 1 (St. Petersburg, 1917), 16. To judge from its rubrics, this manuscript is almost certainly Eastern, not Italo-Greek: the Alleluia verses for the anniversary of the founding of Constantinople. (May 11) are headed 'Οπότε ὁ πατριάρχης ἀνέρχεται ἐν τῷ φόρω. This should mean, of course, that the whole tradition of this particular recension is Eastern.

[11]See, for example, the second version (ἄλλον) of the words ἐκεῖ εὑρέθη φρέαρ from the oikos of the Christman kontakion (Grottaferrata Γ.γ.iii, fol. 9; Sinai 1280, fol. 133) or the two versions of the beginning of the Alleluia verse 'Υπομένων ὑπόμεινα (Vaticanus graecus 345, fol. 22; Sinai 1280, fol. 48). The Paris copy appears not to share this peculiarity.

can a provenance be positively established, although the copies at Grottaferrata, Rome, and Paris are clearly Italo-Greek. The oldest of the four copies is undoubtedly that at Grottaferrata, which is dated "1247." Of the Asmatikon in its simple state I know only two copies:

Grottaferrata, Γ.γ. i;[12]
Grottaferrata, Γ.γ. vii, fols. 1–71.[13]

These also belong to a single tradition, and—as will appear presently—this tradition must go back to the year 1225 at the very latest. I am not altogether persuaded by Rocchi's conjecture that the one copy may have been written in Calabria, the other at Grottaferrata itself. On the contrary, the two copies would appear to me to have a common origin, and—as we shall see—this is quite as likely to have been Messina as any point on the mainland.

Now in the scriptorium at S. Salvatore the contents of these two books, the Psaltikon and the Asmatikon, were consolidated and combined with other material to form a new compilation which, since it seems not to have been imitated elsewhere, may be said to bear the individual stamp of the great monastery with which we are directly concerned. Each of the four known copies exhibits certain peculiarities of content or structure. Thus the older of the two at Messina (S. Salvatore 129)[14] presents the most extensive and varied repertory. Nearly as extensive and as varied is the copy at Grottaferrata (Γ.γ.v);[15] but whereas S. Salvatore 129 arranges the bulk of its contents according to the calendar, with the Proper chants for each festival grouped together in sequence as a sort of Office, Grottaferrata Γ.γ.v is laid out in two parts, the first with the Proper antiphons, responds, and kontakia in the order of the church year, the second with the remainder of the contents— Proper or Ordinary—in a systematic arrangement. The two later copies, Vaticanus graecus 1606[16] and S. Salvatore 120,[17] follow

---

[12]Rocchi, *op. cit.*, p. 432; Tardo, *op. cit.*, pl. xxiv.
[13]Rocchi, *op. cit.*, p. 437. A manuscript exhibiting some, but not all, of the characteristics of an Asmatikon is Grottaferrata E.α.xiii. I have not seen the fifteenth-century copy on Mount Athos, Laura Γ.3.
[14]A. Mancini, *Codices graeci monasterii messaniensis S. Salvatoris* (Messina, 1907), pp. 187–188.
[15]Rocchi, *op. cit.*, p. 435–436; Tardo, *op. cit.*, pl. xxvi.
[16]C. Giannelli, *Codices vaticani graeci*, IV (Rome, 1950), 262–264.
[17]Mancini, *op. cit.*, p. 192.

the structure of S. Salvatore 129 but are rather more modest in scope; indeed S. Salvatore 120 excludes in principle all borrowings from the Asmatikon and is mentioned here only because of other characteristics that it shares with the remaining manuscripts of the group and as having been copied by the writer of Vaticanus graecus 1606. One might summarize all this by saying that the Psaltikon and Asmatikon are most successfully integrated in S. Salvatore 129 and Vaticanus graecus 1606, less successfully in Grottaferrata Γ. γ.v, not at all in S. Salvatore 120. In S. Salvatore 129 and Vaticanus graecus 1606 the Great Troparia of the Christmas and Epiphany Vigils are followed by their verses, with rubrics prescribing choral performance for the one,[18] performance by a soloist for the other;[19] similarly treated are the daily Vesper graduals, for which Vaticanus graecus 1606 gives first the half refrain of the soloist, then the verses, and finally the full refrain of the choir.[20] Once again the melodic tradition is remarkably uniform—so uniform, indeed, that all four manuscripts must go back to a common original. And, fortunately for us, the Grottaferrata copy is dated and signed. On folio 117ᵛ, at the end of the first part, it is said to have been completed in the year 1225; on folio 129ᵛ, the writer identifies himself as the Hieromonachos Sophronios of S. Salvatore.

The manuscripts of this little family are so many-sided and are from so many points of view unique that it is difficult to know where to begin—whether with the great cycle of Ordinary and Proper antiphons, the earliest and most comprehensive thing of its kind that we possess; whether with the elaborate provisions for the Gonyklisia, from which we can gather that in the thirteenth century the Italo-Greek rite still retained some features of the Constantinopolitan order; or whether with another equally interesting liturgical survival, the solemn setting of Psalm 31, sung as an introit at the Vespers of Holy Saturday during the entrance of the newly baptized. The mere mention of these features will have to suffice, however, for at the moment we are concerned solely with the general question of the overall musical tradition.

And in this respect, what our manuscripts reveal is not altogether what we might have expected. In so far as they draw upon the

---

[18]Οἱ ψάλτοι.
[19]Ὁ ψάλτης μονοφώνως.
[20]This last is headed ἡ δοχή.

Asmatikon, the manuscripts of Messina are in full agreement with the melodic tradition of the separate book—hence my earlier reference to the year 1225 as the latest possible date for this tradition and to Messina as the place at which it may have originated. But at this point agreement ceases. For in such parts of their contents as are drawn from the Psaltikon, the manuscripts of Messina, although in full agreement with one another, are no longer in agreement with the melodic tradition of the separate book, but follow a tradition of their own. This means that in Magna Graecia we have for the Asmatikon one tradition, for the Psaltikon two; that while there is only one version of each communion melody, there will be two for the melody of each Alleluia verse and each kontakion; and that while for the music of the Asmatikon the text-critical procedure is simple, for the music of the Psaltikon it will be complex.

In order to clarify the precise nature of the difference between the two versions of the music of the Psaltikon and at the same time to show in a general way what this music is like—for until now no really satisfactory transcriptions have been offered at all—I have prepared three short illustrations. In each of these the upper staff gives the quasi-universal reading of the separate Psaltikon, after Vaticanus graecus 345, the lower staff the reading from Messina, after Vaticanus graecus 1606. Obvious errors and omissions of these two sources have been corrected or supplied with the aid of other manuscripts already mentioned. In general, the transcriptions conform to the editorial practice of the Monumenta.[21] Example 1 compares the two versions of the half refrain and first verse of the gradual sung in place of the Alleluia at the Vespers of Holy Saturday. In Example 2 I have compared the two versions of the first of the two verses of the Alleluia for commemorations of single martyrs, the Byzantine counterpart of the Roman Alleluia "Justus ut palma," familiar to every student of the Gregorian chant. My third and final example is a comparison of the opening line and concluding refrain of the Christmas kontakion.

---

[21]I have departed from this in only three respects: notes and groups of notes affected by a gorgon are written in a smaller size; notes affected by a psephiston are marked with a horizontal stroke; a small *kappa* indicates a kouphisma.

Example 1
Mode III Plagal (Barys)   Gradual (Holy Saturday)

Example 2
Mode IV   Alleluia (A Martyr)

Example 3
Mode III   **Kontakion (Christmas)**

These comparisons show the version of S. Salvatore to have been the more elaborate or more developed of the two. They also show that the degree of this elaboration becomes progressively more marked as we proceed from gradual to Alleluia verse and from Alleluia verse to kontakion. The elaboration is effected partly through interpolations, partly through substitutions, some of which, being used over and over again, become highly characteristic. At the same time the essential features of the underlying melodic scheme are never obscured or lost sight of.

Having expressed the opinion that the Psaltikon is a soloist's book, containing nothing beyond what the soloist sings, I ought perhaps to comment also on the ending of the Alleluia verse shown in Example 2, which breaks off just before the end of the line. An examination of the complete cycle of Alleluias— there are fifty-seven numbers in all, with 120 verses—shows that this is invariably the case, and that in each mode the cadential formula with which the manuscripts break off is always the same.[22] There can, I think, be only one explanation of this curious phenomenon:—the endings of the verses must have been sung by the choir and in each mode they must always have been sung in the same fashion. Consideration of the six or seven Alleluias formerly sung in Greek at St. John Lateran and other churches in Rome bears out this view and suggests that there may also have been at least a partial correspondence between the melodies to which these endings were adapted and the Alleluia refrains themselves. We have no way of knowing what these Alleluia refrains were like, for our manuscripts do not give them. But even so we may say that, from a purely formal point of view, the Byzantine Alleluia, with its verses, probably corresponded exactly to the classical Roman Alleluia, with parallel cadences and will in fact have been the original upon which this was modeled.[23]

A final word regarding the tradition of S. Salvatore for the music of the Psaltikon. That this was not simply a local tradi-

---

[22]Only Mode I has two preparatory formulas, one beginning from a, the other from D.

[23]I am accordingly inclined to question the Byzantine origin of the bilingual Alleluia "Dies sanctificatus," studied by Wellesz in his *Eastern Elements in Western Chant* (Oxford, 1947), pp. 36–44. Not only does this depart from the classical type with parallel cadences, it is also nontypical in having a free text, not drawn from the Psalter or the liturgical canticles as is invariably the case with the Byzantine Alleluia.

tion, peculiar to S. Salvatore, is evident from its partial adoption in manuscripts known to have been written at Grottaferrata—in Grottaferrata E.β.vii, with kontakia commemorating S. Nilo and S. Bartolomeo; the founders of the monastery;[24] in Florence, Biblioteca Mediceo-Laurenziana, Ashburnham 64, copied at Grottaferrata in 1289;[25] and in Vaticanus graecus 1562, likewise copied there in 1318.[26] From these sources it appears that at Grottaferrata the tradition for the music of the Psaltikon was a mixed one. On the one hand the responds and Alleluia verses prove to be completely dependent on S. Salvatore, even to the extent of presenting the Alleluia verses in the order of the Messina MS Grottaferrata Γ.γ.v; the kontakia, on the other hand, follow the tradition of the separate Psaltikon, again including the "second versions" already mentioned in this connection.[27] For this part of their contents, the manuscripts of Grottaferrata—E.β.vii and Ashburnham 64—offer the best and most accurate text of any of our sources. Not only this. They contain a number of additional contrafacta and even certain idiomela not to be found in the separate Psaltikon at all. We may infer, then, that there must once have existed a manuscript of the separate Psaltikon more complete than any that we now possess.

[24]Rocchi, *op. cit.*, pp. 421–422.
[25]Tardo, *op. cit.*, p. 234, n. 2.
[26]Giannelli, *op. cit.*, 153–155.
[27]See, for example, the second version from the oikos of the Christmas kontakion cited in n. 11 above: E. β.vii, p. 69; Ashburnham 64, fol. 77[v].

ST. GREGORY NAZIANZUS AND THE PROPER HYMNS FOR EASTER[†]

I N a contribution published some years ago[1] S. Petrides drew attention to the commentaries of the Archimandrite Dorotheus on certain "psalms" of St. Gregory Nazianzus.[2] These seemed to him to throw new light upon the early history of Byzantine hymnography and to offer concrete proof of the early dependence of lyric poetry upon rhetorical prose. The present essay aims to reexamine this evidence with a view to bringing it to bear also upon the early history of Byzantine music.

The commentaries of Dorotheus constitute the twenty-second and twenty-third chapters of his *Didascalia*, an ascetic treatise written about the middle of the sixth century in a monastery situated between Gaza and Maiouma in southern Palestine. It is Easter Sunday and the monks have just finished singing one of Gregory's "psalms"—'Αναστάσεως ἡμέρα καρποφορήσωμεν ἡμᾶς αὐτούς. The archimandrite expounds the text for them, going over it line by line. It proves to have been adapted from the first of Gregory's two sermons *In sanctum Pascha;*[3] Petrides notes that this adaptation is not included among the Easter hymns in the liturgical books as we now have them and suggests that it may have been

†From *Late Classical and Mediaeval Studies in Honor of Albert Mathias Friend, Jr.,* ed. Kurt Weitzmann (Princeton, 1955), pp. 82–87. Reprinted with permission of Princeton University Press.

[1]"Notes d'hymnographie byzantine," *Byzantinische Zeitschrift*, XIII (1904), 421–428, largely reprinted in Cabrol by Leclercq as a part of his article "Hymnes," VI, 2874–2876.

[2]*Pat. Gr.,* LXXXVIII, 1821–1836.

[3]*Pat. Gr.,* XXXV, 396 ff.

crowded out by the familiar canon by John of Damascus, which
begins with the same words and also leans on Gregory to some
extent. Having finished his first discourse, Dorotheus goes on to
commend in general the singing of passages from the sermons of
the Fathers. On festivals of Our Lord, on anniversaries of martyrs
and confessors, indeed on any solemn and outstanding occasion,
this practice, he says, will teach us the very meaning of the commemoration we observe. This leads him to an analysis of a "psalm"
for martyrs which proves in turn to have been adapted from Gregory's sermon *Adversos Arianos;*[4] Petrides identifies this second hymn
with a Martyrikon of Mode IV. The text is still in liturgical use
and may be found printed in the current editions of the Parakletike.

For our present purposes the significant thing is that Dorotheus has transmitted to us, embedded in his commentaries, the
texts of two hymns that were actually being sung in Palestine
about the middle of the sixth century and perhaps still earlier.
What is more, he gives us the exact wording, and since this involves some skipping about and also departs here and there
from the established wording of Gregory's sermons, we may be
confident, on finding either hymn in a later source, that what
we have before us is in fact a composition dating from the sixth
century or earlier, and by no chance a later adaptation. What is
still more, his general commendation of the singing of hymns
adapted from the writings of the Fathers clearly permits the inference that other hymns of this sort must have existed in his
day; thus on finding wholly similar pieces in later sources, particularly when we find them in the company of either of the
hymns for which Dorotheus specifically vouches, we ought at
least to put them to the test and weigh the possibility that they
also may have been among those he knew.

Now although Petrides was entirely correct in saying that the
hymn Ἀναστάσεως ἡμέρα καρποφορήσωμεν ἡμᾶς αὐτούς
is not included in the liturgical books as we now have them, it
is none the less to be found, with its music, in a considerable
number of early manuscripts of the Sticherarion, among them
the following:

---

[4]*Pat. Gr.*, XXXVI, 213 ff.; the passage adapted begins in column 232.

Athens, National Library, MSS 883, 888 (from the Meteoron), 957 (dated 1274), 974; Grottaferrata, E.*a*.vi; Iviron (Athos), MS 953; Laura (Athos), Γ.12, Γ.67, Γ.71, Γ.72, Γ.86, Δ.3 (dated 1304), Δ.15, Δ.28, Δ.68; Paris, Bibliothèque Nationale, gr. 261 (dated 1289), 262, 264; Rome, Biblioteca Vaticana, Barberini gr. 411 and 498, Ottob. gr. 380, Palat. gr. 420; Sinai, MSS 1214 and 1216; Vatopedi (Athos), MSS 1486, 1487, 1488, 1489, 1490, 1492 (from Damascus, dated 1242); Vienna, Nationalbibliothek, Theol. gr. 136.

In most of these sources it is the second of three stichera in Mode I.[5] The first sticheron of the triptych is Σήμερον σωτηρία τῷ κόσμῳ, a text adapted in a similar way from Gregory's second sermon *In sanctum Pascha;*[6] the third, Τῆς λαμπρᾶς καὶ ἐνδόξου, is evidently a free composition.[7]

Leaving trifling variants aside, the text of 'Αναστάσεως ἡμέρα, as given in the MSS, departs from Petrides' careful reconstruction only in adding the line ἵνα ἡμᾶς τοὺς νεκρωθέντας ἐπανάγῃ πρὸς ζωήν, which Dorotheus attributes to Gregory, although it is not from his sermon, and in concluding with the conventional formula ὡς μόνος ἀγαθὸς καὶ φιλάνθρωπος, which may be found in any number of early doxologies. Much the same might be said of Σήμερον σωτηρία; this is made up of two passages, fourteen lines in all, quoted almost literally from the beginning of Gregory's long sermon, with four additional lines in which the adapter alludes to Psalm 106 and, perhaps unintentionally, to the Easter troparion Χριστὸς ἀνέστη.

The transcriptions that follow are based upon Koutloumousi 412 (Fig. 1) and Sinai 1216 (Fig. 2a–b). (See pp. 62–63.)

Surely these two pieces deserve the most careful consideration. As we have seen, the text of *B* goes back to the middle of the sixth century at the very latest. And while one cannot claim this categorically for the text of *A,* when two texts have a common basis and a common tradition, as these texts have, one may at least suspect them of having had a common origin. The situation is unusually

---

[5]Laura Δ.3, Barberini gr. 411, Sinai 1216, and Vatopedi 1488 contain the first two stichera, but not the third.

[6]*Pat. Gr.,* XXXVI, 624 ff.

[7]Sources containing the first and third of the three stichera, but not the second, include Athens, National Library, MS 884 (dated 1341); Milan, Biblioteca Ambrosiana, gr. 733; Paris, Bibliothèque Nationale, gr. 260; and Sinai, MS 1453. Only the first appears in Koutloumousi (Athos), MS 412 and Paris, Bibliothèque Nationale, gr. 242.

favorable—indeed without a parallel. If our sources have preserved for us even the essential features of the melodies with which
these texts were first associated, they will enable us to form an idea,
however partial, of what the earliest stratum of Byzantine music
must have been like.

A

εν Χρι - στω και - νη _____ κτι - σις α - να - και -
νι - ζε - ται · Πα - σχα κυ - ρι - ου Πα - σχα ·
και πα - λιν ε - ρω _____ Πα - σχα _____
τι — μη της τρι - α - δος · 'αυ - τη η - μιν
ε - ορ - των _____ ε - ορ - τη · πα - νη - γυ - ρις
ε - στι _____ πα - νη - γυ - ρε - ων ·
εν _ ταυ - τη γαρ Χρι - στος α - νε - στη εκ νε - κρων ·
φω - τι - ζων τους εν σκο - τει και σκι - α ·
και σω - ζων τους υι - ους των γη - γε - νων ·
ως α - γα - θος _____ και φι - λαν - θρω - πος.

B

Α - να - στα - σε - ως η - με - ρα · καρ - πο -

The problem, in short, is a specific instance of the recurrent central problem of early Christian music. How can we control the evidence of our oldest manuscripts? To what extent does their melodic tradition reflect that of earlier times? Shall we say that, unless there are indications to the contrary, a melody is as old as the liturgical use of its text? Or shall we take the opposite stand and say that a melody is valid only for the time of the manuscripts that contain it? Extreme positions, surely, the one uncritical, the other unrealistic, neither one susceptible of scientific proof or disproof.

In many respects the problem is identical with that which confronts the historian of art who wishes to trace the illustrations in his oldest Greek and Latin manuscripts to their early Christian prototypes. But it cannot be solved in the same way. Throughout the early Christian world an impenetrable barrier of oral tradition lies between all but the latest melodies and the earliest attempts to reduce them to writing. Comparisons will not help us here, for one cannot work out the chronology of one set of melodies by comparing them with those of another set whose chronology is equally uncertain. The same argument also forbids the use of Jewish melodies for comparative purposes. With the fragmentary remains of ancient Greek music we should be on surer ground. But what effective use could we make of remains so meager, so much the result of chance? And the expedient of stemmata would not carry us far enough to be worth resorting to.

Taking the specific case of the Easter hymn 'Αναστάσεως ἡμέρα, let us rather consider, one by one, the various alternatives. Can its sixth-century melody have been improvised? Surely not, for Dorotheus repeatedly implies that it was sung by a choir. Can it have been forgotten or discarded later on, to be replaced sometime before the tenth or eleventh century by a wholly new melody, the one transmitted by our manuscripts? This is remotely possible, perhaps, but most unlikely. Can there have been several older melodies? Again perhaps, but if so it is even less credible that the melody we have should be a wholly new creation. The real question, it would seem, is not so much one of fact as one of degree —not whether our melody reflects some traces of an ancient model but rather how faithfully it reflects them.

In general it should be possible to say that under one set of conditions a melody is more likely to survive centuries of oral transmission; under another set, less likely—that melodies of the Proper and Common are more resistant to alteration than melodies of the Ordinary and less readily dislodged; that prose texts and texts in irregular and unusual meters tend to retain their original melodies while texts in the simpler meters are sung now to one melody, now to another; that music for a choir is more stable than music for soloists. Thus it is on the whole unlikely that our earliest

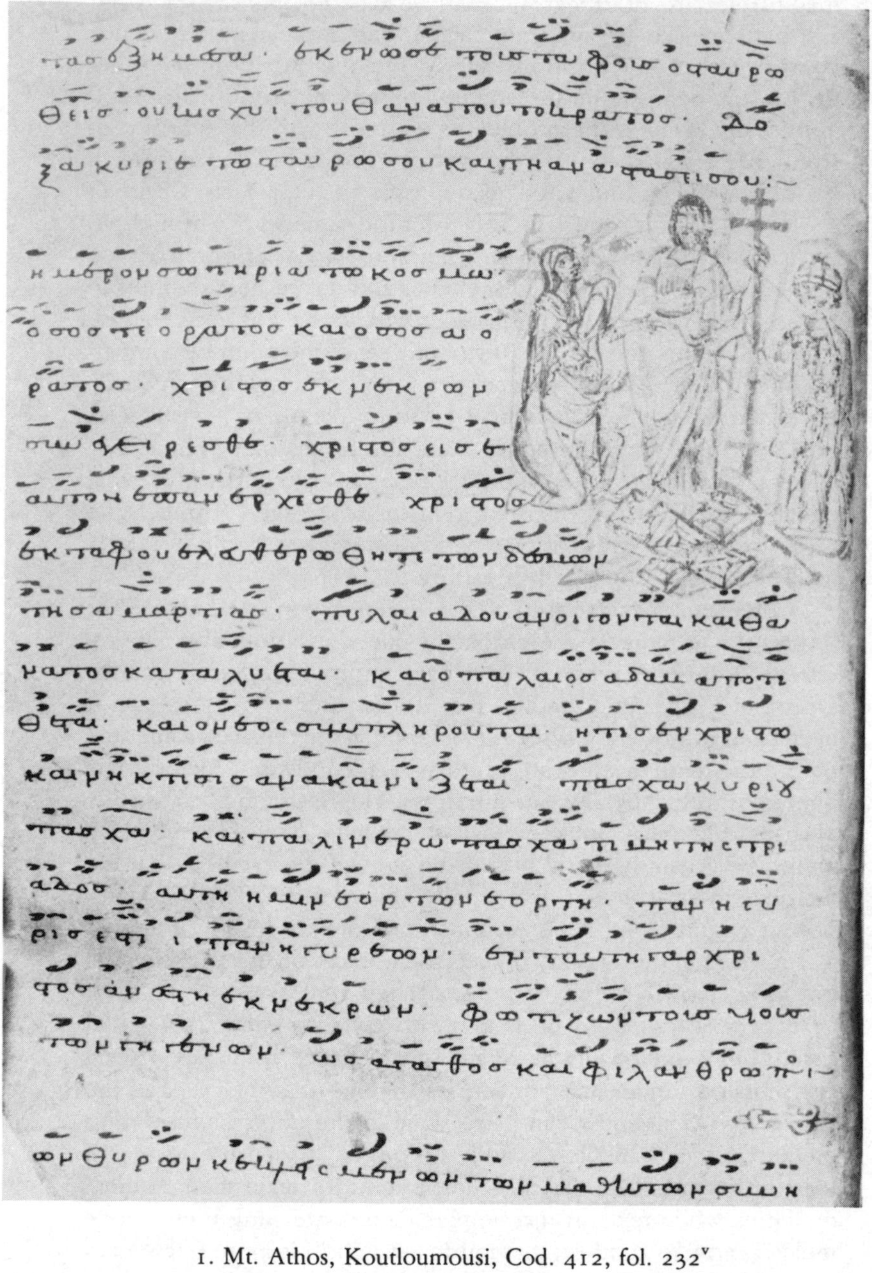

1. Mt. Athos, Koutloumousi, Cod. 412, fol. 232v

2a–b. Mt. Sinai, Cod. 1216, fols. 220ʳ–220ᵛ

recorded melodies for the Cherubic Hymns, for the hymns of St. Ambrose, for the kontakia of Romanos, have anything at all to do with the melodies to which these texts were originally sung. But if each of these examples fails fully to meet our set of favorable conditions, 'Αναστάσεως ἡμέρα meets them all.

In supposing that John of Damascus may have known and sung the second of our two stichera, and that this may have prompted him to compose his Easter canon 'Αναστάσεως ἡμέρα λαμπρυν-θῶμεν λαοί, which may in turn have caused the disappearance of its model from the liturgical repertory, Petrides suggests still another approach to our problem. John's first heirmos, like the sticheron which begins with the same words, takes its cue from Gregory's first sermon *In sanctum Pascha;* the second sermon is the source, not only of the sticheron Σήμερον σωτηρία, but also of John's fourth heirmos and of much of the language of his eighth. As a result of this dependence upon Gregory, the texts of John's three model-stanzas and of our two stichera have much in common. And John has also chosen to write in Mode I. This opens the door to melodic correspondences as well as textual ones, and if we find that such occur in fact, we may reasonably infer a dependence of the one set upon the other. The example that follows compares the parallel passages.[8]

[8]The quotations from the canon after *The Hymns of the Hirmologium, Part I,* revised and annotated by Carsten Høeg, Monumenta musicae byzantinae, Transcripta, 7 (Copenhagen, 1952), pp. 55–57.

Ση - με - ρον   σω-τη - ρι - α — τω   κο - σμω

αυ - τη   η-μιν ε - ορ - των   ε - ορ - τη

και πα-νη-γυ - ρις   ε - στι   πα - νη - γυ - ρε - ων ·

If only the fifth and last of these correspondences is really conclusive, it is at the same time so very striking—particularly since each of the two passages serves in its context as a sort of climax—that one can neither ignore it nor successfully explain it away. It is of course conceivable that the original is the heirmos and not the sticheron. But the opposite view is at once simpler and inherently more plausible.[9]

Yet on the whole I think it unlikely that it was the conflict between John's canon and our stichera which caused these last to drop out of liturgical use. The real explanation would appear to lie elsewhere—in the conflict between the three stichera in Mode I

[9]Still another possibility is that both pieces are the work of the same person. This solution appears to receive some support from a group of early manuscripts—Laura Γ.12, Laura Γ.72, and Vatopedi 1488—which attribute Σήμερον σωτηρία to "Joannes Monachos." Yet it would be a mistake to attach great importance to this. Attributions of this kind are notoriously unreliable; the Athens MS 883, unusually systematic in its ascriptions, gives no author for Σήμερον σωτηρία or its two companion pieces; MS 1486 at Vatopedi describes all three as ἀμνήμα.

and the five very similar pieces in Mode I Plagal that are still in use today:

Πάσχα ἱερόν
Δεῦτε ἀπὸ θέας
Αἱ μυροφόροι
Πάσχα τὸ τερπνόν
'Αναστάσεως ἡμέρα, καὶ λαμπρυνθῶμεν τῇ πανηγύρει.

The pieces of this second group constitute a considerable problem in their own right; to discuss them here would lead altogether too far. Suffice it to say that, like our sticheron B and John's first heirmos, the fifth and last of these pieces is based upon Gregory's first sermon, to the opening clauses of which it adds a connecting phrase and, as a refrain, the Easter troparion Χριστὸς ἀνέστη.[10] These pieces, then, and not John's canon, will have caused our stichera to drop out of sight. Once again, the simple and inherently plausible explanation is that the two sets come from different centers, the one from southern Palestine, the other perhaps from Jerusalem itself, and that when the liturgical books were codified sometime before the year 1100 a choice was made; from thenceforth our stichera will have been copied and sung only when they belonged to a local use.

Through the liturgical use of his sermons, St. Gregory Nazianzus—theologian, orator, and poet—came to play a considerable role in the development of Byzantine art and music, for these popular writings of his were not only read aloud as lessons, they were also illustrated and sung. At one time his two sermons *In sanctum Pascha* were appointed as readings for Easter Sunday and for the Monday to Friday following; throughout the week, salient passages from the lessons read at Morning Prayer were echoed by the choir, just as they were also illustrated in the lectionaries. Nor was this confined to the Easter season. Years ago Cardinal Pitra drew attention to the quotations by Cosmas from Gregory's sermon *In Theophania*.[11] There are further borrowings from his sermon *In Pentecosten* among the hymns for Pentecost,[12] and al-

---

[10]In older sources this refrain also concluded the third and fourth members of the group and a large number of additional pieces.

[11]*L'Hymnographie de l'Église grecque* (Rome, 1867), p. 75.

[12]Pointed out by Jan Sajdak in his *De Gregorio Nazianzeno poetarum christianorum*

though this seems to have escaped notice until now, from his sermon *In novam Dominicam* among those for the Dedication of the Church.[13] Thanks to Dorotheus, we know that some of these borrowed texts were being sung as early as the sixth century. And he has carried us a little closer to the music of that remote time and has taught us that the history of the sticheron—or of the "troparion," as it was called at first—actually begins far earlier than we have generally assumed.

---

fonte (Kraków, 1917).

[13]Published by Egon Wellesz in Monumenta musicae byzantinae, Transcripta, 1 (Copenhagen, 1936), nos. 45, 48, and 49.

THE NOTATION OF THE
CHARTRES FRAGMENT[†]

I N May 1953, at the time of my visit to the monastery of
Vatopedi on Mount Athos, a systematic examination of the MSS
preserved there brought to light an unusually interesting choir-
book, the MS Vatopedi 1488. At my suggestion, and with the kind
permission of the courteous librarian of the monastery, Father
Gennadios, a complete microfilm copy was made for the Library of
Congress by Professor Ernest W. Saunders of the Garrett Biblical
Institute of Northwestern University. To Father Gennadios, and to
Professor Saunders, I should like to express here my most sincere
thanks.

The published catalogue of the Vatopedi library assigns the
MS to the eleventh century.[1] It is a perfect copy of the second
half of the Sticherarion, a choirbook corresponding roughly—
but only very roughly—to the Western Antiphoner, and it is divided, following the usual plan, into three main sections—one
with the idiomela of the Triodion and Pentekostarion (the
Western *Proprium de Tempore*), another with the idiomela and antiphons of the Oktoechos (the Western *Commune Dominicale*), and
a third with the prosomoia of Theodore Studites (a cycle of contrafacta for the weekdays in Lent). Like other early copies,
Vatopedi 1488 is unabridged in that it contains a considerable

†From *Annales musicologiques*, III (1955), 7–37. Reprinted with permission of La
Société de musique d'autrefois.
[1]Sophronios Eustratiades, *Catalogue of the Greek Manuscripts in the Library of the
Monastery of Vatopedi on Mt. Athos*, Harvard Theological Studies, XI (Cambridge,
1924), p. 234.

number of idiomela and other pieces not regularly found in later MSS; most of these occur also in other eleventh-century sources, a few are perhaps unique. And whereas in later MSS the music for a given festival is ordinarily arranged in the order of the modal cycle, in Vatopedi 1488, as in other early copies, it tends to follow the order of the service and to be provided with rubrics indicating its place in that order.

But the most striking feature of the MS is its notation. The whole is the work of a single scribe. Yet for one part of the contents the notation used is the so-called "Coislin" notation, as used in MSS from the later eleventh and earlier twelfth centuries; for another part it is the archaic notation of the Chartres fragment—Professor Tillyard's "Andreatic system."[2]

It was in 1907, in his catalogue of the MSS of Byzantine music in the public libraries of France, that Gastoué first drew attention to the Chartres fragment.[3] The six folios of which this consisted had been brought to Chartres from the Grand Laura on Mount Athos by the librarian and director of the local museum, Paul Durand, who had visited the Balkans in 1840 with Didron, the art historian. Gastoué rightly considered the fragment to be the earliest of the Byzantine MSS that he had seen, and as such he described it in minute detail, giving an itemized list of its contents and reproducing two pages in facsimile.[4] To its archaic musical notation he gave the name *notation paléobyzantine ou athonite,* thus distinguishing it from the notation now usually called "Coislin," to which he gave the name *notation droite.*

---

[2]For the terminology and a discussion of the successive stages in the development of the early Byzantine notation, see Tillyard's recent studies—"The Stages of the Early Byzantine Notation," *Byzantinische Zeitschrift,* XLV (1952), 29–42, and "Byzantine Music about A.D. 1100," *Musical Quarterly,* XXXIX (1953), 223–231. The scheme of classification there set forth is in effect a restatement of that first presented in Tillyard's "The Problem of Byzantine Neumes," *Journal of Hellenic Studies,* XLI (1921), 22–49.

[3]*Introduction à la paléographie musicale byzantine* (Paris, 1907), pp. 96–99, also viii, 13, 52, 60, 65, and pl. iii.

[4]And fortunately so, for the fragment itself was destroyed during a bombardment of Chartres toward the end of the Second World War. Gastoué's plate has been reproduced by Wellesz in his *Byzantinische Musik* (1927), pl. 8, and by Mme. R. Palikarova Verdeil in *La musique byzantine chez les Bulgares et les Russes* (Copenhagen and Boston, 1953), pl. vi. Mme. Verdeil also reproduces (pl. vii) one further page, after a photograph from Gastoué's private collection, until recently the property of the late Professor Masson. I learn from Mme. Verdeil that no further photographs are believed to exist.

If Gastoué was probably not on solid ground when he related the notation of the fragment to the Mozarabic neumes, and if his one transcription from it can only be called naive, it remains to his credit that he fully recognized the genuine importance of the fragment and that his comments on it have for the most part stood the test of time. He was undoubtedly correct in describing its notation as one in which conventional signs often stood for melodic groups, he was undoubtedly correct in relating this notation to that used in the earliest MSS of Russian chant, and he was undoubtedly correct in attaching importance to the liturgical peculiarities of the fragment.

If there were doubts about the provenance of the fragment at Chartres, they were laid to rest in 1912 when Tillyard visited Mount Athos and identified the codex from which it had been detached as the Laura MS Γ.67. This MS, it now developed, had at the end a full-page list of its musical signs, and in 1913 Tillyard published this list in facsimile, with a helpful commentary.[5] The same year also saw the publication of Thibaut's *Monuments,* with photographs of a new specimen of the notation.[6] This was a single folio from the collection of fragments brought back to Russia from Mount Sinai by the Archimandrite Uspensky. It was obviously later than the fragment at Chartres and it illustrated a more developed state of the notation. One had now to admit that the Chartres fragment was not a freak, and that its notation had had a longer life and a wider geographical distribution than Gastoué had supposed. Thibaut's fragment had already been identified by Benešević as a part of the MS Sinai 1219.[7]

In the meantime, Hugo Riemann had published further transcriptions from the Chartres fragment,[8] and to these Tillyard's article of 1913 added others, based on the Athos MS itself. These

[5] "Fragment of a Byzantine Musical Handbook in the Monastery of Laura on Mt. Athos," *Annual of the British School at Athens,* XIX (1912–13), 95–117, pls. xiii and xiv. The table of signs is also reproduced in the monograph by Mme. Verdeil cited above (pl. v). The fragment formerly at Chartres originally belonged between the folios now numbered 81 and 82.

[6] *Monuments de la notation ekphonétique et hagiopolite de l'Eglise grecque* (St. Petersburg, 1913), pp. 77–78.

[7] *Catalogus codicum manuscriptorum graecorum qui in monasterio Sanctae Catharinae in Monte Sina asservantur,* I (St. Petersburg, 1911), 622.

[8] *Die byzantinische Notenschrift* (Leipzig, 1909), pp. 73–78 ("Die Notierung des Fragments von Chartres").

too were failures, for—like Gastoué—Riemann and Tillyard were still trying to read the archaic notation directly, without the help of a control. It was not until 1921 that Tillyard made his first experiments with the method of parallel transcription, which uses late and unambiguous sources to disclose the meaning of earlier ones that are less clear. Applied to the "Coislin" notation, this method led almost at once to significant results, and in subsequent studies Tillyard has used it with ever-increasing assurance and precision.[9] But the notation of the Chartres fragment proved more obstinate and at first resisted even this approach. The earliest results were inconclusive, and it is only in his latest studies that Tillyard has renewed the experiment with some measure of success[10] and has begun to use the method to support his contention that the notation of the Chartres fragment is a genuinely melodic notation and that the melodies it transmits have at least a general resemblance to those found in later sources.

The MS Vatopedi 1488 is well adapted to provide for these claims the confirmation their author invites. Its two notations are kept quite distinct. In no case are they combined in the course of a single melody; there is no trace of a transitional stage. Nor is there anything arbitrary in the choice of the one notation or the other. The "Coislin" notation is used for those stichera of the Triodion and Pentekostarion which form part of the abridged contents of the later MSS; the notation of the Chartres fragment is used for the rest. Only too obviously, the copyist of Vatopedi 1488 worked from two *Vorlagen*—one of them in the "Coislin" notation, the other in the notation of the Chartres fragment, one an abridged copy of the Triodion and Pentekostarion, the other an unabridged copy which contained also an Oktoechos and the Lenten prosomoia. In choosing between his two *Vorlagen* he followed a simple rule. Wherever possible he used the "Coislin" *Vorlage;* the other one, in the notation of the Chartres fragment, he used only when he was forced to do so.

[9]Above all in "Early Byzantine Neumes: A New Principle of Decipherment," *Laudate,* XIV (1936), 183–187, and "Byzantine Neumes: The Coislin Notation," *Byzantinische Zeitschrift,* XXXVII (1937), 345–358.

[10]It is most instructive to compare Tillyard's two transcriptions of the sticheron Πρῶτος ἐν διακόνοις after Sinai 1219, one made in 1921 (*Journal of Hellenic Studies,* XLI, 46–49), the other in 1953 (*The Musical Quarterly,* XXXIX, 229–230).

Thus the MS Vatopedi 1488 points unmistakably to an intimate relationship between contents and notation, and I shall want to return, later on, to this relationship and to what it implies. That the MS constitutes a sort of turning-point is equally clear. At the time it was copied, an old system of notation was being displaced by a new one, and if our MS was one of the first to use the new system, it was also one of the last to use the old. For the comparative study of the two notations it should be the ideal source.

But if the MS is to be used effectively for this purpose it must contain melodies that are ideally comparable, written first in the one notation, then in the other. And fortunately it does. One of the Lenten prosomoia, written in the notation of the Chartres fragment, repeats a melody previously entered in the "Coislin" notation as part of the Triodion.[11] And other stichera from within the Triodion itself, written in the "Coislin" notation, are followed by additional stanzas to be sung to the same melody; for these additional stanzas, the notation is usually that of the Chartres fragment, for they are seldom found in later sources.

A single example will lead us to the heart of the problem. At Lauds, on Wednesday in Holy Week, our MS appoints four stichera—the idiomelon "Ἥπλωσεν ἡ πόρνη and three added stanzas. The "Coislin" notation is used for the model stanza, the notation of the Chartres fragment for those that follow.[12] The four stanzas develop topics taken from Matthew 26:6–16, the Gospel read at Vespers later in the day—the annointing of Christ's feet by Mary Magdalen, the tempting of Judas, the visit of Jesus to the house of Simon the Leper. With its orderly antitheses and its conventional refrain, the text of the model stanza is thoroughly characteristic.

---

[11]This is Δυσημερεύει Λάζαρος (fol. 217), for which the model is Κύριε ἐπὶ τὸν τάφον (fol. 55ᵛ). There should of course be others, similarly comparable, but Vatopedi 1488 contains only a selection from the prosomoia of Theodore.

[12]Other similar sets are Φθάσαντες πιστοί (with two added stanzas), Τοῦ κρύψαντος (with three), and Ὅτι ψυχῆς (with two). And at Vespers on Palm Sunday there are three prosomoia on Ὁ ἔχων θρόνον, an idiomelon sung at the Vespers of the preceding day. In all four cases, the "Coislin" notation is used for the model stanza, the notation of the Chartres fragment for those that follow. Ἡ ἀπεγνωσμένη also has two added stanzas, but in this case the "Coislin" notation is used throughout.

The harlot held out her hair to Thee, the Master; Judas held out his hands to the lawless; she to receive forgiveness; he to receive silver. Therefore we cry out to Thee, betrayed for us and our Redeemer: Lord, glory to Thee!

The first five plates which accompany this study illustrate the various ways in which the melody has been written down. Plate I gives it in the "Round" notation, after Koutloumousi 412, an Athos MS of the thirteenth century.[13] Plates 2 and 3, after Vatopedi 1488, give the model stanza in the "Coislin" notation and the three added stanzas in the notation of the Chartres fragment. Plate 4 gives the model stanza once again, after Laura Γ.67, the MS to which the Chartres fragment belonged, while Plate 5 adds still another Chartres version, after Laura Γ.72, where the piece is ascribed to one "Ioannes," presumably the ubiquitous "Ioannes Monachos." I should like to have shown also the Chartres version of Laura Γ.12, but the neumes of this MS are badly faded and those for "Ηπλωσεν ή πόρνη can barely be made out. Once again I am indebted to Professor Saunders for microfilms made at the Laura during our visit to that monastery, and it is a pleasure to recall also the many kindnesses of Father Panteleimon, the Laura's learned librarian.[14]

The "Round" notation of Koutloumousi 412 presents no difficulties. I transcribe it without comment, copying above my transcription the neumes of the earlier sources. In considering these, it will be simplest to limit the discussion, at first, to the opening phrase of the melody and to the "Coislin" neumes.

[13]For an account of this MS, see p. 23, n. 17, of this volume.

[14]Together with the Laura MSS B.32 and Γ.74, to be mentioned later, these sources are described by Spyridon and Eustratiades in their *Catalogue of the Greek Manuscripts in the Library of the Laura on Mount Athos* (Cambridge, 1925), where they are numbered 152 (B.32), 252 (Γ.12), 307 (Γ.67), 312 (Γ.72), and 314 (Γ.74). Wellesz has a clear reproduction from Γ.12 in his *Eastern Elements in Western Chant* (Boston, 1947), pl. v; see also his folding plates preceding p. 99 and Tillyard's transcription in *Byzantinische Zeitschrift*, XLV (1952), 37–42. Complete microfilms of all five MSS were made by Professor Saunders for the Library of Congress.

Ex. I

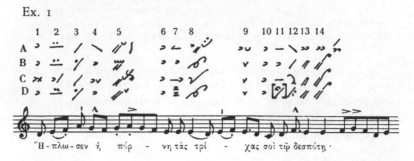

If the reader will take the trouble to compare the "Coislin" neumes from Vatopedi 1488 (A) with the corresponding signs of the "Round" notation, as shown in Plate 1, he will discover for himself that the "Round" notation for a given syllable usually incorporates the "Coislin" sign, sometimes taking it over just as it stands (syllables 2, 6, 7, 10, 11, 13), sometimes combining it with other signs that "spell out" or otherwise clarify its meaning (syllables 1, 4, 5, 9, 12). Where this does not happen, it is either because of the substitution of a sign with a similar but not identical meaning (syllable 3) or because of the substitution of an equivalent sign for one of the elements of a group whose remaining elements are retained (syllables 8 and 14). And just as the "Round" notation incorporates the "Coislin" signs, so it consciously and inevitably incorporates the "Coislin" melody also. Visually, the "Coislin" neumes make the more agreeable impression; compared to their studied and almost classic simplicity, the "Round" notation seems overly cluttered. On the other hand, the "Round" notation tells the singer everything there is to know, while the "Coislin" neumes give him only the merest guidance. If he has heard the melody before, they will help him to recall it; if he has not, he must divine their meaning. And if he is thoroughly familiar with the conventions of Byzantine melody, general and specific, he can do so.

For the fact is that when a body of music is sufficiently conventional, a very simple notation is all that is needed. In this mode, the Second Plagal, the "Coislin" neumes of our first phrase can have only one meaning, and wherever we find them—again in this mode —we shall know what that meaning is. If the reader will turn again to Plate 1, he will find at the bottom of the page the beginning of another melody belonging to the same mode and type, whose first phrase concludes also with the same cadential formula. He can already anticipate its notation in the "Coislin" neumes, and if he had seen this first, he would have known how to read it. I transcribe from Koutloumousi 412, adding the "Coislin" neumes from Vatopedi 1488, folio 77 verso.

Ex. 2

Even more revealing is the first line of the idiomelon, Προσῆλθε γυνή, also shown on Plate 1. This can be divided into two complementary phrases, the first a modification of the opening pattern by now familiar, the second a more or less literal restatement of it. Once again I transcribe from Koutloumousi 412, taking the "Coislin" neumes from Vatopedi 1488, folio 77.

Ex. 3

Here there is no pitch difference between the ending of the antecedent phrase and the beginning of the consequent. Yet, as before, the "Coislin" notation for the consequent phrase begins with the *apostrophos,* which normally represents a lower pitch. In this notation, clearly, one has to think in terms of whole phrases, not single signs.[15]

The notation of the Chartres fragment, to which I now turn, is sometimes called "the notation with the straight *ison,*" and rightly so, for its use of this sign to represent the repeated note or unison is the simplest and most striking characteristic of its later state.

[15]The reader may also compare the use of the compound neume above syllable 8 in Example 1 with its use above the accented syllable of the word ἀπεγνωσμένη in Example 2. In the first case the *apostrophos* with which this begins corresponds to the unison, in the second case it corresponds to the third below.

Characteristic of its earlier state is its neglect of secondary syllables, which it often leaves unprovided for. But since this neglect of secondary syllables is equally characteristic of the "Coislin" notation in its earliest state, while the earliest MSS in the notation of the Chartres fragment make no use of the straight *ison,* we must evidently look further for a persistent and distinctive characteristic. And we can find such a characteristic for the notation of the Chartres fragment in the strange signs it uses to represent melodic groups. Tillyard's table from Laura Γ.67 illustrates some thirty of these and tells us their names. These signs are as old as the notation itself, and they live on until it passes out of use. The "Coislin" notation does not know them, nor does its "Round" derivative. As one result of this, it is impossible to convert successfully from the notation of the Chartres fragment to either of the later systems, although one can easily convert from "Coislin" neumes to "Round" with few outright alterations or erasures, simply by writing in additional signs.[16]

Below the "Coislin" neumes in row A, Example 1 correlates the three Chartres versions of our opening phrase, from Plates 2, 4, and 5. B is the version of Vatopedi 1488—I follow the neumes for Χριστοκτόνων δῆμος, the first of the added stanzas; C and D are the versions of Laura Γ.67 and Γ.72. That A and B have substantially the same meaning is self-evident—the writer of the Vatopedi MS implies as much when he collects the four stanzas and introduces all but the first by abbreviating the word ὅμοιον in the margin. Once this is recognized, it follows sufficiently from the general resemblance that C and D must approximate the "Coislin" melody also.

As we have seen, the distinctive mark of the Chartres notation —the thing that sets it apart and gives it a physiognomy of its own —is its use of unfamiliar symbols to represent melodic groups. Three of these occur in our example, and it will be advantageous to begin with them, taking them up in order before turning to the simple signs.

---

[16]Such converted MSS are actually not uncommon—the Heirmologion Saba 83 is perhaps the most familiar example. For a brief account of this important MS see Wellesz, "Early Byzantine Neumes," *The Musical Quarterly,* XXXVIII (1952), 71–75. There are good facsimiles in his *History of Byzantine Music and Hymnography* (Oxford, 1949), pl. iii, and in Peter Wagner's *Einführung in die gregorianische Melodien,* II, 2nd ed. (Leipzig, 1912), 45.

Above syllable 5 of our example, each of the Chartres versions has a different sign. B uses what appears to be the *tromikon* ("trembling") of Tillyard's table, combining it with the doubled *oxeia* or acute accent.[17] C and D substitute signs common to the Chartres and "Coislin" notations. D's reading—the *xeron klasma*—is identical with A's and is thus to be rendered precisely as in my transcription from Koutloumousi 412.[18] C's reading would not lead to a radically different solution. Above syllable 8 of our example, B and D have the *tinagma* ("shaking"), while C has a sign not shown in Tillyard's table which seems to represent a simpler form of the same progression.[19] Above syllable 14, all three of the Chartres versions have the *laimos* ("throat"), combined with the doubled *oxeia.*

No adequate account of these distinctive signs can be based on a single example. Such an account would have to deal, not with one example, but with many; not with isolated signs, chosen almost at random, but with the whole system to which these signs belong. For our present purposes, however, it is perhaps sufficient that for each of the three signs encountered in our example we have a "Coislin" equivalent, and that each of these equivalents is "spelled out" for us in the "Round" notation. From this it by no means follows that the "Coislin" equivalents we have are the only ones possible or that the way in which they are "spelled out" in the "Round" notation has any validity apart from this particular context. And even after looking at further examples, all one can say is that in this mode and on these steps our "Coislin" equivalents for the Chartres *tromikon* and *tinagma* are the ones usually employed and that—again in this mode and on these steps—the way in which they are "spelled out" in the "Round" notation is the usual way.

With the *laimos,* the third and last of our unfamiliar signs, the situation is far simpler. In countless instances, in every mode and on every step, this corresponds, as it does in our example, to the *kylisma* of the "Coislin" and "Round" notations, so that there can

---

[17]This is a frequent combination—it occurs again on Plate 3 in Ἀρχιερεῖς καὶ γραμματεῖς and on Plate 5 in Ὁ τοῦ ἐλέους κύριος. That it occurs also in Laura Γ.67 may be seen from Gastoué's plate (left-hand page, lines 4, 6, 10, and 14). Here the *tromikon* is formed somewhat differently, beginning from below and ending with a downward stroke.

[18]Laura Γ.12 also has the *xeron klasma* (fol. 31ᵛ), both here and at the corresponding point in the second phrase.

[19]Laura Γ.12 also has the *tinagma,* here and in the second phrase.

be no doubt that the two signs are wholly identical in meaning. The fact is significant. For it is scarcely consonant with the view of the Chartres and "Coislin" notations as constituting earlier and later stages in a single development that two signs should agree in meaning, yet differ in name and outward form. The sign *laimos* cannot very well have "become" the sign *kylisma,* nor does there appear to be any good reason for the change in name. But the difficulty disappears the moment the two notations are viewed as separate and concurrent developments from a common beginning. Thus far, to avoid anticipating, I have spoken of them as though they were successive stages. I can now abandon the use of this device.

As was to be expected, the simple signs of the four versions are in general agreement, particularly in essential matters. In two cases all four signs are the same (syllables 6 and 10); in a third they are equivalent (syllable 13). Above syllables 1 and 3, the Chartres versions add clarifying auxiliaries, rudimentary forms of the later leap-signs, which at this early stage have much the same force as the auxiliary letters used in MSS of Western chant. Above syllable 9, the "Coislin" version adds a clarifying *apostrophos.* Syllables 4 and 12 involve real differences in notation, but little change in meaning. And even here there is at least partial agreement, for above syllable 12 C's sign is simply another form of the *bareia* or grave accent, as used in A.

But at syllable 7 there is general disagreement, and some departure from the "Coislin" melody is almost certainly intended. B has the *apostrophos,* which should take us at least a step below A's *ison,* while C has the straight *ison* followed by the *apostrophos,* thus combining the divergent readings. D abbreviates the syllables *nana,* which serve at this stage of the development as a medial signature indicating the first step of the basic tetrachord—usually a, but often the fourth above or, as here, the fifth below. In this way D lets us know the pitch at which the signs in B and C are probably to be transcribed.[20]

The rest of the phrase is distinctly problematic. It raises fundamental questions, and they demand positive answers. Up to this

---

[20]Laura Γ.72, the source in which this signature occurs, contradicts the general tradition by assigning the idiomelon to the authentic form of the mode. I take this to be a mere slip of the pen. But even if it were intended, it would have no effect on the implications of the medial signature.

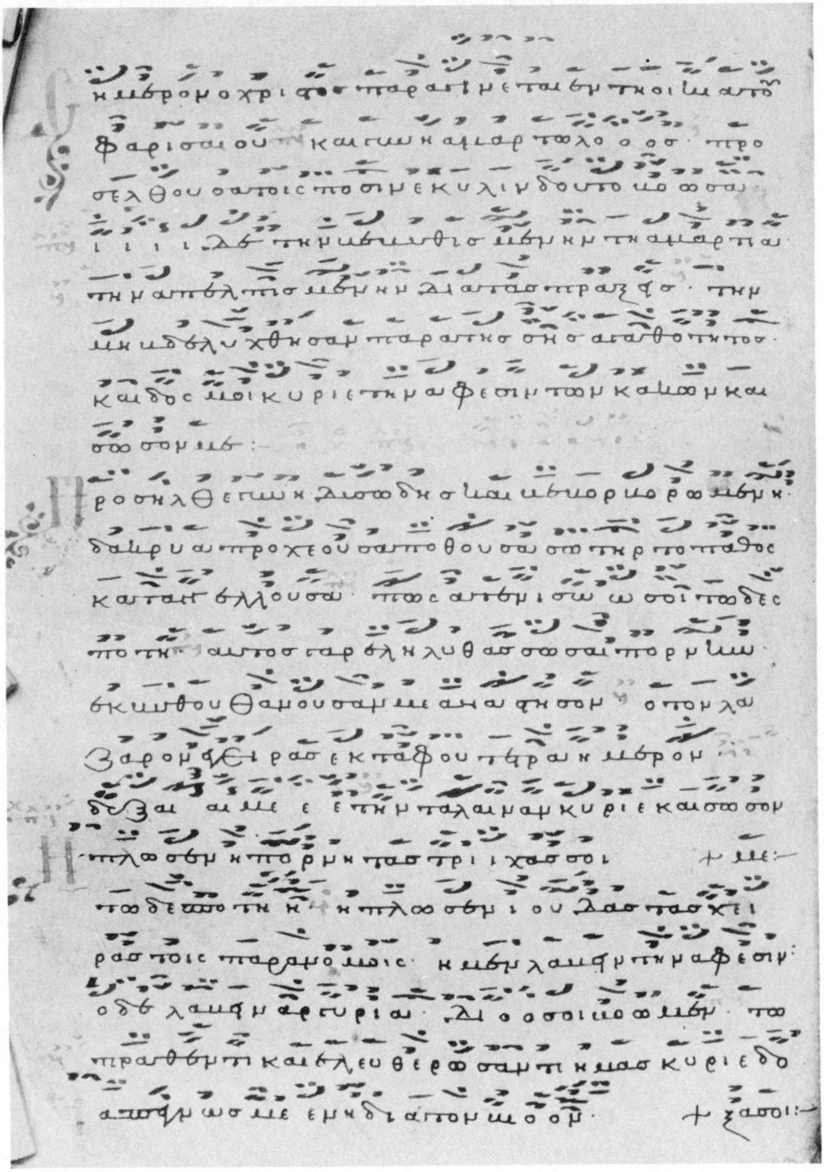

Plate 1: Koutloumousi 412, fol. 214v

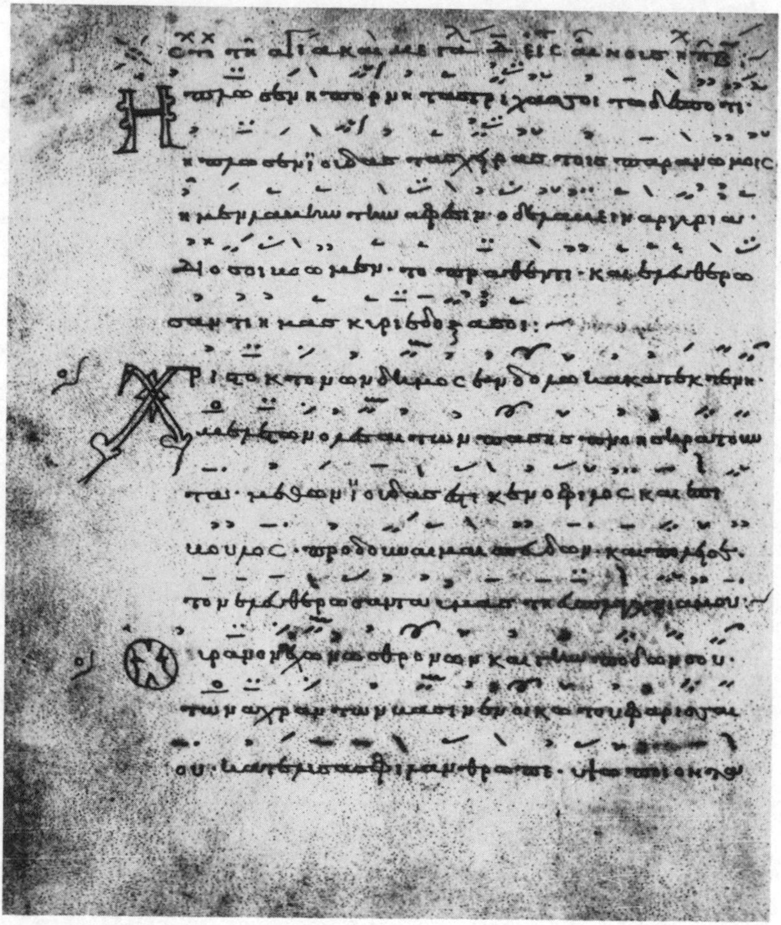

Plate 2: Vatopedi 1488, fol. 74^v

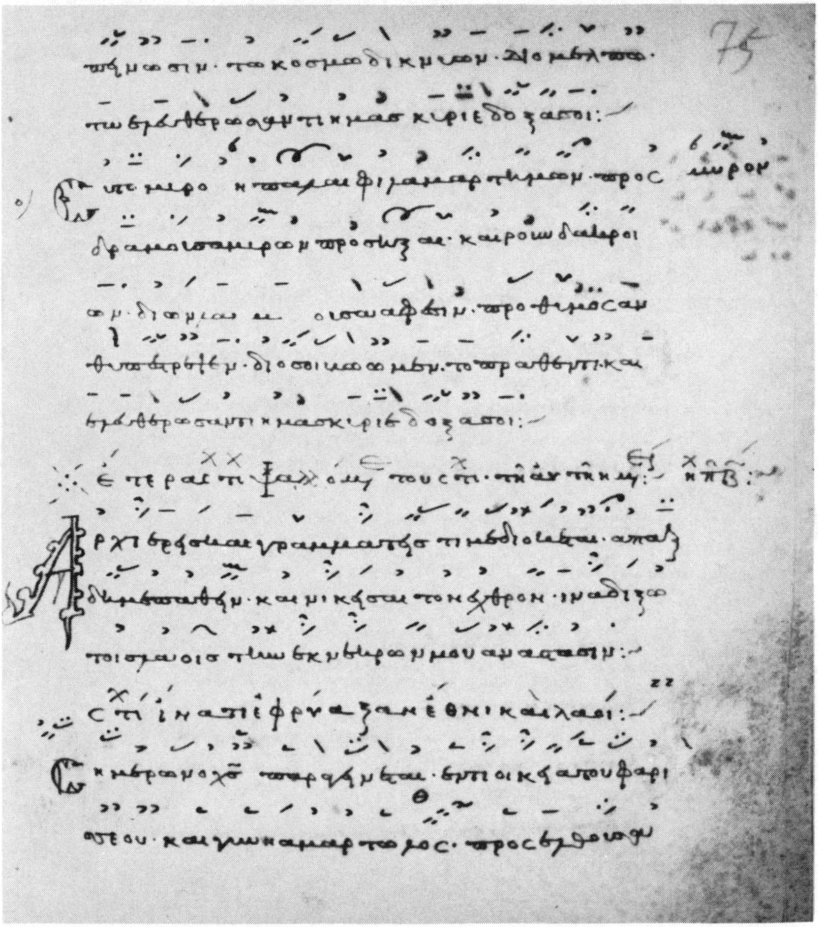

Plate 3: Vatopedi 1488, fol. 75

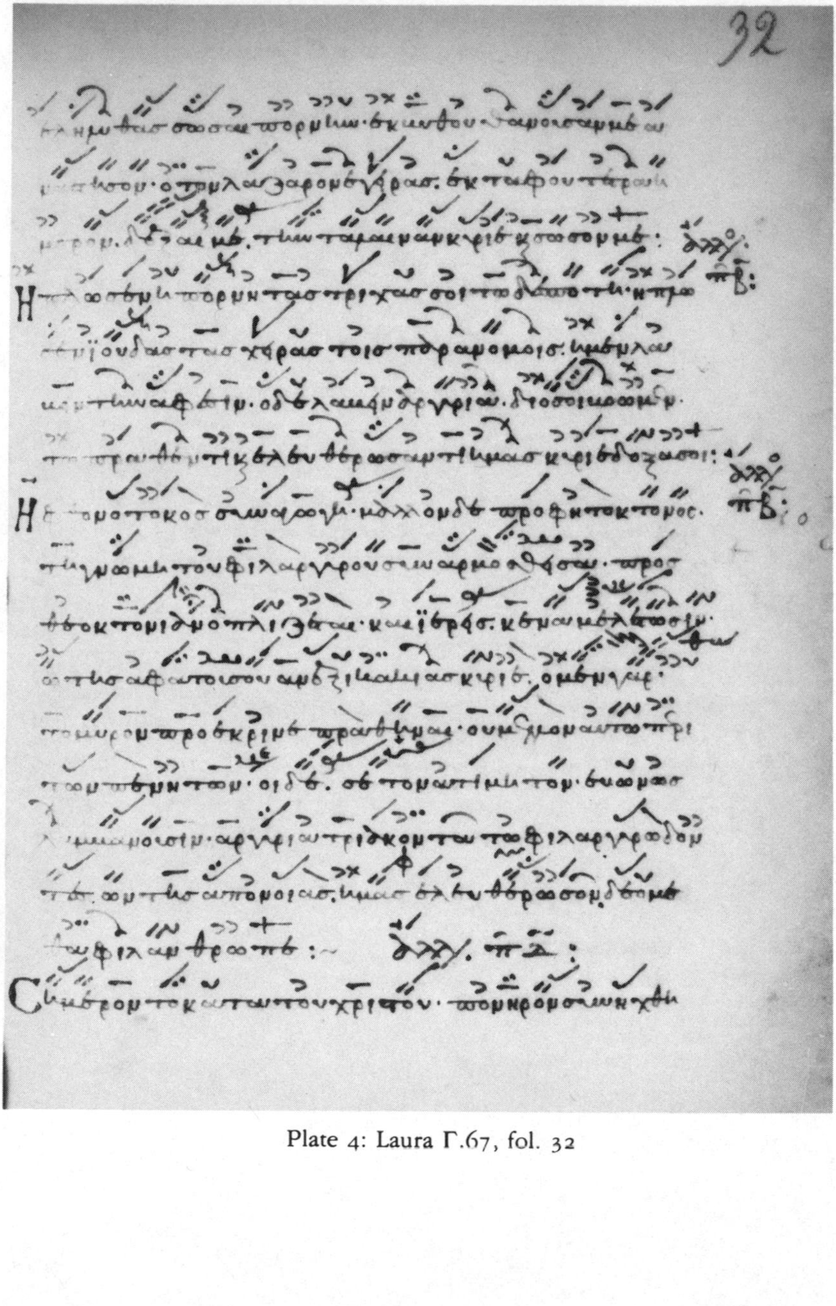

Plate 4: Laura Γ.67, fol. 32

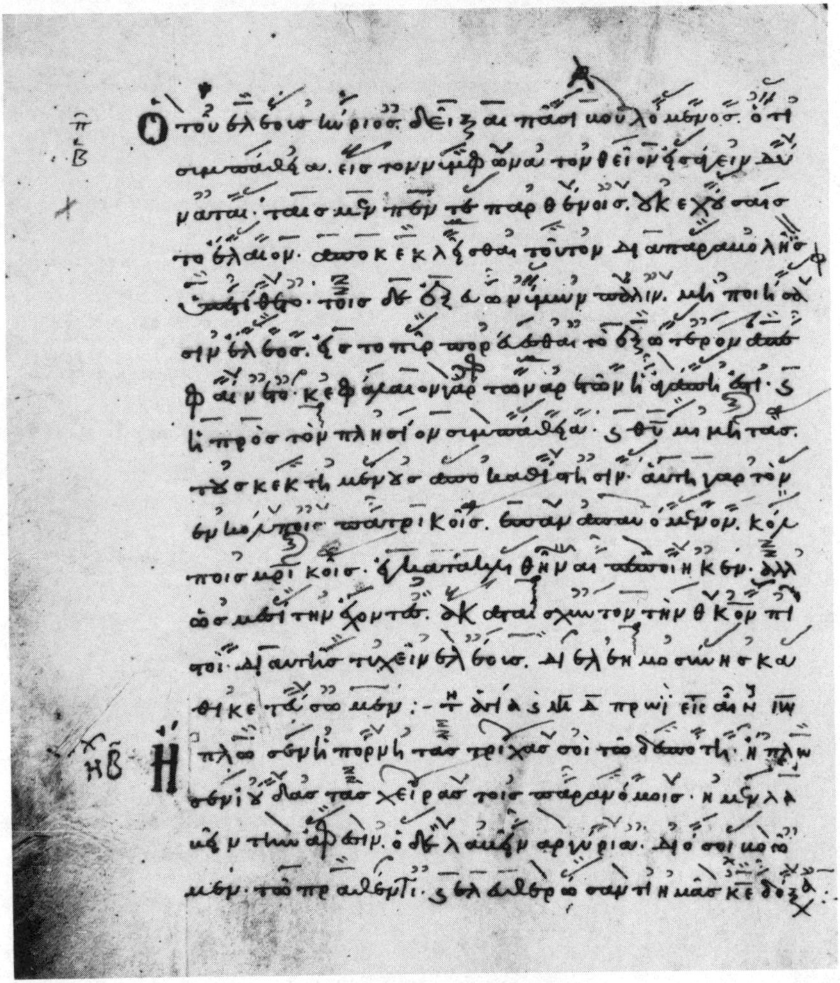

Plate 5: Laura Γ.72, fol. 6^{v}

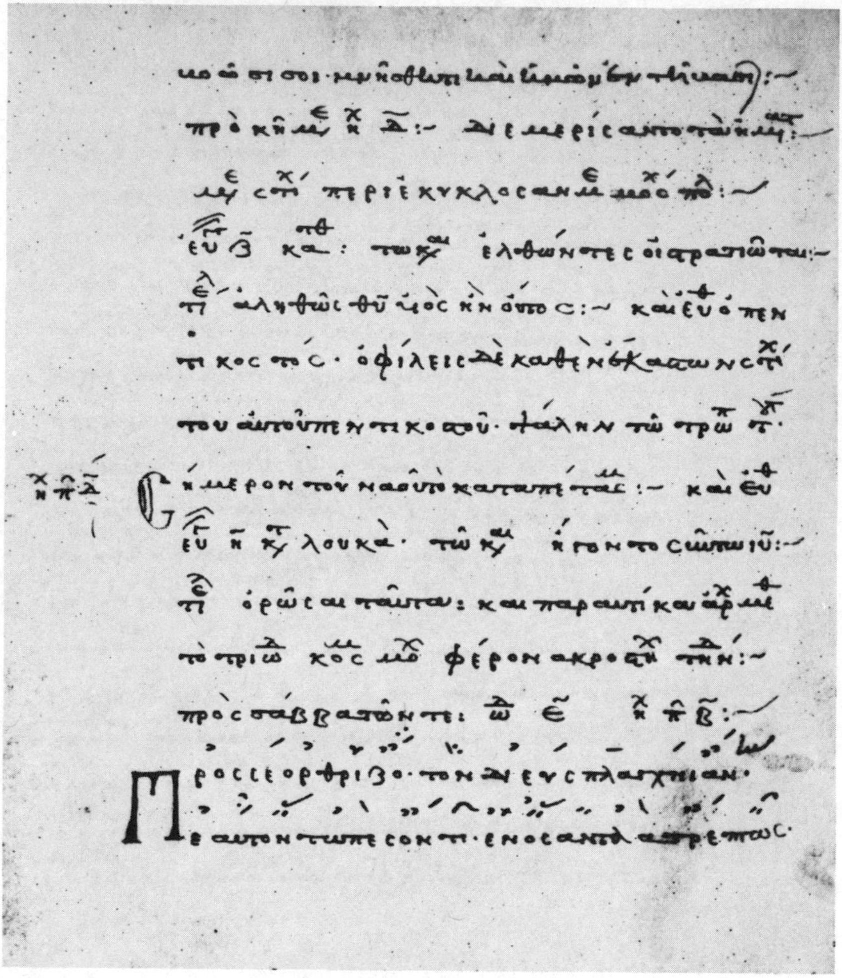

Plate 6: Vatopedi 1488, fol. 104v

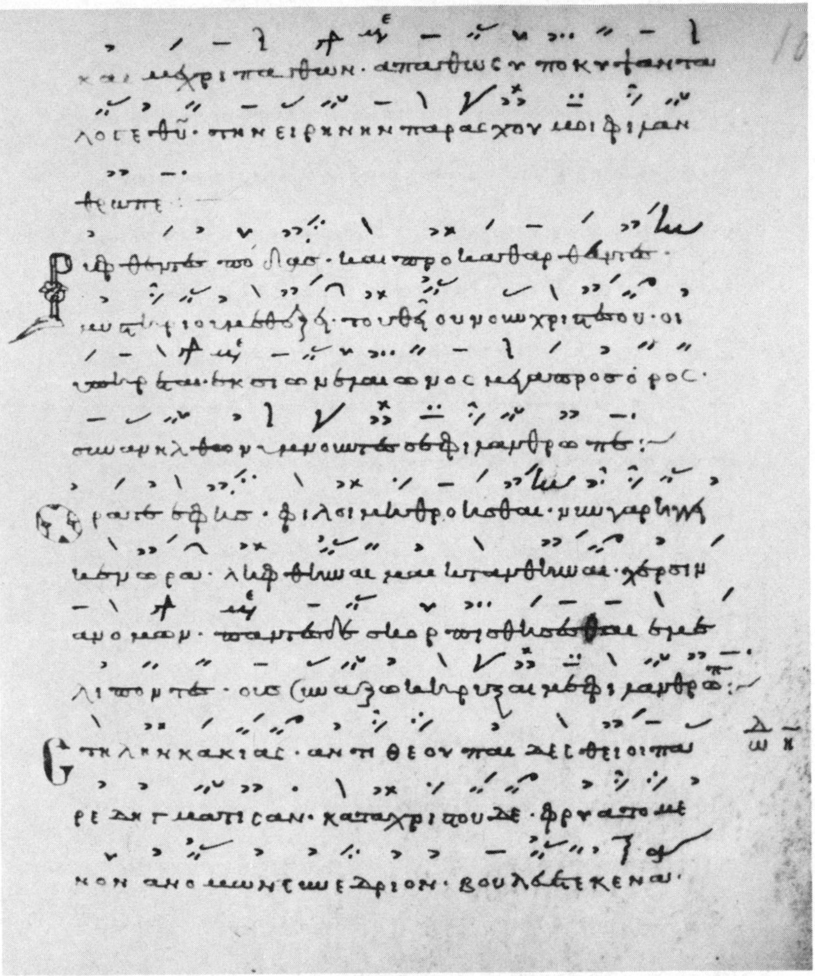

Plate 7: Vatopedi 1488, fol. 105

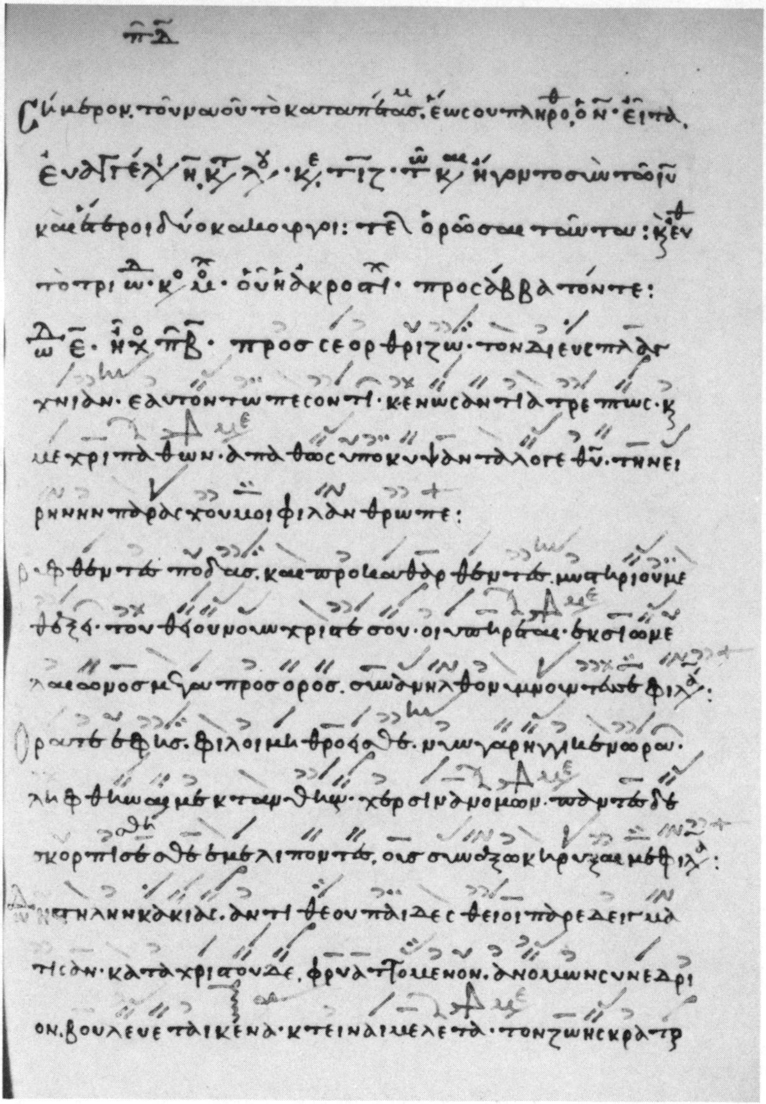

Plate 8: Laura Γ.67, fol. 53

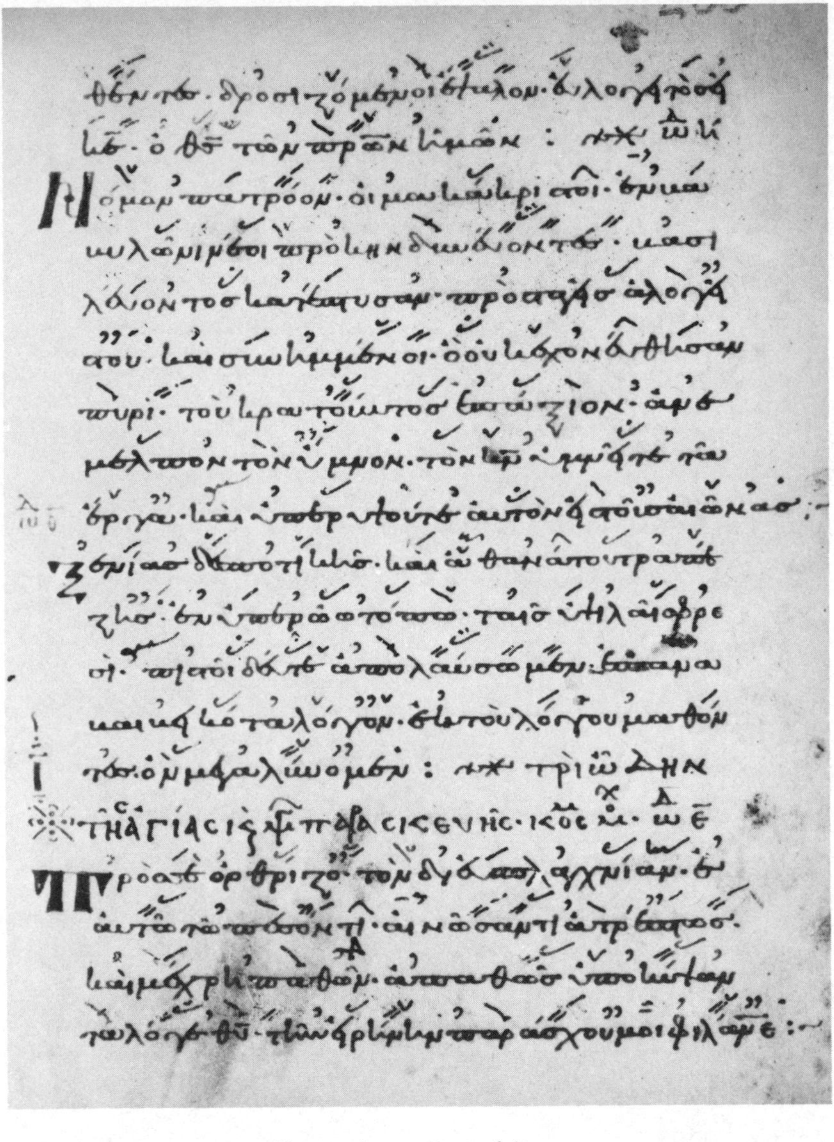

Plate 9: Laura B.32, fol. 200

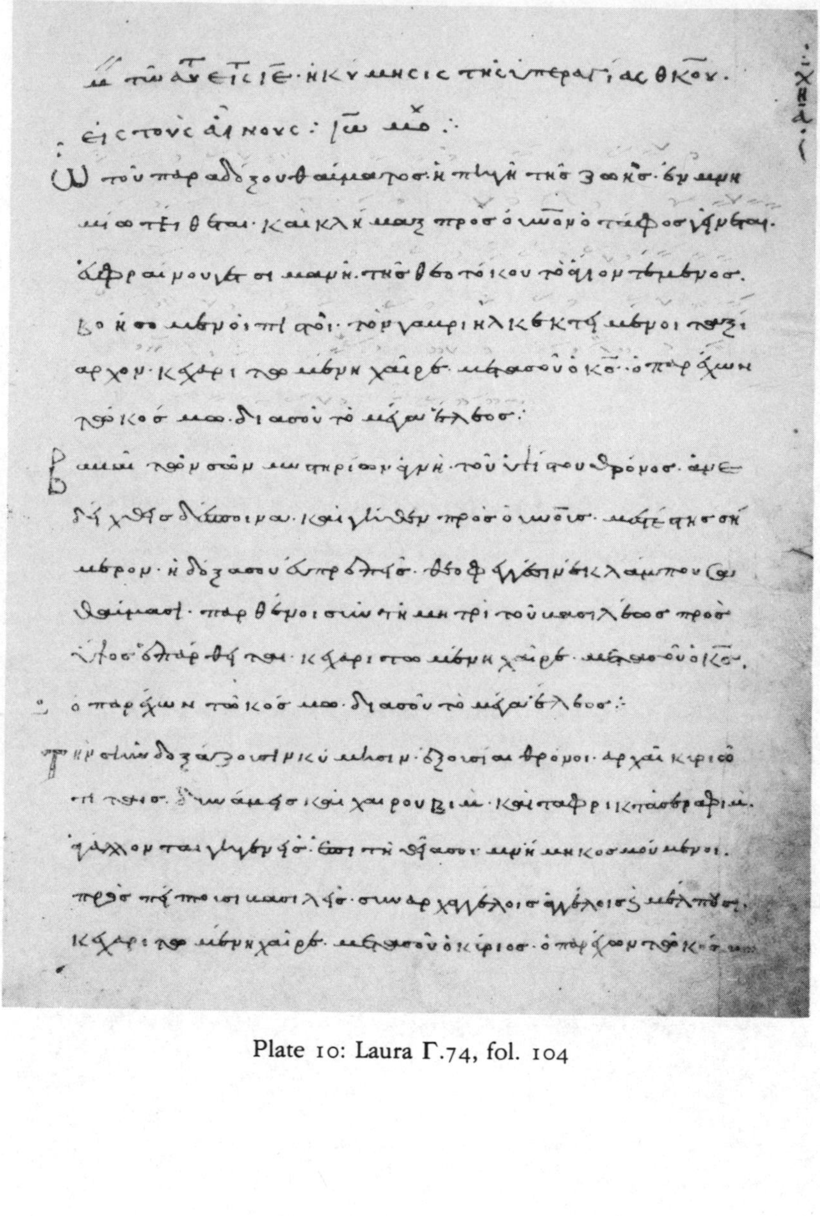

Plate 10: Laura Γ.74, fol. 104

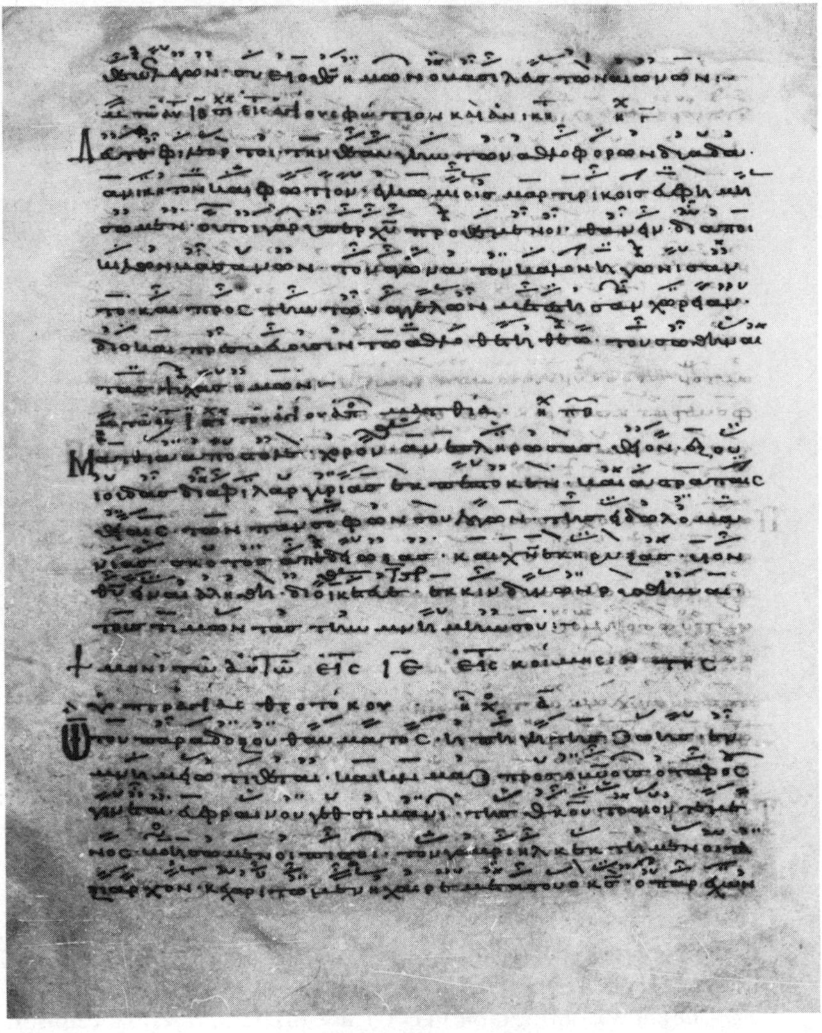

Plate 11: Sinai 1219, fol. 143ᵛ

point, my findings have agreed with Tillyard's or have been at least consistent with them. Here, after weighing his solutions, I find myself obliged to take a different stand. In so far as this denies the absolute directional value of the Chartres *apostrophos,* it tends, of course, to weaken Tillyard's principal thesis in one respect. But in so far as it affirms the essential identity of the melodies transmitted by the Chartres and "Round" notations, it tends at the same time to strengthen it in another.

The first question is one of interpretation. From D's second phrase, a sign must be supplied to fill in the gap above syllable 11. It is an *oxeia,* to which is added an auxiliary somewhat resembling our modern *fermata.* Tillyard identifies this auxiliary with the *argon* and with the *apoderma* and explains it as "a small *tenuto.*" One objection to this view would be that the *apoderma,* like our modern *fermata,* is an unusual sign calling for an unusual effect, while the auxiliary in question is a sign in constant use. As a general rule it occurs only when the "Round" notation proceeds by step. I am accordingly inclined to understand it as a sign calling for stepwise progression—up or down as the case may be—and to identify it with the *oligon* of the table in Γ.67. If this is correct, our auxiliary is simply an abbreviation, formed from the letters *omicron* and *lambda,* conventionalized and so reduced in scale that the *omicron* has become a mere dot. It combines not only with the *oxeia* but also with the *petaste* (or *petasma*) and with the *apostrophos,* thus performing the same function as the Latin auxiliary $g = gradatim.$ This interpretation brings D's reading into agreement with the "Coislin" and "Round" versions. What is more important, it means that in the notation of the Chartres fragment we now have, besides the straight *ison* and the two *kentemata,* a third sign whose diastematic meaning is usually unambiguous.

That the plain horizontal stroke used in our MSS is to be called an *ison,* we know from the table in Γ.67, and that it represents the unison or repeated note is evident, not only from its name, but also from the overwhelming majority of its occurrences in Tillyard's parallel transcriptions and my own.[21] Logically, then, the combination *ison*

---

[21]Surely it is to the straight *ison* that the author of the "Hagiopolite" treatise refers when he says that "in the notation of melismatic music (ἐν τοῖς χειρονο-μήμασι τοῖς ἀσματικοῖς) the *oligon* was called *ison*" (Thibault, *Monuments,* p. 59).

plus two *kentemata* ought to represent the group unison plus ascending second. Tillyard takes it to mean just this, with the result that, at the point affected, his transcription of Παράδοξον μυστήριον, after two sources in the notation of the Chartres fragment, lies a step below the version of his "round" control.[22] In "Ηπλωσεν ἡ πόρνη, as transmitted by B and D, a literal reading will lead to the same result, not only at syllable 2 and at the corresponding point in the phrase that follows, but also in the concluding refrain. There are two possibilities—one is that the eleventh-century version of the melody differed from that current in the twelfth century and later; the other is that, when combined with the two *kentemata,* the straight *ison*—if we may so call it—represents an ascending second. The latter alternative would appear to me to be the more likely, particularly since in "Ηπλωσεν ἡ πόρνη the points affected belong to opening and cadential patterns for which one should be able to assume the highest degree of stability.

The same argument bears even more directly on the difficult question of the *apostrophos.* If at syllable 2 we are to reject as improbable the literal readings of B and D, ought we not also to reject C's reading, which is still more improbable? Are we to suppose that in an otherwise stable pattern a single detail, obstinately unstable, crept gradually upward, step by step, until it finally found its level? To explain the readings of B and D, I suggested just now that as one element of a particular combination the straight *ison* may have represented an ascending second—may, in other words, have taken on the meaning of the "Coislin" *oligon* with which it is identical in outward form. No such explanation can reasonably be offered here. Instead of asking what this particular *apostrophos* means in terms of direction and interval, ought we not rather to ask whether it has any meaning in these terms? Is it not possible that the *apostrophos* was at first a sign without melodic meaning, used to distinguish secondary syllables, and that in the course of time it gradually acquired melodic meaning through association—first in terms of direction, then in terms of interval? This would seem to me to be the only reasonable hypothesis. In dealing with the early Byzantine notations, one soon discovers for

[22]*The Musical Quarterly,* XXXIX (1953), 225, fig. 1, line 5.

oneself that the frequency of the *apostrophos* is determined by the date of the MS. The earlier the MS the more frequent the *apostrophos*, and the gradual decrease in frequency as one proceeds from earlier MSS to later cannot be satisfactorily accounted for by attributing it solely to an increase in the use of other descending signs. Yet it would be absurd to conclude from this that the tenth century was more partial to descending progressions than the eleventh, or the eleventh than the twelfth. Of our three Chartres versions, C is easily the earliest, and it is to this version, the one in which the *apostrophos* is used most frequently, that our difficulty is largely confined. To show just how considerable a difficulty this is, I insert here the remaining phrases of the parallel transcription begun in Example 1.

Ex. 4

θε - ρώ - σαν - τι ἡ - μᾶς· Κύ - ρι - ε   δό - ξα   σοι :

Version D presents no problem. With one exception, every *apostrophos* corresponds to a descending progression, and the one exception—in the concluding refrain, above the first syllable of the word κύριε—is clearly due to a melodic variant, implicit in the preceding *bareia* and confirmed by Version C. Version B is already problematic. In general it agrees with D, but the *apostrophos* above syllable 11 of the opening phrase is distinctly suspect, as is its repetition in the phrase that follows, the more so since the two signs contradict the readings of C and D, not to mention those of the "Coislin" and "Round" versions. With Version C the problems increase. Besides the ambiguous *apostrophos* above syllable 2 and its repetition in the phrase that follows, there are three further ambiguities—one above the first syllable of the word λαβεῖν in the line ἡ μὲν λαβεῖν τὴν ἄφεσιν, a well-established pattern; another above the second syllable of the word λαβεῖν in the following line, the usual cadential formula in this mode; and a third above the second syllable of the word κύριε in the concluding refrain, another form of the same cadence. That the *apostrophos* corresponds to a unison in one of these five cases, and to an ascending step in the four others, is possible and even likely. But in none of these cases can it properly be said to represent a melodic progression of any sort. If one could say of the "Coislin" notation that it is necessary to think in terms of whole phrases, not single signs, one may repeat this here with greater emphasis.

In the commentary that accompanies his transcription of Παρά-δοξον μυστήριον, Tillyard deals at some length with an ambiguous *apostrophos* of the same general type as those just discussed, and one of his suggestions is that the sign is perhaps to be explained as "a conscious archaism." This view is practically identical with my own, and I would modify it only by deleting the word "conscious." Tillyard then goes on to say that such a view will not destroy his main argument or lead to any change in his transcriptions. I quite agree. To deny the absolute directional value of the Chartres *apostrophos* means only that in the notation of the Chartres fragment the *apostrophos* does not invariably stand for a descending progression. It does not mean that the sign is always a purely dynamic or rhythmic indication and never a melodic one; still less does it mean that the Chartres notation as a whole is simply a system of dynamic and rhythmic indications, as Wellesz seems to imply in his latest study.[23]

Not only do I agree with Tillyard that the notation of the Chartres fragment is a genuinely melodic notation, I am ready to go beyond this and to make the same claim for the notation of what is probably our earliest source, the Heirmologion Laura B.32. For the differences between this notation—Tillyard's "Esphigmenian system"—and the notation of the Chartres fragment are differences of detail and of degree, but not of principle. The Laura Heirmologion does not use the straight *ison* and its provisions for secondary syllables are even less systematic than those of the Sticheraria with which we have been occupied. Its treatment of the *apostrophos* is somewhat more archaic. But it forms its simple signs in precisely the same way; it employs the same *fermata*-like *oligon,* the same variants of the *bareia,* and the same v-shaped *klasma;* when its simpler repertory permits, it also employs the ornate signs for melodic groups which constitute the distinctive mark of the Chartres family.

The Heirmologion and the Sticherarion are in principle independent books, the one containing the model-stanzas of the canons, the other containing the stichera sung in connection with the psalms and psalm-verses. Ordinarily there is no common ground and hence no proper basis for comparison. It so happens, however, that this rule does not always hold. Exceptionally a Sticherarion will set forth the Good Friday Office in more than the usual detail, and in so doing a copy of this type will often include the model-stanzas and troparia of the three-ode canon or "Triodion" of the day. Fortunately for us, two of our three Sticheraria are copies of this type, and for this one canon they give the words and music in full.

---

[23]"Early Byzantine Neumes," cited on p. 76 above.

This circumstance makes comparison possible, for the Heirmologion gives the model-stanzas of the Good Friday canon as a matter of course.

The Good Friday canon is the work of Cosmas of Jerusalem, and the initial letters of its 13 stanzas spell out the words Προσάββατόν τε, thus continuing a metrical acrostic which runs through the canons for Holy Week from Monday to Saturday. It is one of the very few canons of the Heirmologion whose full text is still being printed and still being sung. In an expanded form, the heirmos of its ninth ode has become the familiar "Αξιόν ἐστιν, one of the ordinary chants of the Divine Liturgy. Legend attributes the few words of preface which introduce this form of the stanza to an angelic visitation in the year 980, an incident often depicted by the icon-painters and annually commemorated by the faithful.[24] As the story indicates, the poem has enjoyed a long and widespread popularity. The heirmos with which the canon begins, nominally a paraphrase of Isaiah 26:6–20, bears rather more directly on Philippians 2:7–8.

> Unto Thee will I arise, Thou who through compassion didst humble Thyself, unchanging, for him who fell, and who didst submit, unsuffering, until the hour of Thy sufferings, Word of God. Grant me Thy peace, Lover of mankind!

To allow the reader to draw his own conclusions about the notation of Laura B.32, I am reproducing the beginning of the Good Friday Canon in facsimile after all three MSS. Plates 6 and 7, after Vatopedi 1488, give the heirmos and its two troparia in the notation of the Chartres fragment; Plate 8 gives the same three stanzas again, after Laura Γ.67; Plate 9, with the heirmos only, is from Laura B.32. The photographs introduce us to several more of our distinctive signs, and in order to show how these are "spelled out" in the "Round" notation, and at the same time to facilitate the comparative study of the plates, I have correlated the three versions with a parallel transcription after the published facsimiles of the MSS Iviron 470 and Grottaferrata E.γ. ii.[25] The

---

[24]For the legend, see the synaxarion for June 11, as printed in the Athens edition of the Menaia, also E. Lamerand, "La Légende de l'AΞION EΣTIN," *Echos d'Orient*, II (1898–99), 227–230.

[25]Monumenta musicae byzantinae, Principal series 2 and 3.

signs above the final syllables of εὐσπλαγχνίαν and παθῶς are the *echadin* ("little sound" or "modulus") and the *stauros apo dexias* ("cross from the right"); above the first syllable of ἀπαθῶς, the two Sticheraria abbreviate the word *mesos* ("mediant"), thus indicating that the new line is to begin from the third step of the mode, the Second Plagal.

Ex. 5

Λό - γε Θε - οũ. Τὴν εἰ - ρή, - νην πα - ρά - σχου μοι, φι - λάν - θρω - πε :

Admittedly, the two Sticheraria correspond more closely with one another than they do with the Heirmologion. At the same time, the points of total agreement are so numerous and so revealing, and the differences so trivial, that it is difficult to see how a significant distinction can be longer maintained. I am accordingly for extending the meaning of the phrase "notation of the Chartres fragment" to include the Heirmologion Laura B.32, just as I am also for extending the meaning of the term "Coislin" to include the Heirmologion Saba 83 and the related and still earlier fragment Leningrad 557.[26]

In his most recent writings, Wellesz has repeatedly expressed the opinion that it will never be possible to make satisfactory transcriptions from Byzantine MSS earlier than the year 1100 and that transcriptions of this kind ought not even to be attempted.[27] There is something to be said for this point of view. The transcriber may make every effort to reduce the conjectural element in his transcription to a minimum, but a certain fallible residue will always remain, and like transcriptions from Latin neumes *in campo aperto,* the result will never be able to claim the same authority as a transcription from a wholly diastematic source. Why should we make such transcriptions at all? Would it not be wiser and more economical to transcribe only from sources whose meaning is perfectly clear, using our early sources as a

[26]Complete facsimile in Thibaut, *Monuments,* pl. vi–xxi. For the Heirmologion Saba 83, see p. oo above and Høeg's comments on its notation in *The Hymns of the Hirmologium,* pt. I, pp. xxvii–xxviii. Other MSS using this primitive form of the "Coislin" notation are Patmos 55 and Esphigmenou 54.

[27]*A History of Byzantine Music and Hymnography,* p. 232; *The Musical Quarterly,* XXXVIII, 78.

means of determining which later ones to prefer?

The trouble with this point of view is that it loses sight of the enormous number of Byzantine melodies for which no versions later than the year 1100 are known to exist. Something like 40 per cent of the contents of Vatopedi 1488 is not ordinarily to be found in later MSS—indeed it may very well be that when all the early sources for the Sticherarion have been indexed and collated, we shall find that the standard abridged copies contain less than half of the original repertory. And it by no means follows that the part retained surpasses in quality or interest the part discarded. On the contrary, it would appear that the probable purpose of the standardization was to give a quasi-official stamp to a particular local use. Vatopedi 1488 includes stichera by Cosmas for which we have no other source; it includes a unique set of antiphons for the Mandatum; it includes a whole series of idiomela to precede the Great Doxology on Sundays and festivals, Byzantine counterparts of the Latin Gloria tropes, represented in the standard abridged copies by two isolated pieces, one of them a contrafactum.[28] Similar things are to be found also in the two MSS of the Chartres family that contain stichera for the festivals of the calendar year—Laura Γ.74 and Sinai 1219.

Only too obviously, if we are ever to deal with this part of the music at all, we must begin by learning to read the early sources directly, just as they were read by the scribes who wrote them and the singers for whom they were written. And we can succeed in this if only we bring to the task some part of the familiarity with the conventions of Byzantine melody that these scribes and singers must have possessed. In saying this I am simply restating an opinion first expressed by Wellesz himself.

> I am convinced that anybody who knows the cadences of the *echoi* by heart, as the Byzantine singers did, will be able to sing the melodies from manuscripts in the Early Byzantine musical notation, without the help of manuscripts of the Middle period. This knowledge

---

[28]One of these is the Christmas idiomelon Σήμερον ὁ Χριστὸς ἐν Βηθλεέμ (transcribed and translated by Wellesz in his *Eastern Elements,* pp. 148–149); the other, modeled upon it, is the corresponding piece for Epiphany, Σήμερον ὁ Χριστὸς ἐν Ἰορδάνῃ. Another member of this series—the idiomelon Σὺν ταῖς ἄλλαις, for the Sunday of the Women at the Tomb—is shown on Gastoué's plate from the Chartres fragment.

also enables us to detect scribal errors, and to correct them. We have often been obliged to make such corrections in our transcription, and having compared them with the notation of a manuscript containing a faultless version of the melody, we have always found them to be accurate.[29]

To demonstrate the possibilities of this approach—and also its limitations, I am adding a transcription of a melody for which no version in the "Round" notation is known to exist. It is the important automelon in the First Mode, "Ω τοῦ παραδόξου θαύματος, one of the fifteen to twenty model-melodies used for the hundreds of stichera prosomoia, and it was excluded from the standard abridged Sticherarion, not as a thing no longer in use, but as a thing too familiar to require further copying. Even today, centuries after the disappearance of the original melody, any Greek psaltist will be able to sing the modern setting without the help of a book, and in elementary manuals of Neo-Byzantine chant the piece is still being cited as typical of its mode. The model-stanza, with its two original troparia, belongs to the festival of the Assumption; there are further sets of three stanzas for two other festivals of the Virgin, the Nativity and the Presentation, and for the commemoration of St. Anne on July 25. The text of the model-stanza gives a very fair idea of this sort of poetry.

> O marvelous wonder! The source of life is laid in the tomb and the grave is become a stairway to heaven. Rejoice, Gethsemane, holy ground consecrated to the Virgin! We, the believers, shall cry aloud, acknowledging Gabriel as our commander: Hail, Thou who art full of grace; the Lord be with Thee, He who grants to the world through Thee His great mercy!

The original melody is known to me from two sources only— Laura Γ.74 (Plate 10) and Sinai 1219 (Plate 11).[30] I have based my transcription primarily on the first of these, which ascribes the piece to "Ioannes Monachos," but I have also made some

---

[29] *Eastern Elements in Western Chant*, p. 91.

[30] Readers familiar with the facsimiles from Sinai 1219 published by Thibaut (after Leningrad 363) and Mme. Verdeil (*op. cit.*, pl. iii) will notice that Plate 11 shows an entirely different hand. This is the main hand, which beings on fol. 33 (November 25) and continues to the end (August 22). The fragment in Leningrad belongs between the folios now numbered 1 and 2; Mme. Verdeil's plate is fol. 24.

use of the second, which fills in an occasional gap and is often more explicit.

Ex. 6

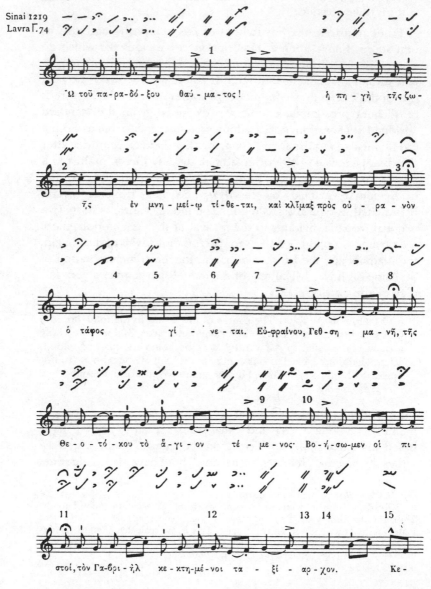

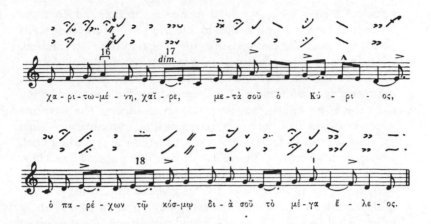

If we were dealing with a Latin melody, written *in campo aperto,* we should have to begin by determining its modality, and if no version on the staff were known to exist, we might easily find ourselves confronted at the outset with a formidable and perhaps insuperable difficulty.[31] No such difficulty confronts us here—the mode is clearly indicated in both our sources. And in this melody, as in "Ἥπλωσεν ἡ πόρνη, an internal repetition considerably simplifies our task. Two lines agree in meter, having the same number of syllables, the same distribution of accents, and the same caesura:

Εὐφραίνου Γεθσημανῆ · τῆς θεοτόκου τὸ ἅγιον τέμενος ·
Βοήσωμεν οἱ πιστοί · τὸν Γαβριὴλ κεκτημένοι ταξίαρχον·

They also agree in melody, for in both our sources the second line is introduced by an abbreviation of the word ὅμοιον.[32] Certain differences in the notation of the two lines are thus revealed as nonessential. Before we have even begun to transcribe, we are in possession of two important facts.

For the transcription itself, the cadences provide an obvious point of departure. In this mode one can easily distinguish two

[31]Dom Suñol, in his *Introduction à la paléographie musicale grégorienne* (Tournai, 1935), pp. 47–49, gives a brief summary of the means by which this difficulty may be overcome.

[32]The internal use of this abbreviation is shown also on Plate 2, from Vatopedi 1488, where it is used to indicate repetitions in the second and third stanzas of "Ἥπλωσεν ἡ πόρνη.

principal forms. When the final neume is the doubled *oxeia* the cadence is on a, when it is the doubled *apostrophos* the cadence is on D, and since the two cadences differ also in their preparation, the neumes which precede will exhibit a corresponding difference. Thus the cadences at 1, 9, and 13 can only be cadences on a; the more positive cadence on D is reserved for the ending. Having fixed these few points, we can go on to fix others. The new line which begins at 10 must begin from a, for the straight *ison* in Sinai 1219 shows that its first note is a repetition of the preceding final, whose pitch we know. This tells us further that the new line which begins at 7 must also begin from a, for we know already that the two lines agree in their melody. This gives us in turn the position of the cadence at 6, for the neume at 7 was a straight *ison.* We now have a whole series of fixed points and we can proceed to connect them. Some means of doing this are already familiar from our study of "Ηπλωσεν ἡ πόρνη. We know, for example, that the straight *ison,* the two *kentemata,* and the Chartres *oligon* are signs whose diastematic meanings are usually unambiguous, and we know how to read the compound sign at 18, where the *ison* and the two *kentemata* are combined. We know also that in each mode, or pair of modes, the meaning of some of the less usual signs depends upon the context, and that this meaning can often be ascertained. This applies with equal force to signs common to the Chartres and "Coislin" notations and to signs peculiar to the one or the other—to the *apoderma* at 3, 8, and 11, to the *tinagma* at 4, to the *rhapisma* at 12 and 15 (Sinai 1219 only), to the *anatrichisma* at 14, and to the *kratema* at 16. Above all it applies to the two forms of the *xeron klasma* at 2, 5, and 17. We know, finally, that all Byzantine melodies are built up from stable patterns, and that these patterns can be recognized and read almost as easily in the early sources as in the later ones. The phrase μετὰ σοῦ ὁ κύριος offers a convenient illustration. In Tillyard's *Hymns of the Octoechus,* Part I, I find this pattern 18 times among the melodies of the First Mode, authentic and plagal; its notation in MSS of the Chartres family may vary from case to case and from MS to MS, but it will never vary sufficiently to cause the reader a moment's hesitation.

Byzantine sacred poetry is so heavily laden with conventional diction, and with reminiscences of Biblical and patristic language, that one rarely finds a stanza that does not contain some familiar allusion or turn of phrase. This simple fact can be useful to us here, for it means that even when no version in the "Round" notation is known to exist, some parts of a transcription may still be open to confirmation and to the most rigid sort of control. Whole lines, particularly opening- and refrain-lines, wander from one hymn to another, and in so far as they form parts of compositions in the same mode, these poetic commonplaces tend to carry their melodies with them. The opening line of our model-melody is a case in point. Where it comes from does not concern us here, nor are we concerned with its frequent appearances in modes other than the First. What does concern us is that it is quoted in the course of a sticheron in the First Mode—the sticheron Δαυΐτικῶς σήμερον (or Ἀσματικῶς σήμερον, for the commemoration of the Prophet Elijah—and that this sticheron forms part of the standard abridged contents of the Sticherarion. I transcribe the line from Koutloumousi 412, copying above my transcription the neumes from Sinai 1219.[33]

Ex. 7

ὦ τοῦ πα-ρα - δό - ξου   θαύ - μα - τος·

In much the same way, a shorter form of the concluding line of our model-melody is used to conclude a number of other stichera in the First Mode, among them several belonging to the standard abridged contents. In this case, it is possible to compare the notation of three distinct appearances, one of them after two sources. A and B give the concluding line of "Ακουε οὐρα-νέ, after Γ.74 and Sinai 1219; C is the concluding line of Ὁ πα-λαιὸς ἡμερῶν, also after Sinai 1219; D is the concluding line of the Alphabetikon Γυναῖκες μυροφόροι, after Γ.67. Below the four lines of neumes I have added Tillyard's transcription of the concluding line of the Alphabetikon, after two MSS in the "Round" notation.[34]

---

[33]In this transcription from Koutloumousi 412 I have preferred the variant to the first version.
[34]*The Hymns of the Octoechus,* pt. I (Copenhagen, 1940), p. 112.

Ex. 8

ὁ πα - ρέ - χων τῷ κόσ - μῳ τὸ μέ - γα ἔ - λε - ος.

In my transcription of "Ω τοῦ παραδόξου θαύματος, and in
the brief and necessarily incomplete account of the reasoning that
underlies it, I have aimed above all to suggest that the success or
failure of such an experiment depends primarily upon the transcriber's familiarity with the conventions of Byzantine melody and
that an excessively cautious adherence to the literal meanings of the
single signs can easily result in distortion. For the First Mode, the
main conventions and their bearing on transcriptions from the
"Coislin" notation have been carefully worked out by P. Bartolomeo Di Salvo in a series of studies in the *Bollettino della Badia greca
di Grottaferrata*.[35] P. Bartolomeo's findings are based upon a
phrase-by-phrase analysis of the entire contents of the Sticherarion
Vienna, Nationalbibliothek, Theol. gr. 136, and I have drawn on
these findings repeatedly in my transcription and in my account of
it. In these same studies, P. Bartolomeo drew attention for the first
time to the ambiguity of the *apostrophos* in the early Byzantine
notations, and while his views on this subject were at first received
with considerable skepticism, it is becoming increasingly clear that
they were not altogether wide of the mark.[36]

My principal source for the transcription of "Ω τοῦ παραδόξου

---

[35]"La notazione paleobizantina e la sua trascrizione," IV (1950), 114–130; "La
trascrizione della notazione paleobizantina. 1. I syndesmoi e i syndesmoi con il
klasma nel modo primo," V (1951), 92–110; "2. Il xeron klasma e il kylisma nel
modo primo," V (1951), 220–235.

[36]Høeg too has noticed that in older sources the *apostrophos* is not invariably a
descending sign. Thus, speaking of Laura B.32, he writes that "an *apostrophos* can
be put not only above a syllable sung on a weak descending note, but also above
a syllable sung on a weak note of the same pitch as the preceding one" (*The Hymns
of the Hirmologium*, pt. I, p. xxvi); of Saba 83, that its writer "used the *apostrophos*
in a more general way . . . as a minus-sign indicating the absence of dynamic stress"
(*ibid.*, pp. xxvii–xxviii); of Iviron 470, that its use of the *apostrophos* is "similar" to
that of the two older MSS just mentioned (*ibid.*, p. xxiv).

θαύματος can claim a special interest, for the MS Laura Γ.74 is the one MS of the Chartres family whose date and provenance can be established with reasonable precision. Under August 16, the MS contains two stichera commemorating the Translation of the Mandilion, a miraculous icon of the Savior, from Edessa to Constantinople. This translation, a lengthy account of which has been attributed to the Emperor Constantine Porphyrogenitus,[37] took place in the year 944. Under December 11, it contains two stichera commemorating the death of the Emperor Nicephorus Phocas, the great patron of the Laura, who was assassinated in 969. And under July 13, it contains an elaborate office for the Emperor's uncle, St. Michael Maleinos, abbot of a monastery at Cymina in Bithynia, Asia Minor, and the "spiritual father" of St. Athanasius, the founder of organized monasticism on Mount Athos and of the Laura itself. All of these entries are in the principal hand and in their proper positions in the MS, which is arranged in the order of the calendar. Yet under July 5, where one would expect to find the office for St. Athanasius of Athos, there is only a marginal note in a later hand, directing the reader to "the end of the book," where the same later hand has entered three stichera commemorating St. Athanasius, with music in the "Coislin" notation. From these facts, one might easily conclude that the MS was written at the Laura sometime between the death of the Emperor Nicephorus, in 969, and the death of St. Athanasius, which occurred not earlier than 997 and not later than 1011.[38] But on closer examination, the case does not appear to be quite so simple, for among the stichera for the commemoration of Michael, several are addressed to Athanasius, and while these make no express mention of the founder's death, the probabilities are that they were not written during his lifetime. If this is true, one can only say that the MS must have been written before the annual commemoration of the anniversary was instituted, and that a date later than about 1025 would appear to be out of the question. And this means that the MS Laura Γ.74 is our earliest source for the stichera of the Menaia. Its companion volume is Γ.72, with the stichera of the Trio-

---

[37] *Patrologia graeca,* CXIII, 424–453.

[38] Philipp Meyer, *Die Haupturkunden für die Geschichte der Athosklöster* (Leipzig, 1894), p. 25.

dion and Pentekostarion. The two MSS are the work of a single scribe—the "humble Anthony" who has signed them both. Together they constitute the earliest known copy of the complete Sticherarion.

Of the remaining MSS of the family, B.32, Γ.12, and Γ.67 are certainly earlier, although I should not want to place any one of them earlier than the year 950. B.32 ascribes an iambic canon in the Second Mode Plagal to the Patriarch Photius.[39] When it is considered that Photius did not become Patriarch until 858, that he may have composed his canon at any time between that year and the year 886, when he was deprived of his office and banished by his pupil, the Emperor Leo, that some time must be allowed for the composition to find its way into the anthologies, and that in B.32, as in most early copies of the Heirmologion, the order of the canons within each mode is roughly chronological,[40] with the canon by Photius occupying the thirtieth place in a series that runs to 53, the likelihood of a date before 950 appears very slim indeed. As to Γ.12 and Γ.67, both of these MSS contain the sticheron Δεῦτε λαοί (or Δεῦτε πιστοί), written for the Whitsunday office by the Emperor Leo, who shared the imperial titles from 886 to 912. To be sure, the Emperor is not specifically mentioned, but his authorship has seldom been questioned, and the language of the poem and the style of the melody are in themselves enough to place the composition in his day. Here again, some time must be allowed for the composition to find its way into the anthologies.[41] And the differences in notation between this group of older sources and the MSS Γ.74 and Γ.72 are scarcely of sufficient moment to warrant the assumption of a greater interval.

This last argument can be brought to bear also on the date of the MSS Vatopedi 1488 and Sinai 1219. That these are the youngest

[39]The texts of the heirmoi are published by Eustratiades in his edition of the Heirmologion (Chennevières-sur-Marne, 1932), p. 183.

[40]To put it more precisely, each mode consists of an "old layer," which is followed by a series of additions whose arrangement evidently represents the order in which the added canons came to the compiler's attention.

[41]In addition, the MS Γ.67 contains the Emperor's cycle of Heothina, in two versions, the second incomplete, and the Exaposteilaria usually attributed to his son Constantine Porphyrogenitus. The paschal table on fols. 106–106[v], covering the period 1226 to 1250, is in another hand.

members of the Chartres family has been more than evident from our study of their notation. But they lie rather closer to Γ.74 and Γ.72, and to the year 1025, than they do to our earliest dated MS, the Sticherarion Leningrad 789, written at the Vatopedi in the year 1106, with its fully developed "Coislin" notation and its sharply differentiated modal signatures.[42]

As we know, the MS Vatopedi 1488 represents an attempt to compile a complete Triodion and Pentekostarion by adding to the contents of the standard abridged version a considerable number of items for which this version had found no place.[43] To date this MS "about 1050" is to say also that by "about 1050" the standard abridged version was already in circulation. It remains to determine where the version came from, and if we can determine this, we shall also have determined where the "Coislin" notation came from, for the two phenomena are very evidently related. Another possibility would be to work in the opposite way and to begin by attempting to determine where the "Coislin" notation came from. Still another possibility would be to work from both ends. Then, if we find strong indications pointing in one direction, we may be pretty sure that we are on the right track.

Inevitably, the Byzantine arrangement of the church year began by reflecting the local use of Constantinople, and our earliest documents indicate that this arrangement had been generally accepted throughout the Empire by the beginning of the eighth century. It is thus in no way remarkable that the standard abridged Sticherarion, when it finally took shape, should itself have preserved some remnants of Constantinopolitan usage, as it does on July 2 and August 31 in including music for the veneration of relics of the Virgin formerly preserved in two of her churches in the capital, the Blachernae and the Chalkoprateia. What is remarkable, in the stan-

---

[42]There are excellent reproductions in Kirsopp and Silva Lake, *Dated Greek Minuscule MSS to the Year 1200,* VI (Boston, 1936), pls. 437–439.

[43]To prevent misunderstanding, I may say that, from about 1050 on, most copies of the Sticherarion represent the standard abridged version or depart from it only to a very limited extent. Koutloumousi 412 represents it almost exactly; the Vienna copy published in facsimile by the editors of the Monumenta departs from it only in adding commemorations of John of Damascus (Dec. 4), Menas and companions (Dec. 10), Isaacius and companions (Aug. 3), and Titus (Aug. 25).

dard abridged version, is its treatment of the music for the Dedication of a Church. All stichera having to do with such occasions are brought together here under September 13, the dedication-date of the Church of the Resurrection in Jerusalem.[44] Yet only one of the ten pieces bears directly on this particular dedication;[45] the rest are universally applicable, and in earlier times the date or dates of their performance would of course have been determined locally. And having thus betrayed its Palestinian origin, the standard abridged version goes on to include the troparia composed for the three great vigils by Sophronius, Patriarch of Jerusalem from 634 to 638, pieces which would appear to have been almost unknown in Constantinople before the eleventh century and whose performance involves liturgical arrangements that conflict with Constantinopolitan practice.

Palestine, then, is the place where our search for the first traces of the "Coislin" notation ought logically to begin. And Palestine is where we find them—in two copies of the Heirmologion, one of them from the influential monastery of Mar Saba, not far from Jerusalem, the other so closely related, in the arrangement of its contents and in its notation, that it too must have come from the same environment.[46] The fragment Leningrad 557, which ends each heirmos with a little cross, does not use the hooked *ison* at all; the MS Saba 83 uses it only at cadences, chiefly at final cadences. In both MSS, notably in Leningrad 557, the treatment of the *apostrophos* is decidedly archaic, and many secondary syllables are left unprovided for. There is no *oligon*. But in all other respects, the notation of the two MSS agrees with that usually called "Coislin" —the signs used are the same, they are formed in the same way, and one finds none of the distinctive characteristics of the notation of the Chartres fragment.

Occasional traces of this primitive form of the "Coislin" notation are also to be found in the remarkable set of Menaia from the

---

[44]Egon Wellesz, *Die Hymnen des Sticherarium für September* (Copenhagen, 1936), nos. 42–51.

[45]*Ibid.*, no. 44, beginning Τὸν ἐγκαινισμὸν τελοῦντες, τοῦ πανιέρου ναοῦ τῆς σῆς Ἀναστάσεως, σὲ δοξάζομεν Κύριε ("Celebrating the all-sacred temple of Thy resurrection, we glorify Thee, O Lord").

[46]See pp. 76 and 91 above.

monastery of the Prophet Elijah at Carbone, near Chiaramonte in Calabria, preserved today in the library at Grottaferrata.[47] In general, the notation used in these volumes is the moderately developed "Coislin" notation of the later eleventh century; the primitive form is used only for a few exceptional pieces, such as Διὰ τὴν παράβασιν τὴν ἐν Ἐδέμ and Θεὸς ἐφάνη ἐπὶ γῆς, two stichera included among the music for the Christmas office, as published in facsimile by Petrescu from the December volume, Grottaferrata Δ.α.xiv.[48] But these few pieces are enough to show that the "Coislin" notation, in its primitive form, had reached Southern Italy by the year 1000. And what has just been said of the "Coislin" notation applies with equal force to the notation of the Chartres fragment, which is used, in the MSS of this same series, for three isolated stichera—one for St. Demetrius (Δ.α.xiii, f. 67ᵛ), one for the Epiphany (Δ.α.xv, f. 73), and one for the Purification (Δ.α.xvi, f. 8). That none of these pieces is contained in the standard abridged version is surely significant. If we did not already know it, we might infer from this evidence alone that the standard abridged version was in circulation by 1050 and that it was connected, not with the "Coislin" notation in its primitive form or with the notation of the Chartres fragment, but with the "Coislin" notation in its moderately developed form.

In tracing the primitive form of the "Coislin" notation to Palestine and Mar Saba, we have taken a first step toward localizing the notation of the Chartres fragment and have begun to delimit the territory within which it was once known and used. If we now attempt to determine the center from which it spread, we shall naturally think first of Mount Athos and Mount Sinai. But neither of these localities can very well have been the point at which the development began. At Mount Sinai, the evidence thus far uncovered is too meager and too late,[49] and it is in any case unlikely that

[47]Antonio Rocchi, *Codices Cryptenses* (Grottaferrata, 1883), pp. 312–319.

[48]*Les idiomèles et le canon de l'office de Noël* (Paris, 1932), pls. ii and vi. It was to these plates that I referred, in my brief survey for the International Congress of 1950, when I said that "in some instances, one can even distinguish, within a single MS, an earlier layer and a later one" (p. 42 of this volume).

[49]That the notation of the Chartres fragment was known and used at Mount Sinai

this isolated spot can ever have exerted an active influence. On Mount Athos, organized monastic life began only in 963, with the foundation of the Laura; the earliest MSS of the Chartres family were perhaps not written here at all, and even if they were, we should have to assume that still earlier specimens of the notation, written elsewhere, must once have existed. At the same time, it is on Mount Athos that the early evidence is concentrated. The true center, then, cannot be far away, and to find it we have only to find the center of the territory upon which Mount Athos was dependent —Thessaly, Macedonia, Thrace, the Aegean islands, and the coast of Asia Minor. And this brings us in the end to the great capital cities of Thessalonica and Constantinople, not only because of their commercial, political, and ecclesiastical importance, but also because it was from Thessalonica and Constantinople, about the year 860, that the brothers Cyril and Methodius, "the apostles of the Slavs," set out on their missions, taking with them the primitive form of the notation of the Chartres fragment which we find in the earliest Slavic MSS.[50]

I had hoped to complete this study by adding a brief description of the one remaining member of the Chartres family—MS 18 at the Russian Skiti of St. Andrew on Mount Athos. This was seen and studied by Professor Tillyard in 1912, and there are frequent references to it in his later publications. Unfortunately, however, the MS is no longer accessible. In 1954, Professor H. G. Lunt of Harvard University tried in vain to locate it for me at St. Andrew's, and my own attempt, made in September 1955, was likewise fruitless. Father Michael, the present Abbot of St. Andrew's, is unable to produce the MS and professes to know nothing whatever about its past history or present whereabouts. It would not at all surprise me to learn that it

---

is evident, not only from the MS Sinai 1219, but also from the important table at the end of the MS Sinai 8, which "spells out" the ekphonetic signs in a curious mixture of the "Coislin" and Chartres notations; for this table, see Carsten Høeg, *La notation ekphonétique* (Copenhagen, 1935), pp. 20–22, 26–35, and pl. iii.

[50]That these Slavic MSS, of the eleventh century and later, conserve the Chartres variety of the early Byzantine notation in its most archaic form is a thesis first advanced by Mme. Verdeil in two contributions to *Byzantinoslavica*, published in 1949 and 1950.

has been for some years in private hands. A single photograph kindly placed at my disposal by Professor Tillyard (f. 115, from the office for St. Stephen) shows a MS with an unusually small format (13 lines to the page, averaging 24 characters to the line). To judge from the writing of the text and the state of the musical notation, it should date from about the year 1050.

THE BYZANTINE OFFICE
AT HAGIA SOPHIA†

I N the year 1200, on the eve of the capture of Constantinople by the Latins, a Russian pilgrim from Novgorod—the monk Anthony—visited Hagia Sophia and recorded his impressions of the Great Church and its marvels. Not the least of these, to judge from his account, was the order of service followed by the Greek clergy in their celebration of the morning and evening office.

When they sing Lauds at Hagia Sophia, they sing first in the narthex before the royal doors; then they enter and sing in the middle of the church; then the gates of Paradise are opened and they sing a third time before the altar. On Sundays and feastdays the Patriarch assists at Lauds and at the Liturgy; at this time he blesses the singers from the gallery, and ceasing to sing, they proclaim the polychronia; then they begin to .sing again as harmoniously and as sweetly as the angels, and they sing in this fashion until the Liturgy. After Lauds they put off their vestments and go out to receive the blessing of the Patriarch; then the preliminary lessons are read in the ambo; when these are over the Liturgy begins, and at the end of the service the chief priest recites the so-called prayer of the ambo within the sanctuary while the second priest recites it in the church, beyond the ambo; when they have finished the prayer, both bless the people. Vespers are said in the same fashion, beginning at an early hour.[1]

†From *Dumbarton Oaks Papers*, 9–10 (Cambridge, 1956), 175–202; a revised and extended version of the paper read at the Dumbarton Oaks Symposium of 1954. Reprinted with permission of the publisher.

[1] *Publications de la société de l'Orient latin*, Série géographique, V (1889), 97. I am obliged to Professor Roman Jakobson of Harvard University for his suggestions regarding the translation of this document.

That our visitor took the trouble to set all this down is in itself enough to tell us that what he saw and heard was new and strange to him. And even if we had no other evidence, we should know from his references to the procession from the narthex to the middle of the church, to the preliminary lessons, and to the ambo, that at the beginning of the thirteenth century the conduct of the morning and evening office at Hagia Sophia did not conform to the monastic rite.

Two hundred years later, Symeon, Archbishop of Thessalonica, included in his monumental treatise *On Divine Prayer*[2] an elaborate exposition of the ceremonies that the Russian pilgrim had witnessed, together with a minute analysis of the differences between the liturgical practices of the Great Church and those of the monasteries. But by this time, the situation throughout the Empire had deteriorated to such an extent that these practices, once the glory of Hagia Sophia and the other great churches, had largely fallen into disuse. Rightly or wrongly, Symeon places the blame squarely upon the Latin conquerors:

> After Constantinople had been enslaved [he says], and the clergy driven out and settled elsewhere, these ceremonies were neglected; it became customary not to perform them, and when the clergy returned after many years, their practice ceased; from the one church [Hagia Sophia], as from a mother, this was handed on to the rest.[3]

In his day, the Archbishop tells us, the secular clergy had almost universally accepted the monastic rite;[4] in Constantinople itself the old order was followed at Hagia Sophia only three times a year,[5] and even on these occasions its use appears to have been merely permissive; in his own great church in Thessalonica, the second Hagia Sophia, the ancient rites of Constantinople had found their last haven;[6] in himself, they had found their last champion. What he defended was already an anachronism, unintelligible to many,

---

[2] *PG,* CLV, 536–669.

[3] *De sacro templo, loc. cit.,* 325. Strictly speaking this passage has to do only with the custom of commemorating the anniversary of a dedication. But Symeon says much the same thing in other connections; cf. *De sacra precatione, loc. cit.,* 553, 625; *Responsiones, loc. cit.,* 908.

[4] *De sacra precatione,* 556.

[5] On the feasts of the Exaltation, of the Assumption, and of St. John Chrysostom. *Ibid.,* 553.

[6] *De sacro templo,* 328; *De sacra precatione,* 556, 624; *Responsiones,* 908.

appreciated by few. Even in Thessalonica there were some who professed an inability to distinguish between the old order of Vespers and the Liturgy, and Symeon tells us that visitors from Constantinople, who might have been expected to know better, were still more perplexed.[7] Some compromises had already been made; Symeon made others.[8] And on March 29, 1430, only six months after the Archbishop's death, Thessalonica fell to the Turks, its great church was made a mosque, and the old order came suddenly to an end.

With this an ancient conflict was finally laid to rest—the conflict between the rival claims of the city of Constantine and the city of David, between the rival claims of two more or less independent and incompatible liturgical practices. This is a conflict which affects virtually every area within the general field of Byzantine studies. Not only does it affect all study of liturgical developments; it also affects the study of Early Christian art and architecture, of Old Testament text-criticism, of canon law. In recent years it has prompted a whole series of noteworthy monographs, in which Baumstark,[9] Malickij,[10] Schneider,[11] and Antoniades,[12] scholars representing the widest variety of interests, have sought to define and distinguish the two practices more sharply. Each has brought to the task a special competence; each has had his particular contribution to make. Yet when one adds all these together, the sum falls short of a total solution; much remains unexplained, and there are disturbing contradictions to be resolved.

Now in Symeon's time there was a well-established name for the office of the Great Church. It was called the ἀκολουθία ἀσματική—the "chanted" or "choral" office. From this we may

[7] De sacra precatione, 625.

[8] Ibid., 556, 628, 648.

[9] "Das Typikon der Patmos-Handschrift 266 und die altkonstantinopolitanische Gottesdienstordnung," Jahrbuch für Liturgiewissenschaft, VI (1923), 98–111; "Denkmäler der Entstehungsgeschichte des byzantinischen Ritus," Oriens Christianus, 3. Serie, II (1927), 1–32.

[10] Le Psautier byzantin à illustrations marginales du type Chludov est-il de provenance monastique?" L'Art byzantin chez les Slaves, 2me recueil (Paris, 1932), 235–243.

[11] "Die biblischen Oden in Jerusalem und Konstantinopel," Biblica, XXX (1949), 433–452.

[12] "Περὶ τοῦ ἀσματικοῦ ἢ βυζαντινοῦ κοσμικοῦ τύπου τῶν ἀκολουθιῶν τῆς ἡμερονυκτίου προσευχῆς," Θεολογία, XX–XXII (1949–51).

certainly infer that it involved more singing than was usual in the monasteries, and to say this is to reduce the distinction between the two liturgical practices to its simplest terms. Precisely this same simplification is made by the Archbishop when he contrasts the two forms of worship. In the "chanted" office, he says, we have an office requiring a considerable personnel, for although he repeatedly connects the disuse into which it has fallen with the Latin occupation, he adds at one point that the shortage of priests and singers may have been a contributing factor;[13] to this he opposes the monastic office, which can be carried out by one person alone.[14] In the "chanted" office, he says again, we have an office that is sung throughout, no words being recited without singing except the prayers and petitions of the priests and deacons;[15] to this he opposes the monastic office, which was often performed without singing at all.[16] Thus it appears that the problem of the "chanted" office is fundamentally a musical problem, and that it will not be possible to solve it satisfactorily without taking music into account. It likewise appears that the music of the "chanted" office constitutes a central and crucial chapter in the history of Byzantine music and that until this chapter is written our conception of Byzantine music is bound to remain one-sided and incomplete.

The manuscript sources for the music of the "chanted" office are neither numerous nor well known. Three belong to monasteries on Mount Athos. At the Laura, MS. E.173, a bulky miscellany dated "1436," devotes some ten folios to the "chanted" office as it is sung at Vespers of outstanding feasts and at the Vespers and Lauds of the feast of the Exaltation.[17] Parts of its contents are duplicated in a second miscellany at the Laura, the MS.E.148,[18] and in a similar though smaller miscellany at Vatopedi, the MS. 1527, dated "1434."[19] From these three sources alone one could learn a good deal, and they would be well worth our attention if they were not

[13]*De sacra precatione*, 553.
[14]*Ibid.*, 556.
[15]*Ibid.*, 624.
[16]*Ibid.*, 556.
[17]Fol. 247–257^V.
[18]Fol. 325–328^V.
[19]Fol. 310^V–321^V.

completely overshadowed by a fourth manuscript, one of the more than 1,200 added to the collection at the National Library in Athens since the publication of the printed catalogue in 1892. This is the MS. Athens 2061.

Unlike the three monastic sources, the MS. Athens 2061 is concerned with the "chanted" office only. Its first folios are devoted to what a Western book would have called an "Ordinarium"; this contains music for the psalms and canticles as they are sung at the daily Vespers and Lauds throughout the week. It is followed by a second "Ordinarium," similar to the first and likewise covering a week, so that in principle each psalm or canticle is represented twice. A third section adds ordinary and proper chants for certain great feasts—for Easter, for feasts of Apostles, for the two Sundays before Christmas with the Saturdays that precede them, for Christmas, for Epiphany, and for the feast of the Exaltation. A fourth and final section adds a few familiar pieces, common to the two practices, for which earlier and purer sources are available.[20]

When was this manuscript written and where does it come from? Its date is fixed between the years 1391 and 1425 by the acclamations for the Emperor Manuel II Palaeologus and his wife Helena which follow the Vespers for the feast of the Exaltation. These acclamations of the Emperor and Empress are accompanied by others addressed to an archbishop.[21] He is not named, but he presides in person at the ceremony, for one rubric directs that he is to pronounce the opening benediction, and another that he is to

[20]The Athens MS. was photographed for me by Miss Alison Frantz, of the American School of Classical Studies, to whom I am particularly indebted for her extraordinary helpfulness; acknowledgment is due also to the American School itself, to Mr. Peter Topping, Librarian of the Gennadius Library, to Mr. Georgios Kournoutos, Curator of MSS. in the National Library, and to Professor Ernest W. Saunders, of the Garrett Biblical Institute, Evanston, Ill., and Father Gregorio Nowack, of Athens, who photographed for me the pertinent folios of the MSS. on Mount Athos.

[21]These acclamations do not differ materially from those addressed to John VIII in 1433, published by Tillyard after the MS. Pantocrator 214 in his paper on "The Acclamation of Emperors in Byzantine Ritual," *Annual of the British School at Athens,* XVIII (1911–12), 239–260, and often reprinted, most recently by Wellesz in his *History of Byzantine Music and Hymnography* (Oxford, 1949), pp. 103–106. Tillyard's shrewd suggestion that the examples he published might be an adaptation of earlier music is thus borne out. Indeed the fact is that this music can be traced as far back as the year 1336, when it was used for acclamations addressed to the Emperor Andronicus III (Athens, National Library, MS. 2458, fol. 144).

give the singers who acclaim him his blessing. From these directions we may infer that the manuscript comes from an archiepiscopal church, and from other directions found in the same context we may draw the further inference that it was a church possessing a sizable and accessible dome, for at the beginning of the ceremony the psaltists, bearing lights, are described as going up into the dome, and it is from here that they sing their acclamations. This archiepiscopal church with a sizable and accessible dome can only be the Great Church of Thessalonica, Hagia Sophia, for we know from Symeon, whose treatise is roughly contemporary with our manuscript, that in his day this was the one place where the "chanted" office was extensively used. I may add that the manuscript came to Athens from the library of the Gymnasium in Salonika, and that MS.E.148 at the Laura, in duplicating a part of its contents, describes it as "The office as it is sung in Thessalonica on the feast of the Exaltation of the Precious and Life-giving Cross."[22]

Here we must make a choice, for two courses lie open to us. What is to be our point of departure? The Constantinopolitan Hagia Sophia and the ninth century? Or the Thessalonican Hagia Sophia and the year 1400? Shall we begin with early documents from Constantinople, drawing on Symeon's treatise and the Athens manuscript only when a detail remains obscure or when an illustration is needed? Or shall we begin with our late provincial sources, relying at every turn upon earlier ones from the capital to insure the validity of our reconstruction? The second course may seem roundabout, but in the end it will prove to be the more direct. And it has this to recommend it: our late provincial sources, Symeon's treatise and the Athens manuscript, are ideally complementary, for they belong to the same time and place, and the one is in effect a commentary upon the text of the other.

Everyone recognizes that the primary purpose of those who founded the office as a form of Christian worship was to provide for the daily recitation of the Psalter and to fulfill the injunctions of the Psalmist, who would have us sing praises seven times a day,

---

[22] I am indebted to Professor H. G. Lunt of Harvard University for having kindly verified this reference for me at the time of his visit to the Laura in 1954.

at evening, at morning, and at noon. Whether we think of the Apostolic Constitutions, of Basil, of Cassian, or of Benedict, all early attempts to regulate the conduct of the office reflect this purpose. It is from the Psalter that an office derives its structure and, in the last analysis, the differences between one office and another are rooted in differences in the method of distributing the contents of this one book. To simplify my presentation, I shall build it around this central fact; the subordinate details will then fall into place of themselves.

It will be recalled that the Athens manuscript devotes its first folios to a sort of "Ordinarium," and that this contains music for the psalms and canticles as they are sung at the daily Vespers and Lauds throughout the week. In principle, each of these services begins with eight selections from the Psalter. As a rule one finds only the first line, but we know from other sources that the whole selection was usually sung and that each selection was followed by a doxology. Such a selection from the Psalter, when used liturgically, is called in Greek an "antiphon," and it is of course through a radical extension or change of meaning that this same term comes to be applied in Latin to a refrain sung in a psalmodic context.

The first of the Vesper antiphons is invariably the eighty-fifth psalm, "Bow down thine ear, O Lord, and hear me." Symeon describes its performance in some detail.

> After the priest has pronounced the opening benediction [he says] and has recited the Great Litany and the "Uphold, save, have mercy," the psaltists at once begin to sing the words "And hear me: Glory to thee, O God." And this singing is essential, for it contains both prayer and praise, the one from the psalm "Bow down thine ear, O Lord, and hear me," the other from the angelic hymn "Glory to God in the highest." . . . Then the priest says "Calling to remembrance the all-holy, undefiled," and raising his voice, he praises God in the Trinity, saying: "For unto thee is due all glory, honor, and worship." . . . And thus the whole psalm "Bow down thine ear, O Lord," is recited verse for verse by the two choirs in turn, with the "Glory to thee, O God," at every verse. . . . Then they sing the "Glory be to the Father" with the "Glory to thee, O God," and the other choir sings the "And now and ever."[23]

---

[23] *De sacra precatione,* 625, 628, 629.

Example 1   PSALM 85

From this it is clear that the recitation began with a sort of pre-amble, interpolated before the final petition of the litany, and that following the doxology of the prayer, the psalm itself was sung antiphonally by the two choirs, each taking a verse in turn. But Symeon is not correct in assigning the preamble to the psaltists; it was sung by a single precentor, or domestikos, who also sang the "Amen" after the doxology of the prayer and then went on to sing the whole first line of the psalm with its refrain. Only at this point did the choirs take over.[24] The Athens manuscript shows just how

[24]In his account of the "chanted" Lauds (*ibid.*, 637), Symeon describes these procedures more accurately.

this was done. From among its many settings I choose the one that opens the Vespers on Monday of the first week [Plate 1].

From the photograph alone one can see that the precentor sings in one style, the choir in another—that while the soloistic preamble and first line are relatively elaborate, the choral first line maintains a studied simplicity, most syllables bearing only a single neume. A transcription will bring out this antithesis more clearly (Ex. 1, p. 119).

It will pay us to stop a moment over this one example, for it can tell us a good deal about the procedures characteristic of this kind of psalmody. First of all, it enables us to see that, in the psalmody of the "chanted" office, the cadence formulas obey the general rule of the Byzantine psalm-tone: they are regularly made up of four elements, and these four elements are mechanically applied, without regard to accent or quantity, to the last four syllables of the text. In this respect, as also in many others, the Byzantine psalm-tones are more conservative than those of Western chant and lie closer to the beginnings of stylized recitation. The cadence formula is the all-important factor in music of this kind, and to recognize this is to recognize also the purpose of the precentor's preamble. This serves to establish the pitch, to establish the mode, in this case the Second Plagal, and to establish the melody of the refrain. But above all it serves to establish the cadence formula, and it is for this reason that so short a text is used and that it is drawn from the end of the line and not from the beginning. In this particular case, the choirs use a simpler cadence and a simpler refrain. But this does not always happen, and we may safely assume that it was not the original practice.

The Athens manuscript is a late source, written at the last possible moment, at a time when the tradition of the "chanted" office was about to die. What assurance have we that the music it contains is not a late creation, perhaps contemporary with the manuscript itself? In so far as it affects the melismatic recitation of the precentor, I see no simple way of answering this question. But recalling that the cadence formula is the all-important factor in music of this kind, it is easy to show tht the syllabic psalm-tone of the choir goes back to the first half of the thirteenth century at the very latest. For adapted to the first line of Psalm 148, one finds this same psalm-tone among the proper antiphons of a manuscript at Grottaferrata, written—as its colophon informs us—in the monastery of S. Salvatore di Messina in the year 1225.[25] The comparison speaks for itself.

Example 2

So much for the music of our example. As to its text, the use of Psalm 85 as the first antiphon of the "chanted" Vespers unquestionably preserves an old tradition. It is specifically and repeatedly called for in the Patmos copy of the Typikon, or rule, of Hagia Sophia,[26] a text which Baumstark places in the years between 802 and 806.[27] And Symeon himself makes the acute observation that the first of the evening prayers, beginning "O Lord, full of compassion and gracious, long-suffering and plenteous in mercy," is in effect a patchwork of quotations from Psalm 85, the simultaneous singing of which it obviously presupposes.[28] This prayer is already contained in the Barberini Euchology, a manuscript of the eighth century and the earliest document of its kind, and the use of Psalm 85 as the first antiphon of the "chanted" Vespers must of course go back still further. In the monasteries, Psalm 85 is read at Nones, and although the first of the evening prayers is the same as in the "chanted" office, the psalm which follows it is Psalm 103.

These provisions for the first antiphon of the "chanted" Vespers have their exact counterpart at Lauds, which also has its invariable first antiphon, consisting of Psalms 3, 62, and 133, sung under one doxology, and once again Symeon supplies a detailed account of its performance.[29] We can afford to pass over it without comment,

[25]The MS. Γ.γ.V (446). The antiphon is assigned to September 1 and November 8, and to most feasts of Our Lord and of the Virgin, and it occurs also in the MS.S. Salvatore 129 in the library of the University of Messina.

[26]Published by Dmitrievskii in his useful collection of texts, Описаніе литургическихъ рукописеи, I (Kiev, 1895), 1–152.

[27]"Das Typikon der Patmos-Handschrift" (cited in n. 9 above), 111.

[28]*De sacra precatione,* 628.   [29]*Ibid.,* 637.

for it agrees in every respect with what we have just seen; as at Vespers, the refrain is "Glory to thee, O God."

Like the fixed psalms of Matins, Lauds, and Compline in the West, the first antiphons of the "chanted" office are set apart from what I may call the "distributed" Psalter, and the same is true of the final antiphons (τὰ τελευταῖα) and of a few other psalms with special functions to fulfill. The remainder of the Psalter is then divided into sixty-eight antiphons, roughly equal in length, each antiphon containing from one to six psalms. A further division splits these sixty-eight antiphons into two groups—the odd-numbered antiphons, with the refrain "Alleluia," and the even-numbered antiphons, with a variety of little refrains not unlike those used for the Western litanies. In all, there are ten of these refrains, and it will be simplest to illustrate them here, together with transcriptions of the melodies with which they are most commonly associated.

Example 3   Refrains

Οἰ—κτεί—ρη—σόν   με , κύ—ρι—ε .   Σῶ—σον   ἡ—μᾶς , κύ——ρι—ε .
'Ε—πά—κου—σόν   μου, κύ—ρι——ε .   Φύ—λα—ξόν   με ,   κύ——ρι—ε .
'Ε—λέ—η—σόν   με, κύ—ρι—ε .   Μνήσθη—τί   μου , κύ——ρι—ε .
Βο—ή— θη—σόν   με , κύ—ρι—ε .
'Αν—τι—λα—βοῦ   μου, κύ—ρι——ε .
Εἰ—σά—κου—σόν   μου, κύ—ρι——ε .
'Ι—λά—σθη—τί   μοι, κύ—ρι—ε .

It is not difficult to recognize in the "distributed" Psalter of the Athens manuscript, and in its system of refrains, the arrangement set forth in the "Canon of the Antiphons of the Great Church," a document published many years ago by Cardinal Pitra after an eleventh-century manuscript at the Vatican (Vat. gr. 342).[30] The two divisions are indeed identical, and with the help of the Athens manuscript we can even supply the defects of Pitra's source.[31]

---

[30] *Iuris ecclesiastici graecorum historia et monumenta,* II (Rome, 1868), 209. It was reprinted by H. Leclercq in his article "Antienne (Liturgie)," Cabrol, *Dictionnaire d'archéologie chrétienne,* I, 2301–2303.

[31] Some additions and corrections have already been made by L. Petit in his article "Antiphone dans la liturgie grecque," Cabrol, *loc. cit.,* I, 2467–2468. For a reconstruction of the canon after Athens 2061, see Appendix I below.

What is more, the manuscript clears up for us an apparent inconsistency of the canon which would otherwise remain a puzzle. The evident intention is that the two sorts of refrain should alternate, and that each "Alleluia" antiphon should be followed by one sung with a little refrain. At two points the canon departs from this orderly arrangement. But there is no mistake—the Athens manuscript reveals that in either case an antiphon is to be taken out of order.

	Corrected Canon		Athens 2061
Ps. 4–6	Οἰκτείρησόν με, κύριε.	Ps. 4–6	Οἰκτείρησόν με, κύριε.
Ps. 7 and 8	Σῶσον ἡμᾶς, κύριε.	Ps. 9	Ἀλληλούϊα.
Ps. 9	Ἀλληλούϊα.	Ps. 7 and 8	Σῶσον ἡμᾶς, κύριε.
Ps. 10–13	Ἀλληλούϊα.	Ps. 10–13	Ἀλληλούϊα.
Ps. 33	Οἰκτείρησόν με, κύριε.	Ps. 33	Οἰκτείρησόν με, κύριε.
Ps. 34 and 35	Ἐπάκουσόν μου, κύριε.	Ps. 36	Ἀλληλούϊα.
Ps. 36	Ἀλληλούϊα.	Ps. 34 and 35	Ἐπάκουσόν μου, κύριε.
Ps. 37 and 38	Ἀλληλούϊα.	Ps. 37 and 38	Ἀλληλούϊα.

That this system of antiphons and refrains is in fact the system of Hagia Sophia is borne out by a whole series of additional documents,[32] and one finds it also in a number of early Psalters, among them several illustrated copies well known to the historian of Byzantine art. Cardinal Pitra himself drew attention to its presence in the eleventh-century Psalter Barberini 285, and Malickij has more recently discussed its bearing on the provenance of the ninth-century "Chludov" Psalter in Moscow and its companion piece at the Bibliothèque Nationale, the MS. Ancien fonds grec 20. In all three of these sources the make-up of the antiphons and the refrains with which they are to be sung are consistently indicated in the upper or lower margins. Thus, to take an example, the "Chludov" Psalter makes one antiphon of Psalms 97 to 100 and directs that

[32]Among them a Euchology at the Bibliothèque Nationale dated 1027, the MS. Coislin 213, cited by Malickij (n. 10 above).

it is to be sung with the refrain "Alleluia" [Plate 2]. A second hand has gone over the faded uncial text of the psalms and their titles, but has left the marginal direction untouched. The same direction —and the same illustrations—can be seen also on the corresponding folio of the Psalter at the Bibliothèque Nationale [Plate 3]. The Athens manuscript supplies the music for the first line of this antiphon also (Ex. 4). To take another example, the "Chludov" Psalter

Example 4   PSALM 97

makes one antiphon of Psalms 136 and 137, and directs that it is to be sung with the refrain "Forgive me, Lord" [Plate 4]. The same direction can be seen also on the corresponding folio of the Barberini Psalter [Plate 5]. Once again the Athens manuscript supplies the music, and the fragmentary manner in which it does so is typical of its treatment of these even-numbered antiphons.

Example 5   PSALM 136

Like Pitra's canon, the "Chludov" and Barberini Psalters adopt a different procedure for the fixed psalms. In the "Chludov" Psalter, Psalm 85 is simply headed "At Vespers," and there is no indication of a refrain [Plate 8]. And in the Barberini Psalter, Psalm 133, the last psalm of the first antiphon at Lauds, is given similar treatment [Plate 6]. The designation "monastic," for Psalters of this type, could scarcely be less accurate.[33]

As will have been evident from the foregoing, the psalm-tones of the "distributed" antiphons do not differ essentially from those used for Psalm 85 and for the first antiphon at Lauds. But there are differences in the manner of their performance. As before, the odd-numbered antiphons are preceded by the recitation of a litany—in this case, the so-called "Little Litany." But in introducing them, the precentor no longer draws, for his preamble, on the text of the psalm to follow. Instead he employs a set phrase—the words Τὴν οἰκουμένην· ἀλληλούϊα ("The earth: Alleluia")—adapted in each case to the cadence formula which he will afterward use in singing the first line of the antiphon itself. Symeon interprets this phrase as a sort of gloss on the preceding petition of the litany.

> For seeing that the priest addresses God with the words "Uphold, save, have mercy, and preserve us, O God, through thy grace," the psaltist adds [in effect] "Uphold, save, have mercy, and preserve *the earth*, O God, through *thy presence.*" For the word "Alleluia" signifies God's presence, his coming, and his being made manifest, and it is set apart as the special praise of his dispensation.[34]

As to the even-numbered antiphons, these are without preamble and no "Amen" is ever indicated. We may safely infer that they followed directly upon what preceded and that there was no intervening litany or doxology.

Now and then the Athens manuscript gives two first lines for an odd-numbered antiphon—the melismatic first line of the precentor and the syllabic first line of the choir. When this happens, the syllabic first line can sometimes be compared with a psalm-tone from the Grottaferrata MS. of 1225, and as a rule the two settings will agree, at least in their essential features. The first line of Psalm 17 provides a particularly instructive

---

[33]For photographs from the "Chludov," Paris, and Barberini Psalters I am indebted to Professor Kurt Weitzmann and Professor Ernest T. DeWald of Princeton University. Other Psalters with indications of the Constantinopolitan system of antiphons and refrains are listed by Heinrich Schneider in his article "Die biblischen Oden seit dem sechsten Jahrhundert," *Biblica,* XXX (1949), 249, n. 9.

[34]*De sacra precatione,* 629.

Example 6   PSALM 17

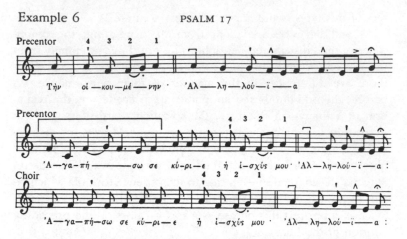

example. In this case, the precentor's announcement is only slightly more elaborate than the choral entrance and the two cadence formulas are identical, as are the refrains. In turn, the choral setting is in substantial agreement with the psalm-tone of the Grottaferrata MS., which, as we know, represents the practice of S. Salvatore di Messina (Ex. 7).[35] And in this mode, the "Low Mode" or ἦχος βαρύς, the precentor's intonation can also be traced to an earlier source. Taking the same formula, as adapted

Example 7

in the Athens manuscript to the first line of Psalm 37, I compare it with a solo verse of the common prokeimenon or gradual of the

[35]This psalm-tone, which belongs to the monastic psalmody of the Sunday Lauds, is found also in the MSS. Messina, University Library, S. Salvatore 120; Vaticanus graecus 1606; and Grottaferrata Γ.γ.vii (904).

mode, as given in a number of thirteenth-century manuscripts, among them one at Grottaferrata dated "1247." This confirmation is the more welcome in that the manuscripts containing the pro-

Example 8   PSALM 37

keimenon undoubtedly conserve a Constantinopolitan tradition.[36]

Symeon tells us very little about the use of these sixty-eight antiphons at Vespers and Lauds and almost nothing about the number to be recited at any one service. Of Vespers, he says only that in his day the antiphons were no longer being sung, excepting on Saturdays and during Lent, at which season the traditional complement of six antiphons was still being maintained; he calls this "weak and negligent," and adds that the constant "grumbling of the lazy" has forced him to reduce this complement, on Saturdays, to a single psalm. In his account of Lauds, he deals only with the Sunday arrangements, which constitute a special case.[37] But combining this meager evidence with the implications of the Athens manuscript, we might perhaps assume that the theoretical complement for either service was normally six antiphons—or if we counted the first and final antiphons, eight. This would agree well with the number of the evening and morning prayers. It would also agree with the views advanced by Father Nilo Borgia in his reconstruction of the "chanted" Vespers,[38] and up to a certain point it would agree with the more recent conclusions

[36]Sinai 1280; Patmos 221; Paris, Bibliothèque Nationale, Ancien fonds grec 397; Vaticanus graecus 345; and Grottaferrata Γ.γ. iii (372).

[37]*Ibid.*, 637, 640.

[38]In his 'Ωρολόγιον *"diurno" delle chiese di rito bizantino*, 2nd ed. (Grottaferrata, 1929), 84–103. The basis of this reconstruction was the work of Father Sofronio Gassisi.

of Antoniades.[39] There can be little doubt that it would closely approximate the practice of Thessalonica about the year 1400.

But one has only to consult the Typikon of the Great Church to recognize that the practice of Constantinople in the ninth century was altogether different. This is already evident from the infrequent and unsystematic indications of the Patmos copy, the one text now available in print.[40] And with the aid of the more complete and more explicit text of the copy at the Greek Patriarchate in Jerusalem,[41] the details of the earlier practice can actually be pieced together. A single example will make this clear. Under August 15, the Patmos copy gives one of its brief and infrequent directions: "From this day on we sing at Lauds 10 antiphons and at Vespers 15."[42] Of itself, this does not help us much. But the Jerusalem copy, in repeating the rubric, makes a significant addition: "About this time there is added to Lauds one antiphon, making 10, and 15 antiphons are recited at Vespers."[43] The inference is plain—at some earlier date the number of antiphons at Lauds was nine. Turning back to July 31 we find this confirmed: "[Today] there is added to Lauds one antiphon, making 9, and there is subtracted from Vespers one antiphon, making 16."[44] Again turning back, we find a further direction under July 16: "On or about the Monday after this commemoration there is added to Lauds one antiphon, making 8, and there is subtracted from Vespers one antiphon, making 17."[45] With this the pattern is unmistakable, and even though we lack some of the pieces, we can restore the whole. (For details of the early practice, see the table below). The purpose and meaning of this arrangement will be immediately apparent. During

---

[39]Θεολογία, XXI (1950), 199, 341. Relying on Symeon's account of the Sunday arrangements, Antoniades concludes that, counting the first antiphon, the number of antiphons at Lauds was either four or seven, depending on whether the three divisions of Psalm 118 are reckoned as three antiphons or as six.

[40]Dmitrievskii's edition is cited in n. 26 above.

[41]Hagiou Staurou, MS. 40, microfilmed for the Library of Congress in 1949 and 1950 by the American School of Oriental Research. The first folios of this MS. were published by Dmitrievskii in the third volume of his collection of texts (pp. 766–768), a project interrupted in 1917.

[42]Dmitrievskii, loc. cit., I, 105.

[43]Fol. 203 (August 14).

[44]Fol. 196.

[45]Fol. 188ᵛ.

the greater part of the year—roughly from All Saints, or Trinity Sunday, to the beginning of Lent—the daily complement was

Number of Antiphons at Lauds and Vespers

——	7	18	*Lent*	
July 16	8	17	First Monday	12 12
July 31	9	16	Second Monday	11 12
August 14–15	10	15	Fourth Monday	10 12
——	11	14	Fifth Monday	9 12
September 14	12	13	Sixth Saturday	8 12
	13	12		
October 11	14	11	*Eastertide*	
October 21	15	10	Easter Monday	7 13
——	16	9	Beginning of May	7 14
November 10	17	8	——	7 15
December 25	18	7	——	7 16
January 7	17	8	June 4	7 17
——	16	9		
January 20	15	10		
——	14	11		
——	13	12		

twenty-five antiphons, including the first and final antiphons of Morning and Evening Prayer. But the division of this assignment between the two services varied with the season. When the days are longest, in late June, the heavier burden falls to Vespers; when they are shortest, in late December, it falls to Lauds. During Lent the daily complement is gradually reduced; after Easter it increases again. And unlike most other systems of this kind, which aim to provide for the weekly reading of the whole Psalter, or for two such readings, the ancient system of Hagia Sophia makes no attempt to synchronize the recitation of the sixty-eight antiphons with a period of seven days or with any other predetermined period. At Lauds of the First Monday in Lent,[46] and again at the Vespers of Easter Sunday,[47] the Typikon directs a beginning from Psalm 1. But apart from these two points of adjustment, there is no co-ordination, for the period of the sixty-eight antiphons—roughly three days and

---

[46]Hagiou Staurou, MS. 40, fol. 206.
[47]*Ibid.*, fol. 229ᵛ; Dmitrievskii, *loc. cit.*, I, 136.

a fraction, or a little more, depending on the season—is not commensurable with the calendar.

If we proceed now to a comparison of these provisions with those worked out in the monasteries, we shall find them different in every conceivable respect. To the sixty-eight antiphons of the Great Church, a division of only 140 of the 150 psalms, the monasteries oppose a division of the whole Psalter into twenty sessions (καθίσματα) and sixty stations (στάσεις). At the Great Church the recitation of the sixty-eight antiphons does not coincide with any predetermined period; in the monasteries the whole Psalter is recited once a week, or—during Lent—twice. The elaborate system of refrains set forth in Pitra's canon is wholly foreign to monastic psalmody, which knows only the one refrain, "Alleluia." A further difference affects the text of the Psalter itself. For the "chanted" office this is arranged by whole verses which correspond roughly to the verses of the Authorized Version; for the monastic office it is (or was) arranged by short distinctions or half verses.[48] This of course brings with it a difference in the manner of recitation —in the monasteries the choirs alternate more frequently, and when refrains are used, they are more frequently interpolated. One might suppose that it would lead also to the introduction of medial cadences in the psalm-tones of the Great Church. But this does not happen, and the long verses of the Constantinopolitan text are recited straight through, without a noticeable break. Still another difference helps to explain Symeon's statement that the "chanted" office was sung throughout, as opposed to the monastic office, which was often performed without singing at all. For the sixty-eight antiphons of the Great Church are designed for daily use, and the Athens manuscript provides music for every one of them. In the monasteries, on the contrary, the chanting of the "distributed" Psalter was restricted to the Saturday Vespers, the Sunday Lauds, and the Vespers of great feasts; the monastic books provide music only for the few psalms used on these occasions—the rest of the

---

[48]On this point see Rahlfs, *Verzeichnis der griechischen Handschriften des Alten Testaments* (Stuttgart, 1914), pp. 18–19, 225; and Schneider, "Die biblischen Oden in Jerusalem und Konstantinopel" (cited in n. 11 above), 451. Many early Psalters include a more or less elaborate colophon comparing the total number of verses in the two versions. For the Constantinopolitan or "Ecclesiastical" Psalter the total is usually 2,542; for the Palestinian or "Hagiopolite" Psalter it is usually 4,782 or 4,784.

Psalter was simply read.[49] These are impressive differences with far-reaching implications. We shall find others, equally impressive, if we turn now from the Psalter to the canticles of the Old and New Testaments. Since neither the number nor the order of the canticles is predetermined, we may expect to find these differences still more significant.

On this point Symeon says only that at the Sunday Lauds the second canticle of the Holy Children followed the singing of the final antiphon, and that on week days at Lauds the canticle of Zacharias came at the end, between Psalms 148 to 150 and the Gloria or Great Doxology.[50] The other well-known canticles of the Old Testament he does not mention, nor does he say anything at all about the use or position of the Magnificat. Now at the Sunday Lauds, as we know from Symeon, the regular antiphons of the "distributed" Psalter were displaced by the great acrostic psalm, Psalm 118.[51] The Athens manuscript confirms this. At the same time it discloses that a similar displacement occurred at the Saturday Lauds, at which time, instead of the regular antiphons, one sang a series of seven canticles. That this was also the practice of the ninth century in Constantinople is evident from a direction found in the Typikon of the Great Church. For on the Saturday of the Akathistos Hymn, one of the few Saturdays it treats in any detail, the Patmos copy has this rubric: "At Lauds we sing 8 antiphons—the first antiphon and the 7 canticles."[52]

In largely restricting the singing of the canticles to a particular day of the week, the Great Church places itself once again in direct opposition to the monasteries, where the canticles were read every morning, and it proclaims its independence not only in this respect but also in choosing different texts and in arranging them in a different order. In the monasteries the sequence of canticles begins with the two canticles of Moses from Exodus and Deuteronomy;

[49]This view is based not only on the MSS. referred to in n. 35 above, but also on MS. L 36 sup. (476) of the Biblioteca Ambrosiana in Milan, which provides only for the psalms sung at the Saturday Vespers during Lent, and on a considerable number of sources, among them the one just cited, that give the beginnings of the troparia sung with the Psalter at Lauds, restricting themselves in this to the Lauds of Sundays.

[50]*De sacra precatione*, 640–641, 648–649.

[51]*Ibid.*, 637–644.

[52]Dmitrievskii, *loc. cit.*, I, 124.

then come the canticles of Hannah, Habakkuk, Isaiah, and Jonah, followed by the first canticle of the Holy Children. But in the Athens manuscript the canticle of Hannah comes after those from Habakkuk and Isaiah, and it is coupled with the Magnificat, just as two or more psalms are often combined in a single antiphon. After this follows the Prayer of Hezekiah, which forms no part of the monastic canon, while the canticle of Jonah is passed over in silence.

The order is strange, but it is not unique. With the aid of Schneider's exhaustive study of the canticles and their liturgical use, one can trace it to the commentaries of Hesychios, as contained in a manuscript of the eleventh or twelfth century at the Biblioteca Marciana in Venice, and from thence to a seventh-century source, the celebrated "Purple Psalter" of the Stadt-Bibliothek in Zürich. Relying on marginal indications of the Barberini Psalter, Schneider correctly identifies this ordering of the canticles with the use of Hagia Sophia. And his sources complete the series for us. That the Magnificat was coupled with its Old Testament prototype, the canticle of Hannah, we know already from the Athens manuscript. It now appears that the canticle of Jonah and the Prayer of Manasseh were similarly treated, and that just as Mary followed Hannah, so Jonah followed Isaiah, and Manasseh Hezekiah. Thus our seven canticles are in reality ten.[53]

Like the antiphons of the Psalter, the seven canticles are also provided with refrains. The canticles from Exodus and Daniel form these from their first lines. The long canticle from Deuteronomy has several, of which the first and principal one is "Glory to thee, O God." The remainder draw on the common stock, selecting their refrains from among those used earlier for the even-numbered antiphons of the "distributed" Psalter.[54] It follows logically that these refrains ought also to be indicated in the margins

---

[53]"Die biblischen Oden im christlichen Altertum," *Biblica*, XXX (1949), 28–65, especially 58 and following.

[54]In the Athens MS. the canticles of Hannah and Mary are also preceded and followed by a troparion. On the first Saturday this is "Holy Mother of the unutterable Light," on the second Saturday it is "All-holy mother of God, protecting wall of Christians." As troparia for the Psalter at Lauds, both texts can be found in the current Athens edition of the *Parakletiké* (pp. 119 and 273). Additional troparia of the same sort are found on fol. 57 and 99^V of the Athens MS. in connection with the Lauds of the two Saturdays before Christmas.

of the "Chludov" Psalter and its descendants. And of course they are. Thus the "Chludov" Psalter directs that the prayers of Hezekiah and Manasseh be treated as one antiphon and sung with the refrain "Forgive me, Lord" [Plate 9]. In this source the order of the canticles departs from the use of Hagia Sophia, in that the two royal prayers, numbered "7" and "8," follow immediately after the canticle of Jonah.[55] But the refrain is the correct one, and it is noteworthy that the later hand, having gone over the faded uncial text from Jonah, leaves the first of the two prayers untouched. The same is true of the second, for neither prayer belongs to the monastic canon [Plate 7]. As before, the Athens manuscript supplies the music.

Example 9   Prayer of Hezekiah

Once more we are confronted with a proof of independent origin. For in former times the monasteries too had a system of refrains for the canticles, and it has been preserved for us in the conventional headings of the texts themselves and in the concluding lines of many troparia from the Heirmologion. Thus for the canticle of Habakkuk the monasteries once used the refrain "Glory to thy strength, O Lord." But at Hagia Sophia the refrain was "Hear me, Lord," a refrain used also for several antiphons of the Psalter.

If the Great Church sang the canticles only once a week, choosing its own texts, ordering them in its own way, and interpolating its own refrains, what place can it have found for those unique expressions of the monastic spirit, the stanzas of the canons? Symeon tells us that at Hagia Sophia they formed no part of the original order.[56]

---

[55]The order is that of the Turin MS. of the commentaries of Hesychios, as given by Schneider on p. 64 of the article cited in n. 53 above.

[56]*De sacra precatione,* 648.

But wishing that order to be preserved and kept from harm [he adds], we ourselves have introduced the canons as a sort of spice or sweetening, so that no lazy or indifferent person, grumbling about beauty and knowing nothing of the order, may find a pretext to destroy it, alleging that he does not hear the familiar canons that are sung by all.[57]

Symeon's solution, as he explains it, was to place the canons in the second half of the service, between the fiftieth psalm and the Lauds themselves. The Athens manuscript adopts a different plan for the one canon it appoints. This is the well-known canon by Cosmas of Jerusalem for the feast of the Exaltation, and its eight model-stanzas are to be interpolated after the last eight of the twelve antiphons of the "distributed" Psalter provided for this exceptional occasion. Thus the stanzas of the canon, conceived by Cosmas as poetic paraphrases of specific canticles, are made to alternate with groups of psalms to which they stand in no intelligible relation whatsoever. The sheer incompatibility of the two liturgical practices could scarcely have been made more obvious.

What is true of the canons and their model-stanzas ought also to be true of the stichera, even though Symeon specifically directs the singing of such pieces, both at Vespers and at Lauds.[58] At Hagia Sophia, the successive verses of the evening psalm, or Κύριε ἐκέκραξα, were sung with a refrain which varied from day to day and from week to week.[59] This leaves no appropriate place for further interpolation, and none is called for in the Typikon of the Great Church. Similar considerations forbid the interpolation of stichera at the morning office, whether with Psalm 50 or with the Lauds themselves. Thus, like the stanzas of the canons, the stichera are fundamentally incompatible with the "chanted" order, and if they were at length admitted to it, as Symeon tells us they were, it must have been reluctantly and as a drastic compromise.

To round out my account of the Lauds at Hagia Sophia, I ought now to touch on the final antiphon or introit, which our visitor

---

[57] Ibid., 556.
[58] Ibid., 632, 649.
[59] Symeon (ibid., 629) names only those for alternate Sundays, but the Athens MS. has them all, and our other sources give an occasional proper refrain for an outstanding feast. For the refrains of the Κύριε ἐκέκραξα and Psalm 50, as given in Athens 2061, see Appendices II and III below.

from Novgorod heard sung as the choirs entered the Great Church from the narthex and grouped themselves in the center; to proceed as he did to the second canticle of the Holy Children, chanted before the altar as the doors of the sanctuary were opened; then to continue with Psalm 50 and with the concluding rites of Morning Prayer—the Lauds themselves, the canticle of Zacharias, and the Gloria or Great Doxology—which lead on Sundays to a troparion commemorating the Resurrection and to the prokeimenon and morning Gospel. In a similar way I ought also to round out my account of the Vespers, beginning with the final antiphon, the evening psalm, and the prokeimenon, and proceeding to the supplication and petitions, the lessons from the Old Testament, and the troparion of the day. But to do this properly would require another paper and would involve the use of quite different sources, for in principle the Athens manuscript does not follow either service beyond the central psalm, from which point the "chanted" Lauds and Vespers begin to agree in most respects with the monastic rite.

In most respects, but not in all. For there remains one highly individual feature of the "chanted" Vespers—the so-called "Little Antiphons" which follow the supplication and petitions of the deacon. Our manuscripts provide for these,[60] and Symeon pays high tribute to their fitness and to the thought behind them.

> Observe in these three antiphons [he says] the well-ordered arrangement of the hymns of the church: in the first, it invokes the intercession of the Virgin; in the second, aspiring higher, it implores him who was born of her to be propitious through the mediation of his saints; in the third and last, it sings the Trisagion with the angels, glorifying God, asking his forgiveness, and ascending a further step toward the sublime.[61]

The three antiphons draw their texts from Psalms 114, 115, and 116. Each has four verses and each is followed by a doxology. For each there is a special refrain, as Symeon implies, and for each a special prayer. The whole construction offers an exact parallel to the preliminary antiphons of the Liturgy. Here too the first and second antiphons are addressed, through their refrains, to Mother and Son. Here too the second doxology leads to a poetic summary

---

[60]Athens 2061, fol. 48ᵛ; Vatopedi 1527, fol. 312ᵛ; Laura E. 173, fol. 248.
[61]*De sacra precatione,* 633.

of the Constantinopolitan Creed, the troparion "Only-begotten Son and Word of God." And here too, though in a different way, the whole is crowned by the Trisagion. That the parallel extends also to the music can be shown quite simply. Let us take the refrain of the second antiphon: "Save us, Son of God, thou who didst rise from the dead, we who sing to thee Alleluia." Though they stand

Example 10

in different modes, the two melodies are in other respects very much alike.[62]

The little antiphons of the "chanted" Vespers have left a permanent impression on the monastic rite. Even today the prayers they were designed to accompany are read once a year, at the Vespers of Pentecost. And at first, on this one Sunday evening, the monasteries sang the antiphons as well. As one result of this, one finds occasional traces of the "chanted" office in early monastic books. Thus the texts of the three little antiphons are contained in a manuscript at Vatopedi, written about the year 1050.[63] But although a rubric directs that they be sung, no music is given for them at all. For the rest, the service is purely monastic, as will be evident from the opening directions [Plate

[62]The melody sung at the Liturgy can be found in any number of fourteenth-century sources as a refrain for the introit. I transcribe it here after a MS. at the Laura dated "1377" (Laura, I.178, fol. 212[V]).

[63]Vatopedi 1488, fols. 168–168[V].

10]. These prescribe the singing of Psalm 103, as usual in the monastic rite; after this follows a group of stichera, by Cosmas of Jerusalem, to be sung with the evening psalm. Again without music, the texts of the three little antiphons are found also in a number of manuscripts from Sicily and Calabria, of which the earliest, at Grottaferrata, was written about the year 1100.[64] But in these sources, despite monastic interpolations, the whole framework of the service is Constantinopolitan. And this framework has music throughout. In the copy at Grottaferrata, the Vespers begin from the benediction used at Hagia Sophia: "Blessed be the kingdom of the Father, Son, and Holy Ghost, for ever and ever" [Plate 11].[65] Then follows the usual litany, and after this, with musical notation, the first and final antiphons of the "chanted" Vespers.[66] Except for isolated phrases, we cannot read the notation of this source. But one thing is certain. Although the melodies are different from any of those we know, their general behavior conforms exactly to the pattern of our later sources.

By the eleventh century, then, the monasteries were already borrowing procedures from the "chanted" office and making them their own. At the same time, and even earlier, the influence of the monastic rite was making itself felt at Hagia Sophia. By the year 1200 the Great Church had abandoned the celebration of the Liturgy on Good Friday, our visitor from Novgorod informs us.[67] And in an eleventh-century manuscript at the Laura, almost certainly written in Constantinople or within its orbit, the Palestinian hour-services for Good Friday have displaced the service called for in the Typikon of the Great Church [Plate 12]. In this source, the monastic hours are specifically identified as "conforming to the tradition of the Holy City." The conflicting service called for in the Typikon is then relegated to an appendix [Plate 13]. Nor is the Typikon itself altogether free from monastic borrowings, even in

---

[64]Grottaferrata, Γ. β.xxxv (409), fols. 59ᵛ–67. Other Italo-Greek MSS. giving the text of the three little antiphons are Messina 129, Grottaferrata Γ. γ.v, and Vaticanus graecus 1606.

[65]Compare Symeon, *De sacra precatione*, 624–625.

[66]The beginning of the final antiphon, as given in this source, is reproduced in facsimile by Father Lorenzo Tardo in his *L'Antica melurgia bizantina* (Grottaferrata, 1938), pl. xvi.

[67]*Itinéraires russes en Orient* (cited in n. 1 above), 105. For the earlier custom, see Dmitrievskii, *loc. cit.*, 131, and Symeon, *Responsiones*, 905–908.

its ninth-century state. On Maundy Thursday, as Baumstark has pointed out,[68] the commemoration of the washing of the feet of the disciples already involves the singing of troparia taken over from the local use of Jerusalem.

Thus it appears that we do not in fact possess either office in its pristine form and that the intermingling of monastic and non-monastic practices antedates our earliest documents. Long before the Latin occupation, the conflicting claims of the two practices had clashed, and in the ensuing contest the imperial city did not prove itself the stronger part. By 1204 the rites of the Great Church had lost their hold. Their life was almost spent. May we not recognize in this the surest sign of their venerable antiquity?

The principal sources upon which this study is based are those which came to my notice in the spring of 1953, at the time of my first visit to Athens and Mount Athos. Following a second visit during the summer of 1955, made possible by grants from the John Simon Guggenheim Foundation and from Princeton University, I can direct attention to a number of additional sources which, without affecting my earlier conclusions in any significant way, show that the music of the "chanted" office was somewhat more widely disseminated than I had at first supposed.

Thus, on Mount Athos, music for the "chanted" Vespers of outstanding feasts is found, not only in Laura E.173 and Vatopedi 1527, sources already mentioned, but also in Koutloumousi 456 (folios 466 to 469), an otherwise normal compilation dated "1446." Additional sources from the fourteenth and fifteenth centuries with more or less complete versions of the "chanted" Lauds for the feast of the Exaltation are Iviron 947 and 1120, Koutloumousi 457, Laura I.185, and Vatopedi 1529. In Iviron 1120, a voluminous anthology compiled and copied in 1458 by Manuel Chrysaphes, this music is assigned to the Lauds of the Sunday before Christmas, and it is preceded by the little liturgical drama of the Holy Children whose text has been published by P. N. Trempelas, after Athens 2406, in his Ἐκλογὴ ἑλληνικῆς

---

[68]"Denkmäler der Entstehungsgeschichte des byzantinischen Ritus" (cited in n. 9 above), 21.

ὀρθοδόξου ὑμνογραφίας (Athens, 1949).

But by far the most important of these additional sources is a manuscript belonging to the National Library in Athens and, like Athens 2061, it is a manuscript that has come to Athens from the Gymnasium in Salonika. The MS. Athens 2062, which devotes its first 137 folios to the "chanted" office and to special music for the feast of St. Demetrius, is in most respects a duplicate of Athens 2061. But it is the earlier manuscript of the two, for its polychronia place it not later than the year 1385, during the lifetime of Andronicus IV. Unlike Athens 2061, it has only a single Ordinarium, that for the first week. In compensation, however, it is sometimes more complete. It contains several settings of Psalm 50 and gives the music for two of its refrains. It shows us how the refrains for the canticle of Zacharias were sung, and is the only source to tell us that this canticle was regularly coupled with the canticle of Symeon, the Nunc dimittis. Finally, it fills in serious gaps in Athens 2061, which has lost a number of folios.

While my own study of the "chanted" office was being written and prepared for publication, an independent study of the same problem was appearing serially in the Greek periodical Θεολογία. Published under the title Αἱ εὐχαὶ τοῦ ῎Ορθρου καὶ τοῦ ῾Εσπερινοῦ, this is the work of Professor P. N. Trempelas of the University of Athens, who has since reprinted its several installments in the second volume of his Μικρὸν Εὐχολόγιον (Athens, 1955). Like myself, Professor Trempelas draws heavily on the text of Athens 2061, from which he publishes a number of useful extracts. He also makes some use of an earlier study by Alexander Lavriotes, published in the ᾽Εκκλησιαστικὴ ᾽Αλήθεια for 1895, from which he reprints the text of the Vespers for outstanding feasts, as given in Laura Λ.165, a manuscript of the seventeenth century. Considering that Professor Trempelas was no more aware of my work on the problem than I was of his, I think it remarkable that our two solutions should agree as closely as they do.

Appendix I

The Antiphons of the Psalter

1. The "Distributed" Psalter

1	1–	2 : Ἀλληλούϊα.	35		70 : Ἀλληλούϊα.
2	4–	6 : Οἰκτείρησόν με, κύριε.	36	71–	72 : Ἀντιλαβοῦ μου, κύριε.
3		9 : Ἀλληλούϊα.	37	73–	74 : Ἀλληλούϊα.
4	7–	8 : Σῶσον ἡμᾶς, κύριε.	38	75–	76 : Φύλαξόν με, κύριε.
5	10–	13 : Ἀλληλούϊα.	39		77 : Ἀλληλούϊα.
6	14–	16 : Φύλαξόν με, κύριε.	40	78–	79 : Ἱλάσθητί μοι, κύριε.
7		17 : Ἀλληλούϊα.	41	80–	81 : Ἀλληλούϊα.
8	18–	20 : Ἐπάκουσόν μου, κύριε.	42	82–	83 : Ἐπάκουσόν μου, κύριε.
9		21 : Ἀλληλούϊα.	43		84 : Ἀλληλούϊα.
10	22–	23 : Ἐλέησόν με, κύριε.	44	86–	87 : Μνήσθητί μου, κύριε.
11	24–	25 : Ἀλληλούϊα.	45		88 : Ἀλληλούϊα.
12	26–	27 : Βοήθησόν με, κύριε.	46	89–	90 : Φύλαξόν με, κύριε.
13	28–	29 : Ἀλληλούϊα.	47	91–	93 : Ἀλληλούϊα.
14		30 : Ἀντιλαβοῦ μου, κύριε.	48	94–	96 : Σῶσον ἡμᾶς, κύριε.
15	31–	32 : Ἀλληλούϊα.	49	97–100 : Ἀλληλούϊα
16		33 : Οἰκτείρησόν με, κύριε	50		101 : Εἰσάκουσόν μου, κύριε.
17		36 : Ἀλληλούϊα.	51		102 : Ἀλληλούϊα.
18	34–	35 : Ἐπάκουσόν μου, κύριε.	52		103 : Οἰκτείρησόν με, κύριε.
19	37–	38 : Ἀλληλούϊα.	53		104 : Ἀλληλούϊα .
20	39–	40 : Εἰσάκουσόν μου, κύριε.	54		105 : Ἀντιλαβοῦ μου, κύριε.
21	41–	42 : Ἀλληλούϊα.	55		106 : Ἀλληλούϊα.
22		43 : Σῶσον ἡμᾶς, κύριε.	56	107–108 : Βοήθησόν με, κύριε.
23	44–	45 : Ἀλληλούϊα.	57	109–112 : Ἀλληλούϊα.
24	46–	47 : Ἱλάσθητί μοι, κύριε.	58	113–116 : Ἐπάκουσόν μου, κύριε.
25	48–	49 : Ἀλληλούϊα.	59		117 : Ἀλληλούϊα.
26	51–	53 : Μνήσθητί μου, κύριε.	60	119–124 : Ἐλέησόν με, κύριε.
27		54 : Ἀλληλούϊα.	61	125–130 : Ἀλληλούϊα.
28	55–	56 : Ἐλέησόν με, κύριε.	62	131–132 : Μνήσθητί μου, κύριε.
29	57–	58 : Ἀλληλούϊα.	63	134–135 : Ἀλληλούϊα.
30	59–	61 : Βοήθησόν με, κύριε.	64	136–137 : Ἱλάσθητί μοι, κύριε.
31	63–	64 : Ἀλληλούϊα.	65	138–139 : Ἀλληλούϊα.
32	65–	66 : Οἰκτείρησόν με, κύριε.	66	141–142 : Εἰσάκουσόν μου, κύριε.
33		67 : Ἀλληλούϊα.	67	143–144 : Ἀλληλούϊα.
34	68–	69 : Σῶσον ἡμᾶς, κύριε.	68	145–147 : Ἀντιλαβοῦ μου, κύριε.

2. Psalm 118

Antiphon 1 : Ἀλληλούϊα.
Antiphon 2 : Συνέτισόν με, κύριε.
Antiphon 3 : Ἀλληλούϊα.

3. The Canticles

1. Exodus	Τῷ κυρίῳ ᾄσωμεν, ἐνδόξως γὰρ δεδόξα- σται.
2. Deuteronomy	Δόξα σοι, ὁ θεός.
At Καὶ ἔφαγεν Ἰακώβ	Φύλαξόν με, κύριε.
At Ὅτι πῦρ ἐκκέκαυται	Δίκαιος εἶ, κύριε.
At Ἴδετε ἴδετε	Δόξα σοι, δόξα σοι.
3. Habakkuk	Εἰσάκουσόν μου, κύριε.
4. Isaiah & Jonah	Οἰκτείρησόν με, κύριε.
5. Hannah & Mary	Ἐλέησόν με, κύριε.
6. Hezekiah & Manasseh	Ἱλάσθητί μοι, κύριε.
7. Holy Children	Εὐλογητὸς εἶ, κύριε.

Appendix II

The Refrains of the Κύριε ἐκέκραξα

1. First Week

Sunday. Ἦχος β'.

Ἔνδοξε ἀειπαρθένε θεοτόκε, μήτηρ θεοῦ, προσάγαγε τὴν ἡμετέραν προσευχὴν τῷ υἱῷ σου καὶ θεῷ ἡμῶν.

Monday. Ἦχος πλ. δ'.

Ἐκέκραξά σοι, σωτὴρ τοῦ κόσμου· εἰσάκουσόν μου καὶ σῶσόν με, δέομαι.

Tuesday. Ἦχος πλ. β'.

Τὴν ἔπαρσιν τῶν χειρῶν μου, κύριε, θυσίαν πρόσδεξαι ἑσπερινὴν καὶ σῶσόν με, φιλάνθρωπε.

Wednesday. Ἦχος β'.

Κατεύθυνον τὴν προσευχήν μου, κύριε, δέομαι καὶ σῶσόν με.

Thursday. Ἦχος β'.

Ὅτι πρὸς σέ, κύριε, κύριε, οἱ ὀφθαλμοί μου. φύλαξον καὶ σῶσόν με.

Friday. Ἦχος πλ. β'.

Θεὸν ἐκ σοῦ σαρκωθέντα ἔγνωμεν, θεοτόκε παρθένε· αὐτὸν ἱκέτευε σωθῆναι τὰς ψυχὰς ἡμῶν.

Saturday. Ἦχος γ'.

Τὴν σωτήριόν σου ἔγερσιν δοξάζομεν, φιλάνθρωπε.

2. Second Week

Sunday's refrain agrees with that for the first week.[1]

Monday. Without indication of mode.

Κύριε, ἐκέκραξα πρὸς σέ, εἰσάκουσόν μου· πρόσχες τῇ φωνῇ τῆς δεήσεώς μου.

Tuesday. Ἦχος β'.

Ἐν τῷ κεκραγέναι με, κύριε, τῆς φωνῆς μου ἄκουσον καὶ σῶσόν με.

Wednesday. Ἦχος πλ. β'.

Κατευθυνθήτω ἡ προσευχή μου ἐνώπιόν σου, σωτὴρ τοῦ κόσμου.

Thursday. Ἦχος πλ. β'.

Δέσποτα κύριε, σοὶ μόνῳ ἀναπέμπομεν ἑσπερινὸν ὕμνον· ἐλέησον ἡμᾶς.
Friday's refrain agrees with that for the first week.
Saturday. Ἦχος πλ. β'.
Τὴν ζωηφόρον σου ἔγερσιν, κύριε, δοξάζομεν.

Appendix III
The Refrains of the Fiftieth Psalm
1. First Week

Monday. Ἦχος γ'.
Τῆς ψυχῆς μου τὸν ῥύπον σὺ γιγνώσκεις, κύριε· παράσχου μοι συγχώρησιν πλημμελή-
ματι ὡς ἀγαθὸς καὶ ἐλέησόν με.
Tuesday. Ἦχος πλ. α'.
Διὰ τὰ ἔργα μου τὰ δεινὰ πάσης παρρησίας ἐστέρημαι· καὶ κράζειν οὐ τολμῶ τὸ Ἱλά-
σθητι· ἀλλ' ὡς σὺ μόνος οἶδας, κύριε, ἀφιέναι ἁμαρτίας, ἐλέησόν με.
Wednesday. Ἦχος α'.
Ὁ σταυρὸν ὑπομείνας δι' ἐμέ· φώτισον τὴν ψυχήν μου δέομαι, ὁ θεός, καὶ ἐλέησόν με.
Thursday. Ἦχος γ'.
Ἐκ βυθοῦ τῶν ἀνομιῶν μου ἀνάγαγε, κύριε· ὡς τὸν Πέτρον ἐκ τῶν κυμάτων καὶ ἐλέησόν με.
Friday. Ἦχος δ'.
Πλῦνον τὸν ῥύπον τῆς καρδίας μοῦ· κάθαρον τὰ πλήθη τῶν πταισμάτων μου· τῇ δυνάμει
τοῦ σταυροῦ σου, ὁ θεός, καὶ ἐλέησόν με.
Saturday. Ἦχος πλ. δ'.
Τὸ φῶς τῆς σῆς γνώσεως, κύριε, λάμψον ταῖς καρδίαις ἡμῶν διὰ τῆς θεοτόκου καὶ ἐλέ-
ησον ἡμᾶς.

2. Second Week

Monday. Ἦχος δ'.
Ἀπὸ πασῶν τῶν ἀνομιῶν μου ῥῦσαί με, κύριε· καὶ τῆς σῆς εὐσπλαγχνίας [ἀξίωσον] καὶ
ἐλέησόν με.
Tuesday. Ἦχος πλ. α'.
Εἰς τὸ πέλαγος τῶν σῶν οἰκτιρμῶν ἀφορῶντες βοῶμέν σοι, κύριε.
Wednesday. Ἦχος πλ. δ'.
Ἀπὸ τῆς ἁμαρτίας μου καθάρισόν με, κύριε· καὶ τῆς σῆς εὐσπλαγχνίας ἀξίωσον, σωτὴρ
πολυέλεε.
Thursday. Ἦχος γ'.
Τὸν βυθὸν τῶν πταισμάτων μου σὺ γιγνώσκεις, κύριε· δός μοι χεῖρα ὡς τῷ Πέτρῳ καὶ
ἐλέησόν με.
Friday's refrain agrees with that for Wednesday of the first week.
Saturday. Ἦχος πλ. β'.
Ὁ τὸ φῶς ἀνατέλλων· διὰ τῆς θεοτόκου ἐλέησον ἡμᾶς.

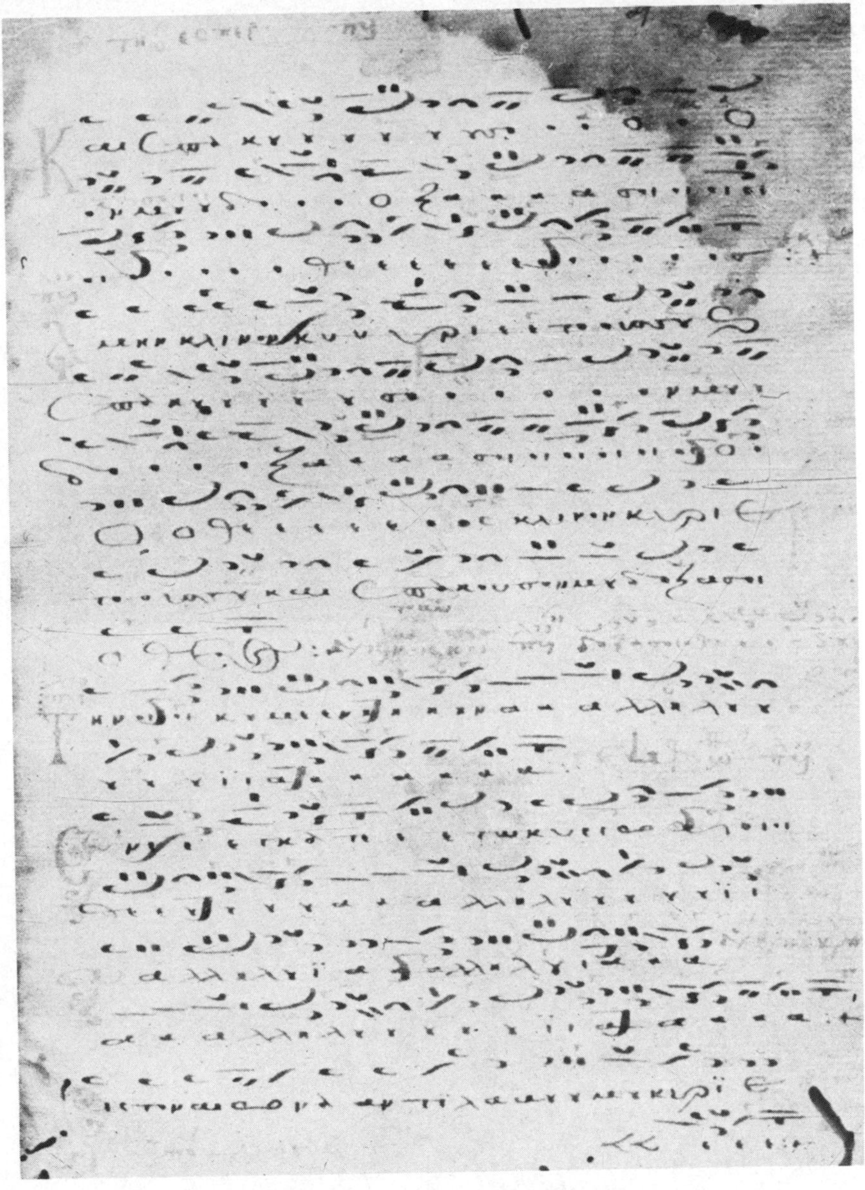

Plate 1. Athens, National Library, MS. 2061, fol. 4

Plate 3. Paris, Bibliothèque Nationale, Ancien fonds grec, MS. 20, fol. 5ᵛ

Plate 2. "Chludov" Psalter, fol. 97ᵛ

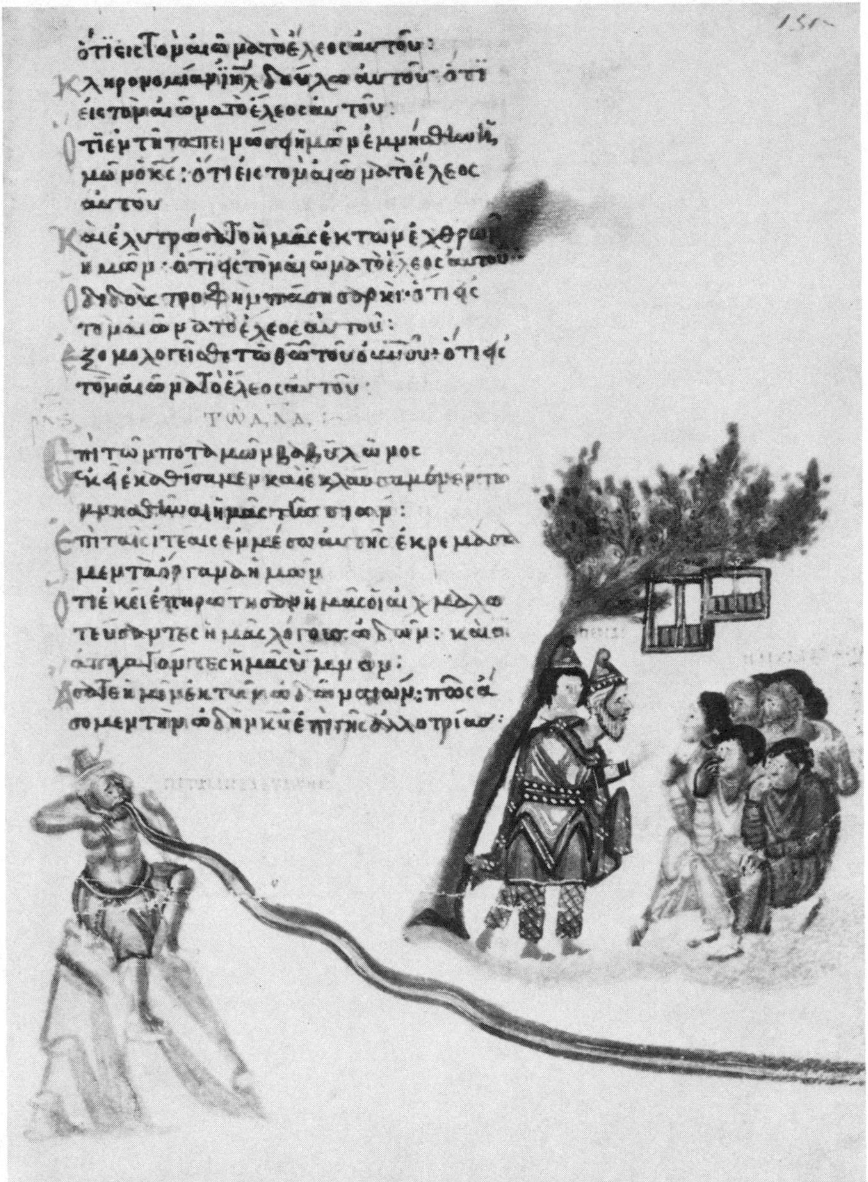

Plate 4. "Chludov" Psalter, fol. 135

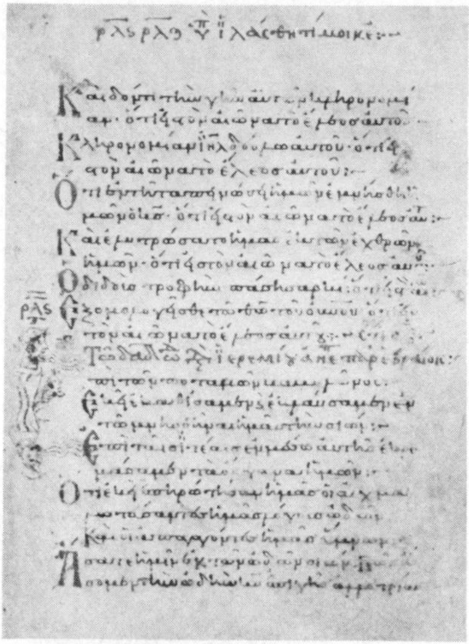

Plate 5. Vatican, Barberini gr. 285,
fol. 129

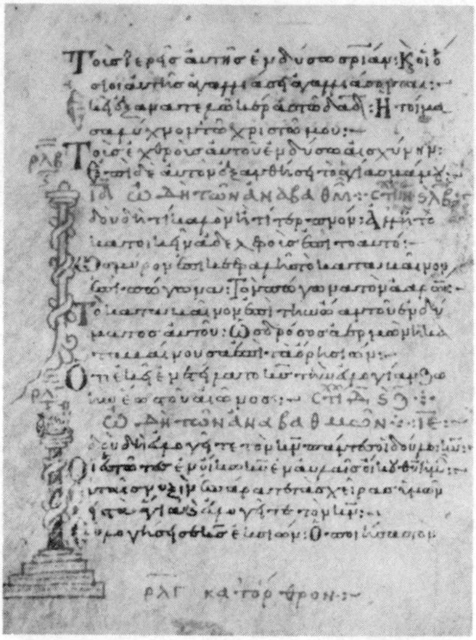

Plate 6. Vatican, Barberini gr. 285,
fol. 126ᵛ

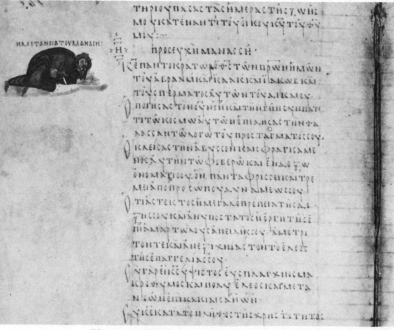

Plate 7. "Chludov" Psalter, fol. 158ᵛ

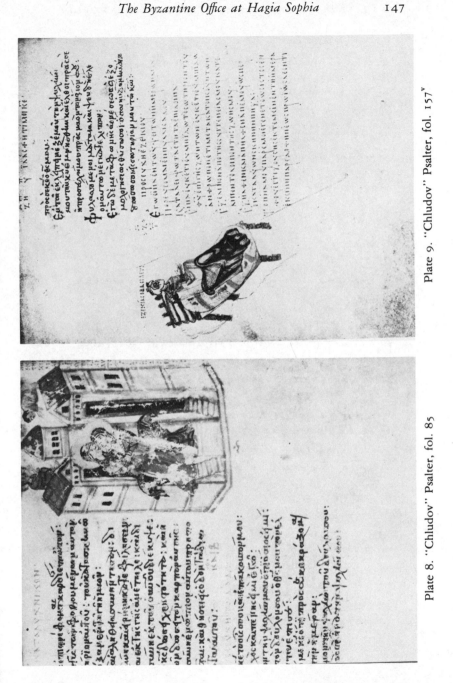

Plate 8. "Chludov" Psalter, fol. 85

Plate 9. "Chludov" Psalter, fol. 157[v]

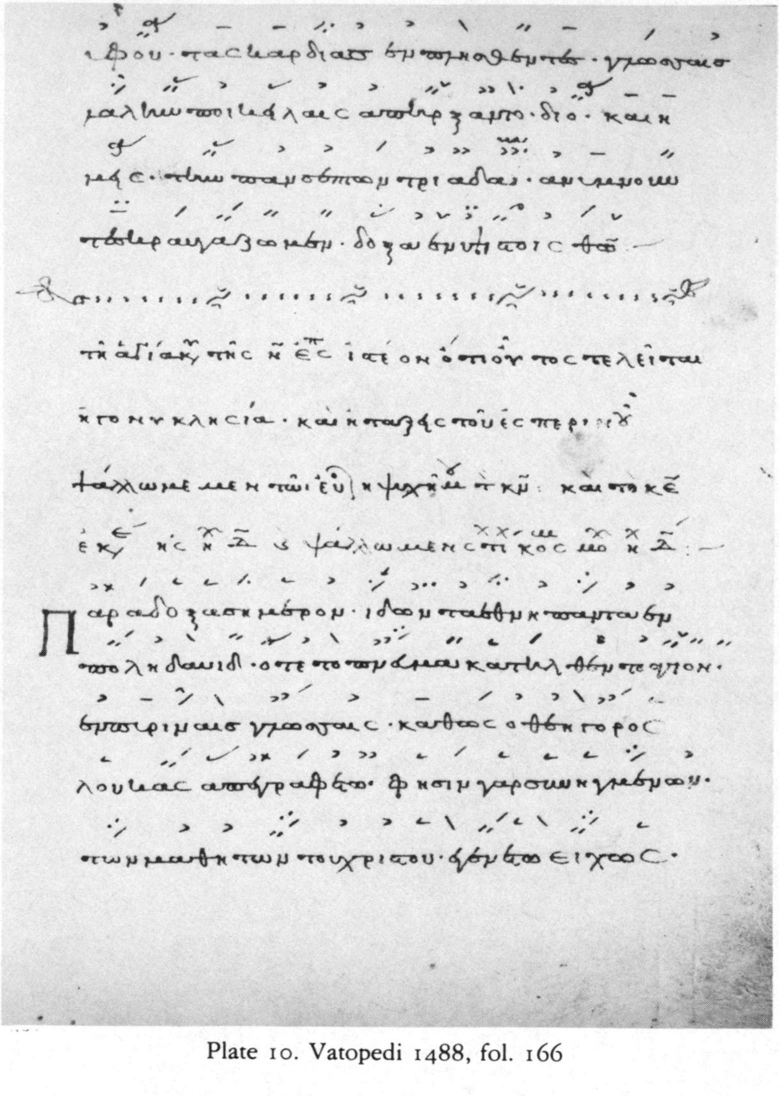

Plate 10. Vatopedi 1488, fol. 166

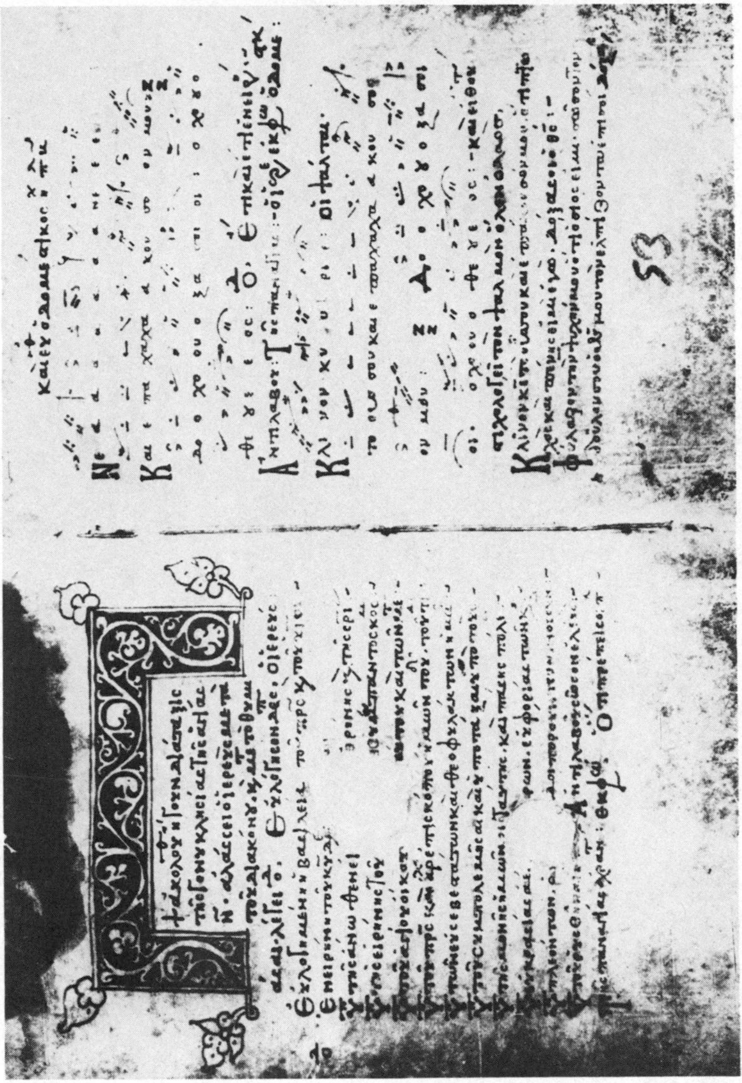

Plate 11. Grottaferrata Γ.β.xxxv, fol. 52ᵛ–53

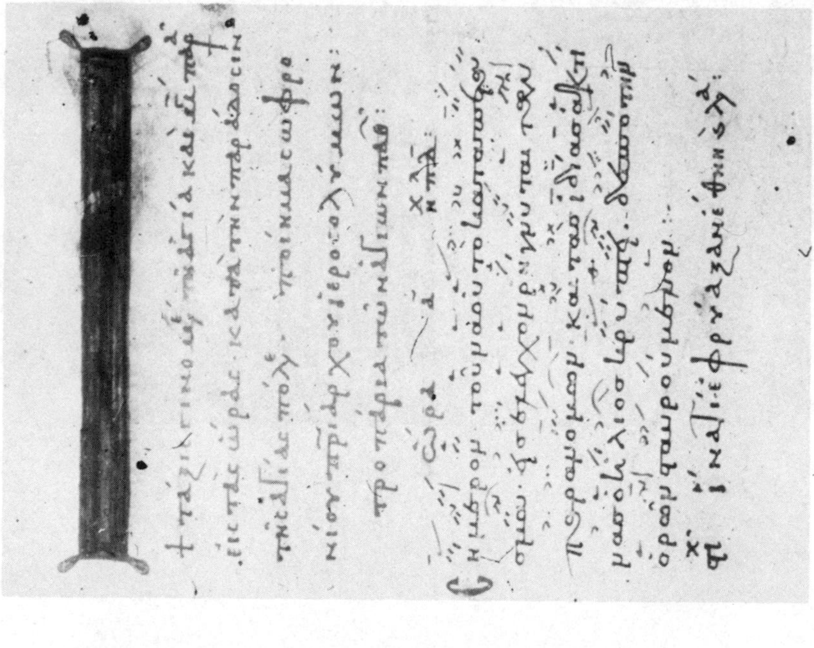

Plate 12. Laura Δ.11, fol. 42

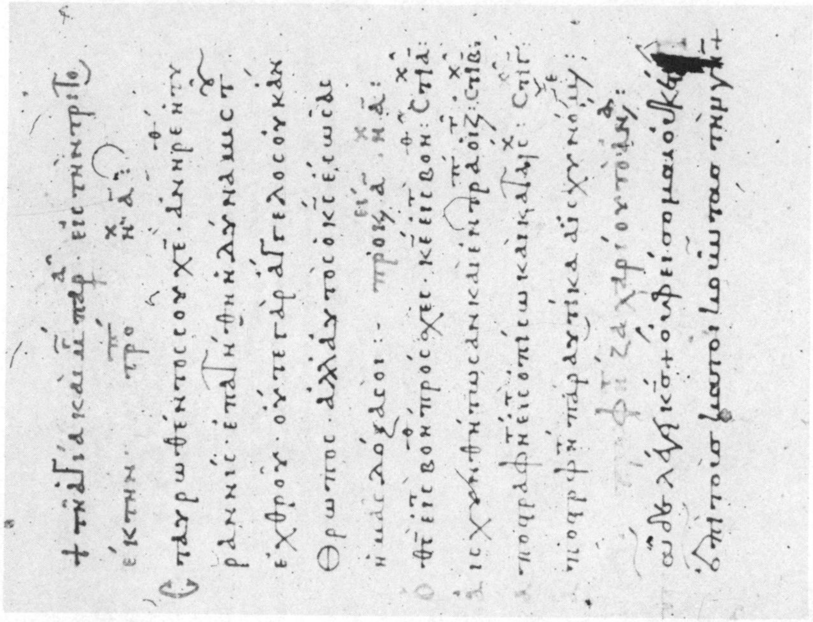

Plate 13. Laura Δ.11, fol. 102

THE INFLUENCE OF THE LITURGICAL CHANT OF THE EAST ON THAT OF THE WESTERN CHURCH[†]

I N a remarkable paragraph of his recent encyclical, the Holy Father reminds us that his tribute to the dignity and usefulness of the Gregorian chant has also a wider application. Within limits, it applies as well to the liturgical chants of the non-Roman rites, and among these His Holiness expressly includes the rites of the Christian East. He draws attention to the necessity of safeguarding this venerable treasure, to be esteemed not only for its antiquity and its intrinsic merit, but also for its great influence on the music of the Latin West.

Surely no one ever questioned the fact of this influence. Yet it is difficult to define it, difficult to measure its extent, difficult to distinguish—in comparing the two bodies of chant—between indications that the one has influenced the other and indications of their common origin. The difficulty increases if one seeks to deal with the relationship in strictly musical terms, without speaking of the influence of rite upon rite, or of the symbolic use of the Greek language in Latin ceremonies, or of the numerous literal translations into Latin from the Greek hymnographers, even of those exceptional cases in which the translated Greek text has actually carried its Greek melody with it. It is,

†Originally published in Italian translation as "Influsso del canto liturgico orientale su quello della Chiesa occidentale," in L'Enciclica Musicae Sacrae disciplina di Sua Santità Pio XII; testo e commento, a cura dell'Associazione Italiana S. Cecilia (Rome, 1957), pp. 343–348. Reprinted with permission of the publisher.

however, in strictly musical terms that the relationship must be dealt with if one is to convey any idea of its genuinely pervading and deep-seated vitality.

If, then, we look beyond chance borrowings, however interesting and significant these may be, searching instead for common qualities and traits, for the underlying points of contact, we shall naturally think first of the eight-mode system. And to think of the eight-mode system is to think also of all that this implies—the diatonic basis, the possibility of transpositions to the fourth and fifth, the use of characteristic opening and cadential patterns, the centonate constructions to which the use of such patterns inevitably leads. The essential identity of the two modal systems, Eastern and Western, follows sufficiently from these two instances of direct borrowing, recently uncovered by Wellesz and Handschin.

But the identity thus revealed is confirmed for us by the musical theorists of the early Middle Ages, who also tell us in plain language that the Western modes are of Eastern origin.

The first full account of the eight-mode system to be written in the West was the *Musica disciplina* of Aurelian of Réomé. We can date this "about 843," for in that year the Abbot Bernard, to whom the treatise is dedicated, was one of the signers of a letter of privilege extended to the Abbey of Corbie. Aurelian makes no secret of the source of his teaching. As he puts it, he has drawn water from the Greek well and plucked flowers from the Greek garden. To this he adds that when the arrogance of the Greeks—constantly boasting about their eight modes—became intolerable, the Emperor Charlemagne ordered the number to be increased to twelve, whereupon the Greeks, not to be outdone, likewise brought forth an equal number of equally superfluous additions. Aurelian's whole terminology is Greek, or rather Byzantine, as are those of his immediate successors, Hucbald and the author of the *Musica enchiriadis;* and as late as the first quarter of the eleventh century Guido of Arezzo is still insisting, in his *Micrologus,* that to say "Tonus primus" rather than "Authentus protus" is an abuse.

Having introduced his readers to an Eastern theory and an Eastern terminology, Aurelian goes on to acquaint them with an Eastern practice—the use of the eight formulas of intonation. He is puzzled by the mysterious texts that accompany these little introductory phrases and uncertain about the proper text to use with the plagal modes—whether Noeane or Noeacis. A Greek acquaintance has informed him that these words are meaningless and that the number of syllables is determined solely by the length of the phrase.

Even for Aurelian, the eight-mode system is something more than a theoretical construction—it has an eminently practical purpose. It underlies the methodical arrangement of the Gregorian psalm tones, and for each antiphon or respond it determines the appropriate psalmodic context. This being the case, we ought obviously to ask whether the Gregorian psalm tones themselves do not also show traces of Eastern influence.

Before pursuing this question, however, we shall need to return for a moment to the Byzantine modal formulas, for these provide the essential connecting link. Their purpose is to announce and prepare the singing of troparia, and since the troparia of a particular mode have various ways of beginning, the endings of the single formulas exhibit a corresponding variety. In this significant respect, the Byzantine modal formula closely resembles the Gregorian psalm tone, for just as the endings of the formulas are determined, from case to case, by the beginning of the following troparion, so the endings—or differences —of the psalm tones are determined, from case to case, by the beginning of the following antiphon. Here, for the first time, we find the two bodies of chant obeying a single law of musical style. The resemblance turns on identity of function, not on literal agreement, although this too is often present, as in these examples from the Tonus quartus or Second Plagal.

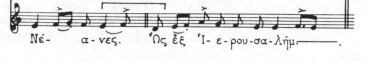

The parallel could scarcely be more exact or more suggestive. Not only does it establish a relation, it establishes a strong presumption of cause and effect, for the Byzantine modal formula was at one time known throughout Western Europe.

The next step follows naturally. Like the Latin antiphon, the Greek troparion is normally sung in a psalmodic context, either in association with the fixed psalms of the daily Office, or in association with Proper verses, appropriate to the feast, and in earlier times the orderly recitation of this psalmodic context was governed by established traditions not unlike those familiar to us from the Western choir books. Already we have traced a connection between the Gregorian psalm tone and the Byzan-

tine modal formula. Can we now go on to extend this to the
Byzantine psalm tone itself? The example that follows makes
this extension for us. It quotes the openings of four troparia,
two in the Third Authentic, two in the Fourth Plagal, each in
its proper psalmodic setting, and it shows us that the endings of
the verses, like the endings of the modal formulas, were determined in each instance by the beginning of the troparion that
followed. Indeed, the several endings illustrated are all of them
used also as endings of modal formulas, so that it now appears
that the foreshadowing of the psalmodic cadence was one of the

chief functions with which these formulas were charged. Although the verses just quoted are drawn from a relatively late
source, the Sticherarion Grottaferrata E.a.ii, a manuscript of the
thirteenth century, the antiquity of the tradition that they represent lies beyond question. It is confirmed for us by the psalmodic beginnings of the troparia on the gradual Psalms, written
shortly after the year 800 by Theodore Studites, a comprehensive cycle of little pieces whose written tradition can be traced
back as far as the late tenth century. Not less significant is its
confirmation in an early Slavonic source, the eleventh-century
Typografskii Ustav in Moscow.

What was true of the modal formulas is also true of the

psalm tones—this much is evident. It is likewise evident that these psalm tones belong to a familiar type whose characteristic feature is its cadence—a cadence of four elements, mechanically applied to the last four syllables of the text, without regard to accent or quantity. This type is represented in the Gregorian chant by the monastic Tonus irregularis and in the Ambrosian chant by a similar tone, likewise irregular, frequently used with tenors on *mi* and their transpositions to the fourth and fifth. That it was known also to the Mozarabic chant is evident from many pages of the recently published facsimile of the *Antifonario de Leon*. Here, indeed, one finds no other type. The conclusion is inescapable. Psalm tones of this well-defined and somewhat arbitrary variety can scarcely have sprung up independently in Toledo, Milan, Rome, and Byzantium. The evidence before us points unmistakably to a transmission from a single center. And in the light of what we have already seen, this center can only be Byzantium.

Thus we see an Eastern theory and an Eastern practice brought into the West, touching Western theory and practice at a vital point, exerting a shaping influence not only on chants of later composition, but also on the transmission of existing ones, and contributing in a significant way to the development of psalmodic recitation. Perhaps one may claim even more. For while it is perfectly possible that the rigidly organized psalm tones brought in from the East represent an end product, a last step in a gradual process of stylization, it is at least equally possible that they represent a starting point, with the gradual process working away from stylization rather than toward it, and that the traces they have left in the Gregorian, Ambrosian, and Mozarabic Antiphoners are all that remains of the oldest Western practice.

SOME OBSERVATIONS
ON THE MUSIC
OF THE KONTAKION[†]

W HEN was the kontakion scaled down in actual practice to two stanzas, the prooimion and the first oikos? No official document answers this critical question for us, and our earliest liturgical documents, when they throw any light on it at all, reveal only that by the tenth century the reduction was already an accomplished fact. Yet it seems obvious that this radical change in the structure of the Morning Office must have been reflected almost at once in kontakion poetry. To date the change we have, then, only to determine when the poetry itself began to change. Theodore Studites was the last poet of any stature to write extended kontakia, comparable in scale to those of Romanos, and on his death in 826 the anonymous kontakion for his commemoration ran in the original to at least eleven stanzas. The change first becomes evident in the work of the next generation. Joseph the Hymnographer reduces his kontakia to the smallest scale compatible with acrostic poetry. An early example is the kontakion in which he commemorates his "spiritual father," Gregory Dekapolites; written shortly after 842, this has five stanzas (with the acrostic Ἰωσήφ). And in other works Joseph is already using the three-letter acrostic Ὠδή. It seems quite clear that the reduction of the kontakion must have taken place during the second quarter of the ninth century.

---

†A paper presented at a private conference in Copenhagen, August 13, 1958, previously unpublished.

Music, too, must have reflected this change in structure, although we cannot expect it to have reflected it quite so promptly. My own view would be that its effect on music was probably not felt until the tenth century, and that it led at that time to the composition of original melismatic music for the kontakia still in use.

No manuscript devoted exclusively to the music of the kontakion is known to have been written within the empire before the time of Koukouzeles, for until the compilation of the kalophonic kontakarion it was the practice in Byzantium to collect all music for the solo singer in a single volume. I am assuming that this association of the kontakion with the hypakoe, prokeimenon, and Alleluia verse goes back to the time when the music of these related classes was first collected and written down.

Of this one-volume compendium there are copies on Patmos, on Mount Athos, and at Mount Sinai,[1] and the book is preserved also in a number of copies written in those parts of Italy where Greek was spoken. All copies of the book derive from a single archetype. They have the same contents and they arrange it in the same somewhat arbitrary order. Their homogeneity is further borne out by their marked tendency to transmit identical variants. From its choice of prokeimena it is evident that the book was intended for the use of public churches and the secular clergy; from its choice of Alleluia verses and from their rubrication it is equally evident that its provenance can only have been Constantinople. Most copies that have not lost their first and last folios bear the title Psaltikon.

To be distinguished from this nonmonastic or Constantinopolitan form of the Psaltikon, and from Italian copies of it, are the specifically Italian forms of the book developed at Messina and Grottaferrata. These adapt it to local monastic requirements, suppressing some part of its contents and adding much that is new. In copies deriving from Messina the melodic version is more elaborate throughout; those written at Grottaferrata follow Messina in their versions of the hypakoe and Alleluia verse, Constantinople in their versions of the kontakia.

---

[1]Since this paper was presented, one further copy has come to light—the MS Ochrida, Musée National, 59.

And there are characteristic differences in arrangement and calendar.

Despite these differences, however, our sources have one revealing common trait—they arrange the kontakia for the fixed and movable feasts in a single series, placing the kontakia for the movable feasts between those for the months of February and June, and interpolating the kontakia for March and April at fixed points within the Triodion and Pentekostarion. There are no significant departures from this arrangement, and the calendars are separated only in two of our latest sources—the copies of the kalophonic kontakarion at Mount Sinai and in Athens.

No such arrangement is found in any known copy of the Sticherarion, and if it was ever used for the lectionaries, it must have been abandoned at a very early date.[2] It is not found in our principal source for the poetry of the kontakion, the MSS Patmos 212 and 213, and the same may be said of most other manuscripts of this class. Significantly enough, however, one does find it in two of the earliest—in the older part of Sinai 925, a manuscript of the tenth century, and in Corsiniana 366, an eleventh-century Italian manuscript with other archaic features.

The obvious inference is that the archetype of our sources with musical notation cannot be dated later than the tenth century. We could scarcely date it earlier, for to do so would carry us beyond the beginnings of the written tradition as we now know them. Thus, to the view that the music of the kontakion is an original creation of the tenth century, there is now added the further view that the music of the kontakion was first committed to writing in the tenth century. The second view confirms the first, for it is, I think, impossible that melodies of such length and such complexity could ever have been transmitted orally.

The view that the music of the kontakion is an original creation of the tenth century is not inconsistent with what we already know

---

[2]To be sure, the principle underlying the arrangement of the Biblical readings in the several lectionaries is that of the *lectio continua;* an intermingling of the readings for the fixed and movable feasts would accordingly be inconvenient and inappropriate. Even so, there are rare exceptions. All of them early, these are intended for imperial use and restricted to lessons for the principal feasts.

about the music of that time. Beginning about 850, radical changes were taking place. Particularly for doxastika and other liturgically outstanding pieces, a new and more elaborate style was being developed, and composers were beginning to think of themselves as virtuosi and to expect virtuosity of the singers who sang their music. These tendencies are already evident in the Heothina (Ex. 1), in the great Doxastikon of Pentecost,[3] and above all in the processional pieces written for the mid-Lenten ceremony of the Adoration of the Cross.[4] They are also evident in the alterations made at this time in the opening phrases of certain troparia of the Good Friday Hours (Ex. 2) and in the rapid development of the musical notation, which had constantly to meet more exacting demands.

In a word, the development is toward the kalophonic style and toward the notation associated with that style, and in my view the music of the kontakion and the way in which it is written down constitute important first steps in this direction. Our earliest sources for these two kinds of music belong to the same time and they use the same notation. There are distinct stylistic analogies also: both kinds of music show a fondness for the descending melodic sequence; both tend in the same way to free established groups from their traditional association with particular modes and particular steps of the system (Ex. 3). As a general rule, the kalophonic technique is applied only to liturgically outstanding pieces. Thus it is not surprising that in the end it should have been applied to the kontakion also once its melodies had come to be regarded as "ancient." Most kalophonic Sticheraria contain embellished versions of one or more kontakia, sometimes based on the older melodies, sometimes freely composed, and whole collections of pieces of this kind were ultimately assembled in a special book.

In rare instances, a sticheron belonging to the accepted repertory quotes more or less literally from the text of a kontakion, usually from its refrain, and when this happens, the sticheron and the kontakion from which it quotes are regularly in the

---

[3]See H. J. W. Tillyard, *The Hymns of the Pentecostarium* (Copenhagen, 1960), no. 96.

[4]For an elaborate, freely composed melisma from one of these pieces, see page 306 below.

same mode. It is a fair inference, surely, that these quotations extend also to the music, thus preserving for us a few phrases from syllabic melodies used for kontakia in the eighth and early ninth centuries. Comparisons show, however, that there is no correspondence whatever between these phrases and the corresponding phrases of the Psaltikon (Ex. 4).[5] The same conclusion imposes itself when we compare the melismatic setting of a conventional refrain, as found in the Psaltikon, with its established and familiar syllabic setting.

Thus the view that the music of the kontakion is an original creation of the tenth century commends itself as simple, as reasonable, and as the one open to the fewest objections. It fits the facts and it is also consistent with the broad view of the tenth century already formulated by students of Byzantine art and literature.

In so far as these conclusions are applicable to the kontakion, they are equally applicable to the hypakoe. But it need not follow that they apply also to the prokeimenon and Alleluia verse, for the texts of these two classes have quite a different history and their melodies, while agreeing with the melodies of the kontakion in some respects, disagree with them in others. One possible view would be that the tenth-century creators of the kontakion melodies adopted the style of the prokeimenon and Alleluia verse as their point of departure.

[5]In Copenhagen, this point was also illustrated by the examples to be found on page 315 below. For another example, see Kenneth Levy, "An Early Chant for Romanus' Contacium Trium Puerorum?" *Classica et Mediaevalia,* XXII (1961), 172–175, and for a syllabic setting of the entire prooimion of the Romanos kontakion on the Woman of Samaria (Maas-Trypanis no. 9), the transcriptions of Tillyard cited above, no. 47, here provided with an additional refrain.

Ex. 1 Syllabic cadence and its florid elaboration in Heothinon 6

Ex. 2 Simple and florid versions of troparia of the Good Friday Hours

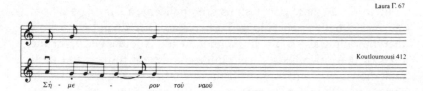

Ex. 3 Comparison of phrases from the kontakion Τὸν δι' ἡμᾶς and the Koukouzeles exercise in the eight modes

Ex. 4 Quotations from the kontakion Ψυχή μου in the sticheron Βασιλεῦ οὐράνιε

THE ANTIPHONS
OF THE OKTOECHOS †

I N the Byzantine rite, at the Sunday morning office, immediately
following the recitation of the Psalter and just before the prokeimenon and morning Gospel, the two choirs alternate in singing
the Anabathmoi of the mode, a set of three to four little antiphons
on the Gradual Psalms(αἱ ᾠδαὶ τῶν ἀναβαθμῶν).[1] In all, there
are eight such sets—one in each of the eight modes, one for each
of the eight Sundays of the modal cycle. Some sources, among them
the Vienna MS published in facsimile by the editors of the *Monumenta musicae byzantinae,* name as the composer of these pieces St.
John of Damascus. Other sources prefer Theodore Studites,[2] and
their testimony is confirmed by Nicephorus Callistus, the mid-14th-
century author of a commentary on the Anabathmoi, who records
the tradition that Theodore wrote the antiphons in Thessalonica at

†From *Journal of the American Musicological Society,* XIII (1960), 50–67; written
in honor of the eightieth birthday of Otto Kinkeldey. Reprinted with permission
of the American Musicological Society.

[1]Earlier studies of the music of the Anabathmoi include H. J. W. Tillyard's "The
Antiphons of the Byzantine Octoechus," *Annual of the British School at Athens,*
XXXVI (1935–36), pp. 132–141, and P. Lorenzo Tardo's "L'ottoecho nei manoscritti melurgici," *Bollettino della Badia greca di Grottaferrata,* I–II (1947–1948), especially I, 34 and 133. A complete transcription is published in Tillyard's *Hymns of
the Octoechus,* P. I (Copenhagen, 1940), pp. 145–183.

[2]The earliest source in which I have seen the attribution to Theodore is Sinai
778, an 11th-century text of the Parakletike. It is also found in these later MSS with
musical notation: Athos, Koutloumousi 403 and 411; Athos, Laura Δ.30; Jerusalem,
Greek Patriarchate, Holy Sepulcher 533; Milan, Ambrosiana A. 139 sup. (gr. 44);
Sinai 1216 and 1471.

the time of his first exile.³ This would place their composition somewhere between the years 794, or shortly thereafter, and 797.

In Byzantine liturgical usage, the word "antiphon" means a selection from the Psalter, followed by a doxology. Such a selection may consist of several psalms, not necessarily consecutive, it may consist of one psalm only, it may even consist of single verses. The presence of a refrain is not essential, but when we find one it will be called ὑπόψαλμα, ἐφύμνιον, ὑπακοή, or τροπάριον—the name "antiphon" is never given to the refrain itself, as it is in the West.⁴ At first glance, Theodore's antiphons appear to constitute an exception to this general rule. In most later manuscripts and in all printed editions, each antiphon of the Anabathmoi consists of three troparia, and of three troparia only—no verses from the Psalter are indicated. But on turning to earlier sources one will find that the general rule applies.

The written tradition for the verses of the Anabathmoi goes back to our oldest copies of the music of the Oktoechos—Laura Γ.67 (late 10th century) and Vatopedi 1488 (about 1050), two Athos manuscripts using the notation of the Chartres fragment.⁵ It may be followed in the Coislin copies of the late 11th and early 12th centuries, of which the Grottaferrata MS E.a.xi (dated "1113") is an outstanding example.⁶ From these sources we learn that in former times each antiphon of the Anabathmoi possessed four verses—two for the first troparion and two for the second. Follow-

---

³P. N. Trempelas, Ἐκλογὴ ἑλληνικῆς ὀρθοδόξου ὑμνογραφίας (Athens, 1949), pp. ιε', ιη'.

⁴In the Greek translation of the Dialogues of Gregory the Great, usually attributed to Zacharias of Calabria, pope from 741 to 752, there is a passage that throws a revealing light on this difference between the Eastern and Western meanings of the word "antiphon." Chapter 35 of Book 4 tells the story of a monk of Spoleto who foretold the day and hour of his own death. When the time came, he received Holy Communion, and calling the brothers to him, asked them to join him in song. And he himself intoned the antiphon for them, saying: Aperite mihi portas justitiae (Ps. 117:19). Gregory's own wording is: Quibus tamen antiphonam ipse per semetipsum imposuit. But Zacharias translates Οἷς ἀντιφωνῶν τὸ τροπάριον αὐτὸς περὶ ἑαυτοῦ ὑπέβαλε—"Answering them antiphonally, he himself intoned the troparion." (Patrologia latina LXXVII, 375–378.)

⁵For an account of these MSS, with several facsimiles, see my "Notation of the Chartres Fragment," pp. 68–111 of this volume.

⁶For a facsimile, see P. Lorenzo Tardo, L'antica melurgia bizantina (Grottaferrata, 1938), p. xvii. I have also consulted two other Coislin sources—Sinai 1214 and 1241.

ing an orderly and symmetrical plan, the antiphons of the authentic modes draw their verses from the first twelve Gradual Psalms; those of the plagal modes begin again from Psalm 119, using the same psalms and in principle the same verses as their authentic parallels.[7] The whole scheme works out as follows:

Protos and Plagios protos	Psalms 119, 120, 121
Deuteros and Plagios deuteros	Psalms 122, 123, 124
Tritos and "Low mode"	Psalms 125, 126, 127
Tetartos and Plagios tetartos	Psalms 128, 129, 130

Disturbing the tidy balance of this arrangement, the Plagios tetartos goes on to add a fourth and final antiphon, with verses from Psalm 132. Only too obviously, this lies outside the main series, and if the Grottaferata copy did not tell us that the piece had a special function, we might easily infer it. The rubric in E.α.xi is Ἀντίφωνον ψαλλόμενον εἰς μνήμην ἀγίων—"An antiphon sung at the commemoration of Saints."[8] Thus, while the first twenty-four antiphons are for ordinary use, the twenty-fifth and last was at one time reserved for feasts of a particular class.[9]

How the verses were to be performed and where they were to be fitted in, our sources do not tell us. No verse has musical notation, and one cannot be quite sure whether the single troparion is to precede its verses or to follow them, for the physical arrangement of the single antiphon varies from one copy to another. But it is easy to show that the verses were intended to be sung, and our best and earliest sources agree in entering each pair

[7]Even in Γ.67, our earliest source and the only one to contain its full complement of verses, there are several cases of disagreement between the verses of corresponding authentic and plagal antiphons, and as one turns to later and later MSS, the disagreements become more numerous and one begins to contend also with omissions and ambiguities. Thus, in Vienna Theol. gr. 181, which is dated "1223," each antiphon has one verse only, and one of these verses is drawn inappropriately from Psalm 6 (or 37). The inescapable conclusion is that by the time our first MSS with musical notation were written, the verses of the troparia were already beginning to pass out of use.

[8]In a shortened form, the rubric of the Grottaferrata MS is found again in Sinai 1231.

[9]Psalm 132 has in the East a special association with certain feasts of brother or companion martyrs—Sergius and Bacchus, Marcianus and Martyrius, Cosmas and Damian, Cyrus and John. For all four of these feasts it supplies the Alleluia verses, and it is also quoted or paraphrased in two of the four offices.

of verses after the troparion to which it belongs and in indicating the position of the doxology by a conventional direction, placed after the final troparion of each antiphon. The whole construction has a close parallel in the proper antiphons that displace the regular psalmody of the morning office on Good Friday. In former times, these antiphons also arranged their verses in pairs, one pair for each troparion, and each troparion was sung twice, once before the first of its paired verses, once before the second. We may safely conclude that the troparia of the Anabathmoi were also repeated in this manner.

Unlike the Latin trope, the Byzantine troparion seldom has any bearing on the sense of the official text with which it is coupled.[10] The troparia are thus more or less interchangeable, and the particular context in which a given troparion is sung can easily vary from one locality to another. To this general rule, the troparia of the Anabathmoi constitute a notable and striking exception, for each troparion is a close paraphrase of the first of its two verses and is introduced by a literal quotation from it. The first two troparia of each antiphon begin by quoting the last three or four words of the odd-numbered verses which follow them, and since the verses of the corresponding authentic and plagal antiphons agree, the quotations with which they begin will agree also. The third troparion begins invariably with the phrase Ἁγίῳ Πνεύματι, quoted from the end of the half-verse of the doxology which follows it, and to keep to this plan Theodore has had to contrive twenty-five different tributes to the Trinity, all beginning with the same two words. A translation will give an idea of the extent to which these troparia are dependent upon their verses and will at the same time serve to clarify the over-all design of the single antiphon. I use for this purpose the final antiphons of the Protos and its plagal parallel, with verses from Psalm 121.[11]

---

[10]Cf. John of Damascus, De hymno Trisagio epistola (Patrologia graeca, XCV, 36): "When we recite a text—from a psalm, perhaps, or a canticle—we often add to it a troparion or refrain having no bearing on its meaning"—Οὖν ῥητὸν λέγοντες, ψαλμοῦ τυχὸν ἢ ᾠδῆς, ἐπιλέγομεν πολλάκις τροπάριον ἢ μελῴδημα, μὴ τῆς τοῦ ῥητοῦ διανοίας ἐχόμενον.

[11]I have completed the second verse, for which my sources give only the first half.

Protos
When they said unto me, let us walk into the courts of the Lord, my spirit was glad and my heart rejoiced.

Plagios Protos
When they said unto me, let us draw nigh unto the courts of the Lord, filled with many joys, I sent up prayers.

1. I was glad *when they said unto me.*

When they said unto me, let us walk, &c.

When they said unto me, let us draw nigh, &c.

2. Our feet shall stand within thy gates, O Jerusalem.

Upon the house of David there is a mighty fear, for when the thrones have been set, all the tribes and tongues of the earth shall be judged.

Upon the house of David fearful things are brought to pass, for there is a fire consuming every evil purpose.

3. For there are set thrones of judgment, the thrones *upon the house of David.*

Upon the house of David there is a mighty fear, &c.

Upon the house of David fearful things are brought to pass. &c.

4. Pray for the peace of Jerusalem.

To the Holy Ghost one should offer honor, worship, glory, and power, as is due to the Father and to the Son, for the Trinity is one in nature, but not in persons.

To the Holy Ghost, as also to the Father and to the Son, belongs the life-ruling virtue which animates every being.

Glory be to the Father and to the Son and to the Holy Ghost.

To the Holy Ghost one should offer honor, &c.Both now and

To the Holy Ghost, as also to the Father and to the Son, &c.

Both now and ever, world without end. Amen.

Whether they displaced some older feature of the morning office or whether they were arbitrarily added to the existing order, Theodore's antiphons must have impressed his contemporaries by their novelty. As liturgical innovations, they agree well with what we know of Theodore as a reformer of monastic rule and as an editor of the office books who also added to them. His antiphons have no exact parallels among the other antiphons of the Byzantine rite. Their troparia approach the Western trope more closely than those of any other class. And they have still another claim on our attention which transcends any of these—they enable us to trace back to the beginnings of the written tradition, and beyond, the underlying conventions of Byzantine psalmody, with many of its specific formulas. Herein lies their special importance. In themselves, they can tell us very little. But they can be made to tell us a great deal when we combine them with later documents. If we now work backward from these, we shall end by placing the melodies of the Sticherarion and Heirmologion in their original and proper setting. What is more, we shall have strengthened the foundation upon which the comparative study of Eastern and Western chant must ultimately rest.

The first manuscripts to treat the Byzantine psalm-tones in a comprehensive and systematic way are the early copies of the anthology compiled toward the end of the 13th century, or at the beginning of the 14th, by Joannes Koukouzeles, a monk of the Laura. Often referred to, somewhat loosely, as Ψαλτική, Παπαδική, or Μουσικόν, the compilation had at first the specific title Ἀκολουθίαι—"Orders of Service." If one thought only of its provisions for the office, one might describe this volume as a musical counterpart of the Horologion. But it provides also for the three Liturgies and contains much of the music required for their celebration—melodies for the Trisagion, the Cherubic Hymns, and the various parts of the Proper of the Mass. In its day, this useful little book must have been in the hands of every psaltist, for an extraordinary number of copies has been preserved. For the 14th century alone I can name eight. Two of these are precisely dated by their colophons—MS 2458 of the National Library in Athens ("1336") and Laura I.178 ("1377"). The others are approximately dated by their acclamations of the ruling Emperor or Empress-regent and of the various co-emperors and their wives—they fall between the year 1341, when Anne of Savoy began her regency, and the death of Andronicus IV, which occurred in 1385. Three of them were written during the lifetime of Anne, who died in 1360 or thereabouts, the three others after her death.

1341 to ca. 1360	Ca. 1360 to 1385
Ambrosiana L. 36 sup. (gr. 476)	Ambrosiana Q. 11 sup. (gr. 665)
Laura I. 185	Vatopedi 1495
Athens 2622	Koutloumousi 457

In turning out new copies of this book, each scribe felt free to add and to discard, for that part of the contents which consisted of original work was always in need of being brought up to date. But he left the underlying plan as he found it, and in so far as changes in the conduct of the services themselves did not dictate the outright suppression of this or that item, he reproduced the traditional

Ex. 1

part of the contents without altering it in any essential way. Thus, on proceeding from the earliest copies to related manuscripts of relatively recent date, although one can recognize a gradual change in make-up and style which leads in the end to the development of the more or less new type represented by Fleischer's "Codex Chrysander,"[12] one can also recognize an ultra-conservative resistance to change of any kind. Those things which Koukouzeles took over from older sources or from oral tradition tend to retain the form he gave them, and in this sense one may say that his "Orders of Service" led a long and useful life. All things considered, it is astonishing how little attention has been paid to them. Among Western scholars, only Gerbert seems to have recognized their importance.[13]

For the fixed and variable psalms of the office, as found in the Horologion and the liturgical Psalter, Koukouzeles makes a variety of provisions in a variety of styles. The whole deserves a systematic study; here I can deal only with a part—the simple tones for the fixed psalms of the morning office. In presenting these, Koukouzeles takes up their several uses one by one. First he adapts them to verses from Psalm 50 (the Pentekostos), then he adapts them to verses from Psalms 148 to 150 (the Αἶνοι or Lauds), finally he sums them up in the form of eight doxologies, one for each of the eight modes. I transcribe these from Laura I.185, which was copied, as we know, in the 1340's or 1350's. (See Ex. 1.)

In the normal Sunday order, the doxology of the Lauds is followed by one of the eleven Stichera Heothina, and as though to remind the singer of this, Koukouzeles adds to each of his doxologies a suitable opening phrase from this cycle. In a similar way, he adds to the first verse of Psalm 50 opening phrases from the stichera which most frequently follow it, and adapting each of his eight simple tones to useful verses from the psalms and canticles, he couples these with other opening phrases from the Sticherarion and Heirmologion, appropriate to the context. Thus it appears that the simple psalmody of the office has a twofold function: on the one hand it serves for the recitation of Psalm 50 and the Lauds, on the other, for the verses of the stichera and the canons. To illustrate the psalmody of these troparia, I transcribe the model verses of the Protos, from the morning office, and to these I add the first verse

[12]After Fleischer's death, the "Codex Chrysander" was acquired by the Prussian State Library, where it received the signature Mus. MS. 40614. Since the second World War it has been housed in the University Library at Tübingen.

[13]De cantu et musica sacra, I, 587–588, pl. v.

Ex. 2

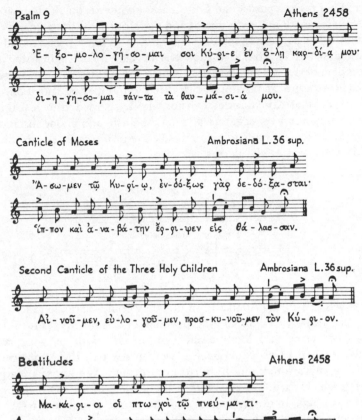

of the Beatitudes, from the office of the Typical Psalms. We shall
see presently that these same tones served also for the verses of the
Anabathmoi. (See Ex. 2.)

Needless to say, the simple psalm-tones of the office were not
invented by Koukouzeles. They belong among the things he took
over from the existing written or oral tradition, and one can actually find them in slightly earlier sources, always in less detail, often
in a less satisfactory form. One such source is the Sticherarion Paris

gr. 261 (dated "1289"), with doxologies and simple tones for the fixed psalms as a part of the Oktoechos; another is the Sticherarion Grottaferrata E.a.ii, with verses and doxologies for the troparia of the Christmas and Epiphany Hours.[14] If I have preferred the Koukouzeles version to these, it is because of its authority, its completeness, and the ease with which the omissions or mistakes of a given copy can be supplied or corrected. It may be said at once, however, that Koukouzeles has not wholly succeeded in resisting the temptation to exaggerate and to embellish, and in one instance we can actually eliminate his embellishment of a cadence with the aid of his own model verses.

Ex. 3

It was said of the Anabathmoi that they could be made to tell us a great deal if we combined them with later documents. Returning to them now, and looking at them in the light of what we have learned from Koukouzeles, we can see that their construction involves something hitherto unsuspected. We know already that each troparion begins with a literal quotation from a psalm or doxology. It now appears that these quotations are treated psalmodically, that they take the form of psalmodic cadences, and that these cadences, like those of the simple tones for the fixed psalms, are "syllabic" or "cursive" cadences which apply their four elements mechanically to the last four syllables of their text, taking no account of tonic accent. In principle the final element coincides with the end of the quotation, and in the oldest

[14]The Grottaferrata MS may be dated quite precisely, for—as P. Ignazio Pecoraro of Grottaferrata has pointed out to me—the copyist of E.α.ii and its companion volume E.a.v is the same Symeon of Grottaferrata who copied and signed the MS Ashburnham 64 at the Laurenziana in Florence in the year 1289. For transcriptions of four of its verses, see my "Influsso del canto liturgico orientale su quello della chiesa occidentale," pp. 151–56 of this volume.

sources, as though to emphasize this, the quotation is usually set off from what follows by a mark of punctuation (·), even when this runs counter to the grammatical construction. Should a quotation extend to more than four syllables, as often happens, the cadence is preceded by a brief recitation, and in rare instances this recitation is itself introduced by a conventional *initium* or *inchoatio*. An incidental result of this psalmodic treatment is that the troparia of the Anabathmoi cannot readily be fitted into any general scheme of melodic classification, for while they make extensive use of familiar opening patterns, these are associated, not with the beginning of the quotation, but with the beginning of the poetic paraphrase which follows.

It will be simplest to begin with the troparia of the Protos, even though two of these (Troparia 4 and 5) do not conform to type—the mode is otherwise regular and the cadence formula most frequently used is the one that Koukouzeles prescribes. Only Troparion 8 uses a formula of its own. As a psalmodic cadence I do not find it elsewhere, but it is formed in the usual way and its use in this context is readily understood—Troparion 8 continues in the highest register, closing on the upper finalis, and it was evidently thought that it required a special preparation. (See Ex. 4, p. 176.)

Like most of those that follow it, our example is based upon the complete transcriptions of the Anabathmoi published by Professor Tillyard in the first volume of his *Hymns of the Octoechus.* These are transcriptions from 13th-century manuscripts in the round notation,[15] whose versions are related to those of the Chartres and Coislin manuscripts very much as fully diastematic versions of Latin melodies are related to those written *in campo aperto.* But it is not as though the Chartres and Coislin notations were successive stages in a single straightforward development—on the contrary, they are two distinct and largely independent notations which developed concurrently from a common beginning. The round notation derives from the Coislin notation, not from the Chartres, and in much the same way the round versions derive from the Coislin versions

[15]Tillyard's primary sources are Athens 974 and Vienna 181; he makes incidental use of Vatopedi 1499 and Patmos 220.

Ex. 4

and agree with the Chartres only when the Chartres and Coislin
agree with one another. To recognize this, one has only to compare
Tillyard's transcriptions of the two atypical openings (Troparia 4
and 5)[16] with transcriptions made directly from the Chartres and
Coislin sources.[17] (See Ex. 5.)

[16]For Troparion 5 I have preferred the reading of Vienna 181; Tillyard follows
Athens 974.
[17]For the method of transcription, see the article cited in n. 5 above.

Ex. 5

In cases like these, the original intention must remain in doubt, and just as it is a fair inference that signs peculiar to the one early notation or the other are of later origin than those that are common property, so it should follow also that the two early versions lie closer to the original intention when they agree, further removed from it when they do not.

Among the troparia of the Protos we have just seen an illustration of the way in which the opening pattern at the beginning of the free paraphrase may determine the choice of psalmodic cadence. We shall find others among the troparia of the corresponding plagal mode, and in coordinating these I add in each case the beginning of the appropriate paraphrase.[18] (See Ex. 6.)

The preparatory function of the psalmodic cadence and its subordination to what follows could scarcely have been made more clear. In Troparia 1 to 8, only the final element of the cadence has been modified in an essential way. Where the paraphrase begins from G (as in Troparia 2 and 8), this final element is simply a D; where the paraphrase descends to the low C after a beginning on D (as in Troparia 1, 3, 6, and 7), the final element becomes the group D–E; where the paraphrase begins directly from the low C (as in Troparia 4 and 5), the final element modifies the group D–E by prolonging the D and accenting the E which follows. Finally, in Tropa-

[18]For Troparion 4 I have preferred the simpler reading of Vienna 181, without the *kylisma;* Tillyard follows Athens 974.

Ex. 6

rion 9, where the paraphrase begins in a manner characteristic of the authentic form of the mode,[19] Theodore devises a special cadence to meet a special requirement.

Even from these few examples it is quite evident that in Byzantine music the psalmodic cadence is subject to the same laws that govern the modal formula and its abbreviation in the modal signature. When a heirmos or sticheron of the Plagios protos begins from the low C, as sometimes happens, the modal formula which introduces it regularly takes the special ending whose earlier and later forms are shown in the example below.

[19]It agrees with the beginning of the paraphrase in Troparion 2 of the Protos.

As in the cadences of Troparia 4 and 5, only the final element is modified, and it is modified in the same way and for the same reasons. (See Ex. 7.)

Ex. 7

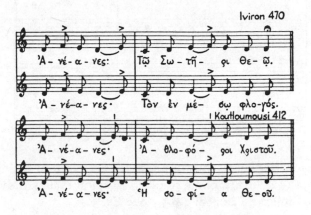

To turn now to the body of the cadence, as distinguished from its final element, there can be little doubt that the form this usually takes in Tillyard's manuscripts is a later form that has gradually crowded out an earlier one. In this later form, the cadence is in essential agreement with the one prescribed by Koukouzeles for the Plagios protos, and if one were to transpose it to the fifth above, it would agree with his Tritos cadence, as shown in Example 3. Vatopedi 1488 uses this form for Troparion 2, Grottaferrata E. α.xi for Troparion 7. But the form preferred by our three early sources is the one seen in Tillyard's transcription of Troparion 2, and in Laura Γ.67, our earliest source, it is the only form admitted.[20] One finds it used also, both early and late, for certain troparia of the F modes, authentic and plagal.[21] (See Ex. 8.)

[20]We have already encountered it in the two atypical openings of the Protos (Ex. 4, Troparia 4 and 5), where it was not co-ordinated with the quotations from the Psalter in the expected way.

[21]Finally, it ought probably to have been used, in both forms of the F mode, for Troparion 5. This is the plain implication of the Chartres and Coislin sources, and in the "Low mode," Vienna 181 actually has this reading.

Ex. 8

Koukouzeles knows this form too, for he uses it in his version of Psalm 102, the first of the so-called "Typical Psalms." My transcription follows Vatopedi 1495. (See Ex. 9.)

Ex. 9

As these last examples suggest, the cadence formulas used in Byzantine psalmody are associated, not so much with particular modes, as with particular steps of the system. A given formula may be used in several modes, and as one result of this, there is established a sort of intermodal relationship, usually at the third. We shall meet with this same relationship again, and with an entirely new set of formulas, if we turn now from the modes on D and F to those on E and G. Among these remaining modes, the Plagios tetartos is at once the simplest and the most instructive. In coordinating its troparia, I omit those of Antiphon 4, which treats its quotations from the Psalter and the Doxology in

Laura Γ. 67, fol. 114, recto and verso · The Antiphons of the Deuteros

Moscow, *Typografskii Ustav*, fols. 98 and 102ᵛ (After Metallov)

a special style suited to its special purpose. (See Ex. 10.)

Once again the cadence formula most frequently used is in essential agreement with the one prescribed by Koukouzeles. Once again the final element of this cadence has sometimes been accommodated to the opening pattern at the beginning of the free paraphrase. Normally, this final element is simply a G (as in Troparia 5 to 8); where the paraphrase ascends by step after beginning from the low *D* (as in Troparia 1 to 3), the final element becomes the group *G–a,*[22] where the paraphrase leaps up a fourth after begin-

Ex. 10

[22]Troparion 3 offers a somewhat different solution, but it agrees with Troparia 1 and 2 in its insistence on *a* as preparation for D. Tillyard follows Athens 974; in Vienna 181 the last two elements of the cadence agree with those of Troparion 9, as shown in the example above.

ning from the low D (as in Troparion 4), the final element becomes the group G–E–F. And as before, these special forms of the psalmodic cadence correspond to special forms of the modal intonation and modal signature, regularly associated in the Heirmologion and Sticherarion with the same opening patterns.[23] (See Ex. 11.)

Ex. 11

Troparion 9 appears at first glance to constitute a special case. Abandoning the cadence used elsewhere, Tillyard's manuscripts adopt a new one, and in so doing they faithfully reproduce the tradition of Grottaferrata E.α.xi and the other Coislin sources. But Vatopedi 1488 and Laura Γ.67 make no change and give the familiar cadence its normal ending. The distinction may seem trivial, but it is none the less worth making, for it is only when the Chartres and Coislin versions disagree that the descent of the round versions becomes apparent. (See Ex. 12.)

This cadence too belongs to the step, rather than to the mode, and—as anticipated—one finds it again, and at the same level, in

---

[23]The intonations, signatures, and opening patterns of the Plagios tetartos are studied more closely in my "Intonations and Signatures of the Byzantine Modes," p. 19 of this volume.

certain troparia of the Deuteros. Two of these troparia reproduce
it exactly; in a third case our sources disagree, with the Chartres

Ex. 12

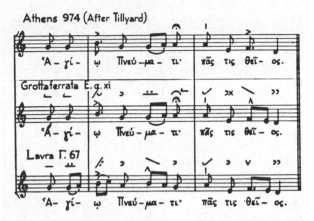

MSS preferring the familiar form, the round and Coislin MSS an
embellishment of it.[24] (Ex. 13.)

Not less important for the troparia of the E modes is the peculiar
cadence used to prepare an opening pattern common to the authentic and plagal varieties.[25] (See Ex. 14.)

In an embellished form, this cadence is also used by the round and
Coislin sources for Troparion 8 of the Deuteros. In Vatopedi 1488
and Laura Γ.67 it is just the other way—Troparion 8 has the simple
cadence, while the embellished form is reserved for Troparion 4.

This cadence belongs undoubtedly to what was once called the
Mesos deuteros—a modal variety halfway between authentic and
plagal and combining characteristics of both.[26] (See Ex. 15.)

[24]For this embellished cadence, see also (in Tillyard's publication) the first
troparion of the final antiphon of the Plagios tetartos, paraphrasing the first line of
Psalm 132.

[25]For Troparion I of the Plagios deuteros I have preferred the reading of Vienna
181; Tillyard follows Athens 974. I do not understand Tillyard's note on this
opening. Vienna 181 has the familiar Nenano signature and its first line reads
readily from *a*.

[26]In my study of "The Byzantine Office at Hagia Sophia," p. 121 of this
volume, wishing to demonstrate the antiquity of a psalm-tone quoted from a source
of the late 14th or early 15th century, I could show only that it was found also in

At this point I may safely leave the curious reader to pursue the investigation for himself. He has already looked at more than half

Ex. 13

the troparia—if he looks at the rest he will discover a wealth of variety, with many special cadences, infrequently used, but he will discover little outright irregularity, provided only that he bears in mind that what appears to be irregular in a later source will often prove to be a mere distortion of something that in an earlier one is not irregular at all.

Thus our two sets of documents confirm and complete each other most satisfactorily. The "Orders of Service" enable us to recognize in early copies of the Anabathmoi the oldest written record of Byzantine psalmodic practice. In turn, Theodore's troparia enable us to recognize that the doxologies and model verses of Koukouzeles preserve the essentials of that practice more faithfully than

a dated MS from the year 1225. It is now evident, however, that this same psalmtone goes back at least as far as the beginning of the written tradition, for Theodore uses it to open Troparia 3 and 6 of the Plagios deuteros.

Ex. 14

Ex. 15

might have been expected. In a few cases, the quotation with which Theodore begins a troparion is a complete quotation, not a partial one,[27] and in these cases he has fixed for us an entire psalm-tone, not simply a cadence. Combining these exceptional beginnings of Theodore's with the doxologies and model verses of Koukouzeles, we can readily deduce their underlying principles, and having deduced them, we can as readily apply them, in any mode, to any verse. And having worked out the recitation appropriate to a particular verse, we can give to its cadence the ending required by the context, for the Byzantine system of modal intonations and modal signatures shows us how to do it.

[27]These complete quotations open the troparia on the first verses of Psalms 123, 124, 126, and 132.

How can we be certain that in its essentials the manner of recitation prescribed by Koukouzeles is in fact the one used in Theodore's day when no Greek manuscript earlier than the 13th century shows us how any verse of any troparion was sung? And how can we be certain that this manner was applied also to the verses of the Anabathmoi when Koukouzeles himself does not tell us that it was? If the survival of an archaic form of cadence in the practice of the 14th century is not in itself enough to settle these two questions, there remains another way of settling them. We have only to consult the Slavonic sources, which are often more explicit than the Greek, and which tend, as peripheral documents, to lag conservatively behind, preserving vestiges of archaic liturgical and musical practices.

Among the oldest of these Slavonic sources is the so-called *Typografskii Ustav,* a Kontakarion of the late 11th or early 12th century. At the end of this MS an entire section is devoted to a sort of Oktoechos in which certain ordinary chants of the Sunday office are brought together and arranged in the order of the modes. For some of these chants the notation used is the elaborate and somewhat enigmatic notation peculiar to the Slavonic Kontakaria. For others, it is the simpler notation of the earliest Slavonic Heirmologia and Sticheraria, a notation not unlike—indeed, obviously derived from —the primitive Coislin notation found in certain Greek Heirmologia of the 10th and early 11th centuries.[28] Among the chants of this latter group are the antiphons of the Anabathmoi, and from two plates published by Metallov in his *Russkaia Semiografia*[29] one can see just what form these took. (See Plate 2, p. 182.)

The more interesting plate of the two is T. III (f. 98), toward the foot of which one finds the general heading and the beginning of the first antiphon of the Protos. First comes the Slavonic translation of Troparion 1, adapted to a melody closely resembling its Greek prototype. After this follows the first of the four verses, and this verse has musical notation throughout. Its Slavonic text is from Psalm 119:1 and it runs to nine syllables. Above each of the first five the scribe has written the short horizontal hook sometimes identified with the Greek *ison;* added to the first of these hooks is

[28]Notably Leningrad 557, Patmos 55, Saba 83, and perhaps also Esphigmenou 54.

[29]Moscow, 1912. The first of the two plates (T. III) is reproduced by Mme. R. Palikarova Verdeil in *La musique byzantine chez les Bulgares et les Russes* (Copenhagen and Boston, 1953).

an auxiliary dot, or *kentema,* evidently to indicate that the recitation is to begin from the upper finalis. Following this recitation is the four-syllable cadence, set off from the body of the verse by a little space, and above this cadence the scribe has repeated the neumes already written above the four-syllable cadence at the end of the translated quotation with which the preceding troparion began. My example compares the Greek equivalent of this Slavonic verse with the form it would presumably have taken if Koukouzeles had included it among his models. (See Ex. 16.)

Ex. 16

Instead of stopping here, as might have been expected, the scribe goes on to repeat, with minor changes, the neumes of the free paraphrase, adapting them now to the text "Alleluia! Alleluia!" A similar thing happens on T. IV (fol. 102ᵛ), at the head of which one finds the ending of the final antiphon of the Deuteros, with Verses 2, 3, and 4, Troparion 9, and an abbreviated doxology. Here the verses are without musical notation and no Alleluia refrains are indicated. But in copying the abbreviated doxology, the scribe has repeated above the Slavonic equivalent of the words Ἁγίῳ Πνεύματι the neumes already written above these same words at the beginning of the preceding troparion, and once again, instead of stopping, he has gone on to add an Alleluia refrain, this time a threefold Alleluia. It has no musical notation, but the plain inference is that it is to be treated exactly like the one on the previous plate. The melody of the earlier paraphrase was a short one and fell naturally into two distinctions; the one to be adapted here is longer and falls naturally into three. And from the meaningless extra syllables that have been interpolated to lengthen the Alleluias, one can actually see how the adaptation is to be made— the first two Alleluias, with 10 and 4 plus 4 syllables, correspond to the distinctions whose Greek equivalents are προσπηγάζει πᾶσα σοφία and ἔνθεν χάρις ἀποστόλοις; the third Alleluia corresponds to the remainder of the paraphrase.

We may draw two conclusions. In the Slavic-speaking countries the verses and doxologies of the Anabathmoi were at first recited to the same simple tones that were used for the verses of other troparia. And they were followed by Alleluia refrains adapted to the melodies of Theodore's paraphrases. The first of these conclusions should be equally valid for Byzantium. And it would seem that the second must be valid also, despite the silence of the Greek sources on this point, for unless it is, the single antiphons, ending as they do with the half-verse "Both now and ever," will break off inconclusively with a preparatory cadence, leaving an unsatisfactory impression. To sing the Anabathmoi with Alleluia refrains would be to tie them in with the readings from the Psalter that precede them, for in former times the psalms recited on Sunday mornings were regularly chanted with Alleluia refrains that followed each distinction of the text.

This is not the place to enlarge upon the implications of the Anabathmoi for the comparative study of Eastern and Western chant. One would be simplifying matters unduly, and claiming at once too much and too little, if one were to ascribe to the Laura copy of Theodore's antiphons a position analogous to that occupied in the West by the Tonarius of Regino, the *Commemoratio brevis,* or the Hartker Antiphoner. In some respects it is a comparable document. But there is one respect in which it is not. As a record of psalmodic practice, it is an involuntary record, for its writer did not consciously seek to transmit information on this point. All he sought to do was to transmit a cycle of compositions by an 8th-century author, and it was no concern of his that, imbedded in that cycle, were incidental allusions to the psalmodic practice of its author's day. Something of the same kind may be said also of Theodore Studites. He is an involuntary witness, for in writing a poetic commentary on the Gradual Psalms and setting it to music, he sought only to enrich the rite of his church, and if he consciously alluded in this work to the psalmodic practice of his day, this was for him a means and not an end. In a word, while our record belongs to the 10th century, it records the testimony of an 8th-century witness, and if the record and the witness are equally ingenuous, they are by the same token equally and ideally trustworthy.

MELODY CONSTRUCTION
IN BYZANTINE CHANT [†]

I N his paper for the Congress, as also in a number of earlier
studies,[1] Professor Wellesz has rightly and persuasively emphasized the universal and unifying role of centonization in the liturgical chants of the Christian East and West. If in so doing he has
tended inevitably to underemphasize the pervasive influence of
poetic structure on musical structure, particularly in Byzantium, we
cannot take it amiss. For, just as Wellesz was the first to explore the
one approach to our central problem, he was also the first to explore the other, and in the foreword to his transcriptions of the
hymns for September, published exactly twenty-five years ago, he
defined the relationship "Wort und Ton" in a few pages that have
since then been a constant stimulus and inspiration to his younger
colleagues.[2]

While stressing the universal applicability of centonization—of
the formula principle—to the structure of all liturgical melody,

---

[†]From *Actes du XIIe congrès international d'études byzantines* (Belgrade, 1963),
365–373; read in Ochrida at a meeting of the congress, September, 1961. Reprinted with permission of the Institut d'étude byzantines.

[1]Particularly in Pts. II and III of his *Eastern Elements in Western Chant* (Oxford,
1947), in ch. XII of his *History of Byzantine Music and Hymnography* (Oxford, 1949),
and in the introduction to his transcription of the Akathistos Hymn (Copenhagen,
1957).

[2]See for example the analysis of one of the stichera dogmatika in Carsten Høeg's
Musik og digtning i byzantisk kristendom (Copenhagen, 1955), Jørgen Raasted's
"Some Observations on the Structure of the Stichera in Byzantine Rite," *Byzantion,*
XVIII (1958), 529–541.

Professor Wellesz concedes that its most extensive development belongs to Byzantium, and in conceding this he suggests by implication a direction that our present discussion and our future studies might profitably take. If a particular way of working is more extensively cultivated in one environment than in another, we ought surely to ask ourselves why this is so. What was there about that way of working that made it so peculiarly congenial? What was there about that environment that made it so peculiarly receptive?

To work with traditional melodic formulas is to take an ultra-conservative view of one's function as a composer. It implies a deep-seated respect for tradition. It is at the same time an enormously sophisticated way of working, susceptible of infinite refinement. Using analogies drawn from patristic theology and icon-painting, Professor Wellesz argues that it was inherently suited to the Byzantine climate. To these analogies I venture to add another, drawn from ecclesiastical poetry. Not only does it often happen that the text of a heirmos or sticheron is a mere patchwork of quotations and paraphrases—from the Psalter, from the Gospels, from the Liturgy, from the Fathers—but in rare instances what the poet offers is little more than an artful rearrangement of the lines of an existing hymn. Of the twenty-four alphabetic stichera of the Oktoechos, more than half can be shown to have been built in just this way from older poems belonging to the cycle of Anatolika. Since the first stanza of the one cycle reworks the first stanza of the other, it will be simplest to use these two texts in illustration, setting them side by side. To do so is to illustrate also the technique used

Anatolikon 1	*Alphabetikon 1*
Εὐφράνθητε οὐρανοί	Ἀγαλλιάσθω ἡ κτίσις
σαλπίσατε τὰ θεμέλια τῆς γῆς	οὐρανοὶ εὐφραινέσθωσαν
βοήσατε τὰ ὄρη εὐφροσύνην	χεῖρας κροτείτω τὰ ἔθνη μετ' εὐφροσύνης
ἰδοὺ γὰρ ὁ Ἐμμανουήλ	Χριστὸς γὰρ σωτὴρ ἡμῶν
τὰς ἁμαρτίας ἡμῶν	τῷ σταυρῷ προσήλωσε
τῷ σταυρῷ προσήλωσε	τὰς ἁμαρτίας ἡμῶν
καὶ ζωὴν ὁ διδοὺς	καὶ τὸν θάνατον νεκρώσας
θάνατον ἐνέκρωσε	ζωὴν ἡμῖν ἐδωρήσατο
τὸν Ἀδὰμ ἀναστήσας	πεπτωκότα τὸν Ἀδάμ
ὡς φιλάνθρωπος.	παγγενῆ ἀναστήσας ὡς φιλάνθρωπος.

in all similar cases, where—as here—the relationship is a line-for-line relationship, with the structure of the copy an exact reproduction of the structure of the model.[3]

A further question. To what extent, in the process of being received and assimilated, was the congenial principle altered or transformed? Was there in the end something specifically Byzantine about the way in which it came to be applied? These questions can best be answered by studying the way in which Latin and Slavonic translations of Greek texts are handled when they are provided, locally, with independent musical settings. Professor Wellesz has touched briefly on two celebrated instances of borrowing in which Greek texts, literally translated into Latin, have carried their Greek melodies with them. If, instead of looking at these, we were to look at those numerous other instances in which Latin translations from Greek, provided locally with melodies of their own, have found their way into the Gregorian, Ambrosian, and Mozarabic repertories, we should soon discover that the Latin melodies, while built up from formulas, are not built up in precisely the same way as the Greek melodies they have displaced. To approach the same question from another quarter, we might compare the melody that Professor Wellesz has quoted from the Serbian Oktoechos with the original melody for the Greek text from which the Slavonic was translated, or—for that matter—with the melody that is sung today in Athens and on Athos. Once again we should soon discover that, despite their underlying general similarity, there are radical and revealing differences.

In touching on the phenomenon of ornamental accretion, Professor Wellesz raises still another question that we might with profit pursue a little further. The melody of the Good Friday troparion "Ότε τῷ σταυρῷ, which begins melismatically in Byzantine sources written after the year 1050, or thereabouts, is found also, with a syllabic beginning, in a number of Beneventan and other North Italian MSS of the eleventh century, provided there with transliterated Greek text and Latin translation. Since the incorpora-

---

[3]So strictly is this technique applied in those alphabetic stichera whose models I have succeeded in identifying that I can only suppose that the remainder (letters *zeta* to *omicron,* and *rho*) were formed in the same way from models still to be traced. The dependence of copy upon model is seldom reflected in the music.

tion of this alien element into the Beneventan rite cannot well have taken place much later than the year 800, the syllabic form of the incipit is clearly the original one, the melismatic form a later accretion. When and why was the melody elaborated?

If we date the change about the year 1000, we shall not be wide of the mark, for Byzantine sources written just before and after this turning-point make us witnesses of the phenomenon itself. For Ὅτε τῷ σταυρῷ, the syllabic form is still preferred. But for other troparia of the same set, one source prefers the syllabic form, another the melismatic; sometimes both forms are given, with the melismatic form as a marginal or interlinear afterthought; in all these sources, the final troparion takes a form that represents an ultimate in elaboration, subsequently rejected by a later time. The late Beneventan sources are peripheral, as is also the Triodion Chilandari 307, the one Slavonic source conveniently accessible, and this Slavonic source not only prefers the syllabic form throughout, but actually preserves for one of the twelve troparia a syllabic incipit that has no counterpart in any Byzantine MS.

To understand this phenomenon, to explain why it occurred, we shall need to recognize it as part of a new attitude. Beginning about 850, radical changes were taking place. Particularly for doxastika and other liturgically prominent pieces, a new and more elaborate style was being developed, and composers were beginning to think of themselves as virtuosi and to expect virtuosity of the singers who sang their music. These tendencies are already evident in the Heothina, in the great doxastikon of Pentecost, and above all in the processional pieces for the mid-Lenten ceremony of the Adoration of the Cross. They are evident also in the rapid development of the musical notation, which had constantly to meet more exacting demands. They are evident, finally, in the creation of an unprecedented and extraordinarily florid tradition for the music of the kontakion, and they led in the end to the rise of the kalophonic style.

Since 1939, when Tillyard first drew attention to the phenomenon, the existence of two distinct yet cognate traditions for the music of the Heirmologion has constituted a perennial problem. It raises a whole series of fundamental questions, and to some of these questions Professor Wellesz offers new answers in the closing paragraphs of his paper. Beyond this, it has an immediate and critical bearing on the central theme of our discussion, also, as it appears, on a related and not less interesting theme—the interplay of oral and written tradition. It will pay us to take a closer look at it.

With two distinct sets of melodies for the poetry of the Heirmologion, one might suppose that the analyst of their structure would find himself at a disadvantage. Actually, the reverse is true, for the two sets are cognate as well as distinct; here and there they coincide, and when they do, the analyst recognizes their ultimate common origin. No matter how he explains their existence— whether he thinks in terms of local idiom, of gradual evolution, or of deliberate and arbitrary revision—he will conclude that their points of agreement are essential points, their points of disagreement non-essential ones. In the end, the existence of the two traditions becomes for him a positive advantage.

In 1952, Høeg began his inquiry into the tradition for the music of the Heirmologion by asking whether the impression we had of its diversity might not to some extent be due to our lack of familiarity with the parallel tradition for the music of the Sticherarion. On the whole, he thought not, and it is true, of course, that in general terms the tradition for the music of the Sticherarion is extraordinarily uniform. Høeg's question was a shrewd one, none the less, for on closer examination it turns out that this extraordinary uniformity, so often demonstrated, extends only to the contents of the standard abridged version. The moment one turns from this part of the repertory to what I may call the "marginal" part, that is, to those sets and categories of stichera found only in a few exceptional copies, one meets with a diversity quite as bewildering as that met with in the Heirmologion, if not even more so. Any one of these sets or categories could be used in illustration; if I limit myself here to the 64 Stichera Anastasima, it is because some part of the evidence for this set is already available in transcription.

Tillyard's transcriptions of 24 of these pieces, published in 1949, are based on the "Codex Peribleptus," a MS presented in 1940 to the library of University College, Cardiff. Shortly before their publication, Father Lorenzo Tardo had drawn attention to three other sources for the Anastasima, one at the Biblioteca Nazionale in Naples, two at the Biblioteca Ambrosiana,[4] and in 1955, using these

---

[4]"L'Ottoeco nei manoscritti melurgici," *Bollettino della Badia greca di Grottaferrata*, I (1947), 37–38 (nn. 11 and 12), 141.

three sources, he published independent transcriptions of the entire set. If one compares Tardo's transcriptions of the Stichera Anatolika with Tillyard's, published in 1940, one will discover that—apart from variants of little consequence—the differences between the two editions arise entirely from differences in editorial assumptions. These pieces belong to the standard abridged version. But on turning to the "marginal" Anastasima one finds quite another picture. Indeed, the differences are now so striking that, for whole phrases at a time, often for several consecutive phrases, the two editors are simply not transcribing the same melody. This applies particularly to the stichera of the first three authentic modes, where Tardo's source is Naples II.C.17; from this point on he follows Ambrosiana gr. 44, a MS whose readings are less distantly related to those of the "Codex Peribleptus." Tillyard transcribes only the first three pieces of each mode. Had he transcribed the entire set, further discrepancies would have come to light, above all in the pieces for the Orthros, where Tardo's source is Ambrosiana gr. 733, which belongs to another branch of the family.

Despite their general family resemblance, now less distant, now more so, the four MSS touched on in the preceding paragraph are representatives of four distinct traditions. On adding other MSS, we discover that three of these traditions enjoyed a certain currency. To make this clear, I introduce at this point a list of all earlier sources that have come to my notice, with a tentative classification, based in some instances on comparisons of a few test pieces only.

1. *Allied to Ambrosiana gr. 733:*
   Iviron 953
   Sinai 1471
2. *Allied to the "Codex Peribleptus":*
   Dionysiou 564
   Vatopedi 1493
3. *Allied to Ambrosiana gr. 44:*
   Sinai 1230
4. *More or less independent:*
   Naples II.C.17
   Laura Γ.71
   Sinai 1228

The example that follows compares three versions of a single phrase from the third Anastasimon of the Deuteros, Σὺν

'Αρχαγγέλοις ὑμνήσωμεν. Line 1 gives the reading of Iviron 953; Sinai 1471 is concordant and presumably Ambrosiana gr. 733 as well. Line 2 gives the reading of Sinai 1230; Ambrosiana gr. 44 is concordant, also for this particular phrase the "Codex Peribleptus" and presumably Dionysiou 564 and Vatopedi 1493. Line 3 gives the reading of Naples II.C.17; for this particular phrase Sinai 1228 happens also to be concordant.

Now the striking thing about this example, indeed the compelling reason for its inclusion, is that the phrase shown in Line 2 is identical with the phrase quoted from the heirmos 'Εξήνθησεν ἡ ἔρημος in the final line of Wellesz's Example 13.

There it was transcribed from the Heirmologion Saba 599; several other Heirmologia have the same reading, among them Sinai 1256 and Palatina gr. 243. This suggests, of course, that there is a significant relation of some kind between the traditions for the Anastasima represented by the "Codex Peribleptus" and Ambrosiana gr. 44 on the one hand and the tradition for the Heirmologion represented by Saba 599 on the other. Preliminary tests leave no doubt that the suggested relation indeed exists, that it is far-reaching and firmly rooted, and that the tradition most deeply involved—involved almost to the point of virtual identity—is the one represented by Ambrosiana gr. 44, where in the plagal modes there are frequent and literal recurrences of the irregular and highly individual cadences characteristic of Saba 599 and its relatives, familiar from Tillyard's *Twenty Canons*.

It was said earlier that the existence of two distinct yet cognate traditions for the music of the Heirmologion had an immediate and critical bearing on the interplay of oral and written tradition. Now that we have encountered a similar diversity in the tradition for the music of the Sticherarion, we can more readily recognize what that bearing is. With the Sticherarion, it was only the "marginal" part of the contents that was affected. And this "marginal" part of the contents consists of two sorts of pieces. On the one hand are those pieces that have fallen into general disuse or have a purely local application—the "apocrypha," as they were sometimes called. That these pieces should have been excluded from the standard abridged version is only natural. On the other hand are those pieces that must be sung repeatedly throughout the year or throughout a particular season—the automela, the Anastasima, the Στιχηρὰ τοῦ Πάσχα, to mention only the most important. Experienced singers knew these pieces by heart, and their melodies were accordingly excluded from the standard abridged version as sufficiently familiar. They were transmitted orally, and it was only by way of exception that an enterprising scribe attempted to capture in writing the particular form of the oral tradition with which he was familiar. Once he had done so, written tradition might take over, but this did not always happen, and when it did, it happened only in a limited way. That these various attempts should differ as often and as materially as they do reveals only too clearly how unstable a thing an oral tradition actually is.

By contrast, the tradition for the standard abridged version of the Sticherarion was a written tradition, and a written tradition upon which there had to be absolute reliance in practice. The great bulk of the contents consists of melodies that are sung only once a year. To suppose that any substantial part of this contents was ever committed to memory by singers whose memories were already overburdened would be utterly unrealistic. The enormous number of extant copies obliges us to infer that the singers who sang these melodies sang them from a book, and the same inference is forced upon us by the extraordinary uniformity of the tradition these copies transmit.

With the Heirmologion, the situation is more complex. Here too a quasi-official version, comparable in many respects to the standard abridged version of the Sticherarion, was put into circulation about the year 1050, and for roughly two centuries the tradition it transmitted was the dominant one. Høeg believed and Tillyard has convincingly demonstrated that this tradition stems from the one found in our earliest sources; that it is in close agreement with the archaic Slavic tradition is equally clear from the comparative charts published by Velimirović. It is a tradition perfectly consistent with the one familiar to us from the standard abridged version of the Sticherarion, employing the same initial and cadential patterns, the same ornaments, the same melismas; troparia pass from the one collection to the other without changing their shape;[5] when the Sticherarion interpolates a series of heirmoi, as sometimes happens, it interpolates them in this quasi-official version;[6] when a sticheron quotes or paraphrases a heirmos, it is this quasi-official version that is involved.[7] It enjoyed the widest dissemination, extending from Grottaferrata, where it was copied as late as 1281, to the Saba monastery, where the fourteenth-century scribe who revised the notation of the old Heirmologion Saba 83 used a copy as his *Vorlage.* Yet, unlike the standard abridged version of the Sticherarion, this quasi-official version of the Heirmologion was a book for teaching and study, not a book for practical use. Since the melodies it contained had usually to be adapted to texts other than those of the heirmoi themselves, and since these melodies were frequently combined in orders wholly different from those in which they were copied, the singers who sang them were obliged to sing them from memory. The relatively limited number of extant copies bears out this conclusion emphatically.

With the Heirmologion, then, of two conditions essential to the survival of stability, one was lacking, and despite the deceptive uniformity of the written tradition, which continued for a time, the melodies did not stand still. Written and oral tradition were work-

---

[5]Compare for example the published transcriptions of Ἡ ἄσπιλος ἀμνάς as a sticheron (*The Hymns of the Octoechus,* Pt. II [Copenhagen, 1949], pp. 167–168) and as a heirmos (*The Hymns of the Hirmologium,* Pt. I [Copenhagen, 1952], p. 43).

[6]The Triodion for Good Friday is found with musical notation for the heirmoi, and sometimes for the troparia as well, in many older copies of the Sticherarion. The Sticherarion Vienna theol. gr. 136 goes even further in interpolating also the heirmoi for the four preceding days in Holy Week.

[7]Compare for example the sticheron Χριστὸς ὁ ἐρχόμενος (one of the Proeortia of Christmas) with the heirmos from which it quotes (from the canon for Palm Sunday).

ing at cross purposes. By 1257 the contradiction between what was written and what was sung had evidently become intolerable, for in that year the Heirmologion Sinai 1258 puts forward a new tradition that in many respects anticipates the later tradition of Saba 599 and its relatives, although it is by no means identical with it.[8] With the turn of the century the tradition of Saba 599 becomes the dominant one, to remain so until at least as late as 1500. Perhaps the most striking single fact about this latest tradition is its association with Joannes Koukouzeles, a monk of the Laura, whose own "edition" of it survives in two dated copies, Leningrad 121 ("1302") and Sinai 1256 ("1309"), and who draws on it also for the heirmos incipits quoted in his Akolouthiai, or "Orders of Service," easily the most popular handbook of the time.[9]

Much of the foregoing is admittedly conjecture. Even so, the conclusions to which conjecture has led us are inescapable; no other explanation will really fit the facts. Of the two traditions for the music of the Heirmologion, one is amazingly uniform, the other at best loosely so. How shall we account for this antithesis unless we recognize, in the one tradition, a written tradition descended from a single archetype, in the other, a random selection from among the various forms of an oral tradition independently recorded at various times and places? And how shall we evade this recognition after we have encountered, in the tradition for the music of the Sticherarion, a similar and parallel antithesis for which we could account in no other way?

One significant new fact has emerged from our inquiry. The tradition for the music of the Heirmologion represented by Saba 599 and its relatives is related in the most intimate way to the traditions for the Anastasima represented by Ambrosiana gr. 44 on the one hand and the "Codex Peribleptus" on the other. The fact can be useful to us here, for it places at our disposal new evidence bearing on the date and provenance of these related traditions.

Of the five sources for the Anastasima that are involved in this relationship, four are dated—Ambrosiana gr. 44 ("1342"), Sinai 1230 ("1365"), Dionysiou 564 ("1445"), and the "Codex Peri-

---

[8]Concordant with Sinai 1258, and supplying some part of what that MS has lost at the beginning, is the Heirmologion Saba 617.

[9]For a brief account of this compilation, with a list of early copies, see my "Antiphons of the Oktoechos," pp. 161–91 of this volume, especially pp. 170–72.

bleptus" ("1447").[10] No source suggests an early date, and while this does not prove the related traditions to be late ones, it is certainly not calculated to support the opposite view. Likewise unambiguous are the indications of provenance. Of Ambrosiana gr. 44, it can at least be said with assurance that its relative, Sinai 1230, comes from Trebizond. The "Codex Peribleptus" points to Mount Athos and its orbit, as do its relatives Dionysiou 564 and Vatopedi 1493; all three contain offices for the commemoration of St. Athanasius of Athos on July 5. Not one of these sources has anything remotely to do with the Holy Land.

All things considered, it is now time to abandon the attractive theory that the tradition for the music of the Heirmologion represented by Saba 599 and its relatives is an early tradition of Palestinian origin. All we know about the history of Saba 599 is that it was brought to the library of the Greek Patriarchate in Jerusalem in the 1880's, together with other MSS from Mar Saba. There is nothing to show that it was actually written at the Saba monastery, and it is far easier to suppose that it was brought there from within the Empire than to suppose that Koukouzeles, about the year 1300, should have sought to introduce on Mount Athos a Palestinian tradition.

[10]Strictly speaking, the year 1447 is the year in which the "Codex Peribleptus" was brought to the monastery of the Nea Peribleptos, not the year in which it was copied. Even so, the general appearance and character of the MS, and its intimate connection with Dionysiou 564, suggest that the date is close enough for our present purposes.

A FURTHER NOTE
ON THE PROPER HYMNS
FOR EASTER[†]

T HIS little paper returns to a topic with which I occupied myself
some years ago and attempts to answer a few of the questions
that I then left open. Unlike my earlier study,[1] which dealt with
stichera no longer in use and with their dependence upon the sermons of St. Gregory Nazianzus, this one deals with the surviving
stichera of the Easter office, the so-called Στιχηρὰ τοῦ Πάσχα,
and with the problem of their origin and early use. It can aim only
to scratch the surface. When a full-scale treatment of the topic is
undertaken, as it ought to be one day, these single aspects will need
to be re-examined in the context of the whole, and it will be
necessary to deal also with a number of other aspects hitherto
unexplored—the proper offices for the week-days between Easter
and Antipascha, the relation of these offices, and of the Sunday
office itself, to the Sunday offices of the Oktoechos, the singularly
elusive transmission of the melodies and the reasons for the insta-
bility of their tradition, the make-up of the Easter office in the
earliest Slavic sources and the bearing of the melodic tradition
found in them on the tradition of the sources from the center.
Another aspect of the subject has a peculiar significance for the
later development of sacred music in the West, for—as will appear
presently—some part of the music for the Greek Easter is strictly
comparable to the Latin trope.

†From *Classica et mediaevalia,* XXII (1961), 176–181. Reprinted with permission of the publishers.
[1]See pp. 55–67 of this volume.

Normally, the Sticherarion makes no provision whatever for Easter Sunday. The Vienna copy omits the feast entirely, and the same is true of the vast majority of the many copies at Sinai. Where a provision is made, it is seldom complete and often restricted to pieces no longer in use. When one first encounters it, this apparent deficiency seems strange indeed. Yet there is nothing really strange about it. To understand it, one needs only to think of the frequency with which the Στιχηρὰ τοῦ Πάσχα must be repeated during the season Easter to Ascension. With their appointed verses they must be sung twice daily during Easter Week, morning and evening; they must also be sung at Vespers on every one of the following Saturdays, the Saturday before Antipascha alone excepted; on the Eve of the Ascension the Easter season comes to an end, and to mark this, the five pieces are sung again at the Tuesday Vespers, and once again, for the last time, at the Wednesday Orthros.[2] Clearly, the melodies of the Στιχηρὰ τοῦ Πάσχα belonged in earlier times among those that an experienced singer might be expected to know by heart, and if they were not copied into the choir books, it was because one thought this superfluous.

Only a few exceptional MSS contain all five of these melodies. Among them are three copies in the earlier notations—Vatopedi 1488, Paris gr. 242, and Sinai 1244—and the melodies they transmit are more or less faithfully translated into the later notation in Iviron 953 and Sinai 1471, two closely related MSS of the fourteenth century, written—as it appears—on Crete or Cyprus.[3] Πάσχα ἱερὸν ἡμῖν and Δεῦτε ἀπὸ θέας, the first two melodies of the set, prove to be identical, as was indeed to have been expected, since their texts are identical in metrical structure.[4] How is this identity to be accounted for? And ought we not to infer from

[2] I base this enumeration on the edition of the Pentekostarion published in Rome in 1883. A note on page 110 of that edition allows for further repetitions at the Sunday Orthros, beginning with the Sunday of the Women at the Tomb.

[3] The five melodies were no doubt originally contained also in Laura Γ.72, but this MS has unfortunately lost fols. 44 and 45, on which Πάσχα ἱερὸν ἡμῖν, Δεῦτε ἀπὸ θέας, and Ἀναστάσεως ἡμέρα καὶ λαμπρυνθῶμεν ought to have been entered. Then, with one or more omissions, the melodies are found in a good many other MSS, among them Berlin gr. fol. 49 and Vatopedi 1489. There is a transcription of the last of the five pieces in H. J. W. Tillyard, *The Hymns of the Pentecostarium* (Copenhagen, 1960), after Trinity College 256 and Athens 883.

[4] Even today, the two texts are sung to a single melody, one version of which may be found in the Ἱερὰ ὑμνῳδία of Sakellarides (Athens, 1902), pp. 314–315.

it that these two pieces had at first a function quite different from that of the three independent pieces that follow?

Our first question is partially answered for us by the Jerusalem Typikon of 1122 published by Papadopoulos-Kerameus in the second volume of his *Analecta*.⁵ Here our two texts, followed by a third exhibiting the same metrical structure, are introduced by the rubric: "Ἔτερα στιχηρὰ εἰς τοὺς αἴνους ἦχος πλάγιος α', πρὸς τὸ "Ηχθης δι' ἡμᾶς.⁶ The three stanzas are accordingly contrafacta, borrowing the metrical structure and the melody of an earlier model. As to the model itself, pure chance brought this to light in what is surely our oldest text of the Parakletike, Sinai 1593, an uncial fragment of the ninth or tenth century. Having found it there, it was not difficult to find it also in two eleventh-century texts, Sinai 778 and 780. It is a Staurosimon, a hymn in praise of the Holy Cross which once enjoyed a certain favor as a model, now long since discarded, together with the greater number of the stanzas patterned on it.⁷ In Sinai 780, the best of my three sources, it reads as follows:

> "Ηχθης δι' ἡμᾶς εἰς θυσίαν ὡς πρόβατον·
> καὶ ὡς ἀμνὸς ἄκακος· ὁ Ἐμμανουήλ.
> ἐπὶ σφαγὴν ἑκούσιον μετὰ ἀνόμων λογισθείς·
> δεῦτε ἄσατε· αἱ πατριαὶ τῶν ἐθνῶν·
> καὶ προσκυνήσωμεν· ἐπὶ σταυροῦ κρεμαμένην·
> τὴν ζωὴν τὴν ἀτελεύτητον.⁸

Once again we are reminded that the materials with which we deal are sometimes older than has been generally assumed. Cardinal Pitra did not hesitate to assign Πάσχα ἱερὸν ἡμῖν to the earliest

⁵Ἀνάλεκτα ἱεροσολυμιτικῆς σταχυολογίας, II (St. Petersburg, 1894), 1–254.
⁶*Ibid.*, 197–198.
⁷Apart from the two stanzas that have survived, I have encountered the following:

1. Πάσχα ὁ ἀμνὸς ἡμῖν τέθυται τοῦ θεοῦ καὶ πατρός
2. Πάσχα ὁ ἀμνὸς ἡμῖν τέθυται θεῖον σφάγιον
3. Πάσχα ἱερὸν ἡμῖν σήμερον ἐγκαινίζεται
4. Πόθῳ τὸν σταυρὸν τοῦ κυρίου
5. Χαίροις παρ' ἡμῶν θεοτόκε βοήσωμεν οἱ πιστοί

Stanzas 1–3 are found in Sinai 759 (stanzas 1 and 2 also in Lavra Γ.12 and stanza 2 in Papadopoulos-Kerameus, *op. cit.*, 198); stanza 4, for Holy Women, is in Sinai 1593, as is stanza 5, a Theotokion.
⁸Not previously published; Enrica Follieri, in her invaluable *Initia hymnorum ecclesiae graecae* (II, 92), has only a reference to Papadopoulos-Kerameus.

stratum of Byzantine hymnography.[9] Yet, with its companion piece, it now proves to have been imitated from a still earlier model. How our paired stichera and the three independent pieces that accompany them were originally used is a question that will never be answered. All one can do is to determine their use at a particular time and place, and if I elect to determine this for Athos about the year 1000, it is because this is the earliest use for which I have supporting documents with musical notation. To simplify my presentation I center it about Vatopedi 1488, a MS dating from about the year 1050, drawing on two earlier MSS from the Laura, Γ.72 and Γ.67, for confirmation and, where necessary, for corrections and missing details.[10]

In Vatopedi 1488 the Easter Office is arranged as follows:

Στιχηρὰ τῇ ἁγίᾳ καὶ μεγάλῃ Κυριακῇ τοῦ Πάσχα ψαλλόμενα εἰς τοὺς Αἴνους· 'Ιωάννου μοναχοῦ· ἦχος α'.

1. Σήμερον σωτηρία τῷ κόσμῳ
2. 'Αναστάσεως ἡμέρα καρποφορήσωμεν ἑαυτοῖς
3. Τὸ μακάριον πάσχα

Καὶ εὐθὺς ἄρχονται τὸν στίχον· 'Αναστήτω ὁ θεός [Ps. 67.1]· καὶ τούτου ψαλλομένου ποιοῦσιν οἱ μοναχοὶ ἕνα χορόν, λέγοντες ταῦτα τὰ στιχηρά· ἦχος πλάγιος α'.

4. Πάσχα ἱερὸν ἡμῖν

Στίχος· 'Ως ἐκλείπει καπνός [Ps. 67.2]

5. Δεῦτε ἀπὸ θέας

Εἰς τὸ Δόξα.

6. 'Αναστάσεως ἡμέρα καὶ λαμπρυνθῶμεν τῇ πανηγύρει

Στιχηρά ψαλλόμενα καθ' ἑκάστην εἰς τὸ Δόξα· ἦχος πλάγιος α'.

7. Πάσχα τὸ τερπνόν
8. Πάσχα ἑορτῶν ἑορτή
9. Πάσχα τῶν ψυχῶν
10. Πάσχα χαρμοσύνης
11. Αἱ μυροφόροι γυναῖκες
12. Εὐφραινέσθωσαν οἱ οὐρανοί
13. "Αγγελοι σκιρτήσατε
14. 'Ω φύλακες 'Ιουδαίων
15. "Ονπερ τὸ πρὶν ἡ παρθένος

There are no further provisions. It is noteworthy that each of the ten doxastika (6–15) concludes with the refrain

[9]Hymnographie de l'église grecque (Rome, 1867), p. 37.
[10]For an account of these three MSS, with several plates, see pp. 68–111 of this volume. I am preparing an edition of Vatopedi 1488, in facsimile, for publication in the Monumenta Musicae Byzantinae.

Χριστὸς ἀνέστη ἐκ νεκρῶν· θανάτῳ θάνατον πατήσας.
καὶ τοῖς ἐν τοῖς μνήμασι· ζωὴν χαρισάμενος.

In no case, however, is the text of this well-known troparion written out in full; one finds only the first few words, with or without musical notation.

The presence of a whole series of doxastika for daily use, the single members of the series tied to one another through their use of a common refrain, prompts the inference that our paired stichera —which are in effect aposticha, that is to say, stichera alternating with proper verses—were to be repeated throughout the week, every evening and every morning. This inference is supported by the Jerusalem Typikon of 1122, which specifically calls for these repetitions. It is further supported by the Laura MS Γ.72, whose lavish provisions for the Easter Week Office include similar directions, equally specific. What is more, the Laura MS writes out, each in its proper place, the doxastika that are to be sung at the single services, and since its series is more complete than the Vatopedi series, likewise—as the earlier of the two—more authoritative, I reproduce it in full. The same series, with the single pieces in the same order, is also to be found in Laura Γ.67.

Sunday Orthros	Ἀναστάσεως ἡμέρα καὶ λαμπρυνθῶμεν	?[11]	72ᵛ
Sunday Vespers	Ἐν ἀρχῇ ἦν ὁ λόγος	46	73
Monday Orthros	Ὅνπερ τὸ πρὶν ἡ παρθένος	47ᵛ	73
Monday Vespers	Πάσχα τὸ τερπνόν	48ᵛ	73
Tuesday Orthros	Πάσχα τῶν ψυχῶν	49ᵛ	73ᵛ
Tuesday Vespers	Ἡ παράνομος κουστωδία	50ᵛ	73ᵛ
Wednesday Orthros	Πάσχα ἑορτῶν ἑορτή	52	73ᵛ
Wednesday Vespers	Πάσχα χαρμοσύνης	53ᵛ	74
Thursday Orthros	Ἄγγελοι σκιρτήσατε	54	74
Thursday Vespers	Ὦ πάσχα θεῖον[12]	55ᵛ	74ᵛ
Friday Orthros	Τὸ πάσχα τοῦτο τὸ μέγα	56ᵛ	74ᵛ
Friday Vespers	Ὦ φύλακες Ἰουδαίων	57ᵛ	74ᵛ
Saturday Orthros	Τῆς λαμπροφόρου ἡμέρας	59ᵛ	75

As before, the common refrain is the Easter troparion, of which only the incipit is given.

That this earlier series should include a number of pieces not

---

[11] Presumably entered on one or other of the lost folios (see n. 3 above).

[12] For the Thursday Vespers, Γ.72 has two doxastika—first Ἀκούσατε ταῦτα πάντα τὰ ἔθνη, then the one entered above.

found in Vatopedi 1488 is not in itself surprising. What is surprising is that Vatopedi 1488 should include two pieces not found in the earlier series. To be sure, Εὐφραινέσθωσαν οἱ οὐρανοί and Αἱ μυροφόροι γυναῖκες appear in both MSS at the Laura, but they do not appear there as doxastika nor does either one conclude there with the established refrain. Εὐφραινέσθωσαν οἱ οὐρανοί has no refrain at all, while Αἱ μυροφόροι γυναῖκες, which has survived until this day as a part of the Easter Office, has as its concluding line only these words: Χριστὸς ἀνέστη ἐκ νεκρῶν· χαροποιῶν τὰ σύμπαντα. Thus, among the five surviving stichera, Αἱ μυροφόροι γυναῖκες is the one that has undergone the most drastic changes. As one of the many idiomela of the Easter Office, it at first concluded with the line found in Laura Γ.67 and Γ.72. Then, to adapt it for use as a doxastikon, it was given the Easter troparion as a refrain. Finally, in order that it might serve, with Πάσχα τὸ τερπνόν, to continue the series of aposticha that at an earlier date consisted only of Πάσχα ἱερὸν ἡμῖν and Δεῦτε ἀπὸ θέας, it was stripped of its refrain, as was Πάσχα τὸ τερπνόν, for no anticipation of the refrain of the retained doxastikon, Ἀναστάσεως ἡμέρα, was longer appropriate.

THE LATIN ANTIPHONS
FOR THE OCTAVE
OF THE EPIPHANY †

Cum igitur Graeci post matutinas laudes imperatori celebratas in octava die Theophaniae secreto in sua lingua Deo psallerent antiphonas ejus melodiae et materiae, cujus sunt *Veterem hominem* cum sequentibus, praecipit imperator capellano cuidam suo graecismi perito, ut ipsam materiam in eadem modulatione latine redderet et singulis ejus modulaminis motibus singulas syllabas dare sollicite curaret, ne, quantum natura sineret, in illo dissimiles forent. Inde est, quod omnes ejusdem sunt toni et quod in una ipsarum, pro *contrivit conteruit* positum invenitur.[1]

TWICE, within the past decade, this arresting paragraph from the *Gesta Caroli Magni* has been made to serve as point of departure for a significant study. In 1954, the late Jacques Handschin was able to show that, in so far as Notker's story was open to verification at all, it had the ring of truth.[2] His attention was largely focused on two of the *antiphonae sequentes—Caput draconis* and *Te qui in spiritu*. In the one, the reading *conteruit* proved to be preferred by certain sources remarkable either for their antiquity or for the conservative character of their tradition; in the other, the opening lines proved to agree, word for word, with the corresponding lines of Σὲ τὸν ἐν πνεύματι, a processional sticheron

†From *Recueil de travaux de l'Institut d'Études byzantines, No. VIII: Mélanges Georges Ostrogorsky,* II (Belgrade, 1964), 417–426. Reprinted with permission.
[1]Philipp Jaffé, *Monumenta Carolina* (Berlin, 1877), p. 673.
[2]"Sur quelques tropaires grecs traduits en latin," *Annales musicologiques,* II (1954), 27–60.

from the Byzantine office for the feast of the Epiphany, whose metrical scheme they took over unaltered and whose melody they reproduced without essential change. Building on this foundation, Dom Joseph Lemarié came forward in 1958 with fresh evidence in support of Handschin's position, some of it from an unexpected quarter.[3] For five of the antiphons of the Latin series, it now appeared, exact equivalents were to be found within the Armenian office for the Epiphany Octave. Among them were *Veterem hominem, Caput draconis,* and *Te qui in spiritu.* These were the main points. In what follows I shall need to return to them and to touch also on other findings of Handschin's and Lemarié's that confirm them or open up new paths.

As long ago as 1932, in his useful text-edition of the Heirmologion, Sophronios Eustratiades published under the heading Εἰς τὰ ἄγια Θεοφάνεια the heirmoi of a canon by Andrew of Crete. Two of these heirmoi—those for the fifth and sixth odes—are the Greek originals of *Veterem hominem* and *Caput draconis,* the two antiphons to which Notker makes explicit or implicit reference. [4] In republishing these heirmoi, I follow the Heirmologia Patmos 55 and Saba 83, whose readings are at several points superior to those of Laura B.32, the Athos MS upon which Eustratiades based his text. For the Latin antiphons, I follow Lemarié's critical edition, which reproduces the text of the earliest Western source, the ninth-century Antiphoner of Compiègne (Bibliothèque Nationale, lat. 17436), together with the variant readings of 14 other MSS.[5]

'Ωδη ε'	Antiphona 1
Τὸν παλαιὸν ἄνθρωπον	Veterem hominem
ἀνακαινίζων ὁ σωτὴρ	renovans Salvator
ἐπὶ τὸ βάπτισμα ἔρχεται	venit ad baptismum

[3]"Les antiennes 'Veterem hominem' du jour octave de l'Epiphanie et les antiennes d'origine grecque de l'Epiphanie," *Ephemerides liturgicae,* LXXII (1958), 3–38.

[4]Ἁγιορειτικὴ βιβλιοθήκη, IX, 117–118 (no. 161). Despite Gastoué's shrewd conjecture that the originals of the Latin antiphons were probably stanzas of a canon (*Tribune de Saint-Gervais,* XXV [1928], 10), the texts published by Eustratiades seem not until now to have been cited in this connection. I myself ought to have noticed them years ago. Had I known of them in 1954 I should most certainly have brought them to Handschin's attention, for we talked and corresponded about his study before its publication.

[5]Lemarié, pp. 6–7.

ἵνα τὴν φθαρεῖσαν φύσιν
5 δι' ὕδατος ἀνακαινίσῃ
ἔνδυμα ἀφθαρσίας
μεταμφιάσας ἡμᾶς.

ut natura quae corrupta est
per aquam recuperaret
incorruptibili veste
circumamictans nobis.

Ὠδὴ ϛ'

Antiphona 4

Τὴν κεφαλὴν τοῦ δράκοντος

Caput draconis

ὁ σωτὴρ συνέθλασεν
10 ἐν Ἰορδάνῃ ποταμῷ
καὶ πάντας ἐρρύσατο
ἐκ τῆς τοῦ "Αιδου φθορᾶς.[6]

Salvator contrivit
in Jordane flumine
ab ejus potestate
omnes eripuit.

With texts as concise in their wording and as vivid in their imagery as these two heirmoi of Andrew's, to have expected a translator to match the syllable-count of his originals would have been to expect the impossible, particularly at a time when translators were accustomed to leaving word-order and grammatical structure as they found them and to rendering each individual word by its exact equivalent. Out of twelve lines, only two agree —7 and 11—and even if we read *conteruit* (line 9) and *eripuimur* (line 12) with the Hartker Antiphoner (St. Gallen 390/391), the correspondence still falls short of the ideal.[7] But if this might have been foreseen, one could scarcely have foreseen the failure of lines 11 and 12 to reproduce the sense and sequence of the Greek. Here, strangely enough, the Latin version is rather closer to the Armenian—"et, par sa puissance, il a sauvé tous les hommes"[8]—and we are reduced to supposing that the original wording of these two lines must have been altered at some time between the date of the embassy to Aachen[9] and the date of our earliest Greek source.

As Handschin has already shown, the opening lines of another antiphon from our series agree word for word with the correspond-

[6]All three sources have the ascription to Andrew; the heading Εἰς τὰ ἅγια Θειοφάνεια is found only in Laura B.32. Readings peculiar to Laura B.32 are: line 7, μεταμφιέσει for μεταμφιάσας; line 9, Χριστός for σωτήρ; line 9, συνέτριψεν for συνέθλασεν.

[7]The reading *conteruit* is found also in four other sources (Lemarié, pp. 6, 16).

[8]Lemarié's translation (his study, p. 22).

[9]Handschin (p. 28, n. 4) argues convincingly that the incident described by Notker took place on January 13, 802, at the time of the embassy sent to Aachen by the Empress Irene. According to J. F. Böhmer, *Regesta imperii,* I (Innsbruck, 1899), 153, the envoy was the Spatharios Leo.

ing lines of a processional sticheron by Cosmas of Jerusalem. Here, in lines 1 and 2, the translator has been able to match the syllable-count of his original. But with line 3 the agreement breaks down, and it may be said at once that the melodic agreement to which Handschin drew attention breaks down at this point also.

Ἰδιόμελον	Antiphona 2
Σὲ τὸν ἐν πνεύματι	Te qui in spiritu
καὶ πυρὶ καθαίροντα	et igne purificans
τὴν ἁμαρτίαν τοῦ κόσμου	humana contagia
. . . . . .	Deum et Redemptorem
5	omnes glorificamus.

Cosmas and Andrew have chosen the same mode, the ἦχος τέταρτος. As Notker tells us, the Latin antiphons are all *ejusdem toni.* Beyond a doubt, the melody used by Cosmas was known to the Latin translator. To what extent is this true also of the melodies used by Andrew? The question calls for an answer.

Unlike the sticheron by Cosmas, whose melody is transmitted by hundreds of sources, most of them easily read, the melodies of Andrew's heirmoi are found only in the three copies of the Heirmologion on which we have based our text. Patmos 55 and Saba 83, MSS of the tenth and early eleventh centuries, employ archaic forms of the Coislin notation. Somewhat younger than the Patmos copy, but distinctly older than the one from Saba, Laura B.32 employs an archaic form of the Chartres notation and thus belongs to quite another tradition, as is evident also from its textual peculiarities and its interpolation of additional heirmoi. Strictly speaking, these sources cannot be read at all, and although it is sometimes possible to reconstruct the melodies they transmit, this is attended by special difficulties.

In an earlier study[10] I have tried to show that, under favorable conditions, the more developed forms of the Coislin and Chartres notations can be read directly, without the help of a control. Two circumstances prevent my extending this claim to include their archaic forms. Neither notation, archaic Coislin or archaic Chartres, provides a continuous musical text.[11] And while it is true that

---

[10]See pp. 68–111 of this volume.
[11]Dom Louis Brou has some observations on this characteristic of the archaic Byzantine notations in his "Notes de paléographie mozarabe. I. Les manuscrits mozarabes à notation intermittente," *Anuario musical*, X (1955), 22–29.

the latest stages of these archaic notations are more thorough in their provisions than the earliest ones, this heightened continuity is largely deceptive, resulting in the main from the interpolation of wholly ambiguous signs.

Oddly enough, it is the earliest of our three sources that points the way to a solution. Scattered through the Heirmologion Patmos 55 one finds bits of interlinear text, usually at the beginning of a heirmos, over the first words of the first line, sometimes internally, over the first words of a later line. A study of these interlinear bits shows that they were intended for the guidance of the singer. Occurring largely in unfamiliar pieces, they served to remind him of lines from familiar ones, whose melodies he could supply from memory.[12] One such reminder suggests that there is a relation between Τὴν κεφαλὴν τοῦ δράκοντος, the first line of Andrew's sixth heirmos, and Τὸν φωτισμόν σου Κύριε, the first line of a heirmos from a familiar canon by Cosmas. The two lines are identical in mode, in syllable-count, and in the distribution of their accents, and there is no substantial difference in Patmos 55 between the notation of the one and the notation of the other. With the aid of this reminder, the tenth-century singer could supply the melody, and if we supply it today from the Heirmologion Iviron 470, an unambiguous later source,[13] we shall be coming as close to a transcription of Patmos 55 as we are likely to get. The parallel between Τὴν κεφαλήν and Τὸν φωτισμόν extends only to the end of the first line. For the remaining lines, and for the whole of Τὸν παλαιὸν ἄνθρωπον, we must find our own parallels, and if we can do so, the rest is simple. One has, however, to bear in mind that the validity of an operation of this kind rests on a number of assumptions, all of them implicit in the foregoing, and that the final product is not a transcription, in the strict sense, but rather a reconstruction of the form the melodies would presumably have taken if the twelfth-century copyist of Iviron 470 had found them

---

[12]Interlinear texts of this kind are found also in the Heirmologion fragment Leningrad 557, published in complete facsimile by J. B. Thibaut in his *Monuments de la notation ekphonétique et hagiopolite de l'église grecque* (St. Petersburg, 1913), pp. 65–72 and pl. vi–xxiii. Their significance was pointed out to me by Isaac Thomas, one of my students.

[13]Monumenta Musicae Byzantinae, II (Copenhagen, 1938).

Example 1

in his *Vorlage* and included them in his own copy of it. The preceding reconstruction is designed to explain itself.[14]

[14]Above the reconstruction I have copied the neumes from the two Coislin sources, Saba 83 in the upper line, Patmos 55 in the lower; then, on a second staff, I have transcribed from Iviron 470 the parallel passages on which the reconstruction is based, indicating in each case the location of the passage in Iviron 470 and copying above the transcription the neumes with which these same passages are provided in Patmos 55. To have added the neumes from Laura B.32 would have been to introduce an extraneous element, complicating the picture without clarifying the solution in any material way. A facsimile edition of Saba 83, in color, is being prepared for the Monumenta Musicae Byzantinae by Jørgen Raasted. For microfilms of Patmos 55 I am indebted to the Abbé Marcel Richard of the Institut de recherche et d'histoire des textes, Paris.

Crowded out, perhaps, by the familiar Epiphany canons of John and Cosmas, Andrew's canon was soon forgotten. If some of its stanzas were translated into Armenian, this must have happened at an early date, for there is no trace of a Slavic translation; none of its heirmoi was admitted to the quasi-official redaction of the Heir-

Example 2

mologion put into circulation about 1050.[15] The Latin antiphons were more fortunate. From Aachen, their use spread rapidly to the furthest corners of Western Europe. Six of their number found general acceptance, and by the middle of the fifteenth century these had become so thoroughly familiar that the melody of *Veterem hominem* could be made to serve as cantus firmus for a polyphonic setting of the Ordinarium.[16] In 1568, when the Roman Breviary was systematically stripped of its medieval accretions, their hold was broken. But not altogether, for they have stubbornly survived in a few exceptional environments—in the local rite of Braga and in the monastic rites of the Dominicans, Cistercians, and Premonstratensians.

In working out my reconstruction of the Greek melodies, I made no attempt to force them into agreement with the Latin. To have done so would have been to defeat the whole purpose of this inquiry, and the attempt would in any case have failed, for at best the relation of the one set to the other is somewhat tenuous. To permit the reader to satisfy himself on this point, I reproduce the melodies of the comparable antiphons, taking them from the *Antiphonarium sacris Ordinis Praedicatorum* (Rome, 1933), whose readings do not differ materially from those of the Worcester Antiphoner, the source favored by Handschin.[17] (Ex. 2.)

On the positive side, there is identity of mode; there is, in lines 1 and 3 of *Veterem hominem,* and in lines 1 and 2 of *Caput draconis,* a perceptible resemblance to the corresponding lines of Τὸν πα- λαιὸν ἄνθρωπον and Τὴν κεφαλὴν τοῦ δράκοντος. less marked in the one case, more so in the other; the concluding lines of the two antiphons agree, as do those of the two heirmoi. On the other hand, *renovans Salvator* agrees with *Salvator contrivit,* while ἀνακαινίζων ὁ σωτήρ agrees with ἐν Ἰορδάνῃ ποταμῷ; the later lines of the antiphons have virtually nothing to do with the later lines of the heirmoi; above all, the Latin ruthlessly sup-

---

[15]For this redaction, see Carsten Høeg's remarks on "The H-Group" in his introduction to *The Hymns of the Hirmologium,* Pt. I (Copenhagen, 1952); its principal representatives are Paris, Coislin 220; Grottaferrata, E.γ.III; Patmos 54; Iviron 470; Grottaferrata E.γ.II; Vatopedi 1531.

[16]Published in 1957 by Father Laurence Feininger in his series Monumenta polyphoniae liturgicae S. Ecclesiae Romanae; for the English authorship, see Thurston Dart, "A Footnote for Morley's 'Plain and Easy Introduction,' " *Music and Letters,* XXXV (1954), 183.

[17]*Paléographie musicale,* XII, 58–59.

presses the rhetorical treatment of the Greek word ἔνδυμα. The basis of the Latin melodies is Greek, but without Notker we should never have recognized it in the finished products, so drastically has it been transformed. At the same time, it is of course quite possible that this is due, at least in part, to the special circumstances surrounding this particular contact between East and West and to the way in which the melodies have been transmitted on either side.

After all, each such contact means a new set of conditions and each new set of conditions brings with it a change in the nature of the transmission. In Milan, an idiomelon from the Christmas office, translated into Latin, was made to serve as Transitorium for the Third Sunday after Epiphany.[18] Oddly enough, this too was the work of Andrew of Crete, its mode is again the ἦχος τέταρτος, and its melody is in part made up of phrases already familiar from Τὸν παλαιὸν ἄνθρωπον and Τὴν κεφαλὴν τοῦ δράκοντος. In this case, however, the Latin melody is almost wholly independent: not only does *Laetamini justi* fail to agree with Εὐφραίνεσθε δίκαιοι, it also fails to agree with *Veterem hominem* and *Caput draconis* at the points where the idiomelon agrees with the heirmoi. Either the adapter did not intend to retain the Greek melody or the circumstances surrounding this contact must have differed from those that obtained in Aachen. In Benevento, quite the other way, a troparion from the Good Friday hours, sung both in Greek and Latin, actually carried its Greek melody with it, virtually unchanged.[19] Here, however, Byzantine influence was strong and lasting, and the exceptionally faithful transmission of this melody in the Latin sources suggests that the transfer took place rather later than those in Aachen and Milan, perhaps during the time when the principality of Benevento was under the protection of the Macedonian emperors.

[18]For the idiomelon and its two contrafacta, see J. D. Petrescu, *Les idiomèles et le canon de l'office de Noël* (Paris, 1932), Transcription en notation moderne: pp. 96–99, 102–109; for the Ambrosian Transitorium, *Paléographie musicale*, VI, 134, or the *Antiphonale missarum juxta ritum S. Ecclesiae Mediolanensis* (Rome, 1935), p. 78. Despite their needlessly elaborate conventions for the representation of rhythmic and dynamic nuance, Petrescu's transposed transcriptions are still serviceable.

[19]Studied in detail by Egon Wellesz in his *Eastern Elements in Western Chant* (Oxford, 1947).

In a stimulating chapter on "Byzantium and the West," Talbot Rice[20] has emphasized the cultural importance of the numerous embassies that were interchanged between the emperors of East and West in Carolingian times and of the impression made on Western artists and their patrons by the magnificent presents brought from the East. The envoys to Aachen brought presents too, but the impression their presents left was outweighted by the deeper impression left by the singing of the Greek clergy in their entourage. Later on in the same chapter it is pointed out that it would be a mistake to overemphasize the final influence of these contacts on the West: "however marked the Byzantine influence may have been, the art of the Western world as a whole was Western art, just as that of the Eastern world was Byzantine." Our own inquiry has shown us that this applies, with special force, to music.

Of the Latin antiphons with which we have been occupied, *Caput draconis* and *Te qui in spiritu* have the same five-line structure. *Caput draconis,* as we know, translates a heirmos, while *Te qui in spiritu,* as Handschin has shown, agrees in its opening lines with a processional sticheron, a far longer text with which its concluding lines no longer have anything in common. The Latin texts are sung to the same melody. This ought also to be true of the Greek, as indeed it is. (For *Te qui in spiritu,* see p. 152.)

This demonstration bears out the correctness of the reconstruction. What is more important, it suggests that the opening lines of the sticheron are not in fact the original of the Latin antiphon, but rather a quotation from that original which is far more likely to have been a five-line stanza modeled on Τὴν κεφαλὴν τοῦ δράκοντος. A Heirmologion contains only model stanzas. But in actual practice, the singing of each heirmos is followed by the singing of an indeterminate number of similar stanzas, all of them sung to the model melody. The inference, then, is that the original of *Te qui in spiritu* was a troparion by Andrew of Crete, a part of the sixth ode of his canon Εἰς τὰ ἅγια Θεοφάνεια, and if this inference could be confirmed, we should doubtless find that it was equally applicable to the originals of four of the other *antiphonae*

[20]In his *Byzantine Art* (Penguin Books, 1962).

sequentes—Baptista contremuit, Magnum mysterium, Aqua comburit, and *Peccati aculeus*—all of which have the same five-line structure and the same melody. We might also find that it led us to the originals of the remaining antiphons of the set—*Praecursor Johannes, Pater de caelo,* and *Baptizatur Christus*—even though no one of these longer translations corresponds as we have it with any heirmos of the canon.

Only too obviously, what we need is the complete text of Andrew's canon, and we can expect to find it only in a conservative tenth-or-eleventh-century copy of the January Menaion. There are not many such copies, and only a few are easily consulted. The first that come to mind are the two copies at Grottaferrata, Δ.α.xv (from S. Elia di Carbone) and Δ.α.v (written at Grottaferrata in 1102). Father Marco Petta, Grottaferrata's librarian, most kindly informs me that these do not contain Andrew's canon and he adds that he has also failed to find it in any of the other MSS he has consulted. The search will have to go on.

TWO CHILANDARI
CHOIR BOOKS [†]

I N May of this year [1964], together with Professor Kenneth Levy of Brandeis University, I took part in a symposium held at the Dumbarton Oaks Research Center in Washington under the direction of Professor Roman Jakobson and Father Francis Dvornik. The central topic was "The Byzantine Mission to the Slavs," and my own contribution dealt with two choir books at the Chilandari Monastery on Mount Athos, the Triodion Chilandari 307 and the Heirmologion Chilandari 308. These had been published in 1957 as a part of the series Monumenta Musicae Byzantinae,[1] and since the original impetus for this publication had come from Harvard's Roman Jakobson, from the Slavic department of his university, and from that university's institute in Washington, the Dumbarton Oaks Research Center, it had seemed to me that I could scarcely choose a subject more appropriate.

What I sought above all to suggest, in this contribution of mine, was that the two choir books at Chilandari, like other ancient monuments of Slavic chant, could be shown to preserve vestiges of archaic musical and liturgical practices, that they could be made to

†Published in German translation as "Zwei chilandari Chorbücher," in *Anfänge der slavischen Musik* (Bratislava, 1966), pp. 65–76; read in Bratislava at a symposium arranged by the Slovakian Academy of Sciences, early August, 1964. Reprinted with permission of the academy.

[1]V, *Fragmenta Chiliandarica Palaeoslavica* (Copenhagen, 1957); for additional folios of the two manuscripts, see F. V. Mareš, "Pražská část sticheraria Chilandarského," *Slavia*, XXVII (1958), 538–555, and D. S. Radojicić, "L'heirmologion de Grigorovitch," *Južnoslovenski filolog*, XXII (1957–58), 265–268.

shed new light on the early history of Byzantine music, and that the Triodion, in particular, might even be said to constitute a compensating replacement for a type of Byzantine manuscript that must once have existed, now no longer extant.

It was clear, however, that before I could begin to appraise the two choir books from this point of view, I would need to determine precisely when the Slavs first provided their liturgical books with musical signs. Three means of determining this suggested themselves to me. One might take as a starting point the presumed date of the original translations; one might then go on to ask what our two choir books could be made to tell us about the date of their archetypes; a third and final step would be to ask whether the notation itself did not somehow betray the date of its original adoption.

Neither the first means nor the second led to an acceptable solution. Although Roman Jakobson has sought, in a recent study,[2] to date the translation of the Heirmologion from the Moravian mission of the 870s or early 880s, and although we have every reason to infer that by the year 850, at the very latest, the art of musical writing must have been known and practiced in Byzantium, it is one thing to say that the Slavs and their Greek teachers may perhaps have put this art to their own uses as early as 880 and quite another thing to conclude that this is what actually happened.

Not less ambiguous are the indications that may be extracted from the contents of our two choir books. The Triodion contains a number of items dating from the reign of the Emperor Leo, that is, from between 886 and 912, including at least two sometimes ascribed to the emperor himself.[3] The Heirmologion, which in its original state cannot have contained more than about 650 heirmoi, impresses us by the strict economy of its provisions and by the lengths to which it has carried selectivity; it reflects the state of the Office books about the middle of the tenth century, when the

---

[2]"Methodius' Canon to Demetrius of Thessalonica and the Old Church Slavonic Hirmoi," *Sbornik praci filosofické fakulty Brněnské university* XIV (1965), rada umenovedná F 9, 115–121.

[3]The Theotokion beginning on fol. 55ᵛ translates Ἡ ἄνυμφος μήτηρ, one of the emperor's Staurotheotokia (transcription by H. J. W. Tillyard in his *Hymns of the Octoechus*, Part 2 [Copenhagen, 1949], pp. 204–205); the Easter sticheron beginning on fol. 72A translates Ἄγγελοι σκιρτήσατε, ascribed to the emperor in the MS Ohrid, Musée National, Inv. 39 (cote ancienne 87).

extraordinarily popular canons of the poets Theophanes Graptos and Joseph the Hymnographer had permanently supplanted the greater part of the older repertory.[4] From these indications we could, of course, derive a date for the archetypes of our two choir books, but at best that date would be no more than an earliest possible date, and even as such it would be valid only if we were willing to assume that the two manuscripts had neither added to nor subtracted from the original contents.

To leave myself time to deal in greater detail with the central problem of the notation, I have in the foregoing drastically abridged the first part of my paper for Washington, in which I touched also on that striking peculiarity of the Slavic heirmologion, its reordering of the heirmoi.[5] Much has been made of this innovation since Professor Koschmieder first drew attention to it in his edition of the fragmentary heirmologia from Novgorod. I am myself persuaded that there is no mystery about it, and that the heightened selectivity just referred to made its adoption by the Slavs inevitable.

To simplify the presentation, I shall begin the next part of my paper by summarizing its conclusions. I can then examine with you, perhaps somewhat superficially, the paleographic evidence upon which those conclusions are based. In the limited time at my disposal I can scarcely hope to do more.

In brief, I hold (1) that the archaic Slavic notation is a notation of Byzantine origin; (2) that it must have been introduced well before the year 1000, perhaps as early as 950; (3) that at sometime after the year 1000, perhaps as late as 1050, it was modified in certain respects and that these modifications were again of Byzantine origin; and (4) that in certain other respects it is an original creation in that it restricts the use of some of its borrowed signs in ways quite unfamiliar from Byzantium and in that it has invented at least one sign of its own.

---

[4]The Heirmologion, too, contains at least one late entry—Πάλιν ᾿Ιησοῦς, the Byzantine original of the first heirmos on fol. 34, is ascribed in the tenth-century Heirmologion Laura B.32 to Theophanes Protothronos, the ranking bishop who presided at the consecration of the Patriarch Stephen in 886.

[5]The full English text will be published in a forthcoming volume of the Monumenta Musicae Byzantinae, Series Subsidia.

After all that has been written about the archaic Slavic notation in the past ten to fifteen years, particularly after the parallels published by Professors Koschmieder and Velimirović, I need not elaborate my first point. Of the second it should be enough to say that the paleographic evidence points unmistakably to a derivation, not from the notation of the Chartres fragment, as suggested by Mme. Verdeil and as Høeg and I once believed, nor yet from the developed Coislin notation of the later eleventh century, but rather from that rudimentary form of the Coislin notation exemplified by four Byzantine heirmologia of the late tenth and early eleventh centuries—Leningrad 557, Patmos 55, Esphigmenou 54, and Saba 83.[6] This rudimentary notation—let us call it "archaic Coislin"— differs from the notations of the mid-eleventh century and later in that it transmits only the essential features of the melody, making scant provision, if any, for secondary syllables. It knows only a very few basic signs. It has no oligon and no ison; its apostrophos is virtually meaningless, corresponding—as comparisons with later diastematic sources reveal—now to a descending progression, now to an ascending one, now to a tone repetition; its klasma is frequently used independently, without the support of another sign. In our two earliest sources, the Leningrad fragment and the Patmos heirmologion, the final syllable of each text bears a little cross, the counterpart of the ekphonetic teleia. It is in its ultraconservative retention of many of these primitive characteristics, particularly in its retention of the teleia, that the archaic Slavic notation betrays its tenth-century origin.

Equally unmistakable are the indications of later revision. While retaining the teleia and the unsupported klasma, the archaic Slavic notation also makes frequent and idiomatic use of the kylisma and kouphisma. These signs belong to the developed Coislin system, and by the mid-eleventh century, when one first finds them in Byzantine sources, the use of the teleia and unsupported klasma had already been abandoned. Thus the notation of our two manuscripts is seen to involve a combining of incompatible elements. How shall we explain this seeming contradiction unless we conclude that an essentially archaic basis has been modified, here and there, in the light of later developments?

[6]For the terminology, see pp. 68–111 of this volume, especially p. 97.

A further indication of the same sort can be seen in the example to which I shall turn in a moment. Here, at the beginning of the first and second lines of the heirmos and of each of its four troparia, Chilandari 307 writes the bareia with two kentemata. In this it prefers the later, more developed reading to the earlier, more archaic one, which writes the bareia alone.

Even with these modifications, however, the Slavic notation continues to retain its archaic character, for the revisions to which it was subjected were minor ones, affecting only isolated details. No thoroughgoing revision took place. The Slavs rejected the more drastic innovations of the developed Coislin system; above all, they rejected the oligon and the ison. To be sure, the Slavic notation possesses, in its stopitsa, a sign identical with the Byzantine ison in outward form. The two signs cannot possibly be identical in function or in origin. The ison, which represents the unison or tone repetition, may not follow the klasma, which warns of a descending progression; the stopitsa frequently does so. The ison is never combined with the kentema; the stopitsa is frequently so combined. For the representation of simple ascending progressions involving secondary syllables, the developed Coislin system uses the oligon or the oxeia, for similar descending ones the apostrophos; as is clear from comparisons with diastematic sources from Byzantium, the archaic Slavic notation uses the stopitsa in both these situations, and it is perhaps for this reason that it does not regularly use the oxeia and the apostrophos as independent signs. In a word, it is to the blank spaces and ambiguous apostrophoi of the archaic Coislin notation that the stopitsa corresponds most closely, and the archaic Slavic notation thus stands revealed as one that transmits only the essential features of the melody.

In Byzantine ecclesiastical poetry, when several stanzas are to be sung to a single melody, their texts regularly agree, line by line, in their syllable count and in the distribution of their accents. In Slavic translation, this exact agreement disappears, and naturally so, for the translators were concerned, not so much with syllable count and accent distribution, as with the conservation of the original word order and the literal rendering of the individual word. Not only do the several stanzas of the translation fail to agree with their Greek models, they also fail to agree with one another, and the extent of this failure is often so marked that one is at first left wondering how the successive stanzas could possibly have been made to fit the same music. As an example I take the final ode of the Good Friday Triodion.

Table 1   Ninth Ode of Good Friday Triodion

	Greek Heirmos and all Troparia	*Slavic* Heirmos	Troparia			
			1	2	3	4
Line 1	10	9	15	14	11	12
2	6	6	8	8	7	9
3	8	8	9	10	6	9
4	6	7	7	10	9	8
5	7	7	13	9	10	11
6	7	7	9	10	10	8
7	6	6	8	=8	=8	6

In this particular instance, as sometimes happens, the translated heirmos and its Greek model agree reasonably well. The figures for the troparia tell quite another story. Only two lines agree with the corresponding lines of the translated heirmos, and there are two discrepancies of as many as six syllables. One has also to bear in mind that agreement in syllable count need not carry accentual agreement with it; thus in line 3 the agreement of troparion 4 with troparion 1 will prove on closer examination to be no agreement at all. As to line 7, this is a refrain line, and in troparia 1, 2, and 3 its wording is identical.

Now in Chilandari 307, this final ode of the Good Friday Triodion, like the two odes that precede it, is entered in full, with musical notation for the heirmos and for the troparia as well.[7] Since all that this implies is not immediately evident from the facsimile, I have copied out the words and music of the first three lines, writing the troparia in order below the heirmos. In co-ordinating the several stanzas I have been guided solely by the essential signs of the notation.

My illustration is short and simple, but it is at the same time

[7] Fol. 53 and 53ᵛ of the published facsimile.

Table 2

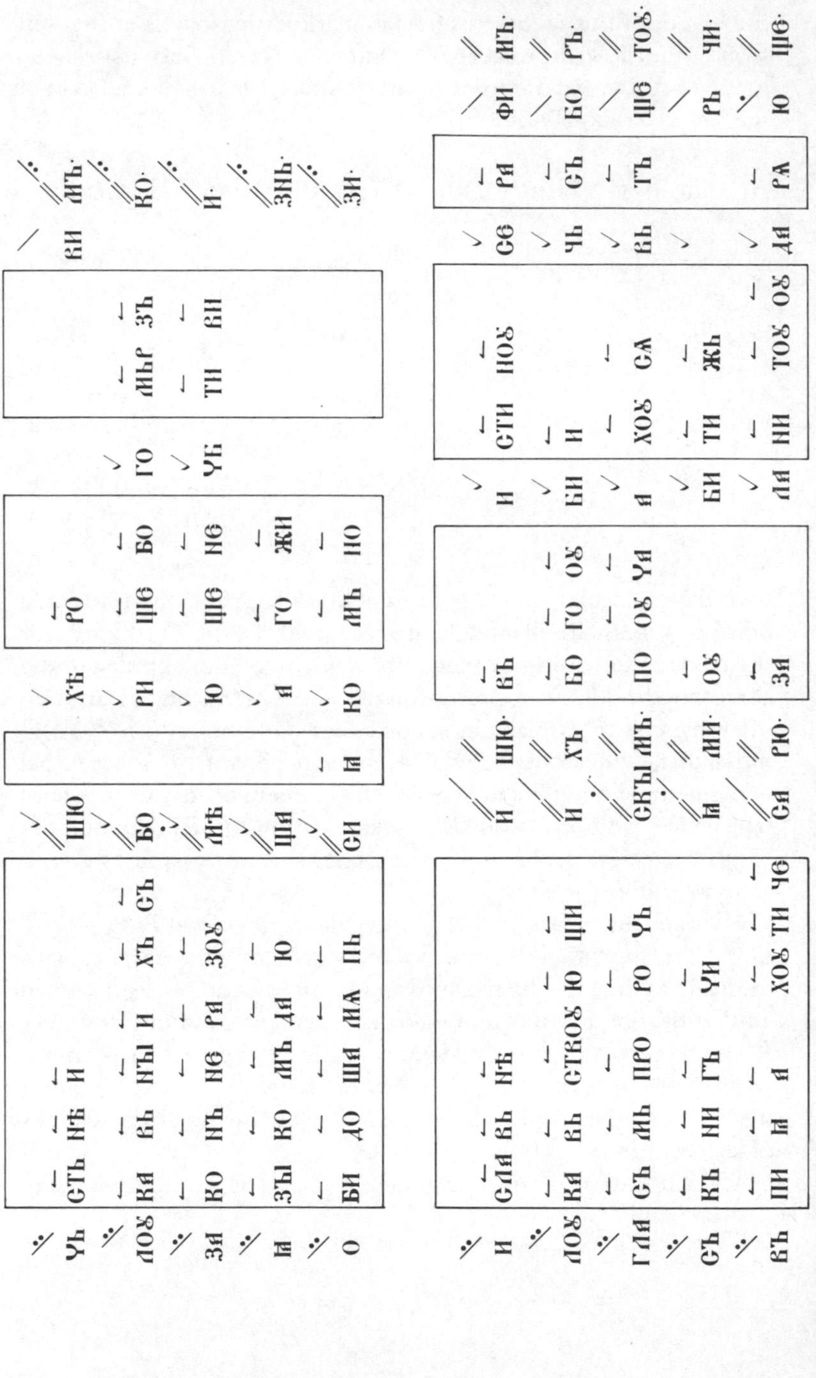
ЧЬ СТЬ НѢ И ШЮ ХѢ РО ВИ ИТЬ
ЛОЎ КЯ ВЬ НЫ И ХЪ СЪ БО РИ ЩЄ БО ГО ИЬР ЗЪ КО
ЗЯ КО НЪ НЄ РЯ ЗОЎ ИТЬ Ю ЩЄ НЄ ЧѢ ТИ ВИ И
Ы ЗЪ КО ИТЬ ДЯ Ю ЩЯ Я ГО ЖИ ЗНЬ
О БИ ДО ШЯ ИЯ ПЬ СИ Ы КО ИТЬ НО ЗИ
И СЛЯ ВЬ НѢ И ШЮ ВЪ И СТИ НОЎ СЄ РЯ ФИ ИТЬ
ЛОЎ КЯ ВЬ СТВОЎ Ю ЩИ И ХЪ БО ГО ОЎ БИ И ЧЬ СЪ БО РЪ
ГЛЯ СЪ ИЬ ПРО РО ЧЬ СКЫ ИТЬ ПО ОЎ ЧЯ Я ХОЎ СЯ ВЬ ЩЄ ТОЎ
СЪ КЪ НИ ГЪ ЧИ Ы ИИ ОЎ БИ ТИ ЖЬ ТЪ РЬ ЧИ
ВЪ ПИ Ы Я ХОЎ ТИ ЧЄ СЯ РЮ ЗЯ ЛЯ НИ ТОЎ ОЎ ДЯ РЯ Ю ЩЄ

typical and highly instructive. It shows us how lines of varying lengths were adapted to the single phrases of a melody that suffered no material change. It shows us that lines of equal length were not always adapted in the same way, and in showing us this it has important implications for the philologist interested in Old Slavonic accentuation. From the penultimate syllables of lines 2 and 3 it is clear that slight differences in notation are not always significant differences; we may safely infer, at these two points, that the addition of the kentema to the oxeia or to the bareia does no more than make explicit what was already implicit without it. Above all, the illustration shows us once again that the archaic Slavic notation is a notation that transmits only the essential features of the melody. What is essential stands outside the rectangles I have enclosed by solid lines; the signs that represent it agree almost exactly with the essential signs of our sources in archaic Coislin. What is nonessential lies within the rectangles; the one sign used here is the stopitsa, and in our sources in Archaic Coislin the corresponding syllables, if they bear any sign at all, bear only the ambiguous apostrophos.

Fortunately for us, the Triodion Chilandari 307 is particularly rich in opportunities for this sort of comparative analysis. Quite apart from the Good Friday Triodion, with its three heirmoi and their ten troparia, it contains more than fifty further contrafacta—stichera and troparia prosomoia—and each of these contrafacta has musical notation throughout. In a few cases the translated model is even shorter than the heirmos we have just considered; more often it is longer and more elaborate. Some models have only one such additional stanza; others have as many as five or six.

Most of these additional stanzas form part of what I may call the marginal contents of the Triodion. This runs in Chilandari 307 to more than sixty-five items, translating texts and transmitting melodies found only in a few exceptional Byzantine copies. One locates their Greek originals with difficulty—in some cases, not at all. Yet it is not on this extraordinary profusion of "apocrypha" that the ultimate value of our manuscript depends, nor is it upon the frequency with which it transmits melodic variants, some of them antedating the readings of our earliest Byzantine sources. A single set of south Italian Menaia, which contains a few stichera copied from older *Vorlagen,* allows us to infer that complete sticheraria in the Archaic Coislin notation must once have existed.[8] Not one such manuscript has been preserved. It is only from Chilandari 307 and other comparable monuments of Slavic chant that we can form any idea of what such a manuscript was like.

Enormous progress has been made during the past ten to fifteen years, and today we stand much nearer to solving our problem than we have ever stood before. What are the prospects of our arriving, sooner or later, at a complete and wholly satisfactory solution? No one who has even begun to grasp the nature of the problem will call these prospects bright. However intimately one may come to understand the workings of an archaic notation like ours, one will never be able to read it. Its high degree of ambiguity forbids this. To think in terms of a positive transcription on the five-line staff is simply to deceive oneself. Under favorable conditions, and with the help of unambiguous, unimpeachable controls, one can as a rule work out a sort of reconstruction; but the operation is attended with real difficulty and the result is, at best, highly tentative. The validity of the procedure rests upon one's acceptance of a whole series of assumptions. If one uses a Byzantine control, and this is what I propose, one has first to assume that there has been no flaw in the tradition and that the melody received and recorded in the twelfth century is indeed the melody that the tenth century sought to transmit; one has then to assume that those who first provided the Slavic books with musical signs sought also to transmit this melody; one has then to assume that the tradition on the Slavic side has been flawless in its turn; one has finally to make due allowance for all perceptible conflicts between these assumptions and the explicit indications of the Slavic notation itself and for the lack of syllable-to-syllable correspondence.

It has seemed to me that the experiment ought to be made. Purely as an experiment, then, I offer a tentative reconstruction of the translated heirmos we were looking at a moment ago. (See Ex. 1 below.) One might call it a controlled experiment, for as a non-Slavist I have no preconceived ideas about the rhythms and

[8]The Menaia of S. Elia di Carbone, now at Grottaferrata (MSS Δ. α.xiii–xvii); for facsimiles of single folios, with isolated "apocrypha" in various stages of the archaic Coislin notation, see J. D. Petrescu, *Les idiomèles et le canon de l'office de Noël* (Paris, 1932), pls. ii and vi, and Lorenzo Tardo, *L'antica melurgia bizantina* (Grottaferrata, 1938), pl. xi.

inflections of Church Slavonic or about its tenth-century accentuation. The transcription on the staff above the Greek text gives the reading of the heirmologion Iviron 470, a manuscript from the twelfth century;[9] above it I have added the Archaic Coislin neumes from Patmos 55 and Esphigmenou 54.[10] The version of the Chilandari Triodion, drawn from the published facsimile,[11] agrees almost exactly with that of Professor Koschmieder's "Fragment B."[12] I have made no attempt to resolve the conflicts between the reading of the Iviron manuscript and the implications of the Archaic Coislin notation. Where these occur, notably at the words χερουβιμ and σεραφιμ, it is with Patmos and Esphigmenou, rather than Iviron, that the Chilandari manuscript agrees.

9 Monumenta Musicae Byzantinae, II (Copenhagen, 1938), fol. 102ᵛ.
10 Fols. 156ᵛ (Patmos) and 63ᵛ (Esphigmenou). For photographs of these two manuscripts I am indebted to the Abbé Marcel Richard of the Institut de recherche et de l'histoire des textes.
11 Fol. 53.
12 *Die ältesten Novgoroder Hirmologien-Fragmente*, I (Munich, 1952), 216.

H. J. W. TILLYARD
AND THE RECOVERY
OF A LOST FRAGMENT †

AMONG the ten to twelve oldest monuments of Byzantine chant, the greater number of them preserved today in monastic libraries on Mount Athos, the Triodion Γ.67 at the Laura occupies a commanding position. With Laura Γ.12 and Laura Γ.72 it is one of our three earliest sources for the idiomela of the Triodion and Pentekostarion—perhaps the earliest of all and, generally speaking, the richest and the most complete. It is our one genuinely early source for the melodies of the Oktoëchos. It is written throughout in the so-called Chartres notation, found also in other early sources, but among these it is the only one to use, for a few melodies, an intermediate stage of that notation, half archaic, half developed.[1] It contains our earliest neume-table.[2] My own belief is that the manuscript was written at the Laura toward the end of the tenth century or that, failing this, it is an early eleventh-century copy of one that was.[3]

†From *Studies in Eastern Chant*, I (1966), 95–103. Reprinted with permission of Oxford University Press.

[1]Some examples of this intermediate stage are included in my forthcoming *Specimina notationum antiquiorum* as pls. 10 and 11; its distinguishing characteristics are that it provides for most secondary syllables, normally by employing the apostrophos, while making almost no use of the Chartres ison and oligon.

[2]First published as pl. xiii in Tillyard's "Fragment of a Byzantine Musical Handbook in the Monastery of Laura on Mt. Athos", *Annual of the British School at Athens*, XIX (1912–13), 95–117; republished by Mme. Palikarova-Verdeil as pl. v in the monograph cited in n. 7 below and by Egon Wellesz in his *History of Byzantine Music and Hymnography*, 2nd ed. (Oxford, 1961), p. 273.

[3]One reason for preferring the second of these alternatives is that while the

On 26 May 1944 the city of Chartres was the target of an Allied aerial bombardment which destroyed the Bibliothèque Municipale and with it the six folios that had been detached from our manuscript and brought to Chartres from Mount Athos in 1840 by Paul Durand, the librarian and director of the local museum. Given the capital importance of our manuscript, the loss of so considerable a fragment was indeed a calamity, the more so since it had been due to this very fragment that the existence of manuscripts of this type and of a distinct and hitherto unknown variety of the early Byzantine notation first came to the attention of Western scholars. I need scarcely repeat all that I had to say about the Chartres fragment ten years ago in a contribution to the *Annales musicologiques*,[4] nor ought it to be necessary to pay tribute again to Amédée Gastoué, the first to recognize the importance of the fragment,[5] or to Professor Tillyard, the first to identify it as a part of the manuscript at the Laura.[6] In one respect, however, my earlier contribution stands in need of correction. In 1955 it was my impression that there remained no trace of the fragment beyond Gastoué's summary list of its contents, his plate reproducing two pages in facsimile, and a single photograph of a third page, formerly in the possession of the late Professor Masson, reproduced in facsimile by Mme. Palikarova-Verdeil.[7] Providentially it now appears that, through the foresight of Professor Tillyard, we have the whole, for at some time before the First World War, probably in 1912, Tillyard visited Chartres, had photographs made of the six pages that follow Gastoué's plate, and copied the remainder by hand.[8] Thus, apart from

---

manuscript uses two inks, black for the text and red for the musical notation, the text is not provided with the breathings and grammatical accents that make the use of two inks obligatory.

[4] See this volume, pp. 68–111.

[5] *Introduction à la paléographie musicale byzantine* (Paris, 1907), pp. 96–99, also viii, 13, 52, 60, 65, and pl. iii.

[6] On p. 96 of the article cited in n. 2 above.

[7] *La musique byzantine chez les Bulgares et les Russes* (Copenhagen), p. 113, pl. vii.

[8] I first learned of the existence of the photographs from Professor Tillyard himself at the time of our meeting with Professor Wellesz in Oxford in June 1964, and I am infinitely obliged to Professor Wellesz, among whose materials they were found, for having permitted me to have them duplicated for the University of Copenhagen's Institute for Medieval Greek and Latin. Later in the same year Mr. Jørgen Raasted drew my attention to the hand-written copies, then already in Copenhagen. Professor Tillyard has published the musical notation for one of the melodies of the fragment in his *Hymns of the Pentecostarium* (Copenhagen, 1960), pp.

crediting Professor Tillyard with having been the first to identify the fragment and to publish plausible transcriptions from its notation,[9] we have now to thank him also for having performed a far greater service—for having preserved for us that part of the contents of the fragment not already preserved by Gastoué.

On the basis of Tillyard's photographs and hand-written copies I insert at this point a table of contents more detailed than the one published by Gastoué,[10] specifying for each of the 28 items its folio number according to Durand's foliation (61 to 66). Beginning in the midst of the office for the second Sunday after Easter, these items include also the office for the third Sunday and the greater part of that for the Wednesday of Midpentecost.

1	β	αι μυροφοροι ορθριαι γενομεναι	61
2	β	αι μυροφοροι γυναικες ορθρου βαθεος	61
3*	δ	το φαιδρον κηρυγμα	61 verso
4	πλ β	αι μυροφοροι γυναικες τον ταφον σου καταλαβουσαι	61 verso
5*	πλ β	των μυροφορων την πολλην αθυμιαν	62
6*	πλ β	ως θνητον εν μνηματι εθεντο	62
7*	πλ β	η ασπιλος και παναμωμος γεννη-τρια	62

54–56 (my table of contents, item 22). The editorial board of the Monumenta Musicae Byzantinae hopes one day to publish, as a single facsimile, the several early sources for the Sticherarion preserved at the Laura, and this facsimile, when it appears, will of course include reproductions of Professor Tillyard's photographs and hand-written copies from Chartres.

Not dissimilar has been the fate of the Latin manuscripts of the Chartres library, in so far as these were of music historical interest. Many years ago the text of Codex 130 was copied for Solesmes by Dom Mocquereau, and Codex 47, one of the capital sources for the Graduale Romanum, has been published in facsimile as vol. XI of the Paléographie musicale. The rest owes its partial preservation to M. le Chanoine Yves Delaporte of Chartres, who had the foresight to photograph, before the war, one or more folios from each Latin manuscript with musical notation. In 1958 these photographs were collected and published as vol. XVII of the Paléographie musicale under the title *Fragments des manuscrits de Chartres,* with a commentary by M. Delaporte himself. In response to an inquiry of mine, M. Delaporte has been kind enough to inform me that, to his great regret, he made no photographs from Codex 1754, the bound volume that contained our fragment.

[9] *Journal of Hellenic Studies,* XLI (1921), 46–49; *Byzantinische Zeitschrift,* XLV (1952), 37–42.

[10] Pp. 97–98 of the monograph cited in n. 5 above. Gastoué has inadvertently omitted one incipit (my table of contents, item 26).

εις το δοξα εν υψιστοις

8*	β	συν ταις αλλαις	62 verso
9*	πλ δ	χαρας ευαγγελια	62 verso

τη γ κυριακη απο το πασχα· εις τον
παραλυτον

10	α	ο τη παλαμη τη αχραντω	63
11	α	αταφος νεκρος υπαρχων ο παραλυ-τος	63
12*	δ	ανεβης ιησου ο θεος ημων	63
13	πλ α	επι τη προβατικη κολυμβηθρα	63 verso
14	πλ α	ανεβη ο ιησους εις ιεροσολυμα	64
15*	πλ β	ανηλθες ο ακαταληπτος τη θεοτητι χριστε μου	64

εις το δοξα (εν υψιστοις)

16*	πλ β	κυριε ο θεος μου ο ιασαμενος πασαν νοσον της ανθρωπινης φυσεως	64 verso
17	πλ δ	κυριε τον παραλυτον	64 verso
18	πλ δ	εν τη στοα του σολομωντος	65

τη δ της μεσοπεντηκοστης
εις το κυριε εκεκραξα· στιχηρα

19	πλ δ	μεσουσης της εορτης διδασκοντος σου σωτηρ	65
20	πλ δ	μεσουσης της εορτης προς του παθους	65
21*	πλ δ	η σοφια του θεου	65 verso

εις το δοξα

22	πλ δ	καθαρωμεν εννοιων	65 verso
23	πλ δ	μεσουσης της εορτης του πασχα	66
24*	πλ δ	φωνης κυριου ακουτισθωμεν βοωσης τρανως	66

του στιχου

25*	πλ β	αδελφοι αγαπητοι	66
26	πλ β	της εορτης μεσουσης	66 verso
27*	πλ β	προ του αχραντου σου σταυρου	66 verso
28*	πλ β	σημερον ο διαταξας εορτας ισραηλ	66 verso

Gastoué was entirely correct when he pointed out, so many years ago, that only one-half of the items contained in the fragment were to be found in later sources. The remainder (distinguished by asterisks in my table of contents) are "apocrypha," that is, items excluded from the standard abridged version of

the Sticherarion, put into circulation about the year 1050. Manuscripts in the Coislin and Round (or Middle Byzantine) notations
do not normally contain such pieces, and as one result of this none
of the items in question is included in Professor Tillyard's volume
of transcriptions, *The Hymns of the Pentecostarium*.[11] Every one of
them can be found, however, in at least one other early source,
usually in Laura Γ.72 and in Vatopedi 1488 as well,[12] less often
in Laura Γ.72 alone,[13] exceptionally in Vatopedi 1488 alone.[14]

Even though we have no unambiguous, diastematic sources
for these melodies, it is usually possible to arrive, with patience,
at a plausible and reasonably dependable transcription. One has
only to bring to the task a certain degree of familiarity with the
conventions of Byzantine melody and to learn to think in terms
of whole phrases rather than of single signs. I offer one such
transcription here, choosing for the purposes of my demonstration
the sticheron Ἀδελφοὶ ἀγαπητοί,[15] which begins on the last of
Professor Tillyard's photographs, to be concluded in his hand-
written copy. The piece is found also, with no variants of any
importance, in Laura Γ.72 (folio 74) and Vatopedi 1488 (folio 144
verso).

Ex. 1

[11]Copenhagen, 1960.
[12]Items 5, 7, 15, 16, 24, 25, and 27.
[13]Items 6, 9, 12, 21, and 28.
[14]Items 3 and 8.
[15]I have not followed up the references to an earlier publication of the text in
the periodical Νέα Σιων, given by Enrica Follieri in her *Initia hymnorum ecclesiae
graecae*.

The text to which this little melody has been adapted is indeed exceptional, beginning as it does with two preliminary phrases of the sort regularly used to introduce the reading of lessons and continuing then with two literal quotations from the Gospel according to John. Since the piece belongs to the office for the Wednesday of Midpentecost, one might expect these quotations to have been drawn from the gospel read on that occasion. But this is not the case: the second quotation is from the gospel for the following day, the first from that for the feast of Pentecost itself. In the English of the Authorized Version, the whole would read as follows:

Dearly beloved, thus spake the Lord:
   He that believeth on me, as the scripture hath said, out of his belly shall flow rivers of living water.

                           —John 7:38.

He that followeth me shall not walk in darkness, but shall have the light of life.

                           —John 8:12.

Before setting this text to music, however, the anonymous composer has permitted himself two tiny liberties. In the first quotation he has altered the accepted word-order—ποταμοὶ ἐκ τῆς κοιλίας αὐτοῦ ῥεύσουσιν ὕδατος ζῶντος. And in the second he has modified the authentic reading—ἀλλ' ἕξει τὸ φῶς τῆς ζωῆς—by interpolating the adjective ἀθανάτου (immortal).

Trivial as these changes may seem, they are none the less instructive, for they can be made to tell us a good deal about the kind of consideration that guided the Byzantine poet-composer in the arrangement of his compositions. The first of the two altered clauses is quoted also in three of the idiomela of the standard abridged version—Hymns 35, 36, and 43 in Tillyard's volume of transcriptions—and in each case the word order is the same as in my example. The accepted text cannot readily be divided into balanced antecedent and consequent phrases, and in the lectionaries with ekphonetic notation it is accordingly treated as a single unit—

ποταμοὶ ἐκ τῆς κοιλίας αὐτοῦ ῥεύσουσιν.[16]

Altering the word-order permits a caesura after ῥεύσουσιν, apt for melodic purposes, and a comparison of the relevant clause of my example with the corresponding clauses in Tillyard's volume of transcriptions will reveal unmistakably that the wish to subdivide is what has prompted the change.[17] What is more, the comparison will serve also to confirm my transcription of the clause in question, for it is essentially the same as that found in Tillyard's Hymn 36, based in turn on unambiguous sources of later date.

Ex. 2

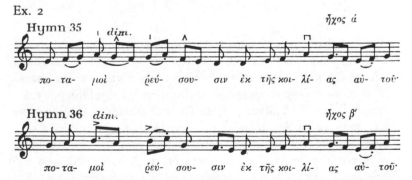

[16]I take the ekphonetic notation from the Evangelion Grottaferrata A.α.x, a manuscript of the eleventh century.

[17]I hope that Professor Tillyard will excuse my having suppressed his b-flats in quoting from Hymns 43 and 44.

In a somewhat different way, the same consideration seems also to have prompted the second change. Here the accepted wording is altogether too short to permit a subdivision and one has only to look at the setting of this wording in Tillyard's Hymn 36 to recognize that, when treated as a single phrase, it brings the melody to too abrupt a conclusion, lacking the weight needed for a final cadence. In my example, on the other hand, and in Tillyard's Hymn 44, the interpolation of the adjective ἀθανάτου permits a caesura after φῶς and a more eloquent and emphatic declamation.

Ex. 3

As we have seen, each of the "apocrypha" contained in the Chartres fragment can be found in at least one other early source. This does not mean, however, that we owe our thanks to Professor Tillyard only for having preserved additional readings for these unfamiliar pieces. The full significance of what he has done for us lies in quite another direction. My table of contents lists fourteen items represented also in the standard abridged version, and six of these (1, 10, 11, 14, 18, and 23) are found with Chartres notation in our fragment alone. For these six pieces the Chartres fragment thus becomes our one genuinely early source, for no Coislin copy of the Triodion-

Pentekostarion antedates the year 1050.[18]

Professor Tillyard was the first scholar to work systematically through the sources of Byzantine chant on Mount Athos and Mount Sinai, on Patmos, in Athens, and in Jerusalem, and he was accordingly the first to see and to describe nearly every one of the manuscripts which stand today in the center of our interests. Through his innumerable publications, above all through his exemplary edition of the *Hymns of the Octoechus,* perhaps the most solid and most useful of them all, he has placed us deeply in his debt. We are now once again indebted to him, perhaps more deeply than ever before, for his providential intervention in photographing and copying by hand the contents of the Chartres fragment while there was still time.

[18]Sinai 1242 (late eleventh century) is perhaps the earliest. Vatopedi 1488 also uses Coislin notation for the pieces in question, reserving the Chartres notation for the "apocrypha" and the idiomela of the Oktoëchos.

BYZANTINE MUSIC
IN THE LIGHT
OF RECENT RESEARCH
AND PUBLICATION †

No one, surveying the research and publication of the last fifteen years in the field of Byzantine music, can fail to recognize that profound and far-reaching changes have taken place. Old problems have in some cases been at least temporarily overshadowed by new ones, while in other cases they have been thrown open to re-examination and reappraisal. Familiar sources have been made more readily accessible than they formerly were, while unfamiliar ones, some of them of capital importance, have been brought to light. Today this branch of musicology is attracting and holding the interest of a small army of able young people, newcomers to the scene, while its development is being followed with closer attention than ever before by musicologists representing other branches of the discipline. For a clear reflection of these various changes, and of some part of the progress that has been made, one has only to compare the two editions of Egon Wellesz's History of Byzantine Music and Hymnography, the first, published in 1949, with 358 pages, the second,

†From Proceedings of the Thirteenth International Congress of Byzantine Studies (London and New York, 1967), pp. 245–254. Reprinted with permission of the British National Committee of the International Association of Byzantine Studies.

¹Among earlier surveys published during the period under consideration, I need mention only H. J. W. Tillyard, "Gegenwärtiger Stand der byzantinischen Musikforschung," Die Musikforschung, VII (1954), 142–149; Egon Wellesz, "The Present State of Studies in Byzantine Chant," in his History of Byzantine Music and Hymnography, 2nd ed. (Oxford, 1961), pp. 23–28; Miloš Velimirović, "Study of Byzantine Music in the West," Balkan Studies, V (1964), 63–76.

published only twelve years later, with 461.[2]

The year 1950 constitutes a sort of turning-point. Not only was it marked by the return of relative stability, political and economic, and of a climate favorable to research, it was also marked by the concurrence of two wholly unrelated developments, each of which played its part in shaping the future course of events. On the one hand, there was the convocation in Rome of an International Congress for Sacred Music, an incidental result of which was the adoption of an amicable working agreement between the Monumenta Musicae Byzantinae in Copenhagen and the Badia greca di Grottaferrata, whose Archimandrite has since served as a member of the Monumenta's Editorial Board.[3] On the other hand, there were the expeditions to Jerusalem and to Mount Sinai, carried out with the co-operation of the Library of Congress in Washington under the auspices of the American Schools of Oriental Research and the American Foundation for the Study of Man; at one stroke, this undertaking placed microfilms of more than 1,750 Greek manuscripts at the disposal of interested scholars, an incalculable boon to Byzantine studies in general and by no means least so to those concerned with Byzantine music.[4]

Also to be traced to the convocation of the congress of 1950 is the spectacular quickening of interest in the melismatic part of the Byzantine repertory. Prior to the turning-point, this whole area, while not unknown, had remained almost uncharted, briefly touched on by Fathers J. D. Petrescu and Lorenzo Tardo in their publications of 1930 and 1938, and treated then in rather more detail by Father Petrescu in a first study of the Christmas konta-

---

[2]See also the review by Constantin Floros in *Die Musikforschung*, XVII (1964), 309–312, which uses this same approach.

[3]Until 1960 the Badia was represented by the Right Reverend Father Isidoro Croce, recently deceased; his successor is the Right Reverend Father Teodoro Minisci, the present Archimandrite.

[4]To the results of these expeditions, briefly summarized by their director, Kenneth W. Clark, in the two check-lists prepared for the Library of Congress in 1952 and 1953, are to be added those of Ernest W. Saunders's more modest expedition to Mount Athos for the Library of Congress in 1953 (*A Descriptive Catalogue of Selected MSS in the Monasteries of Mount Athos* [Washington, 1957]) and those of the Abbé Marcel Richard's periodic missions to Greece for the Institut de recherche et d'histoire des textes, beginning in 1951 and described in a series of reports published in the Institut's *Bulletin d'information*.

kion[5] and by Father P.-A. Laily in a monograph largely devoted to the music of the Alleluia verses.[6] The accident that thrust this previously neglected area into the forefront of scholarly interest was the exhibition during the congress, first at the Biblioteca Vaticana, then at the Badia greca, of the magnificent Psaltikon of the Biblioteca Laurenziana, the MS. Ashburnham 64, written at Grottaferrata in the year 1289. This capital source, immeasurably superior to those consulted by Fathers Petrescu and Laily, immediately attracted the attention of Carsten Høeg and Egon Wellesz. As early as 1953 these two scholars were already presenting the first results of their studies, Høeg in a communication read before the British Academy,[7] Wellesz in a paper published in *Die Musikforschung,*[8] and in 1954, at the Dumbarton Oaks symposium on music and liturgy, Wellesz returned to the subject with a definitive paper on a larger scale—"The 'Akathistos': A Study in Byzantine Hymnography."[9] This first phase of the exploration reached its high point in 1956 and 1957 with the publication of Høeg's sumptuous facsimile of the Ashburnham MS. and Wellesz's critical transcription of the complete Akathistos Hymn, both of these provided with elaborate introductions.[10]

At Grottaferrata, in the meantime, Father Bartolomeo Di Salvo and I had also been surveying this *terra incognita.* What we were seeking was a comprehensive view of the whole, and we began by attempting to deal with the antithesis Psaltikon-Asmatikon, terms once thought to be synonymous, and to discover the reasons for the transmission of the melismatic repertory in two distinct forms and in two distinct yet complementary books. Why was it, we asked ourselves, that certain classes of chant were common to both books, while other classes were peculiar to the one book or to the other? Had either book, at bottom, a standard contents and a standard way of arranging that contents? Was it possible, as at first seemed to be

[5] *Condacul Nasterii Domnului* (Bucharest, 1940).

[6] *Analyse du codex de musique grecque no. 19, Bibliothèque Vaticane (Fonds Borgia)* (Harissa, 1949).

[7] "The Oldest Slavonic Tradition of Byzantine Music," *Proceedings of the British Academy,* XXXIX (1953), 37–66.

[8] "Das Prooemium des Akathistos: Eine Studie zur Melodie der Kontakien," *Die Musikforschung,* VI (1953), 193–206.

[9] *Dumbarton Oaks Papers,* IX–X (1956), 141–174.

[10] Monumenta Musicae Byzantinae, Série principale, 4; Transcripta, 9.

the case, that the two books were preserved only in Italo-Greek copies? How widely had the melodies they contained been in fact disseminated? When and where had they originated and for what liturgical environment had they been intended? By 1955 most of these questions had been at least tentatively answered, and we knew that, while relatively restricted, the number of extant sources was something like three times as great as we had at first supposed.[11]

The pioneer work of the fifties had been largely accomplished by scholars of the older generation. Now was the time for consolidation and for special studies devoted to the single classes of melismatic chant. Since 1960 there have been a number of these, some of them already published, others still in manuscript, all of them the work of younger men. To Constantin Floros we owe a comprehensive study of the kontakion,[12] to Simon Harris an annotated transcription of the koinonika,[13] to Christian Thodberg an exhaustive analysis of the Alleluia verses;[14] Father Mathias Dijker has dealt with the prokeimena,[15] Leonardo Calì with the hypakoai.[16] In other recent studies, melodies belonging to the melismatic repertory have been placed in a larger context. Thus Giovanni Marzi centers his monograph on melody and nomos around an analysis of the Akathistos Hymn,[17] while Kenneth Levy draws on melodies from the Asmatikon in two essays involving comparative methods, one on the Byzantine Sanctus, the other on the Byzantine model for the Ambrosian "Coenae tuae mirabili."[18]

[11]For a preliminary report on these investigations, see pp. 45–54 of this volume. Father Bartolomeo Di Salvo has described the Italo-Greek sources for the Asmatikon in the *Bollettino della Badia greca di Grottaferrata*, XVI (1962), 135–158.

[12]*Das mittelbyzantinische Kontakienrepertoire* (unpublished); see also his contribution to the *Deutsche Vierteljahrsschrift für Literaturwissenschaft und Geistesgeschichte*, XXXIV (1960), 84–106.

[13]*The Communion Chants in the Byzantine Asmatika* (unpublished).

[14]*Der byzantinische Alleluiarionzyklus*, Monumenta Musicae Byzantinae, Subsidia-8 (Copenhagen, 1966); see also his *Tonal System of the Kontakarium: Studies in Byzantine Psaltikon Style*, Det Kongelige Danske Videnskabernes Selskab: Historisk-filosofiske Meddeleser, XXXVII/7 (Copenhagen, 1960).

[15]In a dissertation prepared for the Pontifical Institute of Sacred Music (unpublished.

[16]"Le ipacoè dell'octoichos bizantino," *Bollettino della Badia greca di Grottaferrata*, XIX (1965), 161–174.

[17]*Melodia e nomos nella musica bizantina* (Bologna, 1960).

[18]"The Byzantine Sanctus and Its Modal Tradition in East and West," *Annales*

Perhaps it is not too early to strike a balance. Over the years the gross gains have exceeded the most sanguine predictions, largely because so many of the entries in this column are unexpected dividends. Who could have foreseen, in 1950, that the comparative analysis of melismatic and syllabic chants would prove so effective a means of throwing the essential characteristics of the two style-varieties into sharp relief? Or that the study of the Byzantine Asmatikon would lead in time to a first unraveling of the Paleoslavonic "kondakarion" notation?

Yet on the opposite side of the ledger one has certain losses to record. Naturally enough, the sheer novelty of the melismatic repertory and of the problems it posed seemed at first irresistibly fascinating to those who worked with them. One result, inevitably, has been that the purely musical aspect of melody has been fostered, the study of melody in its relation to poetry neglected. Another result, again inevitable, has been distortion, in that attention has been diverted from the central tradition in order to concentrate it upon one that is special and in the last analysis peripheral.

Any number of questions remain to be answered here and some of them are acutely embarrassing. Why is the number of extant sources so restricted and why is it that the traditions of the Psaltikon and Asmatikon find so little support in manuscripts copied before the adoption of the Middle Byzantine notation?[19] Is it because the melismatic repertory was originally intended for a non-monastic environment? If so, the relative scarcity of sources from within the

---

musicologiques, VI (1958–63), 7–67; "A Hymn for Thursday in Holy Week," *Journal of the American Musicological Society,* XVI (1963), 127–175, with parallel transcriptions of chants found in both the Psaltic and the Asmatic repertories (Exs. 12 and 13).

[19]For the tradition of the Psaltikon I can name only three sources using the Coislin notation: (1) the Euchologion Grottaferrata Γ.β.xxxv, with a single kontakion and oikos, reproduced in facsimile in my *Specimina Notationum Antiquiorum* (Copenhagen, 1966), pls. 33 and 34; (2) the Sticherarion Sinai 1214, with an attempt to add the same melody above a text not originally intended for musical notation, reproduced in facsimile in the same collection, pl. 126; and (3) the Heirmologion Coislin 220, with a marginal entry for the beginning of the first oikos of the Akathistos Hymn, reproduced in facsimile by Egon Wellesz on p. 159 of the study cited in n. 9 above. For the tradition of the Asmatikon no genuinely early sources have been preserved, but from the state of the notation in Paleoslavonic copies of the book one may infer that such must once have existed.

narrower confines of the Empire might be attributed to the sacking
of the great public churches with its attendant destruction of seemingly worthless material objects, first by the Latins, then by the
Turkish conquerors, an explanation that would agree well with the
relative abundance of Italo-Greek copies, which were not exposed
to the same hazards. Or is it because the disfigured remnants from
the two books incorporated in the Koukouzelian "Orders of Service" came in time to supplant the books themselves, making them
less valuable than the parchment they were written on?[20] This
explanation too will seem plausible enough when it is recalled that
the innovations of Koukouzeles and his fellow *maistores* came too
late to have any effect on the musical practice of the Greek-
speaking communities of Sicily and the Italian peninsula. Questions
like these are readily answered, even though the answers may not
wholly satisfy us. But if we are asked to account for the amazingly
poor quality of our extant sources, what shall we say? No one who
has worked intensively with these materials can honestly claim
much for them. Single items may be reasonably well transmitted,
particular modes and particular classes of chant may present fewer
insoluble problems than others, but the overall impression these
sources leave is disquieting, not to say repellent. At best, their
tradition can only be called capricious and untrustworthy. The time
spent on them has been well spent, but I am myself persuaded that
we have already reached the point of diminishing returns.

Turning now from the melismatic to the syllabic part of the
Byzantine musical repertory, it may be said that, while our understanding of the problems posed by the Sticherarion has made notable advances during the past fifteen years,[21] it is on the Heirmologion, which poses problems equally challenging and rather more
elusive, that the attention of recent scholarship has been largely
focused. In 1951 it was Father Lorenzo Tardo's magnificent facsimile of the Heirmologion Grottaferrata E.γ.ii, with its useful index

[20]For the Koukouzelian "Orders of Service," see pp. 165–90 of this volume,
especially pp. 170–74, and the essay by Kenneth Levy cited in n. 18 above, especially 154–171.

[21]I shall limit myself to citing the two volumes of transcriptions published since
1950—Father Lorenzo Tardo's *Ottoeco nei manoscritti melurgici* (Grottaferrata, 1955)
and H. J. W. Tillyard's *Hymns of the Pentecostarium* (Copenhagen, 1960).

of first lines, that marked the return of the Monumenta to active publication after the hiatus of the war years. In 1952 this was followed by Carsten Høeg's transcriptions of the heirmoi of the Protos and Plagios protou, preceded by a masterly introduction in which for the first time the several manuscript traditions for the music of the Heirmologion were critically examined, in which the principal sources as then known were neatly divided into families, and in which a number of fundamental questions bearing on the origin, purpose, and make-up of the Heirmologion were raised and tentatively answered. A further step was the publication in 1956 of H. J. W. Tillyard's transcriptions of the heirmoi of the Barys.

In the meantime our understanding of the book itself has gained in breadth and depth. Once Slavic philology had turned its attention to the Paleoslavonic Heirmologion in its relation to its Greek model—and I think here primarily of the published and unpublished studies of Erwin Koschmieder[22] and Roman Jakobson[23]—Høeg found room within the framework of the Monumenta for a facsimile of the Paleoslavonic Heirmologion Chilandari 308 (1957) and for a study of its contents by Miloš Velimirović (1960). The chance discovery of the intimate and deep-seated relation between a divergent late tradition for a part of the "marginal" contents of the Sticherarion and the equally divergent tradition for the music of the Byzantine Heirmologion transmitted by one of Høeg's branches has placed the manuscripts belonging to this particular branch in an entirely new light.[24] Add to this that, since 1950, our control of the sources for the music of the Heirmologion has grown in assurance and in coverage. Thanks to the missions of the Library of Congress and of the Abbé Richard, we now have microfilms of Sinai 1256 and 1258 and of Patmos 55 and Esphigmenou 54, to mention only the more important sources not avail-

---

[22] *Die ältesten Novgoroder Hirmologien-Fragmente*, Bayerische Akademie der Wissenschaften. Philosophisch-historische Klasse. Abhandlungen. Neue Folge, Hefte 33, 37, 45 (Munich, 1952–58); see also Høeg, "Ein Buch altrussischer Kirchengesänge," *Zeitschrift für slavische Philologie*, XXV (1956), 261–284.

[23] Jakobson's interest in the problem dates from 1917, but his principal contribution to it has still to appear. For recent summaries of his views, see his contributions to the *Actes du XIIᵉ Congrès international d'études byzantines*, I (Belgrade, 1963), 249–267, to the *Mélanges G. Ostrogorsky*, I (1963), 153–166, and the *Sborník Prací Filosofické Fakulty Brněnské University*, F 9 (1965), pp. 115–121.

[24] See pp. 194–201 of this volume.

able in 1952, and in the light of these significant gains we can recognize today that Høeg's introduction, masterly though it is, already stands in need of some revision. With Patmos 55 and Esphigmenou 54 at hand, we can see that Høeg's treatment of the earliest sources was one-sided and incomplete. Knowing that Grottaferrata E.γ.iii belongs to the branch represented by Coislin 220, as Høeg suspected, and that in Patmos 54 we have still another member of the same family, we can attach even more importance to this central tradition than Høeg dared to claim for it. Finally, we have learned that the divergent late tradition to which reference has already been made is far more likely to have stemmed from Sinai 1256 than from Saba 599, the manuscript which Høeg found himself obliged to consider its most characteristic representative, and this amounts to saying that it is far more likely to have originated on Mount Athos than in the Holy Land.

I have elected to deal at some length with the problem of the Heirmologion, for it is precisely in this area that the musicologist and the philologist must work hand in hand. The Heirmologion, as Høeg succinctly put it in 1952, is only an auxiliary book, of no value to the singer unless he has access at the same time to a collection of canon texts.[25] Rightly understood, this means that we cannot isolate the development of the Heirmologion either from the development of the canon or from that of the office-books— the Menaia, Triodion, Pentekostarion, and Parakletike. The development that interests us as musicologists is simply a reflection— more accurately, perhaps, a distant echo—of developments that are the proper concern of Byzantine hymnography.[26] Consider, for example, the effect of the Studite revision of the Triodion and Pentekostarion on the make-up of the Heirmologion.[27] Or con-

---

[25] *The Hymns of the Hirmologium*, Pt. I (Copenhagen, 1952), p. xvii.

[26] In contrast, the Sticherarion, not being an auxiliary book, develops independently. By the middle of the eleventh century its contents have been settled once and for all, and in principle they remain unaltered until the book itself passes out of use. It is for the same reason that the melodic tradition of the Sticherarion is extraordinarily stable, while that of the Heirmologion rapidly deteriorates.

[27] The Triodia added to the Pentekostarion by the brothers Joseph and Theodore are no longer in use, but they cannot have failed to leave their mark on earlier copies of the Heirmologion. For their texts, see Vitali's edition of the Pentekostarion σὺν τοῖς Τριῳδίοις μετὰ τὸ Ἀντιπάσχα (Rome, 1738), additional pages α'–ρβ'.

sider, to take another example, the effect—even more decisive, perhaps—of the ever-increasing popularity of the canons of Joseph the Hymnographer and Theophanes Graptos, which tended more and more to supplant the canons of such older poets as Andrew of Crete and the Patriarch Germanos and, in supplanting them, to render obsolete the heirmoi on which they were based. I have repeatedly expressed the opinion that these were the principal factors that brought about the gradual changes in the content and arrangement of the Heirmologion that one encounters in progressing from tenth-and eleventh-century copies to those of the twelfth and thirteenth centuries, and from these to still later ones, and that they are largely responsible also for the gradual reduction of its bulk.[28] I believe this to be true, but without the help of my friends among the students of hymnography I cannot prove it so.

After reminding his readers that the Heirmologion is only an auxiliary book, Høeg went on to define its contents as consisting of "canons" that are in reality not canons.[29] The quotation marks are his. True—they are ἀκολουθίαι, sets or sequences of heirmoi, and ἀκολουθία is indeed the designation regularly used in the earlier and more authoritative copies. Κανών, on the other hand, is the designation used in the office-books, where one finds it in the headings or titles of longer poems based on sets or sequences of this kind. Now it is one thing to find in an office-book a heading setting forth that a particular canon has been written for a particular use by a particular poet, and quite another thing to find such a heading prefixed to a set or sequence of heirmoi in a Heirmologion. In the latter case we may understand it, surely, as meaning that the set or sequence of heirmoi to which it is prefixed has been chosen by a particular poet as the basis for a canon for a particular use. It need not mean that the poet in question is also the author of the texts of the heirmoi and the composer of the melodies to which they are sung, and I am persuaded that it is seldom to be so understood.[30] To admit this is to admit also that, as a general rule,

[28]See pp. 221–22 of this volume.
[29]See n. 25 above.
[30]Obvious exceptions are heirmoi essential to the acrostics of the canons based on them, for example the heirmoi of the iambic canons and those of certain canons by Cosmas, also the heirmoi of those sets or sequences that have a direct bearing on the commemoration mentioned in the heading, for example the heirmoi of the Easter canon.

the texts of our heirmoi are of uncertain authorship and hence of uncertain date, that the same is true of their melodies, and that we have no real way of knowing whether any of our sets or sequences are made up of heirmoi originally designed to follow one another. That these are radical conclusions I readily concede.[31] At the same time they seem to me inescapable. How else shall we account for the innumerable duplications and cross-references within the single sources for the Heirmologion, for the frequency with which the text of a heirmos wanders from one mode to another, or for those headings that specify a particular use to which the texts of the hirmoi that follow stand in no intelligible relation?

In the last analysis, the preceding paragraphs stem from two perceptive observations of Carsten Høeg. Using these as points of departure, I have endeavored to reach the ultimate conclusions to which they point. I shall hope that Professor Schirò will touch on these conclusions in his supplementary report. Yet I should be indeed ungrateful if I were to ask here for his collaboration without first thanking him, in the name of all those concerned with Byzantine music, for the substantial help he has already given us, above all for his intensely stimulating contribution to the proceedings of the Cretan congress of 1961—"Caratteristiche dei canoni di Andrea Cretese." And by the same token I have also to pay tribute to Enrica Follieri, whose invaluable *Initia Hymnorum Ecclesiae Graecae* enables us not only to distinguish readily between the heirmoi that are actually printed in the various editions of the office-books and those that have long since passed out of use, but also to determine, among the heirmoi of the first of these two classes, the precise degree of frequency with which a given heirmos has been used as a model.

In an earlier reference to essays by Kenneth Levy making use of comparative methods I have already touched in passing on another set of problems whose definitive solution will require considerable inter-disciplinary teamwork.[32] At first a special branch of liturgics, the comparative study of the Eastern and Western rites soon began to attract the attention of musicology also, and in recent years this

---

[31]Father Bartolomeo Di Salvo has arrived independently at somewhat similar conclusions and has published an account of them in *Orientalia Christiana Periodica,* XXXII (1966), 271–275.

[32]See n.18 above.

kind of study, which touches on and overflows into so many other kinds, has become a central concern for all those working in the area of early Christian music. Particularly since the publication in 1936 of the Beneventan Gradual edited for the *Paléographie musicale* by Dom Hesbert, of Egon Wellesz's *Eastern Elements in Western Chant* (1947), and of Dom Brou's "Chants en langue grecque dans les liturgies latines" (1948, with a first supplement in 1952),[33] it has called forth a whole series of larger and smaller studies, some of them written from the viewpoint of the West, others from that of the East, still others contributed by scholars who have taken the whole domain of medieval music as their province;[34] some of them dealing with common traits, others with origins and influences, still others constituting first attempts at broad syntheses. Symptomatic, surely, was the program of the Eleventh International Congress (Munich, 1958), which devoted an entire session to the topic "Byzantinisches in der karolingischen Musik," with reports by Jammers, Schlötterer, Schmid, and Waeltner.

At the time, it was said of this topic that its comprehensive formulation precluded treatment by a single writer; as Schlötterer observed, it embraced a complex of distinct problems, often reaching out beyond the boundaries musicology has set for itself.[35] True, even though the topic being considered was only a part of the whole. Given the present state of the research, no single individual is likely to be equally competent in all the areas into which this complex of problems overflows. The student of Eastern chant will not find it easy to identify the appropriate Western parallels or to comprehend them fully, while the student of Western chant will encounter similar difficulties in attempting to deal with Eastern phenomena. Both may lack the requisite familiarity with comparative liturgics. Only too obviously, they will need each other's help, and the help of experts in comparative liturgical history, if they are to avoid the ever-present dangers of *parti pris* in approaching the

---

[33] *Sacris Erudiri*, I (1948), 165–180; IV (1952), 226–238.

[34] I think here not only of the late Jacques Handschin and his significant study "Sur quelques tropaires grecs traduits en latin," *Annales musicologiques*, II (1954), 27–60, but also of Heinrich Husmann, whose little essay for the Gurlitt Festschrift, "Sinn und Wesen der Tropen," *Archiv für Musikwissenschaft*, XVI (1959), 135–147, deals in a highly original way with the related concepts Tropus and Troparion.

[35] "Eine Frage . . . die ein Komplex verschiedener, den Bereich der Musikforschung oft überschreitender Probleme ist."

perennial problems of "origins" and "influences" and of dilettantism in the construction of grandiose syntheses. Fortunately for everyone concerned, students of Latin chant have always been generous about placing their special knowledge at the disposal of their colleagues among the Byzantinists, while help from this quarter is more readily available today than it used to be.

Among the several partial problems of which this complex whole consists, some continue to confront us while others have still to be examined for the first time. Despite Thibaut's *Origine byzantine* (1907), despite Peter Wagner's valiant attempts in the second edition of his *Neumenkunde* (1912), even despite the recent contribution of Ewald Jammers to the report of the Munich congress (1958), we know no more about the relation of the Western neumes to the Eastern than we did sixty years ago, unless it is that the problem is more complicated than was at first supposed. As to the relation of the Western systems of psalmodic recitation to those of the East, any attempt to deal with this fundamental question today would be premature—the study of Byzantine psalmody has only just begun,[36] and we know very little about the psalmodic practices of the Ambrosian and Mozarabic rites.

In one area there has been real progress. While we have known for years that certain texts found in the choir-books of the Latin rites were literal translations of poems by Byzantine hymnographers, it is only recently that we have begun to realize how numerous these are and how frequent also are the cases in which a Greek original may be at least suspected. In the meantime, after concerning themselves at first with textual parallels only, those working in this area have begun to ask whether in some instances the translated Greek text may not have carried its Greek melody with it.

Today it is as a rule relatively easy to place the Latin and Greek melodies side by side. The delicate task is to interpret the confrontation, giving due weight to dissimilarities as well as to similarities and resisting the strong and ever-present temptation to rest a foregone conclusion on evidence too weak to support it. A vaguely discernible resemblance is not enough; one needs also to deter-

[36]See Egon Wellesz, *A History of Byzantine Music and Hymnography*, 2nd ed., pp. 341–348, or my "Antiphons of the Oktoechos," pp. 165–90 of this volume.

mine whether the details of the melodic constructions agree,
whether the syllables chosen for melismatic development correspond, whether the Latin melody may not in fact be related more
closely to other Latin melodies belonging to the same rite than to
its presumed Byzantine model. One has also to ask oneself what the
circumstances surrounding the presumed transmission are likely to
have been. The decisive factors are time and place. Were the Latins
who sought to take over the Greek melody capable of writing it
down at once or were they obliged to rely for years upon their
memory of it? Was their environment such as to permit their having heard the melody repeatedly, or is it more probable that they
can only have heard it once or twice? To gauge the effects of factors
like these on melodic transmission, one has only to contrast the two
best-known and best-authenticated examples—"O quando in
cruce" and the antiphons of the group "Veterem hominem." On
the one hand the late-ninth or early-tenth century, on the other the
year 802; on the one hand the Byzantine protectorate of Benevento, on the other Aachen and the court of Charlemagne. And on
the one hand an exceptionally faithful copy of the Byzantine model,
on the other copies so unlike their models that one would hesitate
to accept them as copies if their transmission were not so well
documented.[37]

What we have learned about such phenomena in recent years we
owe in large measure to M. Michel Huglo, whose first contributions to the comparative study of Eastern and Western chant—"La
mélodie grecque du 'Gloria in excelsis' et son utilisation dans le
Gloria XIV"[38] and "La tradition occidentale des mélodies byzantines du Sanctus"[39]—were published in 1950, the year with which
I have elected to begin this survey. Equally at home in the chants
of the Roman, Ambrosian, and Mozarabic rites, M. Huglo has
undertaken to supplement this part of my report by bringing Dom
Brou's list of parallels up to date, making it at the same time more

[37]For the transmission of "O quando in cruce," the date "late ninth or early
tenth century," first proposed in my contribution to the *Mélanges G. Ostrogorsky* (p.
217 of this volume), seems to me distinctly more plausible than "not much later
than the year 800," the date I suggested in 1961 (p. 194 of this volume).

[38]*Revue grégorienne*, XXIX (1950), 30–40.

[39]In *Der kultische Gesang der abendländischen Kirche, . . . aus Anlass des 75. Geburts-
tages von Dominicus Johner* (Cologne, 1950), pp. 40–46.

useful by considering the single items, wherever possible, in terms of music. In so doing, he will be performing a signal service for us all.

In order to lend to this survey of mine some semblance of shape and continuity, in order also to keep it within the prescribed limits, I have had to abandon any thought of making it all-inclusive. Recent research or publication that has fallen outside the areas on which I have chosen to concentrate has had to go unnoticed. Two topics that have assumed new importance since 1950 I could safely leave untouched: the contribution of Byzantine chant to the music of the Slavic world is fully covered by Professor Velimirović in another report, while the problems posed by the earlier Byzantine notations, to which Professor Tillyard and Father Bartolomeo Di Salvo have given so much time and thought in recent years, are restated and re-examined in my own *Specimina Notationum Antiquiorum,* published only a few months ago. Even so, the plan adopted has obliged me to make many sacrifices. It has prevented my referring, even in passing, to Lukas Richter's study of the classical elements in Byzantine musical theory[40] or to Gábor Dévai's two papers on the celebrated "Lehrgedicht" of Joannes Koukouzeles.[41] I should have liked also to have had something to say about the recent contributions of my young Danish colleagues Gudrun Engberg[42] and Jørgen Raasted,[43] and to have thanked them, and with them Professor Günther Zuntz, for their steady, self-sacrificing application to the work on the critical edition of the lectionaries with ekphonetic notation, a monumental undertaking conceived and initiated almost thirty years ago by Carsten Høeg. To have considered the special problems that arise in cataloguing without considering them at length would have served no useful purpose, and I have accordingly omitted all reference to the catalogue of the manuscripts of Byzantine music in the Bodleian Library, compiled in 1963 by Nigel Wilson and Dimitrije Stefanović, or to the analo-

[40] *Deutsches Jahrbuch der Musikwissenschaft für 1961*, VI (1962), 75–115.

[41] *Acta Antiqua Academiae Scientiarum Hungaricae,* III (1955), 151–179; VI (1958), 213–235.

[42] "Les Credos du Synodicon," *Classica et Mediaevalia,* XXIII (1962), 293–301.

[43] I shall limit myself to citing the most recent: *Intonation Formulas and Modal Signatures in Byzantine Musical MSS,* Monumenta Musicae Byzantinae, Subsidia 7 (Copenhagen, 1966).

gous catalogues for Mount Sinai, Grottaferrata, and Messina being prepared by the Monumenta for the Répertoire international des sources musicales. Yet it may be helpful if I at least enumerate a few of the more pressing problems that have still to be explored —the problem of the interplay of oral and written tradition, under which I include such special questions as the stichera automela, the stichera "apocrypha," and the unwritten part of the repertory; the problem of establishing a definitive text where the presence of hundreds of sources obliges us to establish and agree upon some rational basis for selection; and the problem of the later development of Byzantine and Metabyzantine chant, beginning with the kalophonic repertory and proceeding step by step to the repertory in actual use today, for what often appears to us to have been an outright break in the tradition may conceivably prove in the end to have been nothing more than the result of a gradual process of transformation.

P. LORENZO TARDO AND HIS
OTTOECO NEI MSS. MELURGICI

Some Observations on the Stichera Dogmatika†

O N reading the name of Lorenzo Tardo, Jeromonaco di Grottaferrata and founder of the Scuola Melurgica of the Badia
greca, one thinks involuntarily of his role as pioneer in the practical
revival of medieval Byzantine chant and of his enormously useful
publications—his *Antica melurgia bizantina* (1938), his *Hirmologium
Cryptense* (1950), and his series of studies on the manuscripts of
Byzantine music in Italian libraries. Students who have worked in
the library at Grottaferrata will think of him gratefully as the man
who assembled the extensive collection of mounted photographs
in bound volumes that permits ready access to important sources
housed elsewhere;[1] many such students are indebted to him also
for helpful counsel gladly given.[2] Perhaps the last thing that will
come to mind is his edition of the Oktoechos,[3] for by the time this

---

†Italian translation published in *Bollettino della Badia greca di Grottaferrata*, XXI
(1967), 21–34. Reprinted with permission of the publisher.

[1] This runs today to fifty-four volumes, with complete reproductions of twenty-
nine manuscripts from Florence, Jerusalem, Messina, Milan, Naples, Padua, Paris,
Rome, Udine, Venice, and Verona.

[2] In 1953, knowing of my interest in locating copies of the Psaltikon in the
libraries of Greece and the Near East, Father Lorenzo drew my attention to the
Psaltikon Patmos 221, incorrectly described as a Sticherarion in the published
catalogue of the library's manuscripts, and generously allowed me to copy his own
notes on it, made at the time of his visit to Patmos in 1934. As a direct result of
this incident, the Patmos Psaltikon has been repeatedly studied in recent years.

[3] *L'Ottoeco nei mss. melurgici: Testo semiografico bizantino con traduzione sul penta-
gramma* (Grottaferrata, 1955); see also G. Schirò in *Bollettino della Badia greca*, XIII
(1959), 165.

appeared, the earlier and in some respects more practical edition by Professor H. J. W. Tillyard[4] was already so solidly established and so widely diffused that scholars tended to think of its younger competitor as a mere duplication.

The fact is, however, that the two editions, although nominally editions of a single text, are at the same time a good deal more than this. Father Lorenzo's introduction, first published in substantially the same form in the volumes of the *Bollettino* for 1947 and 1948, goes far beyond Tillyard's in depth and in detail. And if Father Lorenzo elects not to include the Stichera Heothina or the cycle of Staurotheotokia, both of them conveniently accessible in Tillyard's second volume, he compensates for this by transcribing the complete cycle of Anastasima, of which Tillyard gives only a part. Both editors include representative Dogmatika—Tillyard thirty-two, Father Lorenzo eight—but here again the two editions supplement one another in the most useful way, for they have only one piece in common.

In my *rapport complémentaire* for the congress in Ohrida,[5] comparing the versions of the Anastasima published in the two editions— Tillyard's based on the "Codex Peribleptus," Father Lorenzo's on manuscripts in Naples and Milan—I drew attention to the extraordinary variety of the written tradition for these pieces, observing that for whole phrases at a time, often for several consecutive phrases, the two editors were simply not transcribing the same melody. Recalling that the written tradition for the Anastasima began only in the fourteenth century, I concluded that in earlier times their melodies had been transmitted orally and that the scribes who first sought to write them down had worked independently at various times and in various places. Thus the written tradition, when it finally appeared, was in fact a collection of distinct yet cognate traditions, and it seemed probable that while no one of these contained the whole truth, each contained at least a part of it. Evident, too, was the tendency of certain of these traditions to modernize and to simplify by accommodating themselves to the new melodic idiom introduced about the year 1300 by the

---

[4] *The Hymns of the Octoechus,* Pts. I and II, *Monumenta Musicae Byzantinae,* Transcripta 3 and 4 (Copenhagen, 1940–49).

[5] See pp. 194–201 of this volume.

Heirmologion of Joannes Koukouzeles. I suggested, finally, that what was true of the Anastasima was also true of the "marginal" contents of the Sticherarion as a whole. I aim in this study to show that it is true of at least one other part of that "marginal" contents—the Stichera Dogmatika, or "Marian antiphons," as one might call them, hymns to Our Lady designed to be sung at Vespers and at the Orthros in association with the doxology following the ordinary psalms, the processional stichera, or the aposticha.

As Father Lorenzo more than once reminds us, copies of the Sticherarion differ widely in their treatment of the Stichera Dogmatika.[6] Some copies omit them entirely. Others arrange them by the modes and add them to the Oktoechos as a sort of appendix, the extent of which will vary from copy to copy and, within the single copies, from mode to mode.[7] Still others, in addition to such an appendix, interpolate a specific Dogmatikon for each mode within the main corpus of the Oktoechos, placing it in each mode after the final Anatolikon of the Saturday Vespers.[8] In principle, no two copies contain exactly the same pieces in exactly the same order. Each scribe has made his own selection. Some pieces are frequently found, others infrequently or not at all. Unlike the Anastasima, whose written tradition was nonexistent until relatively late, the Dogmatika can in most cases be traced to our earliest sources—indeed, the Triodion Laura Γ.67, the earliest and richest of them all, contains within its Oktoechos as many as ninety-four.[9] Yet this written tradition, seldom unbroken, is at best erratic, and we have every reason to expect that on examination it, too, will prove full of variety and contradiction.

[6]As cited in n. 3 above, pp. xi, xvii, xxix.

[7]When a Sticherarion includes an appendix of Dogmatika, this appendix will inevitably be one of its last sections if not the last of all, and many copies have lost one or more of their last gatherings. It is thus impossible to estimate at all accurately the relative frequency of copies with and without such an appendix. A cautious estimate, based solely on Paleobyzantine copies, indicates that the number of copies omitting the Dogmatika is roughly equal to the number including them, with copies defective at the end constituting about one third of the whole.

[8]So far as my own observations go, this type of arrangement appears to be confined to manuscripts that provide the Stichera Anastasima with musical notation.

[9]I include in this total all Theotokia contained within the Oktoechos, regardless of designation.

I take as my principal example the Ordinary Dogmatikon of the Protos, Τὴν παγκόσμιον δόξαν, the one melody transcribed by both editors, Tillyard after Athens 974, Father Lorenzo after Milan, Ambrosiana gr. 44; and to provide myself with a basis of comparison, also as a convenience to the reader,

Example 1

Vaticanus gr. 1562

I insert at this point an independent transcription of a third version, after the MS Vaticanus gr. 1562, a full Oktoechos compiled at the Badia greca di Grottaferrata by the Deacon Niphon in the year 1318.[10] Without a single variant, the same version is found also in a little fragment still preserved at the Badia, the MS E.α.xii.

For the first four lines the three transcriptions are identical, or substantially identical, but with line 5 (my numbering) Ambrosiana gr. 44 strikes out on a path of its own.

Example 2

From this point on, while for the most part in general agreement save for frequent transpositions to the fifth above or below, the versions of the Athens and Milan manuscripts are at times in open contradiction—three lines (7, 11, and 15) are totally different, two others (10 and 14) drastically altered. The Grottaferrata version lies somewhat closer to Athens than to Milan, but from line 6 to the concluding exhortation (lines 18 to 21) it cannot be said to agree at all well with either.

If one accepts the premise that the text-critical value of a source in Middle Byzantine notation is directly proportionate to the fidelity with which it transmits the readings of the Coislin archetype, one will not hesitate to give the preference to the version of the Athens manuscript, although even here the transmission falls short of the ideal.[11] The Milan version includes rather more that

---

[10]Antonio Rocchi, *De Coenobio Cryptoferratensi* (Tuscolo, 1893), pp. 67, 280; Lorenzo Tardo, "I Codici melurgici della Vaticana," *Archivio storico per la Calabria e la Lucania*, I (1931), 244; Ciro Giannelli, *Codices Vaticani graeci (1485–1683)* (Vatican City, 1950), pp. 153–155; Alexander Turyn, *Codices graeci Vaticani saeculis XIII et XIV scripti annorumque notis instructi* (Vatican City, 1964), pp. 114–115, pl. 93–94; M. G. Malatesta Zilembo, "Gli Amanuensi di Grottaferrata," *Bollettino della Badia greca*, XIX (1965), 156–157.

[11]For the Coislin readings I have consulted Sinai 1241, Grottaferrata E.γ. iii,

is spurious, while that from Grottaferrata fails even to reproduce the parallel structure called for by the poem, which develops, in lines 10–13 and 14–17, the argument begun in lines 8–9. It is noteworthy, however, that the opening and closing sections of the melody are more or less faithfully reproduced in all three versions. Where there has been reliance upon memory, as there has been here,[12] the beginning and end of a melody will be remembered longer and more accurately than what lies between, and in this particular case the beginning of the melody is made doubly memorable by the striking correspondence of its structure to the logical and metrical structure of the poem:

$$
\begin{array}{lllllll}
\text{T}\grave{\eta}\nu & \pi\alpha\gamma\text{-} & \kappa\acute{o}\text{-} & \sigma\mu\iota\text{-} & o\nu & \delta\acute{o}\text{-} & \xi\alpha\nu, \\
\tau\grave{\eta}\nu \ \ \grave{\epsilon}\xi & \grave{\alpha}\nu\text{-} & \theta\rho\acute{\omega}\text{-} & \pi\omega\nu & \sigma\pi\alpha\text{-} & \rho\epsilon\hat{\iota}\text{-} & \sigma\alpha\nu \\
\kappa\alpha\grave{\iota} \ \ \tau\grave{o}\nu \ \ \delta\epsilon\text{-} & \sigma\pi\acute{o}\text{-} & \tau\eta\nu & \tau\epsilon\text{-} & \kappa\hat{o}\hat{\upsilon}\text{-} & \sigma\alpha\nu, \\
\tau\grave{\eta}\nu \ \ \grave{\epsilon}\text{-} & \pi\text{ov-} & \rho\acute{\alpha}\text{-} & \nu\iota\text{-} & o\nu & \pi\acute{\upsilon}\text{-} & \lambda\eta\nu. \\
\end{array}
$$

On widening the scope of the inquiry, drawing on a considerable number of additional sources, it becomes evident that the versions of the Athens and Milan manuscripts prefigure the two principal forms of the tradition. It was with line 5 that these versions parted company. Agreeing with Athens in line 5, and tending to agree with Athens in all that follows, are Coislin 42, Jerusalem (Panagiou Taphou) 528, and Sinai 1471. Characteristic of this form of the tradition, the more conservative of the two, is its tendency to remain in the lower and middle registers, with occasional cadences on the lower finalis. Agreeing with Milan in line 5, and tending to agree with Milan in all that follows, are the "Codex Peribleptus"[13] and Sinai 1220, 1228, and 1230. Characteristic of this form of the

---

and Coislin 220, sources that are in full agreement on all essential points; for the validity of the concept "Coislin archetype" where the "marginal" contents of the Sticherarion is concerned, see p. 167 below.

[12]That the Stichera Dogmatika are often omitted entirely has already been noted, and the specific example in which we are interested is sometimes represented by its first lines only, as in Sinai 1231 and Coislin 41. In the MS Messina, S. Salvatore 51, a full Oktoechos with Coislin notation for the Anatolika, Anabathmoi, and Heothina, the eight Dogmatika of the Saturday Vespers, like the Anastasima, are without notation.

[13]For this manuscript see the full description by Dimitrije Stefanović in *Mélanges Georges Ostrogorsky,* II (Belgrade, 1964), 393–398.

tradition, the less conservative of the two, is its predilection for the upper register—like Milan, none of these sources even touches the lower finalis.

At the same time, the version adopted for line 5 is not invariably decisive—Ambrosiana gr. 733 and Sinai 1224 agree here with Athens, Naples II.C.17 and Vatopedi 1499 with Milan, but for the rest these four sources tend to agree now with the one version, now with the other; they are perhaps best classed as transitional, particularly since the version of the Vatopedi manuscript, dated "1292," foreshadows to some extent the tradition represented by Tardo's source ("1342"), Sinai 1230 ("1365"), and the "Codex Peribleptus" ("1447").[14] The version of Grottaferrata is clearly an arbitrary one, for it finds no real support in any of the manuscripts consulted.

Commenting on the version of the Athens manuscript, Tillyard has this to say: "The neumes are clear, but the hymn is not free from difficulties, as Lines 17 to 21 seem to be a fifth too low."[15] Comparison with the readings of the three sources most closely related bears out the correctness of this observation, although it also shows that the trouble lies rather earlier. My example compares the treatment of lines 12 and 13 in the Athens manuscript with their treatment in Coislin 42.

Example 3

By closing line 13 with the upper finalis, rather than with the lower, Coislin 42 preserves the parallel construction already referred to, bringing lines 10–13 and 14–17 at the same level, with lines 13 and 17 acting as half and full cadences. The Athens manuscript, on the other hand, by closing line 13 with the lower finalis, destroys the correspondence of lines 13 and 17, bringing

[14]For the date of the "Codex Peribleptus," see p. 201, n. 10, of this volume.
[15]As cited in n. 4 above, II, 112.

the entire consequent a fifth below the antecedent. Jerusalem
(Panagiou Taphou) 528 and Sinai 1471 offer a somewhat different solution.

Example 4

The Milan version is instructive in its own way. Commenting in
my paper for the congress in Ochrida on its versions of the Stichera
Anastasima, I described them as related to those in Sinai 1230,
observing further that, of all traditions for the Anastasima, theirs
was the one most deeply involved in relationships with the Heirmologion of Koukouzeles.[16] All this is equally true of their versions of our Dogmatikon. My example from line 9 compares the
readings of the Athens manuscript and its close relatives with those
of the Milan manuscript and Sinai 1230.

Example 5

The melodic formula just illustrated, a familiar commonplace,
occurs over and over again in heirmoi of the Protos—for instance,
in one of the refrains of the Christmas canon by Cosmas. Comparing the reading of the Iviron Heirmologion for this refrain[17] with
that of the Heirmologion of Koukouzeles one finds that, as in the
preceding example, a kratema has been replaced by a tromikon

---

[16]See p. 197, of this volume.
[17]Carsten Høeg, *The Hymns of the Hirmologium,* pt. I (Copenhagen, 1952),
p. 66.

group. And as though this were not sufficiently conclusive, the tromikon group is followed, as it was in the preceding example, by a stressed descent. Velimirović has published the passage in context, with a wealth of comparative material, in the appendix volume of his *Byzantine Elements in Early Slavic Chant.*[18]

Example 6

In his edition of the Oktoechos, to demonstrate the stability of the written tradition for the Sticherarion, Father Lorenzo offers two instructive examples.[19] One of these is a multiple transcription of the opening line of the first Anatolikon of the Protos, the other—in the same mode—a similar transcription of the first Alphabetikon in its entirety, the number of sources consulted being in the one case twenty, in the other sixteen. The two examples are provided with perceptive commentaries and, after having invited his readers to observe the "quasi assoluta identità melodica, ritmica e grafica in tutti i mss.,"[20] Father Lorenzo sums up as follows:

> Tutti i testi melurgici da qualsiasi *scriptorium* provengano, sia dell' Oriente propriamente detto che della Magna Grecia Bizantina, nel passaggio dalla semiografia paleobizantina a quella successiva neobizantina, riportano le stesse melodie, con gli stessi segni di chironomia e con gli stessi gruppi melodici, benchè espressi con forme lievemente differenti.[21]

As we have seen, and as Father Lorenzo himself is quick to point out,[22] this conclusion is not universally applicable. Far from exhib-

---

[18](Copenhagen, 1960), p. lxiv. Velimirović does not include the readings of the Trinity College Heirmologion, for which see H. J. W. Tillyard, *Twenty Canons* (Boston, 1952), pp. 11 and 118; line 6 ought probably to be emended on the basis of my example. For the use of the petaste in descent, characteristic of the Koukouzeles Heirmologion and its relatives, see Høeg, as cited in n. 17 above, p. xxxvii.

[19]As cited in n. 3 above, pp. xxxiii–lv.

[20]*Ibid.,* p. liii.

[21]*Ibid.,* p. liv.

[22]*Ibid.,* p. lv.

iting the "quasi assoluta identità" of which Father Lorenzo speaks, our sources for the Dogmatika, like those for the Anastasima, are —as expected—full of variety and contradiction.[23]

What are the causes of this phenomenon? I have already suggested two. They are related causes, so interdependent, so tightly bound together, as to be almost inseparable. The more reliance there is on memory, the less apparent the need for written transmission. And where written transmission is sporadic, particularly in its early stages, it leaves little or no impression, and reliance upon memory becomes in effect inevitable. Among contributory causes one has above all to weigh the possibility that the variety and contradiction characteristic of the end of the tradition may actually have been present from the beginning. In isolated instances, they undoubtedly were.

Some part of what lies below the surface here can readily be brought to light. One of our capital sources for the music of the Heirmologion, the MS Grottaferrata E.γ.iii, includes in moderately developed Coislin notation a cycle of Dogmatika that must originally have consisted of something like sixty-four items.[24] The ending of this cycle has been lost, but there are two additional folios with the remains of a second cycle, evidently copied from another Vorlage. Two of the items of which this consists are repetitions of items already copied—Πύλας μὲν παρθενίας is found both on folio 329 and folio 312. Χαίροις

[23]N. D. Uspenskii has published Slavonic versions of Τὴν παγκόσμιον δόξαν in facsimile in his Древнерусское Певческое Искусство (Moscow, 1965), pl. xviii and xix, after Leningrad, Public Library, Q. I. nos. 94 and 95, manuscripts of the fifteenth and sixteenth centuries; see also the commentary and analysis, pp. 84–94. For the later history of the piece, see Dimitrije Stefanović in Actes du XIIᵉ congrès international d'études byzantines, I (Belgrade, 1963), 375–384, especially 378–381, and in Studies in Eastern Chant, I (Oxford, 1966), 71–88. As Stefanović notes, the present-day Serbian melody has been published by S. S. Mokranjac in his Osmoglasnik (Belgrade, 1908), pp. 6–7. Still another version will soon be available in P. Bartolomeo Di Salvo's Canti ecclesiastici della tradizione italo-albanese, I, in the course of publication by the Monumenta Musicae Byzantinae.

[24]The same cycle, no longer intact, but with a number of additions at the end of each mode, is found also in the Heirmologion at the Bibliothèque Nationale (Coislin 220, continued by the little fragment Suppl. gr. 1092, fol. 6–11); see Jørgen Raasted, "A Hitherto Unidentified Fragment of the Heirmologion Coislin 220," Classica et Mediaevalia, XXII (1961), 167–171.

ἁγία παρθενομῆτορ Μαρία, which follows on folio 329, is found also on folio 310. In either case the melodies are distinct and —although perhaps related—irreconcilable, and the significance of this is not lessened by their having been entered in the same manuscript by the same scribe, using the same notational system.[25] We may confidently infer that by the year 1100 there were in circulation at least two written traditions for these particular Dogmatika.

A further instance will strengthen this inference and widen its application. On pages 16–18 of his second volume Tillyard transcribes the prosomion Ὦ τοῦ σταυροῦ σου τῇ δυνάμει, a contrafactum by Theodore Studites for the Thursday of the first week in Lent, using as his principal source the MS Vienna, Theol. gr. 181. Reference to any edition of the Triodion will show that Theodore's model was the Dogmatikon Ὦ τοῦ μεγίστου μυστηρίου, a composition that Tillyard transcribes on pages 113–114 of the same volume, this time from another source, the "Codex Peribleptus."[26] At first glance, the two melodies appear to be wholly unrelated, as will be evident from my example, which co-ordinates the opening lines of Tillyard's transcriptions.

Example 7

On closer examination, however, one will recognize that, beginning differently and continuing more or less independently for some time, the model and the copy gradually arrive at a degree of unanimity and that in their closing lines they are for all practical purposes identical. My example shows only the beginning of their coincidence.

[25] I am indebted to P. Bartolomeo Di Salvo for having brought these conflicting versions to my attention.

[26] This transcription forms the basis of Carsten Høeg's perceptive analysis in his *Musik og digting i byzantinsk kristendom* (Copenhagen, 1955), pp. 98–103.

Example 8

What has happened here? Is it that Theodore has arbitrarily rejected the opening phrases of the model, substituting new ones of his own composition? Certainly not, for the melody he uses is in substantial agreement with that given for the model in our earliest sources, whether Coislin or Chartres.[27] Or is it that the "Codex Peribleptus," written more than two centuries later than the Vienna manuscript of 1221, has reproduced the model melody in a corrupt form? By no means. Not only is this same form to be found occasionally in earlier Middle Byzantine Sticheraria—for example, in Vatopedi 1499—it is also the form transmitted by the paleo-Slavonic tradition. On folios 67ʳ–68ᵛ the Triodion Chilandari 307 enters three "apocryphal" prosomoia on Ὦ τοῦ μεγίστου μυστηρίου. That these transmit the model melody in the form found in the "Codex Peribleptus" is immediately suggested by their florid treatment of their initial syllables. It becomes certain from their treatment of the lines corresponding to παρθενίας δὲ κλεῖθρα;[28] here again they prefer the florid form of the half

Example 9

[27]In addition to the Coislin sources enumerated in n. 11 above, I have consulted the Chartres MSS Laura Γ.67 and Vatopedi 1488. In so far as any of these include both model and copy, the melodies given are the same.
    [28]See the published facsimile (Monumenta Musicae Byzantinae, Série principale 5ᵃ), fol. 67ᵛ, line 1; fol. 67ᵛ, lines 13–14; 68ʳ line 13.

cadence, as found in the "Codex Peribleptus," whereas the Vienna manuscript, supported by our earliest sources in Coislin and Chartres, prefers the rigorously syllabic form.

In this instance, then, the latest possible date for the emergence of a dual tradition may be set back at least a hundred years, for the one form can be traced to our earliest source for the Oktoechos, the Triodion Laura Γ.67, a manuscript of the tenth century, the other to a paleo-Slavonic source using an archaic notation borrowed from tenth-century Byzantium by the Slavs.[29] With this difference, the inference is as before.

Confronted with evidence of this kind, one asks oneself whether the concept "archetype" has any real validity for the "marginal" contents of the Sticherarion. It has none for the Anastasima, this we know, and in another connection I have tried to show that it has only a limited validity for the heirmoi of the Good Friday Triodion in so far as copies of the Sticherarion include them.[30] It now appears that it has little or no validity for the Stichera Dogmatika. And that this should be the case is in one sense fortunate, for the resulting variety and contradiction give us unwittingly a welcome insight into the hidden interplay of oral and written tradition.

[29]See pp. 220–30 of this volume.
[30]See my *Specimina Notationum antiquiorum,* Pars suppletoria (Copenhagen, 1966), pp. 18–19.

TROPUS AND TROPARION [†]

I N his highly original and intensely stimulating contribution to the *Festheft Wilibald Gurlitt,* "Sinn und Wesen der Tropen,"[1] Heinrich Husmann argues persuasively that the earliest tropes were invitatory prefaces whose function it was to introduce the singing of a particular liturgical chant. As such, they were specific manifestations of a general tendency, for invitatory prefaces of this sort are the common property of every Christian rite. In the last analysis, then, the process of troping was not invented in the West, nor yet imported from the East, and in dealing with the related concepts Tropus and Troparion[2] one needs to think in terms of analogies and not of origins.

At the same time it would be misleading to insist upon these

†From *Speculum Musicae Artis. Festgabe für Heinrich Husmann,* ed. Heinz Becker and Reinhard Gerlach (Munich, 1970), pp. 305–311. Reprinted with permission of the Wilhelm Fink Verlag.
[1] *Archiv für Musikwissenschaft,* XVI (1959), 135–147.
[2] As a technical term, the word "troparion" is used both generically and specifically. Generically, it may be applied to most poetic texts intended for singing and for liturgical use, thus to the entire contents of the Heirmologion and Sticherarion, but it is seldom applied to Biblical texts, and never to the Trisagion, to the Cherubic Hymns, to non-Biblical texts used as communions, to the stanzas of the kontakion, or to short refrains. Specifically, it is applied to the troparia sung before the dismissal at Vespers and with the Θεὸς κύριος, to the "Great Troparia" of the Christmas and Epiphany vigils, to the troparia of the Christmas, Epiphany, and Good Friday hours, to the troparia on the gradual psalms (οἱ ἀναβαθμοί), and to the stanzas that follow the heirmoi of the canons. Throughout this paper, with a few obvious exceptions, I have used the word in the broadest possible sense.

analogies without giving due weight to the fundamental differences between the two concepts. In principle, the Latin trope belongs to the Mass, the Byzantine troparion to the Office. The Latin trope is seldom much longer than the official text to which it attaches itself and on whose grammatical construction it often depends, while the Byzantine troparion is invariably long enough to constitute a self-sufficient stanza. When an official text is broken up into lines and subjected to systematic interpolation, the two practices differ again: in the West the final line is never followed by a trope; in the East it is always a troparion that brings the alternations to an end. In such a construction each of the Latin tropes will have a melody of its own, while the Byzantine troparia are as a rule contrafacta—so-called prosomoia—arranged in groups, each member of any single group being sung to the same model-melody. Granted that the Latin tropes are to a certain extent interchangeable, they have no independent existence; in this respect the Byzantine troparion comes closer to the Latin antiphon in that some troparia have lost their parent texts through the familiar process of attrition, while others, appointed for processional use, may have been independent from the moment of their conception. The Greek translator of the Dialogues of Gregory the Great renders the word *antiphona* as τροπάριον,[3] and when, as sometimes happens, a Byzantine troparion is translated into Latin, the translation becomes an antiphon and not a trope. Even so, whenever a trope or a troparion is in effect an invitatory preface, the analogy holds good, and it is precisely here that we may expect to meet with striking correspondences.

To illustrate the Byzantine use of the invitatory preface, Husmann quotes from the Horologion the two preambles that introduce the singing or recitation of the Gloria in excelsis at the end of the Orthros.[4] Other illustrations come readily to mind, and in what follows I shall comment only on a few of those whose resemblance to the Latin introductory trope is so close that it amounts to virtual identity.

---

[3] *Patrologia latina,* LXXVII, 375–378; see also p. 166 of this volume, n. 4.

[4] Strictly speaking, the first of these is a refrain formerly sung with the closing lines of Psalm 150; cf. Symeon of Thessalonica in *Patrologia graeca,* CLV, 648–649, also P. Nilo Borgia, 'Ωρολόγιον *"diurno" delle chiese di rito bizantino,* 2nd ed. (Grottaferrata, 1929), p. 69.

In printing the texts of the nine Biblical canticles appointed for singing or reading at the Orthros, the Horologion prints also the refrains (ὑποψάλματα), now largely out of use, that in earlier times were sung or read responsorially after the single verses.[5] That it was the practice of providing these refrains with invitatory prefaces that led to the creation of the canon as a poetic form is at least a plausible hypothesis and one that finds support, in the Heirmologion, in the wording of innumerable heirmoi and, in the collections of canon poetry, in the wording of many of the troparia modeled upon them. The point is perhaps best illustrated by the refrain for the prayer of Habakkuk, the fourth canticle of the series. Among the 190 akolouthiai of the Heirmologion Iviron 470 there are, for this canticle, 27 heirmoi that end with its traditional refrain, Δόξα τῇ δυνάμει σου, κύριε, and if we were to include also those heirmoi whose last lines make inconsequential departures from the traditional wording—perhaps by altering the word-order or by omitting the word κύριε—the number would be considerably increased. As a rule, the refrain is introduced by some form of the verbs βοάω, κράζω, or κραυγάζω—to proclaim, cry out, or shout. A thoroughly typical example is this heirmos from the canon by Cosmas for Palm Sunday.

Iviron 470, fol. 66ᵛ

On consulting the Triodion,[6] one finds the same refrain used also to end each of the three troparia that follow this heirmos. Whether the melody adapted to these four occurrences of the traditional refrain-text is likewise traditional, one simply cannot know—one cannot even know whether the refrain-text was limited, in each of the eight modes, to a single traditional melody. Suffice it to say that the melody with which the foregoing example concludes is used also, in Iviron 470, to conclude the corresponding heirmoi of this mode in Akolouthiai 3, 6, 8 and 25.

What is true of the heirmoi and troparia of the canons is equally true of those of the Beatitudes (οἱ μακαρισμοί), which most copies of the Heirmologion include as a sort of appendix. Here the refrain is the appeal addressed to the crucified Jesus by the Good Thief (Luke 23:42), and in one form or another it concludes a great many of these little pieces. An example is scarcely needed, for there is no essential difference between the heirmoi of the Beatitudes and those of the canons; indeed the heirmoi of the Beatitudes are in some cases contrafacta, borrowing their melody and metrical structure from the Heirmologion proper.[7]

For an illustration whose resemblance to the Latin invitatory preface is still more striking, we may turn to the Sticherarion and to the Easter doxastikon Ἀναστάσεως ἡμέρα.[8] Often omitted from the choir-books in Middle Byzantine notation as too well known to require copying, this composition is in effect an introductory trope of the Easter troparion:[9]

Χριστὸς ἀνέστη ἐκ νεκρῶν
θανάτῳ θάνατον πατήσας
καὶ τοῖς ἐν τοῖς μνήμασι
ζωὴν χαρισάμενος.

Only this single preface for the Easter troparion has survived the standardization and abridgment of the liturgical books that

[6]Rome, 1879, pp. 608–609.

[7]Thus Νῦν τοῦ λῃστοῦ is based on Δεῦτε λαοί, Λῃστὴν τοῦ παραδείσου on Οἱ ὅσιοί σου παῖδες.

[8]For a transcription after Athens, National Library 883, and Cambridge, Trinity College 256, see H. J. W. Tillyard, *The Hymns of the Pentecostarium* (Copenhagen, 1960), pp. 4–5.

[9]Πεντηκοστάριον (Rome, 1883), p. 6.

took place about the year 1050, but in still earlier times there existed a whole series of similar prefaces, melodically and metrically independent, all of them in the same mode, all of them concluding with the Easter troparion. Thus a distinctive preface could be appointed for the Vespers and for the Orthros of each of the days in Easter week. Since I have dealt with this series at some length in another study,[10] I can afford to pass over it here. In the present context, however, it is significant that in our sources from the tenth and early eleventh centuries the refrain is never written out in full. As in the Latin tropers, the parent text is represented only by its incipit.[11]

We have still before us the closest of all imaginable parallels. As a typical example of the Latin invitatory preface, Husmann draws attention to these widely disseminated verses on the Gloria:

Cives superni   hodie suam
simul et nostram   nunciant mundo
festivitatem.   Gloriam Deo
    resonemus omnes.

Rather more apt for my present purposes would have been the little Gloria trope for the Midnight Mass of Christmas, a prose text published by Gautier after MSS from Nevers and Autun:

Laetentur coeli coelorum et exsultet omnis orbis terrarum, quia hodie Christus de virgine natus est. Iubilemus omnes cum angelis, clamantes et dicentes: Gloria in excelsis Deo.[12]

Not only does this text relate the specific events commemorated to the singing it invites and introduces, it also closes with the actual words with which that singing begins. It is thus strictly parallel, in content and in function, to a well-known text from the Sticherarion, sung on Christmas morning at the Orthros following the Gloria

<hr/>

[10]See pp. 202–07 of this volume.

[11]See my *Specimina Notationum Antiquiorum* (Copenhagen, 1966), pl. 96–97, with reproductions of the Easter office after Paris, Bibliothèque Nationale gr. 242. Here the incipit of the refrain is given also after two other stichera which in later sources are usually found without it.

[12]*Histoire de la poésie liturgique au moyen âge: Les tropes* (Paris, 1886), pp. 255–256. Professor Paul Evans of the University of Pennsylvania, who has kindly examined for me in Paris the two sources used by Gautier, informs me that in the one from Nevers (Bibliothèque Nationale lat. 9449) the Gloria introduced is Gloria IV of the Graduale Romanum, while in the one from Autun (Bibliothèque de l'Arsenal 1169) it is Gloria XI.

Patri of the Lauds (Psalms 148 to 150) and immediately before the Gloria in excelsis itself.

Σήμερον ὁ Χριστὸς ἐν Βηθλεὲμ γεννᾶται ἐκ παρθένου
σήμερον ὁ ἄναρχος ἄρχεται καὶ ὁ λόγος σαρκοῦται
αἱ δυνάμεις τῶν οὐρανῶν ἀγάλλονται
καὶ ἡ γῆ σὺν τοῖς ἀνθρώποις εὐφραίνεται
οἱ μάγοι τὰ δῶρα προσφέρουσιν

οἱ ποιμένες τὸ θαῦμα κηρύττουσιν
ἡμεῖς δὲ ἀκαταπαύστως βοῶμεν
Δόξα ἐν ὑψίστοις θεῷ
καὶ ἐπὶ γῆς εἰρήνη ἐν ἀνθρώποις εὐδοκία.[13]

To follow up all the ramifications of this remarkable piece would lead us far afield. It should be enough to say that it is the model for four prosomoia still in actual use—one for the Nativity of the Virgin,[14] one for the Epiphany,[15] one for the feast of the Three Hierarchs,[16] one for the Purification[17]—and that in former times many other offices included pieces of this sort, some of them prosomoia like those just mentioned,[18] others idiomela concluding with the same refrain-text and—as a rule—with the same refrain-melody, sometimes represented only by its incipit.[19]

Where there is a rubric, it is normally Εἰς τὸ Δόξα ἐν ὑψίστοις, looking forward, then, to the singing that is being introduced. And when the mode is the Deuteros, as it usually is, the refrain-melody will be the one quoted below; when it is the Plagios deuterou, as sometimes happens, the refrain-melody often takes another form,

[13] II (Rome, 1889), 672. There are transcriptions by Egon Wellesz in *Eastern Elements in Western Chant* (Oxford, 1947), pp. 148–149, and by P. J. D. Petrescu in *Les idiomèles et le canon de l'office de Noël* (Paris, 1932), Transcriptions, pp. 116–123.

[14] I (Rome, 1888), 115.

[15] *Ibid.*, III (Rome, 1896), 156.

[16] *Ibid.*, III (Rome, 1896), 446.

[17] As in n. 16. In printed editions of the Menaia, only the first of the four prosomoia cited in this and the preceding three notes concludes with the opening lines of the Gloria in excelsis. But all four of them follow the Gloria Patri of the Lauds, and in such early sources as Grottaferrata Δ.α.v and vi one finds the opening lines of the Gloria in excelsis used also to conclude the stanzas for the Epiphany and the Purification. As to the stanza for the Three Hierarchs, this is a relatively late creation, written for a feast introduced under the Emperor Alexius I Comnenus about the year 1100.

[18] See, for example, my *Specimina Notationum Antiquiorum*, pl. 20 (Σήμερον ἡ παρθένος ἔτεκε and Βλέποντες τὴν ἔνδοξον; the first of these two stanzas has been published also by Petrescu, *Les idiomèles et le canon*, pl. iii.

[19] See, for example, Amédée Gastoué, *Introduction à la paléographie musicale byzantine* (Paris, 1907), pl. iii (Σὺν ταῖς ἄλλαις).

Koutloumousi 412, fol. 77ᵛ

borrowing from an idiomelon of the Christmas office which begins and ends as follows:[20]

Koutloumousi 412, fol. 80ᵛ

Prefaces like these are particularly well represented in MSS using the Chartres notation, two of which—the MSS Laura Γ.67 and Vatopedi 1488—make similar provisions, within the Oktoechos, for the eight Sundays of the Commune Dominicale.[21] More than half these pieces are Staurotheotokia, and as such they develop the theme of the Stabat Mater—the Virgin's lament at the foot of the Cross. In a slightly different form, without the refrain Gloria in

[20]See, for example, my *Specimina Notationum Antiquiorum*, pl. 22 Ὁ τοῦ πατρὸς ὅρος καὶ λόγος; the idiomelon from which this borrows its refrain has been transcribed by Wellesz, *A History of Byzantine Music and Hymnography* (Oxford, 1949), p. 308 (2nd ed. [Oxford, 1961], p. 391), and Petrescu, *Les idiomèles et le canon,* Transcriptions, pp. 83–86.

[21]The two cycles have only four prefaces in common. A third cycle, concordant now with the MS at the Laura, now with the one at Vatopedi, but adding no new item, is found in Coislin notation among the Dogmatika of Sinai 1243.

excelsis, at least three of them function also as Staurotheotokia in the narrower sense; another is a variant of an idiomelon from the Good Friday office. Here, however, they all conclude with the opening words of the Gloria in excelsis, and the remarkable thing is that, in seven of the eight modes, the refrain stands in the Deuteros and uses the first of the two refrain-melodies illustrated above. Only the preface in the Low Mode, or ἦχος βαρύς, evades this general rule. Thus, excepting on the seventh of the eight Sundays of the modal cycle, and on the second, when the mode is in any case the Deuteros, a shift of modality is bound to occur. A single example will show just how this is managed.

Παρεστῶσα τῷ σταυρῷ, the preface given for the Protos in Vatopedi 1488, agrees up to a certain point and in all essentials with a widely disseminated Staurotheotokion.[22] Only the endings differ—at καὶ λάμψον τὸ φῶς σου πᾶσι Vatopedi 1488 strikes out on a path of its own, and before the refrain the shift from Protos to Deuteros is marked by a medial signature, the letter-numeral β'.

Vatopedi 1488, fol. 181

Aside from their interest as Byzantine counterparts to the Latin introductory tropes, these Gloria prefaces, with their virtual insistence on a particular mode, have an additional interest of quite another kind. Surely we may infer that in tenth-century Byzantium the preferred mode for the Gloria in excelsis was the Deuteros.[23] May we infer also that in the first of our two

---

[22]For a transcription after the "Codex Peribleptus," see Tillyard, *The Hymns of the Octoechus,* pt. II (Copenhagen, 1940), pp. 166–167.

[23]In this connection it is noteworthy that, since the thirteenth century, at the very

refrains we have the beginning of a melody—perhaps the principal melody—to which the Byzantine Gloria itself was formerly sung? It would seem so, although there is of course no satisfactory way of answering this question. One thing, however, is certain. If in earliest times an official melody for the Byzantine Gloria did begin as in the first of our two refrains, then it was not the prototype of any of the Latin melodies we know.

latest, the Gloria in excelsis has regularly been preceded on Sundays by a Theotokion of the Deuteros—'Υπερευλογημένη ὑπάρχεις. The problem of modality, as it affects the chants of the Ordinarium Missae, is examined objectively and with a wealth of detail and documentation in Kenneth Levy's "The Byzantine Sanctus and Its Modal Tradition in East and West," *Annales musicologiques,* VI (1958–63), 7–67.

A LITTLE-KNOWN STICHERON
FOR THE TRANSLATION
OF ST. NICHOLAS[†]

No one needs to be reminded that the enormous popularity of the cult of St. Nicholas in the West began in the late eleventh century with the translation of his relics to Bari and the dedication of the great basilica built there to receive them. St. Nicholas does not figure at all in the ninth-century Tonarius of Metz,[1] and his office—dismissed as "assez récent"—is contained in only two of the six early copies of the Roman Antiphoner published in Hesbert's *Corpus*.[2] But by the end of the twelfth century it had found general acceptance, and its appeal was such that the melody of its principal antiphon, "O Christi pietas," had already been adapted as a Sanctus; in 1264, charged with arranging the office for the new feast of Corpus Christi, St. Thomas Aquinas was to adapt this melody once again to the text "O quam suavis."

Nor was it only among adherents of the Latin rite that the arrival of the relics in Bari evoked an ardent and immediate response. Its effect on the Greek-speaking faithful of Sicily and the Italian peninsula was not less marked. With them, however, it took a somewhat different form. Already in possession of a full and solidly estab-

---

†From *La Chiesa greca in Italia dall' VIII al XVI secolo*, III (Padua, 1973), 1261–1269; written for the Convegno storico interecclesiale, Bari, April 30–May 4, 1969. Reprinted with permission of the Casa Editrice Antenore.

[1]W. Lipphardt, *Der karolingische Tonar von Metz*, Liturgiewissenschaftliche Quellen und Forschungen, XLIII (Münster, 1965).

[2]R.-J. Hesbert, *Corpus Antiphonalium Officii. I. Manuscripti "Cursus Romanus,"* Rerum ecclesiasticarum documenta, Series maior. Fontes, VII (Rome, 1963).

lished office for the principal feast of St. Nicholas on December 6, they added the Latin feast of the Translation on May 9 to their calendar also, and the hymnographers among them, writing in Greek on Italian soil, were presently working out a new office for this commemoration within the framework of the Byzantine rite. Once accepted by the Greeks of Southern Italy, the feast of the Translation was then taken over by the Slavs,[3] and if we follow the suggestions made to the Congress by Professor Dujčev[4] and Father Tadin,[5] we may conjecture that it was carried from Bari to the Slavic world by way of the Dalmatian ports, perhaps by way of Cattaro, the Serbian Kotor.

Some years ago, in a full-length study of one of the several Stephens among the Byzantine hymnographers, Giuseppe Schirò published the text of a canon written for the new office, basing it upon manuscripts at Grottaferrata and the Biblioteca Vaticana.[6] Stephen's authorship of this particular canon follows from its acrostic and offers irrefutable proof of his Italo-Greek origin, for as Schirò observes:

> V'è poi da escludere in ogni modo che un canone per la traslazione del corpo di S. Nicola . . . fosse composto da un innografo dell'Oriente, per le cui popolazioni il fatto costituì una ragione di lutto e non di esaltazione.

The same argument might also be used to demonstrate that the two manuscripts in which Stephen's poem is found were written in Italy, for if it is inconceivable that it could have been composed in the East, it is almost as inconceivable that it could have been copied there. Add to this that the manuscript at Grottaferrata,[7] a palimpsest, makes a decidedly Italo-Greek impression, while the one at the Biblioteca Vaticana,[8] likewise a palimpsest, contains readings and kontakia for several saints primarily or exclusively venerated in the West—thus for St. Lucy and for St. Martin of Tours.

---

[3]The Slavic office for the Translation, as printed in current editions of the Slavic Menaia, bears no relation to the Greek.

[4]I. Dujčev, "Riflessi della religiosità italo-greca nel mondo slavo ortodosso."

[5]M. Tadin, "L'arcivescovo di Bari e il suo suffraganeo di Cattaro in Dalmazia."

[6]G. Schirò, "Stefano italo-greco," *Bollettino della Badia greca di Grottaferrata,* I–II (1947–48), especially II, 11–16.

[7]A. Rocchi, *Codices Cryptenses* (Grottaferrata, 1883), p. 213.

[8]E. Feron and F. Battaglini, *Codices manuscripti graeci Ottoboniani Bibliothecae Vaticanae* (Rome 1893), pp. 205–207.

Beyond quoting a few lines from other parts of the new office and considering their possible relation to the canon he is publishing, whether as sources or as derivations, Schirò limits himself strictly to the single text that is surely Stephen's work.[9] Yet if we were to look at the office in its entirety, with its various troparia, canons, kontakia, exaposteilaria, and stichera, we would find that, to the general rule that its texts borrow their metrical schemes and their melodies from older compositions, there is one exception. Expressly identified as an idiomelon in the manuscript at Grottaferrata and provided with musical notation in both our sources, this is the sticheron Τίς ὑμνήσει ὄντως κατ' ἀξίαν. Stephen's canon is Italo-Greek only in a very limited sense, for in writing it its author has employed metrical schemes imported from Byzantium and has had imported melodies in mind. Our sticheron, on the other hand, is Italo-Greek in the widest possible sense, for in so far as stylistic conventions permit it is an entirely original composition.

Thus far, I have encountered this exceptional piece in five sources—in the two text-manuscripts already mentioned and in three copies of the Sticherarion. As a convenience to the reader I list them here, describing each one as briefly as possible.

1. Grottaferrata, Badia greca. B.β.iv. Parchment, 158 ff., 18 × 13 cm. Thirteenth–fourteenth century. Offices for December 6 and May 9. Coislin notation for the melodies of the idiomela. Beginning on f. 154ᵛ there are additions in other hands.
   F. 128ʳ: Τίς ὑμνήσει ὄντως κατ' ἀξίαν.

2. Biblioteca Apostolica Vaticana. Ottoboni gr. 393. Parchment, 98 ff., 23 × 19 cm. Thirteenth century. Synaxarion, September 5 to January 6 (ff. 41ʳ–98ᵛ) and July 25 to August 31 (ff. 1ʳ–14ᵛ), with kontakia for the feasts solemnly celebrated. To this the same hand has added the office for May 9 (ff. 19ʳ–35ᵛ) and a "Martyrion" for June 15 (ff. 37ʳ–40ᵛ). Middle Byzantine notation for the melodies of the kontakia and for the idiomela of the office. On ff. 15–18 and 36 there are additions in other hands.
   F. 19ᵛ: Τίς ὑμνήσει ὄντως κατ' ἀξίαν.

---

[9]Even so, it is doubtful that the kontakion he has published is Stephen's work, for although in Ottoboni gr. 393 it follows the sixth ode of Stephen's canon, its prooemion is found in quite another context in B.β.iv (f. 110).

3. Paris, Bibliothèque Nationale. Ancien fonds gr. 355. Parchment, 330 ff., 22.5 × 16 cm. Thirteenth century. Stichera of the Menaia. Middle Byzantine notation.
   F. 329ʳ: Τίς ὑμνήσει ὄντως κατ᾽ ἀξίαν.

4. Mount Sinai, Monastery of St. Catherine, MS 1471. Paper, 357 ff., 26 × 19.8 cm. Fourteenth century. Sticherarion. Middle Byzantine notation.
   F. 140ᵛ: Τίς ὑμνήσει ὄντως κατ᾽ ἀξίαν.

5. Mount Athos, Monastery of Iviron. MS 953. Paper, ff. not numbered. Fifteenth century. Sticherarion. Middle Byzantine notation.
   Under May 9: Τίς ὑμνήσει ὄντως κατ᾽ ἀξίαν.

Like Grottaferrata B.β.iv and Ottoboni gr. 393, the manuscript Ancien fonds grec 355[10] can only have been written in Southern Italy. It is one of those distinctly atypical copies of the Sticherarion which depart from the norm in adding to the standard abridged contents, stabilized about the year 1050, a certain number of so-called "apocrypha" in order to adapt that universally useful contents to the requirements of a particular community. Such a manuscript can usually be localized with more or less precision, and considering that this one, beyond adding our sticheron for the Translation of St. Nicholas, also adds other similar pieces for Leo of Catania and Nicon of Taormina, saints not solemnly celebrated in the Orthodox East, we need not hesitate to assume its South Italian—and probably Sicilian—origin.

Having said this much, and having already concluded that our sticheron is not likely to have been copied in the East, what are we to make of the two Sticheraria at Mount Sinai[11] and Mount Athos?[12] As we shall see, and as I have previously stressed in other connections,[13] these two sources are intimately related—so inti-

---

[10]A. Gastoué, *Introduction à la paléographie musicale byzantine* (Paris, 1907), pp. 83–84. The manuscript is certainly not from Grottaferrata, as Gastoué supposed.
[11]V. Beneševic, *Catalogus codicum manuscriptorum qui in monastero Sanctae Catharinae in Monte Sinai asservantur,* III/1 (Hildesheim, 1965 = Petrograd, 1917), 56–57.
[12]S. P. Lambros, *Catalogue of the Greek Manuscripts on Mount Athos,* II (Amsterdam, 1966 = Cambridge, 1900), 241.
[13]See pp. 203 and 196 of this volume.

mately that they must have had a common origin. This is in itself enough to eliminate one of their present locations; other considerations will presently eliminate them both.

Where did they actually come from? The copy at Mount Sinai was brought there from Crete, for an annotation on f. 271ʳ identifies it as the property of a certain Gerasimus, a Sinai monk of Cretan origin who was responsible for the copying of a number of seventeenth-century manuscripts in the library at St. Catherine's.[14] But if we now know how the Sinai copy reached its present location, we still do not know where it was written.

Fortunately for us, the two sources at St. Catherine's and Iviron belong to the abnormal type already exemplified by the manuscript at the Bibliothèque Nationale. Each contains upwards of 35 apocrypha, and if we were to compare the one source with the other, we would find little difference in their apocryphal contents. The list is heavily weighted in favor of Cyprus, with nine pieces for commemorations of the Cypriot bishops Epiphanius and Triphyllius, and when one considers that there are no entries for Cretan saints, that St. Catherine's has maintained a metochion on Cyprus, and that the manuscripts from that metochion, the Μονὴ τῆς Βασίλιας, are believed to have been transferred to Sinai,[15] one can no longer doubt that Cyprus is the place where the two sources originated. And with this established, one can understand why it is that they happen to include among their apocrypha our sticheron for the Translation of St. Nicholas, together with similar pieces for other commemorations wholly unknown to the Eastern calendar—on May 10 for St. Cataldus, the patron of Taranto, and on June 15 for Saints Vitus, Modestus, and Crescentia.[16] From 1192 until 1571 Cyprus was under Latin domination, subject first to the house of Lusignan, then to the republic of Venice. During this long period of occupation, Latin congregations—artificially implanted in an Orthodox environment—brought Latin cults with them. But they were evidently accompanied, from Venice or from Southern Italy,

---

[14]Some Sinai manuscripts copied by Gerasimus are nos. 1416, 1438, 1451, 1452, 1490, 1540, 1557, and 2083; once his property, in addition to MS 1471, were nos. 1482 and 1556.

[15]M. Richard, *Répertoire des bibliothèques et des catalogues de manuscrits grecs* (Paris, 1958²), p. 77.

[16]It will be recalled that Ottoboni gr. 393 includes a "Martyrion" for the second of these commemorations.

by Italian adherents of the Greek rite, who for their part brought with them usages until then unfamiliar to the island.

As distinguished from the tradition for the generally accepted contents of the Sticherarion, that for its marginal or apocryphal contents is relatively unstable. This contents must have been transmitted orally, and when an enterprising scribe sought to reduce some part of it to writing, he could only record the particular version with which he was familiar. Once he had done so, other scribes in the neighborhood might copy his version, and the presumed agreement of our two sources from Cyprus is doubtless to be explained in this way. Unfortunately I have no photographs of Iviron 953 and no transcription of its version of our sticheron. But in 1953 and again in 1955 I worked at Iviron with the manuscript itself, and from the list of its marginal contents that I drew up at that time and from transcriptions of other parts of that contents I can be reasonably certain that its version of our sticheron cannot have differed substantially from the version of Sinai 1471. With this single exception, the written transmission of the piece is altogether too contradictory to permit the preparation of a critical text. The transcription that follows is based on Sinai 1471 alone.

Example 1

πλ β'

Mount Sinai, MS 1471, fol. 140ᵛ

To show how widely our various sources disagree, I add the readings of Line 5 found in B.β.iv, Ottoboni gr. 393, and Ancien fonds grec 355. In B.β.iv the melodies are written throughout in the Coislin notation, a non-diastematic system that had passed out of general use by the year 1175, and if in entering the melodies for December 6 the scribe has copied with evident understanding from a *Vorlage* descended from the Coislin archetype, in entering the apocryphon for May 9, presumably unaided, he has been rather less successful, although it is at least clear that his version does not closely agree with any of the others. Apart from the deviations shown in Example 2, the version in Ottoboni gr. 393 ends with Line 8, while in Ancien fonds grec 355, which suppresses or does not yet know the ornamental treatment of the word διό (Thematismos exo), there are striking text-variants that inevitably involve changes in the melody itself: in Line 8, for τὴν τοῦ μύρου σου θήκην, this source has τὴν τοῦ θείου μύρου σου θήκην; in Line 10, for πρὸς σωτηρίαν ἡμῶν, it reads πρὸς σωτηρίαν τῶν ψυχῶν ἡμῶν.

Writing after the year 1087, at a time when the composition of new melodies in the classical style had all but ceased, the author of our sticheron might have been expected to model his poem upon the melody of some one of the thousands of idiomela already in existence. This was the procedure followed at Grottaferrata by S. Bartolomeo in his office for S. Nilo, and in his office for S. Barto-

Example 2

lomeo by the Egumeno Luca. Again at this late date, it frequently happened that an author, having chosen an existing model for his poem, made its original text the basis or point of departure for his own, modifying it only where it proved unsuitable for his new purpose. Thus in Ottoboni gr. 393, in addition to our sticheron, the office for the Translation of St. Nicholas adds on f. 20ʳ a second sticheron with musical notation, Πρέπει τῷ Νικολάῳ ἡ ὑμνῳδία, but although this is identified as an idiomelon, it owes its melody and some part of its text to a familiar sticheron from the office for June 24, Πρέπει τῷ Ἰωάννῃ ἡ εὐωδία. Also made in this way are the stichera found in our two sources from Cyprus for the offices of St. Cataldus and of Saints Vitus, Modestus, and Crescentia.

Departing, however, from the general practice of his contemporaries, our author has preferred to invent a metrical scheme of his own, and if the melody he has provided for his poem is woven entirely from existing materials, these are effortlessly combined to form a new pattern. His composition shows us that in his day a hymnographer could still write an acceptable melody in the traditional Byzantine manner. Beyond this, as already suggested, it has a special value of its own in that it is in the widest possible sense an original Italo-Greek creation. It will not be easy to find other compositions of which this can be said. But we shall have to find them if we are ever to determine the extent to which the Byzantine melodic idiom was modified in the Italian environment.[17]

[17]A problem posed by G. Marzi in his "Cosma il Melodo: Canone per il Natale," *Vichiana*, IV (1967), 139–154.

THE MENAIA FROM
CARBONE AT THE
BIBLIOTECA VALLICELLIANA[†]

I N June, 1969, the Badia greca di Grottaferrata received, for restoration and rebinding, the composite manuscript E.55 of the Biblioteca Vallicelliana in Rome.[1] Father Marco Petta, the Badia's librarian, recognized at once on examining it that the principal Greek item it contained, extending from folio 17 to folio 127 with one interruption, constituted the disordered remains of two volumes belonging to the set of eleventh-century Menaia from the monastery of S. Elia di Carbone, already represented in the library of the Badia by the five volumes Δ.α.xiii to xvii with offices for the months from October to April.[2] Knowing of my long-standing interest in this set,[3] Father Marco promptly drew my attention to

†From *Bollettino della Badia greca di Grottaferrata*, XXVII (1973), 3–9; read at the XIVe Congrès international des études byzantines in Bucharest, September 11, 1971. Reprinted with permission.

[1]E. Martini, *Catalogo dei manoscritti greci esistenti nelle biblioteche italiane*, 2, Catalogus codicum graecorum qui in Biblioteca Vallicelliana Romae adservantur (Milan, 1902), pp. 119–125 (no. 74).

[2]P. Marco Petta, "Codici del monastero di S. Elia di Carbone conservati nella biblioteca di Grottaferrata," *Vetera Christianorum*, IX (1972), 151–171, especially 160–161, 165–167; Antonio Rocchi, *Codices Cryptenses* (Grottaferrata, 1883), pp. 312–319. Rocchi mistakenly locates Carbone in Calabria, rather than in the Basilicata (Lucania), and following him I myself have repeatedly made the same mistake.

[3]See pp. 68–111 of this volume, especially pp. 108–09, and *Specimina Notationum Antiquiorum* (Copenhagen, 1966), Pars principalis, pls. 50–59, Pars suppletoria, pp. 20–27. more recently the five volumes have been studied by Dimitrije Stefanović in his "Daily Menaia from Carbone," *Bollettino della Badia greca di Grottaferrata*, XXI (1962), 41–50, and by Constantin Floros in his *Universale Neumenkunde* (Kassel, 1970), I, 56–57, 311 ff.; III, 33–35, facs. 44–50.

these remains and generously permitted me to make use of his notes on their contents. A little later, at the suggestion of Professor Kenneth Levy of Princeton University, I myself examined another of the Vallicelliana's composite volumes, the manuscript R.32, which—as Professor Levy had suspected—proved to contain eight additional folios from the same complex.[4] In the two manuscripts at the Vallicelliana we have in all 119 folios from Carbone, 14 from the May volume, 105 from the volume for July. Seeing that Father Marco will prepare for publication in the *Bollettino* of the Badia a detailed physical description of these remains with a list of the unfamiliar canons they contain, I may confine myself here to a brief account of their specifically music-historical interest. From what we already know about the volumes at Grottaferrata we may expect this to be considerable.

The work of an uncommonly skillful and conscientious scribe, the Carbone Menaia provide, for each of the Offices they include, a profusion of liturgical poetry—troparia, canons, kontakia, exaposteilaria, and stichera—with musical notation for the stichera idiomela. This musical notation is of two sorts. That used for the idiomela of the standard abridged version is a uniform, relatively developed Coislin notation that brings us as close to the archetype of this particular redaction as we are likely to come.[5] The idiomela excluded from this redaction as no longer in general use, the so-called apocrypha, present quite another picture. The five volumes at Grottaferrata contain upward of forty of these, evidently copied just as they stood from a wide variety of early *Vorlagen;* in three isolated instances the notation used is the fully developed Chartres, for the rest it is the Archaic Coislin, whose successive stages are most of them repeatedly represented.[6] Now it so happens that our extant manuscripts in Archaic Coislin are all of them

[4]Martini, *op. cit.,* p. 200 (no. 12). Neither here nor in his description of E.55 does Martini identify the provenance of the two fragments or connect them with the five volumes at Grottaferrata.

[5]For the concept "standard abridged version," see p. 107 of this volume and *Specimina,* Pars suppletoria, pp. 16, 23–25; also, for a dissenting view, Floros, *op. cit.,* I, 75–91.

[6]For the terminology, see my *Specimina,* Pars suppletoria, pp. 3–7. My attention was first drawn to the presence of these earlier notations in the Carbone Menaia by certain of the plates published by Fathers J. D. Petrescu and Lorenzo Tardo in 1932 and 1938. For a complete list of the apocrypha in Archaic Coislin contained in the five volumes at Grottaferrata, see Floros, *op. cit.,* III, 33–35.

heirmolgia,[7] and it is to this circumstance that the Carbone Menaia owe their peculiar importance. They permit the inference that sticheraria using the Archaic Coislin notation must once have existed, and they enable us to form a clearer idea of what earlier and later copies of such books must have been like than we can possibly form in any other way. In this respect they are unique.

At the Vallicelliana, the meager remains of the May volume include only a few scattered Offices, some of them incomplete and none of them represented in the standard abridged version of the Sticherarion, while the more substantial remains for July, although lacking the important Offices for the Deposition of the Virgin's Veil at the Blachernae (July 2) and for St. Procopius (July 8), make provision for twenty-four feasts and in so doing transmit the melodies of forty-two of the fifty-five idiomela normally assigned to this month in the uniform, relatively developed Coislin notation already familiar from the volumes at Grottaferrata. This same notation is used also for eight September idiomela assigned here to secondary commemorations of St. Euphemia and St. Phocas on July 11 and 22, and under July 11 there is this explicit reference to the lost volume for September—Ζήτει τὰ λοιπὰ Σεπτεμ-βρίου ις΄.[8]

In every respect the remains at the Vallicelliana conform exactly to the pattern established by the volumes at Grottaferrata. Thus they conform also in including a number of stichera apocrypha, three of them left without neumes although clearly intended to bear them, five entered in various stages of Archaic Coislin. These five pieces call for a closer look.

Table 1 The Apocrypha of Vallicelliana E. 55

	Mode				Folio
1	β	Τριάδος τὴν μίαν θεότητα	May 9	Isaiah	107
2	γ	῾Ως νεόφυτον	July 15	Cirycus	45ᵛ
3	γ	᾽Εν θεῷκαρδία	July 22	Phocas	84ᵛ
4	πλ β	Σήμερον καταυγάζει	July 22	Mary Magdalen	85
5	πλ δ	Πατρικὴν ἀθεότητα	July 27	Panteleimon	110ᵛ

[7]The manuscripts Leningrad 557, Patmos 55, Esphigmenou 54, and Saba 83.

[8]Seventeen kontakia from these remains are published by P. G. Nikolopoulos in his ῾Υμνοι (Κοντάκια) σῳζόμενοι εἰς χειρόγραφα τῆς Βαλλικελλιανῆς Βιβλιοθήκης τῆς Ρώμης, ᾽Επετηρὶς ῾Εταιρείας Βυζαντινῶν Σπουδῶν, *ΚΗ* (1958), 286–323. Like Martini, Nikolopoulos does not identify the provenance of the fragments or connect them with the five volumes at Grottaferrata.

Any one of the five might serve to illustrate the general characteristics of the notation. None uses the oligon; except for the final syllable of a stanza, none uses the ison; except in the combination later called xeron klasma, the klasma mikron is usually unsupported. None the less, as a second table will show, there is wide variety here.

Table 2

	1	2	3	4	5
Unsupported klasma	2	2	0	5	8
Dyo kentemata	3	0	0	0	0
Apostrophos-oxeia	0	0	1	0	0
Bareia "spelled out"	2	0	0	0	0
Syllables without notation	0	1	10	31	78
Total syllables	102	87	64	186	146

For an illustration of the earliest conceivable stage of the archaic notation we shall need to turn to the idiomelon for St. Panteleimon (Plate 1). Nearly half its syllables are left unprovided for, and apart from occasional uses of the kentema as an auxiliary and the occurrence of the ison-teleia over the final syllable, the semeiographic material consists solely of the five radical neumes, singly and in combination. In this last respect our apocryphon is simpler than any example from the Carbone Menaia thus far published in facsimile. Noteworthy, too, is the frequency of the diple or double oxeia—of this combination there are eighteen occurrences, while the single apostrophos, usually the commonest sign, has only nine.

Among the pieces occupying the middle ground (nos. 2, 3, and 4), the apocryphon for Mary Magdalen (Plate 2) raises problems more easily stated than solved. It belongs to a type sufficiently familiar from published transcriptions, the distinguishing feature being the repeated salutation (Χαῖρε or Χαίροις), whose three to four occurrences will as a rule be treated melismatically.[9] Our apocryphon is no exception, for the letter *theta,* marking the presence of a melisma of some sort, occurs in all six times, first at καὶ νέφη, then at each of the three salutations, and twice again at μαθητάς· τῇ δειλίᾳ. No single example of Archaic Coislin until

[9]For examples, see September Hymn 74, November Hymn 74, and the Staurotheotokia 5, 7, 8, and 17 in the transcription volumes of the Monumenta.

now published in facsimile can rival it in its degree of elaboration. Yet the Archaic Coislin notation is singularly ill-adapted for the transmission of melismatic music, and if we had no other sources to guide us, we should not know what was intended. Transcription would be mere guesswork, idle self-deception.

Fortunately for us, we do have other sources. The piece has two concordances, one in Chartres notation on folio 134 of Sinai 1219 (Plate 3), the other in relatively developed Coislin on folio 117ᵛ of Patmos 218 (Plate 4). They are in substantial agreement, and they permit us to recognize and name the melismata they call for and to offer transcriptions of them based on parallel passages in Middle Byzantine notation. Those at καὶ νέφη and at the three salutations are simple and extended forms of the Chairetismos, as Joannes Koukouzeles calls it in his well-known "Lehrgedicht"; those at μαθητάς· τῇ δειλίᾳ are the Thematismos exo and the special form of the Koukouzelian Kolaphismos often used in the modes on E and G.[10]

Whether these are in fact the melismata called for by the writer of the *Vorlage* on which our scribe depended, we cannot know. All

[10]No published transcription of the "Lehrgedicht" as a whole is entirely satisfactory. The best source, also the earliest, is Athens, National Library 2458, fols. 3–4ᵛ, published in facsimile by Gábor Dévai in his "Musical Study of Koukouzeles in a fourteenth Century Manuscript," *Acta Antiqua Academiae Scientiarum Hungaricae,* VI (1958), 213–235. Archaic Coislin notation for the more usual form of the Koukouzelian Kolaphismos can be seen in the apocryphon Θεὸς ἐφάνη ἐπὶ γῆς over the words υἱότητος and ἀνακεῖται (Petrescu, *Les idiomèles et le canon de l'office de Noël* [Paris, 1932], pl. vi).

we can say is that at the three salutations he has undoubtedly intended forms of the Chairetismos not unlike those illustrated, for at these three points he has entered above his Archaic Coislin neumes a badly drawn Chartres synagma, summing up their meaning.[11]

From one of my earlier tables it was evident that the first of the five apocrypha belonged to one of the latest stages of the archaic notation. No syllable of its text was left unprovided for; here—and here only—there were occasional dyo kentemata; and at two points the bareia was "spelled out" exactly as it might have been in relatively or fully developed Coislin. Assigned in Vallicelliana E.55 to May 9, the commemoration of the prophet Isaiah, it is found also as an idiomelon for the prophet Zephaniah (Sophonia) in the December volume at Grottaferrata ($\Delta.\alpha$.xiv, folio 10). Direct comparison reveals that the May and December notations of the melody derive in all likelihood from different *Vorlagen* (Plates 5 and 6).[12] The notation of the December volume is the more archaic. Two syllables have been left unprovided for; there are no dyo kentemata; the bareia is never "spelled out"; in addition, there is a single occurrence of the unsupported kentema to mark the end of a line. The comparison should serve also to persuade even the most skeptical reader that the fragments at the Vallicelliana and the volumes at Grottaferrata are indeed parts of the same complex.

[11] Similar instances of the use of Chartres signs to compensate for deficiencies of Archaic Coislin are found also in the five volumes at Grottaferrata; for examples, see Floros, *op. cit.,* I, 331.

[12] Also published in facsimile after $\Delta.\alpha$.xiv by Floros, *op. cit.,* III, facs. 48; with Middle Byzantine notation the piece is found in the manuscript Paris, Bibliothèque Nationale, Ancien fonds grec 265, fol. 51[v].

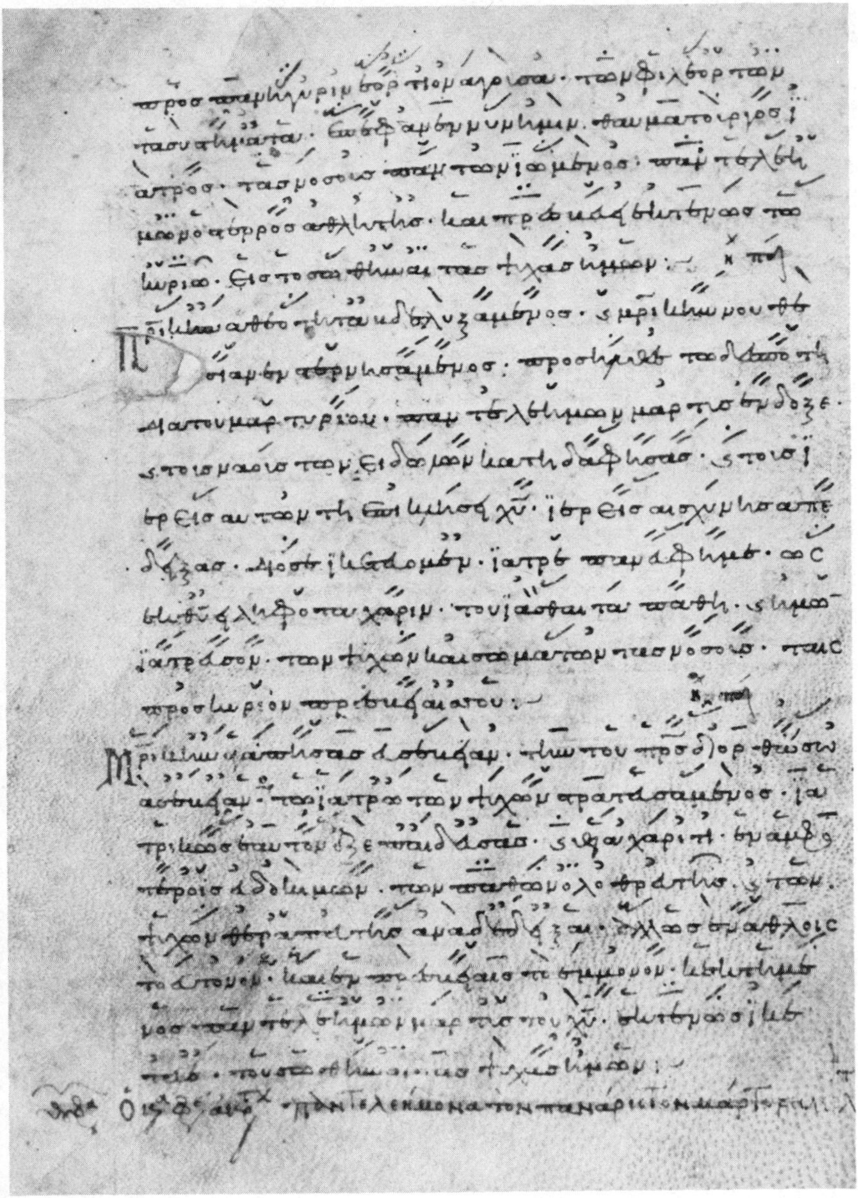

Plate 1: Biblioteca Vallicelliana, E. 55, fol. 110v

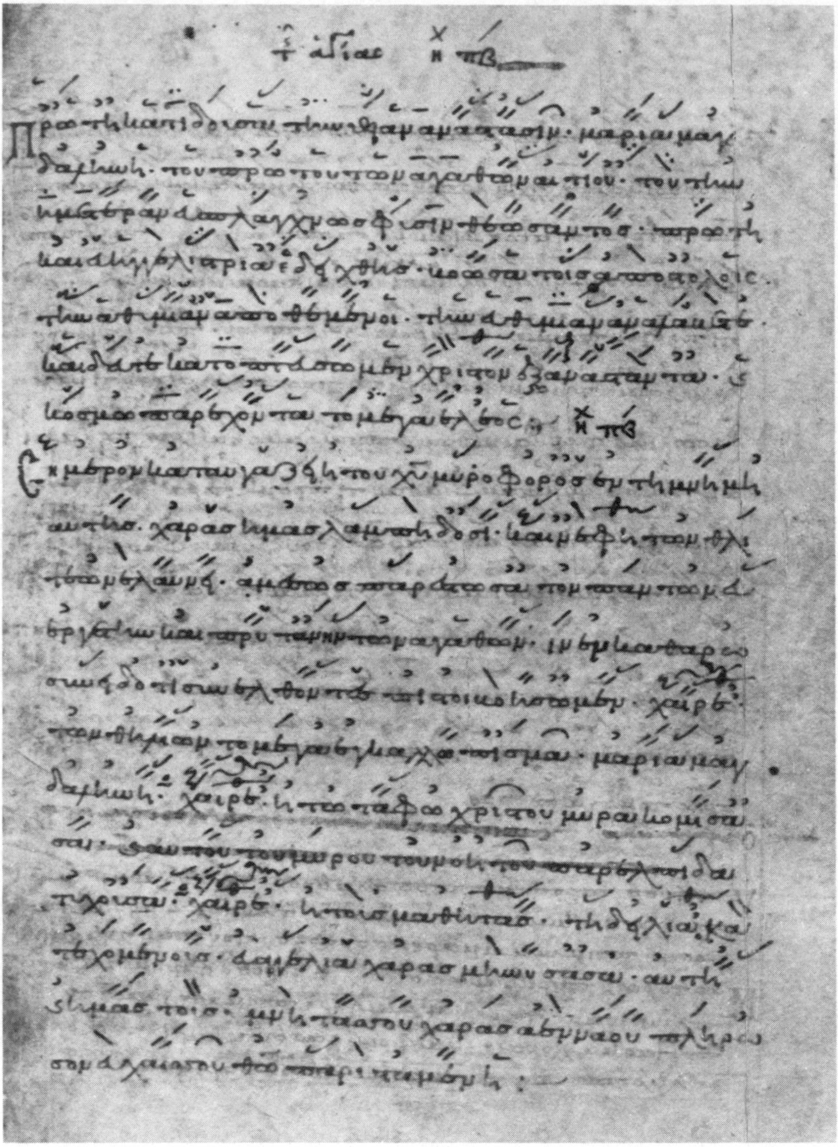

Plate 2: Biblioteca Vallicelliana, E. 55, fol. 85

Plate 3: Sinai, Monastery of St. Catherine, 1219, fol. 134

Plate 4: Patmos, Monastery of St. John, 218, fol. 117ᵛ

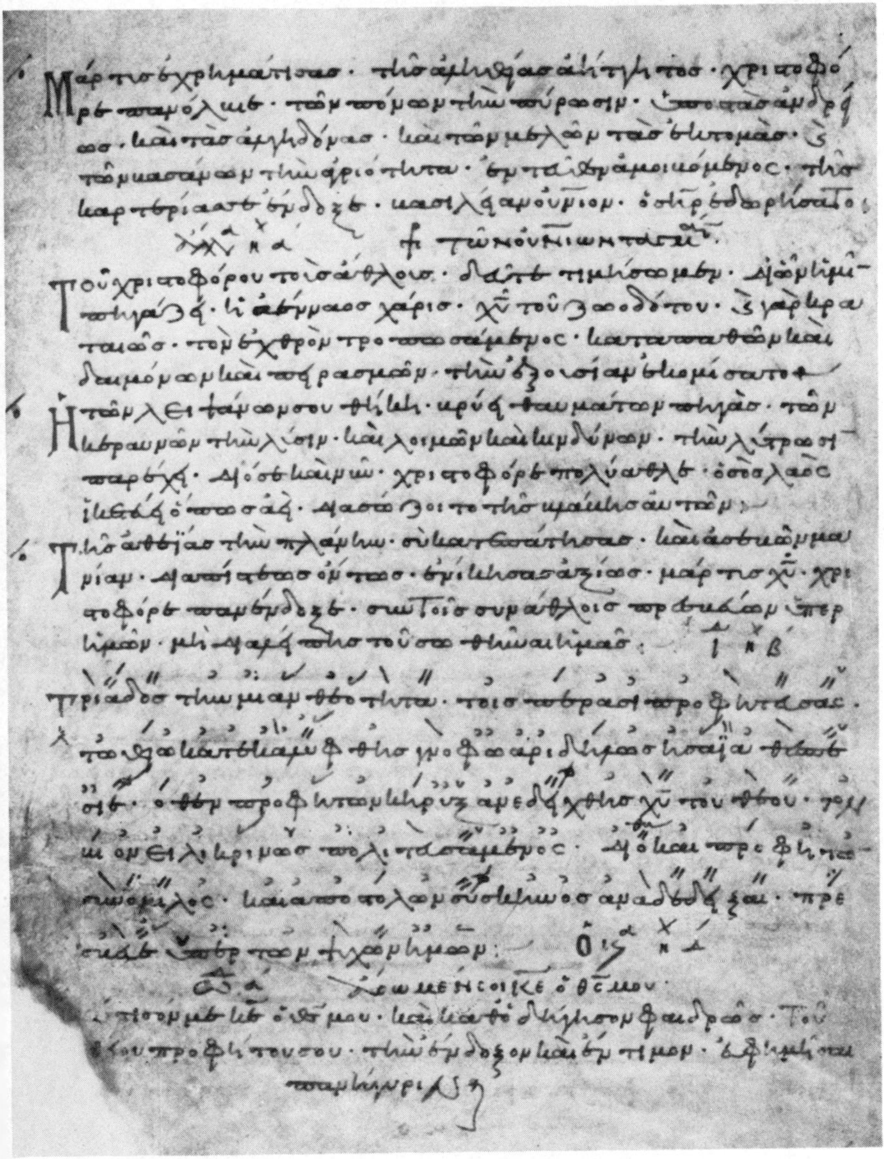

Plate 5: Biblioteca Vallicelliana, E. 55, fol. 107

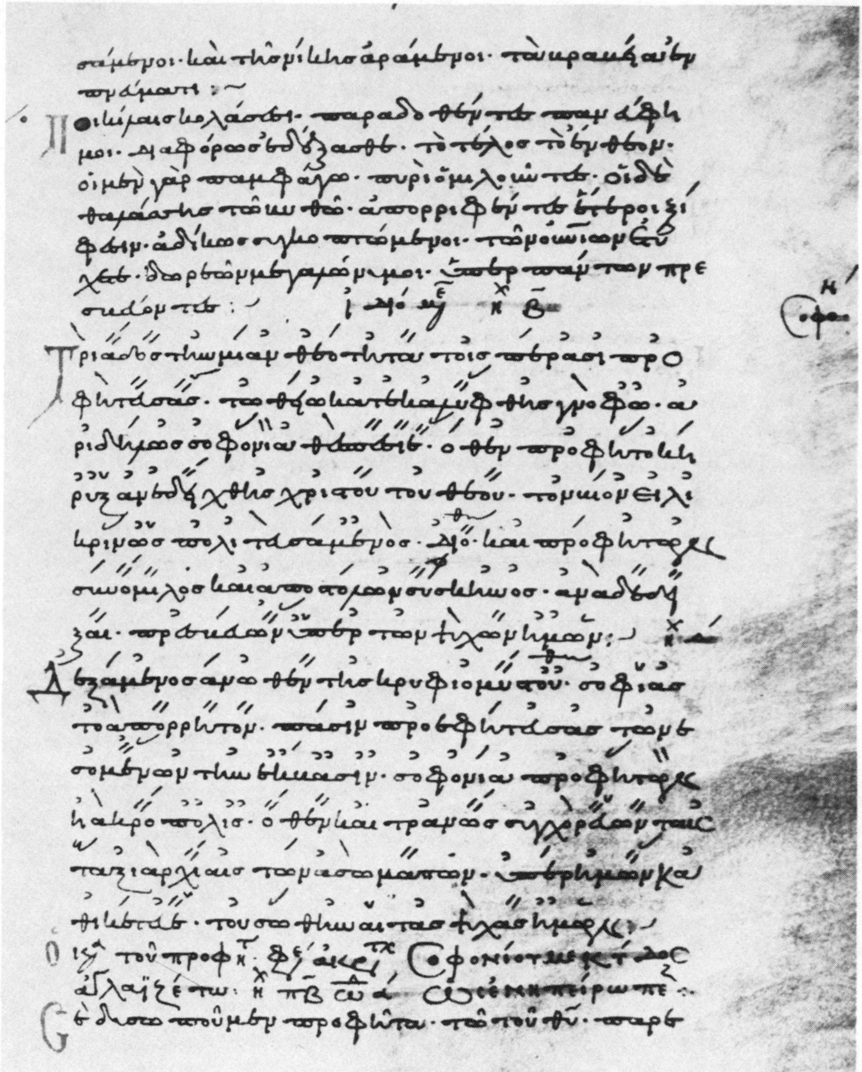

Plate 6: Grottaferrata, Badia greca, E. α. xiv, fol. 10

THE CHANTS OF THE
BYZANTINE-GREEK LITURGY†

I N the second volume of his *Geschichte der Musik* (1864), August
Wilhelm Ambros, usually the most perceptive of music historians, draws a grotesquely distorted caricature of Byzantium and its
civilization and curtly dismisses as unworthy of our notice the music
that that civilization produced.

> Where art becomes the slave of pretentious display and an expression
> of spiritual subordination, withered and mummified in its forms, where
> one seeks the ideally beautiful in empty show and senseless extrava-
> gance, where one supposes the sublime attained through overceremoni-
> ous ritual, where the forces animating state and church are servility and
> superstition, there the ideal arts of poetry and music cannot hope to
> flourish.

And not content with this, on returning to the subject in 1868
Ambros adds:

> For many years the interests of Venice were centered in the Orient,
> where even Cyprus and the Morea were at one time subject to its
> domination, and it was from the Orient that Venice received its earliest
> artistic stimulation. With Byzantium, Venice carried on a lively ex-
> change, as may be seen from the many Byzantine elements in her
> monumental art. Above all, Byzantium supplied Venice with mosaic
> workers who covered the golden walls of San Marco with a colorful

†Originally published in German translation as "Die Gesänge der bysantinisch-
griechischen Liturgie," in *Geschichte der katholischen Kirchenmusik*, ed. K. G. Fellerer,
I (Kassel, 1972), 128–147. Reprinted with permission of the Bärenreiter Verlag.

world of pictures. But well-trained musicians and singers Byzantium could not supply, for it was the most unmusical place in the world.

No one, surely, would write in this style today. Well before Ambros wrote, the Fürstabt Martin Gerbert had treated the subject at greater length and with greater sympathy in his *De cantu et musica sacra* (1774); even as Ambros wrote, F. J. Fétis, basing himself largely on Villoteau, on Chrysanthos, and on Greek informants encountered in Paris, was making a conscientious effort to do justice to the chants of the Eastern rites in a series of chapters published posthumously in the fourth volume of his *Histoire de la musique* (1874). About the middle of the nineteenth century, Western scholars representing a wide variety of disciplines—hymnography, liturgics, art history, political history, and the history of literature—had embarked upon a critical re-evaluation of Byzantine civilization, and by the end of the century men like Cardinal J.-B. Pitra and Wilhelm Christ, Swainson and Brightman, Kondakov, Bury, and Krumbacher had largely swept away the inherited prejudices from which Ambros, in his day, had been powerless to free himself.

Intensive study of Byzantine music may be said to have begun, shortly before the year 1900, with the first publications of the Augustinian Assumptionist J.-B. Thibaut, whose *Origine byzantine de la notation neumatique de l'Église latine* (1907) and *Monuments de la notation ekphonétique et hagiopolite de l'Église grecque* (1913) have left a lasting impression; other early landmarks, scarcely less influential, are Oskar Fleischer's *Spätgriechische Notenschrift (Neumenstudien, III* [1904]) and Amédée Gastoué's *Introduction à la paléographie musicale byzantine* (1907). Thus by the year 1915 the first foundations had been laid, and a new generation of scholars—foremost among them the British philologian H. J. W. Tillyard (1881–1968), the Viennese musicologist Egon Wellesz (1885–1974), and Father Lorenzo Tardo of Grottaferrata (1883–1967)—could take up the work in earnest. Tardo's activities were at first confined to the practical revival of Byzantine chant, and it was not until 1938 that he could come forward with his principal contribution, *L'Antica melurgia bizantina.* In the meantime, working at first independently, then in close collaboration, Tillyard and Wellesz had been propounding and solving the basic technical problems one by one so that by 1930 a refined and generally satisfactory method of transcription had been evolved and one could turn at last to the study of the music itself. Without adequate familiarity with the primary sources this would have been quite impossible, and it is perhaps Tillyard's chief merit to have been the first scholar in modern times to have visited the great libraries on Mount Athos and Mount Sinai, on Patmos, in Athens, and in Jerusalem with a view to examining and describing the manuscripts of Byzantine music they contained. Wellesz, in these early years, distinguished himself particularly with a remarkable series of contributions to the *Zeitschrift für Musikwissenschaft,* extending from 1919 to 1934.

What was needed, only too evidently, was a practical plan for co-ordinating and centralizing the research—an adequate provision for the publication of its materials and its results. The need was met immediately and effectively thanks to the intervention of Carsten Høeg (1896–1961), professor of classical philology at the University of Copenhagen, who had himself entered the field as early as 1922 with an essay on Byzantine musical theory for the *Revue des études grecques.* Respected and looked up to by his fellow Byzantinists, endowed with infinite patience, exceptional tact, and enormous administrative talent, Høeg secured the co-operation of Tillyard and Wellesz, persuaded the Union Académique Internationale to assume sponsorship, and in 1933 founded the Monumenta Musicae Byzantinae, some twenty volumes of which appeared during his lifetime—facsimiles, transcriptions, monographs, and the beginnings of an exemplary critical edition of the Prophetologion, with the Old Testament readings and their ekphonetic notation. Not a few of these volumes—among them the one entitled *La notation ekphonétique,* a study that has become a classic —were the work of Høeg himself. In the introduction to the new edition of the volume on the Byzantine empire in the *Cambridge Medieval History* (1966), Professor J. M. Hussey observes: "Perhaps the most marked advances of this century in Byzantine research have been in the field of music and in administrative and economic history." If one agrees with her, one must attribute much of this advance to the Monumenta. With its founding, Byzantine musicology had come of age.

A complete table of contents for the Monumenta can be found

in the bibliography at the end of this essay, and in what follows there will be frequent references to individual volumes. For an account of recent research and publication, beginning with the year 1950, the reader is referred to the report published in the *Proceedings of the Thirteenth International Congress of Byzantine Studies* (1967), reprinted in this volume, pp. 240 to 254.

How ought we to delimit our subject? Broadly speaking, the concept "Byzantine music" is dependent on the concept "Byzantine rite," and since that concept cannot be defined in terms of ecclesiastical authority or doctrine or language, we may think of Byzantine music as embracing the music of every church that continues to follow the rite developed in Byzantium and its sphere of influence during the later years of the first millennium, without regard to the degree of autonomy it may or may not enjoy and without regard to its teachings and beliefs, no matter whether its liturgical texts are sung and recited in the original Greek or in translations into Church Slavonic, Arabic, or some other language. In the narrower sense, however, seeing that the substitution of translations for original texts inevitably leads in time to the substitution of new melodies for old, we may think of Byzantine music as something confined to those churches that continue to use the Greek language; and since this chapter is addressed to readers primarily interested in Catholic church music, we may wish also to impose a chronological limit, restricting ourselves to the period during which the influence of the Byzantine rite and its music on the West was vital and pervasive and drawing the line—as a matter of convenience—at 1453 and the fall of Constantinople rather than at the formal break between East and West in 1054 or at 1204 and the Latin occupation of a part of the empire.

Byzantine music is a purely vocal music and, during the period we are considering, it was almost certainly a purely monodic music, choral or soloistic, for we have no clear testimony to the practice of ison singing—the improvised addition of a bourdonlike second voice—until after the Turkish conquest. Again during the period we are considering it was a purely diatonic music, despite the failure of our earlier documents to enlighten us on this point and despite the considerable weight of later tradition to the contrary. This is already sufficiently evident from the behavior of the music itself, from the tetrachordal structure of the tonal system that underlies it, from its predilection for literal transpositions to the fourth, fifth, and octave, and from its deliberate avoidance of particular leaps of the fourth and fifth.

And if we turn now from common traits to instances of direct borrowing from the East by the West, the case for a purely diatonic music will be immeasurably strengthened. That the Byzantine Oktoechos, or eight-mode system, had reached the West shortly before the year 800 is amply documented by the Tonarius of Saint-Riquier; that it was Byzantine in its origins is freely admitted by the Latin theorists who first describe it and evident in any case from the terminology they employ; that for all practical purposes the modal systems of East and West were in fact identical follows unmistakably from the Byzantine intonation formulas transmitted in unambiguous letter notations by the author of the *Musica enchiriadis* and by Hucbald in his *De harmonica institutione* and from those Byzantine melodies transmitted in diastematic Latin neumes to which Wellesz and Handschin have drawn attention—the antiphons "O quando in cruce" and "Veterem hominem." As a convenience to the reader there is inserted at this point a comparative table showing the correspondences between the two modal systems and their nomenclatures.

Byzantine	Latin	
	Earliest	Later
Protos	Authentus protus	Tonus primus
Deuteros	Authentus deuterus	Tonus tertius
Tritos	Authentus tritus	Tonus quintus
Tetartos	Authentus tetrardus	Tonus septimus
Plagios protou	Plaga proti	Tonus secundus
Plagios deuterou	Plaga deuteri	Tonus quartus
Barys, or Plagios tritou	Plaga triti	Tonus sextus
Plagios tetartou	Plaga tetrardi	Tonus octavus

To what extent the origins of our modern musical notation are to be sought in the East is a question that has still to be answered satisfactorily. The earliest Byzantine manuscripts with musical notation date from the mid-tenth century and as such are appreciably later than their earliest Latin counterparts; at the same time, the notation they employ would appear to lie rather closer to the remote beginnings of musical writing. Both notations have their roots in grammatical accents; both have made some use of letters as auxiliaries; both underwent considerable development before becoming fully diastematic. To the Latin neumes *in campo aperto* correspond the so-called paleo-Byzantine neumes; to the Latin diastematic neumes, with or without a staff, correspond the neumes of the Middle Byzantine notation; without essential change this last system continued to be used wherever Greek was the liturgical language until the year 1821, when it was supplanted by the drastically simplified notation devised by Chrysanthos.

In Byzantium, the basic or radical neumes of the melodic notation are most of them taken over from the older ekphonetic notation used for the liturgical readings, the signs of the ekphonetic notation having been taken over in turn from the accentual system of the Alexandrian grammarians. But one ought not to conclude from this that the process was one of steady development and refinement. It is rather that signs devised for one purpose came later on to be used for another and that, after having been so used for some time, their purpose was altered once again.

The bulk of the music for the principal hour services—the daily Vespers and Orthros, or Morning Office—is contained in two choir books, the Sticherarion and the Heirmologion. Of those, the more varied and the more important is easily the Sticherarion, a collection embracing, in the standard abridged form put into circulation about the year 1050, upward of 1,400 distinct troparia. The book takes its name from the word *sticheron,* used of a troparion designed to be sung in connection with a verse, or *stichos,* for the single items it contains are for the most part associated with the concluding verses of the Ordinary psalms of the Vespers (140, 141, 129, and 116) and Orthros (148, 149, and 150), or with Proper verses appropriate to the feast, or with the doxologies that follow these arrangements of Ordinary or Proper verses. The first part of the book is devoted to the stichera of the fixed feasts, or Proprium Sanctorum, beginning with September 1 and concluding with August 31; the second part contains the movable feasts of the Proprium de Tempore, beginning with the Sunday of the Publican and Pharisee (the Sunday before Septuagesima) and concluding with the Sunday of All Saints (Trinity Sunday), followed by the Oktoechos, a cycle of eight Sunday Offices, one in each of the eight modes, the Byzantine counterpart of the Ambrosian Commune Dominicale or the Mozarabic Officium de Quotidiano. Contrary to the Western practice, the Sundays in Advent (of the Forefathers and Fathers) and the Sunday after Christmas, as Sundays dependent upon a fixed feast, are included within the Proprium Sanctorum. Our earliest copies of the book, or of one or the other of its two parts, date from the late tenth and early eleventh centuries; a cautious estimate indicates that roughly 650 Sticheraria, copied before the year 1500, are still extant.

If one were to think prosaically in terms of mere number, one might conclude that the upward of 1,400 distinct items brought together in the standard abridged Sticherarion were roughly the equivalent of the 1,235 antiphons with which the Tonarius of Regino credits the Antiphonale Romanum or with the 1,564 found in the Lucca copy. But such a comparison would be almost meaningless, not only because the stichera are, as a rule, more substantial compositions than the antiphons of the Nocturns or those "Ad Laudes et per horas" and "In Vesperis," more readily comparable to the longer canticle and processional antiphons, but also because the standard abridged Sticherarion contains only a part of the repertory. Since it is a book intended to be universally useful, it understandably excludes the so-called "stichera apocrypha," pieces no longer in general use at the time of its compilation, and on similar grounds it also excludes the stichera of the weekdays within the eight-week cycle of the Oktoechos, pieces that even in relatively early times were never sung, as it appears, but simply read or recited. Finally, and what is rather more important, it tends to exclude all pieces thought to be too well known to require written transmission. Thus the Easter Office is, as a rule, omitted entirely; not found in copies dating from before 1300 are the "stichera anastasima," the very heart of the Oktoechos and the oldest of the several cycles of pieces commemorating the Resurrection; and in principle the book contains only those texts that have melodies of their own (the "stichera idiomela"). With few exceptions, the hundreds of contrafacta (the "stichera prosomoia") are rigidly excluded, and with them the ten to twenty model melodies (the "stichera automela") to which they are sung. It is not too much to say that the book leaves out more than it includes.

Nearly 600 stichera, in transcriptions by H. J. W. Tillyard and Egon Wellesz, have already been published in the Transcripta series (1936 to 1960) of the Monumenta Musicae Byzantinae, and Wellesz has included transcriptions of a good many others in his *Trésor de musique byzantine* (1934), in his *Music of the Byzantine Church* (1959), and in the two editions of his *History of Byzantine Music and Hymnography* (1949 and 1961). For further transcriptions, depending in either case on somewhat different editorial assumptions, the reader may turn to Father Lorenzo Tardo's *L'Ottoeco nei mss. melurgici* (1955) or to Father J. D. Petrescu's *Les idiomèles et le canon de l'office de Noël* (1932) and *Études de paléographie musicale byzantine* (1965). But he will wish also to find a transcription here, preferably one not previously published. It is the work of Cosmas of Maiuma (fl. ca. 743), and in its text the reader will readily recognize the Greek original of a celebrated processional antiphon of the Graduale Romanum, one added to the procession preceding the Mass In Festo Purificationis B.M.V. at some time after its introduction into the Roman rite during the pontificate of Sergius I (687–701). As found without neumes in the Codex Blandiniensis (Brussels, MS lat. 10127–10144), a document of the eighth or ninth century, this antiphon and its companion piece "Ave gratia plena" "se présentent sous la forme d'un texte bilingue alterné: chaque incise du texte latin suivant immédiatement l'incise correspondant du texte grec" (Hesbert). The lines of the Latin text, as they follow the Greek, divide as follows, and the lines of the musical example are numbered to correspond.

> *Adorna thalamum tuum, Sion,*
> *et suscipe regem Christum:*
> *amplectere Mariam,*
> *quae est caelestis porta:*
> 5 *ipsa enim portat regem gloriae*
> *novo lumine: subsistit Virgo*
> *adducens in manibus Filium ante luciferum:*
> *quem accipiens Simeon in ulnas suas*
> *praedicavit populis*
> 10 *Dominum eum esse*
> *vitae et mortis,*
> *et Salvatorem mundi.*

Example 1

Although the Greek model has not been published in transcription until now, its relation to its Latin copy has frequently been studied, most recently by Michel Huglo in his "Rélations musicales entre Byzance et l'Occident" (1967). The two versions agree in mode (on the one hand the ἦχος βαρύς or "Low mode," on the other the Sextus tonus) and they agree also in their parallel construction of lines 1 and 2. But if there are "similitudes notables," as Huglo says, there are also revealing differences: in line 6, at "novo lumine," the antiphon suppresses the sticheron's ornamental treatment of νεφέλη φωτός (a literal translation would be "nubes luminis"), and in line 10, at the corresponding words αὐτόν and "eum," the Greek melody reaches its lowest point, the Latin its highest. Clearly, the Latin copy is an extremely free adaptation of its model, if indeed it is an adaptation at all.

Viewed simply as a representative of the poetic and melodic idioms of the Sticherarion, our example is thoroughly typical. Typical is the underlying tripartite scheme of the poem—lines 1 to 4, lines 5 to 9, lines 10 to 12; typical also are the metrical, textual, and melodic parallelisms in lines 1 and 2 and in lines 5a and 5b (line 5a is suppressed in the Latin copy, perhaps to avoid the monotony that an alternating bilingual performance of the piece would entail). Likewise typical are the metrical and melodic correspondences at the principal cadences (lines 4, 5a, 5b, and 12). What a single example cannot show is the characteristically centonate construction of the melody. To recognize how important a role this plays, the curious reader will need to turn to other examples in the same mode, and he can find these conveniently assembled for him in Tillyard's transcriptions of its heirmoi or in the editions of the Oktoechos published by Tillyard and Tardo.

One needs also to consider that the example that has been chosen can represent only one aspect of the Sticherarion's enormous variety. It is, so to speak, a classical example; to represent, at least by a quotation, the extraordinary freedom and virtuosity of the pathos-laden style of the late ninth and early tenth centuries, there is inserted here a transcription of an elaborate melisma on the words Οἴμοι, τέκνον ἐμόν ("Alas, my child") from a sticheron for the mid-Lenten ceremony of the Adoratio Crucis, a piece developing the theme of the Stabat Mater and attributed in some sources to the Emperor Leo VI (886–912).

Example 2

As a book intended to be universally useful, the standard abridged Sticherarion contains no rubrics and leaves it to the individual community to decide how many of the stichera it provides for a given feast it will actually sing and at what points it will fit them into the order of service. There is simply a heading, giving the date and title of the feast, after which the single items follow in the neutral order of the eight modes. In current editions of the service books our sticheron for the feast of the Purification (Hypapante) is assigned to the second half of the Vespers and associated with Proper verses from the canticle of Simeon, but it might equally well have been assigned to the first half and associated with one or more of the concluding verses of the Ordinary psalms. In some early copies of the Typikon, a book containing the rule of a particular community, it is actually so assigned and so associated.

In any case the associated verses must be supplied from a manuscript or printed text, or from memory, and the singers must adapt them on the spot to the appropriate psalm tone. Shortly after the year 1300, psalm tones for the eight modes begin to be illustrated and adapted to model verses in copies of the so-called "Orders of Service" ('Ακολουθίαι), a handbook for the psaltist containing the ordinary chants of the Office and Mass, sometimes in anonymous older settings, sometimes in new ones by composers of the day, and it has been demonstrated that the simple psalm tones these books contain conserve a tradition going back to the year 800 at the very latest. For the demonstration, the reader is referred to the essay "The Antiphons of the Byzantine Oktoechos" (this volume, pp. 159–90), to whose numerous examples, chiefly of the simple psalmody of the Protos, there can now be added one illustrating the adaptation of this same psalm tone to the first of the concluding verses of the ordinary psalms of Vespers (Psalm 141:8):

Educ de custodia animam meam
ad confitendum nomini tuo.

Example 3

From this single example the essential characteristics of Byzantine psalmody will be at once apparent: the reciting tone is moderately inflected to throw the principal accents into relief; there is no medial cadence; and the final cadence is a "cadenza corsiva" (Ferretti)—as in the Tonus irregularis of the Antiphonale Monasticum, the formula is mechanically adapted to the last four syllables of the text, without regard to tonic accent. When the opening of the following sticheron is thought to require special preparation, the ending of the cadence will be modified accordingly, much as in Latin antiphonal psalmody the endings of the cadences may be modified to prepare the return of the antiphon. Thus the two systems of recitation, Greek and Latin, are seen to be governed by a single law of style—Peter Wagner's law of melodic adjustment, the law requiring that when two melodies stand in immediate succession, the first must be accommodated to the second by means of an appropriate treatment of its ending.

While the order of the Byzantine Orthros, or Morning Office, calls for the singing of a number of stichera, its chief emphasis falls on the canticles of the Old and New Testaments, and the central element in its structure presupposes the recitation of nine of these, in three groups of three. The first of these groups comprises the two canticles of Moses from Exodus and Deuteronomy, followed by the canticle of Hannah; the second adds the canticles of Habakkuk, Isaiah, and Jonah; the third concludes the series with the Benedictus es, the Benedicite, and the Magnificat, with which is coupled the canticle of Zacharias. It is this simple fact that lies behind the creation of the canon as a poetic form and behind the development of the Heirmologion, the book containing the heirmoi, or model stanzas, with the melodies to which the stanzas of the canons themselves are sung.

If we open any current edition of the service book for the month of February and turn to the feast with which we have just been occupied, we will find the text of the canon of the day. Once again it is the work of Cosmas of Maiouma, and its mode is the Tritos, the authentic mode corresponding to the plagal one in which our sticheron was composed. As in other canons by Cosmas, the omission of the canticle from Deuteronomy is taken for granted, so that with four stanzas bearing on the content or language of each of the remaining canticles there are thirty-two stanzas in all. Since there is a change of meter and melody at each change in the underlying scriptural basis, the long composition does not become monotonous; at the same time it is held together by its modal consistency, by its subject matter, appropriate to the feast, and by its thirty-two-letter acrostic, a twelve-syllable verse formed by the initial letters of the successive stanzas. In this particular case, the first stanza in each group of four is also the heirmos, and since the acrostic incorporates the initial letters of these first stanzas, along with those of the stanzas that follow, we may confidently infer that the texts and melodies of the eight heirmoi are by Cosmas himself. In further support of this inference, it may be added that the heirmoi of this set are seldom used by other canon poets and then only by such later men as Metrophanes and Joseph the Hymnographer. In Tillyard's Latin translation, the heirmos bearing on the canticle of Isaiah takes this form:

> *Ut vidit Isaias per visionem throno elevato Deum*
> *ab angelis gloriae custoditum:*
> *Me miserum, exclamavit, quod praevidi incarnatum Deum,*
> *aeternae lucis atque pacis Dominum.*

At best, this has little enough to do with Isaiah 26:9–20 or with the subject matter of the feast; but in its refrain line Cosmas implicitly identifies the prophet Isaiah as a prototype of the just man Simeon by juxtaposing the words "peace" and "light," drawn from their canticles, and this identification is then developed and made explicit in the three stanzas that follow.

Example 4

The canon for the feast of the Purification is in no respect exceptional, yet the conventions governing this sort of poetry are loose enough to leave room for wide variety. Not every canon has an acrostic, so that in many instances the poem as a whole can readily be altered, shortened, added to, or otherwise tampered with; not every canon assumes the omission of the canticle from Deuteronomy—indeed the presence or absence of this particular element appears to have been largely determined by local usage; not every canon has thirty-two stanzas—the thoroughly exceptional Great Canon by Andrew of Crete has 250; nor is it essential that the stanzas corresponding to the single canticles should be equal in number. Cosmas provides heirmoi of his own, yet this was by no means the universal practice, and canon writers tended early and late to borrow heirmoi from canons by others. Joseph the Hymnographer and Theophanes Graptos, influential poets of the ninth century, build entirely upon existing heirmoi, and by the mid-eleventh century, when the liturgical books were codified, their canons had found such wide acceptance that they had supplanted any number of older ones, rendering obsolete the heirmoi upon which these had been based.

Not only because it limits itself to the model stanzas with their melodies, but also because the canon texts to which these melodies must be adapted are so often built upon borrowed heirmoi, perhaps on heirmoi borrowed from a variety of contexts and thus not to be found in immediate succession in the book itself, the Heirmologion is by its very nature a book for study and teaching, not for practical use, and the singers who sang its melodies were obliged to commit them to memory. The urge to codify, to make liturgical usage uniform, had led about the year 1050 to the compilation of the standard abridged Sticherarion; it also led—and at about the same time—to the compilation of a comparable redaction of the Heirmologion containing upward of 1,800 heirmoi. But the fate of the two redactions was entirely different. The Heirmologion compiled in the mid-eleventh century is preserved only in a relatively restricted number of copies, and its life was a short one. Written and oral traditions were working at cross-purposes. As early as 1257 a new set of melodies, distinct yet cognate, had been put into writing, and shortly after the year 1300 still another one found favor. Thanks, as it appears, to its association with the celebrated master and innovator Joannes Koukouzeles, this latest tradition soon became the dominant one and remained so until at least as late as 1500. It is above all a simpler tradition, largely freed from melismas, whose authentic melodies tend stubbornly to cling to the upper and middle registers. In the meantime the compass of the book was steadily shrinking, and practical considerations were bringing about a change in the disposition of its contents. At first a book in which the heirmoi of the single modes were arranged in sets or sequences corresponding to their use in particular canons, it became one in which they were arranged, without regard to context, by the single canticles.

It is from a twelfth-century copy of the "classical" redaction that our example has been transcribed. The reader will recognize at once that there is no essential difference between the two melodies by Cosmas, even though for obvious reasons the heirmos is shorter than the sticheron, more compact and less developed (the familiar distinction between the sticheraric and heirmologic styles belongs to a later time). Should he wish to compare the "classical" version of the melody with the "Koukouzelian" one, he may turn to Tillyard's *Twenty Canons from the Trinity Hirmologium* (1952); and to follow the gradual disintegration and transformation of the "classical" tradition, he need only consult the comparative charts in the appendix volume of Velimirović's *Byzantine Elements in Early Slavic Chant* (1960), among which he will find the first heirmos of our canon in the notation of a number of sources, early and late.

If we add their separate repertories together, the Sticherarion and Heirmologion transmit an impressive body of music and contain the bulk of what is required for the solemn celebration of the Office. But they do not contain it all. For the venerable Φῶς ἱλαρόν ("Hail, gladdening light"), the evening hymn of thanksgiving, we have no melody earlier than the seventeenth century, and our older sources tell us virtually nothing about the all-important Common and Proper troparia sung at Vespers before the dismissal and repeated near the beginning of the Orthros with the Θεὸς κύριος ("Deus Dominus"). What we do have is some part of the melismatic repertory, and this is transmitted by two complementary collections, the Psaltikon and the Asmatikon. The first of these is a soloist's book, comparable in some respects to the Latin Cantatorium, although unlike the Cantatorium it concerns itself with both Office and Mass; the second is a book for the choirs, containing those melismatic chants of the Office and Mass that are sung chorally. Certain classes of chant—for example, the hypakoai or responsoria—are common to the two books, existing in two distinct versions, soloistic and choral; others—for example, the great troparia of the Christmas and Epiphany Vigils—are divided between them, with the Asmatikon containing the troparia themselves and the Psaltikon supplying the psalm verses of the soloist; still others are found in one book only—in the Psaltikon but not in the Asmatikon, or vice versa. For the Office alone, the two books inform us not only about the hypakoai, but also about the prokeimena, or graduals, of the Vespers and Orthros, while the Psaltikon devotes more than half its contents to the kontakion, a responsorial chant of the Orthros that serves as an interlude separating the second and third larger divisions of the canon; as a rule one finds melodies for fifty-three of these, roughly 25 per cent of them prosomoia.

Students of hymnography agree that the kontakion represents the supreme achievement of Byzantine ecclesiastical poetry and, despite an undoubted indebtedness to Syriac prototypes, its most original creation. It is a strophic poem, sometimes running to as many as thirty or even forty longer stanzas, linked together by an acrostic that often incorporates the poet's name. Standing outside the acrostic is an introductory stanza or prooimion in another meter, and the refrain with which this concludes is used also to conclude the single stanzas that follow. The subject of the kontakion may be drawn from the Old or New Testament, and when this happens the poem as a whole may have the character of a poetic sermon; again, it may be based on the life of a saint, thus constituting a sort of poetic martyrology. One associates the kontakion inseparably with the name of the poet Romanos, author of the widely imitated kontakion for Christmas Day and of so many others, a Syrian convert who flourished in Constantinople during the first half of the sixth century under the emperors Anastasius, Justin, and Justinian; but a few specimens are believed to antedate his time and, as the iconoclastic controversy was drawing to an end, a kontakion in defense of the icons, with a metrical scheme of its own, could still be written by the patriarch Tarasius (784–806). What liturgical function the kontakion originally fulfilled one cannot say, but by the middle of the ninth century it was already occupying the place it has today, the poem scaled down to its prooimion and a single stanza, and by this time, too, the greater part of the older repertory had fallen out of favor.

By the mid-ninth century, then, it had become customary to limit the singing or reading of the kontakion at the Orthros to the prooimion and a single stanza, the first oikos. But there were exceptions. On the Sunday corresponding to the Roman Quinquagesima, the last Sunday before the beginning of the Orthodox Lent, whose Office appropriately develops the theme of the Expulsion of Adam from Paradise, the kontakion's first oikos is so short that even today the service books prescribe the singing or reading not of one oikos, but of three. The first of these will serve admirably as an example, particularly since it happens to form part of one of those rare kontakia generally held to antedate the earliest productions of Romanos. Its text may be translated as follows:

> *Adam sat aforetime and wept*
> *before the garden of Eden,*
> *striking his face with his hands and saying:*
> *Merciful One, have mercy on me, the transgressor!*

The melody has been transcribed from the MS Ashburnham 64, a magnificent copy of the Psaltikon written at Grottaferrata in 1289 and preserved today in Florence at the Biblioteca Laurenziana. Certain of its unusual features—for example, its threefold treatment of the first word or its optional second version of line 5 (ἄλλο, "another")—are found also in other copies; in line 1, the interpolated syllable νε is used as a pitch indicator—it abbreviates the word "Neanes," the intonation formula of the Deuteros, the authentic form of the mode of the kontakion itself. Since the Psaltikon is a soloist's book, no music is provided for the choral refrain (lines 8 and 9); here the transcription reproduces the soloist's refrain, as found at the end of the prooimion.

Example 5

This melody cannot be the one our fifth-century anonymous had in mind, if indeed he was thinking of any melody at all. It runs counter to the spirit and intention of the poem in that it makes the text almost unintelligible and the argument barely possible to follow; to sing twenty longer stanzas in this style—not to say thirty or forty—would exhaust the listener's attention and consume hours in performance. Obviously, it can only have been composed after the poem had been cut down to size, and a date earlier than the tenth century would appear to be out of the question. Add to this that the melody must be sung from a book and that it thus presupposes a reasonably developed musical notation, and further that no existing copy of the book as a whole can possibly antedate the year 1180. In paleo-Byzantine notation we have only a fragmentary marginal incipit, a single kontakion and oikos, and an abortive attempt to add neumes to a text not originally intended to bear them.

Once again centonization is the basic principle underlying the melodic construction, but it is not the same sort of centonization that we encountered in examples of the syllabic style. The words of the poem are not so much declaimed as adapted to a patchwork of relatively stable melismas, all of which recur again and again in other kontakia of the Plagios deuterou and its authentic counterpart. In transcriptions by Egon Wellesz, two such kontakia are available for comparison—one by Romanos for the Thursday of the Great Canon in *The Music of the Byzantine Church* (1959), the other on St. Symeon Stylite, ascribed to Romanos but probably not by him, in *A History of Byzantine Music and Hymnography* (2nd ed., 1961). And the example before us permits a further and rather more revealing comparison. Two stichera belonging to the Office of this same Sunday incorporate literal quotations from the poem of our fifth-century anonymous. From the first of these the following example reproduces the first and last lines, from the second, "Ηλιος ἀκτῖνας ἔκρυψεν (The sun veiled its rays), the last two. In no other way could the essential antithesis of the two style-varieties, the syllabic and the melismatic, be thrown into such sharp relief. Is it mere coincidence that the mode of the kontakion is also the mode of the two stichera? May we not at least suspect that these quotations have preserved for us some trace of the manner in which our poem was originally sung?

Example 6

Despite everything that has been said about the disparity between the didactic poetry of the kontakion and the elaborately
melismatic music provided for it in the Psaltikon, some copies of
the book actually contain the full text of a single kontakion, with
musical notation throughout, not only for the prooimion and first
oikos, but also for each of the twenty-three oikoi that follow. This
thoroughly exceptional poem, the celebrated Akathistos Hymn, is
one regarded with special reverence by Eastern Orthodoxy. Even
today its twenty-four oikoi are still read aloud at the Orthros of an
appointed day in Lent, either on the fifth Saturday or on some other
day established by local usage or authority; in earlier times it was
evidently customary to sing them, at least in some localities, and to
sing them in the melismatic style that has just been illustrated. In
the Ashburnham manuscript, the whole occupies some forty-eight
large folios, and it was surely not copied without some practical
purpose in mind. The prooimion, of later date than the stanzas it
introduces, has a peculiarly Constantinopolitan flavor. Legend has
it that it was composed by the patriarch Germanus in the year 718,
after the destruction of the Arab fleet that had been threatening the
city, as a thanks offering to the Virgin for Her miraculous intervention. It may be translated as follows:

> To the Invincible Leader the prize of victory,
> the thankful song, as one redeemed from dangers
> I, Thy city, inscribe to Thee, Mother of God.
> And since Thou hast power not to be withstood,
> free me from every sort of peril,
> that I may cry out to Thee:
> Hail, Bride incontaminate!

Wellesz has published a complete transcription, running to eighty-
eight pages, in the Transcripta series of the Monumenta Musicae
Byzantinae (1957), and in the *Muséon* for 1951 one will find the
full text of an eighth- or ninth-century Latin translation, with a
valuable commentary by Michel Huglo.

Even though the Akathistos Hymn is a highly privileged chant,
set apart from all other kontakia wherever the Byzantine rite is
followed, it was local in its origins, its use at first confined to the
church of the Blachernae in the capital. This being the case, we
might suspect the Psaltikon to be a Constantinopolitan product,
and our suspicion would be strengthened if we were to turn to the

kontakion for St. Stephen, which we would find not under December 27, the date of his commemoration according to the Byzantine calendar, but under August 2, the date on which his relics were brought to the imperial city. Turning then to the music for the Mass, or Divine Liturgy, as contained in the two books, we would come upon conclusive evidence of their Constantinopolitan origin. In the Asmatikon, the koinonikon (or communion) for the Dedication of a Church is placed immediately before that for Christmas Day, implying its association with December 23, the dedication date of Hagia Sophia, while the Psaltikon contains proper Alleluia verses for May 11, the day on which the founding of the imperial city is commemorated, and in the older of the two Sinai copies there is actually a rubric directing that they be sung when the patriarch goes up into the forum.

Copies of the Psaltikon and Asmatikon seem never to have been widely disseminated. If we disregard monastic adaptations, which suppress some part of the standard contents, the Psaltikon has been preserved only in eight copies, the Asmatikon in six. Not one of these copies can possibly antedate the late twelfth century; all are of amazingly poor quality; and on first looking into them one may be disappointed to discover how little they actually contain in the way of music for the celebration of the Divine Liturgy. To illustrate this last point, there is inserted here a table comparing, for the variable chants, the combined contents of the two books with the figures given by Bishop Frere for the medieval contents of the Graduale Romanum. Yet it is not that the two books are incom-

Byzantine		Roman	
Introits	1	Introits	150
Prokeimena	30	Graduals	110
Alleluias	59	Alleluias	110
——		Tracts	33
Offertories	2	Offertories	102
Koinonika	26	Communions	150

plete; it is rather that they reflect a rigid economy. In their attitude toward this central part of their formal worship, the churches of the Byzantine rite have remained highly conservative, seldom yielding to the temptation to add to or subtract from the liturgical arrangements codified in the eighth and ninth centuries. Just as the rite provides no proper prefaces, so it provides no proper introits or offertories. For those two parts of what a Western book would call the Proprium Missae, it has only Ordinary chants for which on rare occasions there may be a substitution. The collection of prokeimena seems almost diminutive. Palm Sunday and its vigil, the Saturday of Lazarus, are obliged to share their prokeimena with the Epiphany and the Epiphany vigil; the Christmas prokeimenon serves also for Holy Saturday; of the twelve great feasts, only the Annunciation, the Resurrection, and the Ascension have prokeimena of their own. Much the same thing happens with the Alleluias and koinonika, with the result that those for martyrs and hierarchs are subjected to interminable repetitions. If the melodic tradition of the two books is often untrustworthy, the liturgical tradition to which they bear witness is archaic and extraordinarily revealing.

For the celebration of the Divine Liturgy the Byzantine rite provides three distinct orders. The one regularly used is the Liturgy of St. John Chrysostom; the Liturgy of St. Basil is a more solemn order, used each year on the vigils of Christmas and Epiphany, on five of the Sundays in Lent, on the Thursday and Saturday in Holy Week, and on January 1, the feast of St. Basil; the Liturgy of the Presanctified is a Lenton weekday order, corresponding in intention to the Roman Missa Praesanctificatorum, but it is used also on the Wednesday and Friday in the week preceding Lent and on the first three days in Holy Week (in earlier times its use extended even to Good Friday itself). Fortunately for us, however, music is little affected by the variety of these provisions. The substitution of the Liturgy of St. Basil for that of St. John Chrysostom means only that the Sanctus will be sung in a more elaborate style, while the use of the Liturgy of the Presanctified, which follows on a curtailed celebration of the Vespers of the day, means only that a special offertory will replace the standard one (since there are normally no readings from the New Testament on weekdays during Lent, there will normally be no responsoria, and since there is no consecration, there will be no Sanctus). For the rest, when stripped to its bare essentials, the arrangement of the Ordinary and Proper chants agrees almost exactly with the Roman order.

Byzantine	Roman
Litany and Antiphons	Introit and Kyrie
Trisagion	Gloria
Prokeimenon and Epistle	Epistle and Gradual (or Alleluia)
Alleluia	Alleluia (or Tract)
Gospel	Gospel
Offertory and Creed	Creed and Offertory
Preface and Sanctus	Preface and Sanctus
——	Agnus dei
Koinonikon	Communion

The opening litany, to whose several petitions the choirs respond with the refrain "Kyrie eleison," is preserved for us in Latin paraphrase in such litanies as the Gallican "Dicamus omnes" (a facsimile after Paris lat. 903 in D. J. Grout's *History of Western Music*) and the various "preces" of the Mozarabic and Ambrosian rites, while the correspondence of the three preliminary antiphons (their texts taken from Psalms 91, 92, and 94) to the Roman introit is confirmed for us by the "officium" of the Missa graeca for Saint-Denis, which takes its text from Psalm 94—awkwardly transliterated in the customaries of Saint-Denis as "Zeveta a gallia" (Δεῦτε ἀγαλλιασώμεθα). In the Byzantine rite, the last verse of the antiphon from Psalm 94 is actually designated "introitus" (εἰσοδικόν), for it is sung during the solemn entrance (εἴσοδος) of the clergy with the book of the Gospels. It will be recalled that Amalarius, who visited Constantinople and Hagia Sophia in 813–814, records having heard this psalm sung there "in principio Missae" (*De ordine Antiphonarii,* xxi). Current editions of the Byzantine service books also provide a number of Proper antiphons, but with the possible exception of those for the Exaltation of the Cross, for Christmas, and for Easter, none of these can possibly be genuine, and our earlier sources have music only for the Ordinary third antiphon and introit—a florid psalm tone with the refrain Σῶσον ἡμᾶς, υἱὲ θεοῦ, ὁ ἀναστὰς ἐκ νεκρῶν, ψάλλοντάς σοι· ἀλληλούϊα ("Save us, Son of God, risen from the dead, we who sing to Thee: Alleluia"). Illustration is scarcely necessary.

Following the preliminary antiphons and preceding the scriptural lessons (for in the Byzantine rite the Gloria in excelsis still occupies its time-honored position at the end of the Morning Office), we encounter the venerable Trisagion, common property of all Eastern rites, a chant widely disseminated as early as 451 and the Council of Chalcedon. That its vogue soon spread to the West, first to Mozarabic Spain, then to Gallican France, and from thence to the Adoratio Crucis of the Roman rite, is a story too well known to call for repetition here. For such a chant there is, of course, no "original" melody. The one here illustrated is the one transmitted by our oldest copies of the Asmatikon; it is just possible, however, that one or more settings rather older than this one have been preserved for us imbedded in idiomela of the Sticherarion that quote or paraphrase the official text, with or without Trinitarian "tropes" (the curious reader will find examples in Tillyard's *Hymns of the Sticherarium for November* [no. 27] and *Hymns of the Pentecostarium* [no. 95]). The design AAB, which underlies the setting shown in our example, is also characteristic of all other known versions of the Trisagion, including those transmitted by the Sticherarion and those found in the service books of the Latin rites. The chant is to be sung three times, the Asmatikon directs; then, after a doxology, its final clause is sung once again. On days associated in earlier times with the rite of baptism, notably Epiphany and Holy Saturday, there is substituted for the Trisagion the "Ὅσοι εἰς Χριστὸν ἐβαπτίσθητε ("Quicumque enim in Christo baptizati estis," Galatians 3:27); another substitute, restricted to feasts of the Holy Cross, notably September 14 and the Wednesday of mid-Lent, is Τὸν σταυρόν σου προσκυνοῦμεν ("Crucem tuam adoramus"). For these, too, our oldest copies of the Asmatikon provide settings in much the same melismatic style as that used for the Trisagion itself. Of the two, Τὸν σταυρόν σου προσκυνοῦμεν has found its way into the Latin rites of Benevento, Milan, and Rome; Wellesz has studied the Beneventan version in his *Eastern Elements,* while Huglo, in his contribution to the *Proceedings of the Thirteenth International Congress of Byzantine Studies,* has sought to show that the Ambrosian melody retains some traces of a simpler Byzantine setting.

Example 7

Here we meet for the first time with the so-called "asmatic letters"—the interpolated consonants γγ (or γκ), ν, and χ, and the conventional character ᐃ ; later on we shall meet with them again and in greater profusion. These seemingly arbitrary interpolations constitute an extraordinarily stable feature of the written tradition for the Asmatikon, equally characteristic of paleo-Slavonic copies of the book, for while there may be disagreements from copy to copy over the number of repetitions to be given to the single vowels, the position of the "asmatic letters" appears to have been agreed upon from the first. To demonstrate that their distribution is by no means irrational and haphazard and that the phenomenon itself is intimately and logically connected with the recurrence of melodic formulas would require more extensive illustration than would be appropriate here. Other interpolations seen in the example are the intonation formulas of the Deuteros and Plagios tetartou—"Neanes" and "Nehagie"—and the exhortation λέγετε (Dicite), perhaps sung, like the intonations, by a precentor.

For the responsoria of the Divine Liturgy—the prokeimena and the allelouiaria—we shall need to turn to the Psaltikon. Without exception their texts are drawn from the liturgical Psalter, and again without exception all have at least two verses, some as many as three. Revealing as they are in their bearing on comparative liturgics, these chants have all but disappeared from present-day practice. Today the prokeimenon is simply recited *in tono lectionis* by the reader of the Epistle, immediately before his announcement that there is to be a reading from such and such a book of the New Testament, while the Alleluia verses, often omitted altogether, are at best chanted by a precentor on an uninflected reciting pitch. It is noteworthy, too, that in presenting the prokeimena of the liturgy the Psaltikon limits itself to those clauses of the verses and refrain that are sung by the soloist; thus what we have is fragmentary and inconclusive, and illustration here would serve no useful purpose.

In the Psaltikon, the responsoria of the liturgy are arranged by the modes rather than by the calendar, and in some copies each modal series within the section devoted to the allelouiaria is introduced by a setting of the Alleluia refrain. Its brevity and the absence of a jubilus need occasion no surprise, for it is evident that it restricts itself to the opening of the refrain, as sung by the soloist; the verses, too, break off at the point where the choirs take over. Thus what we have is again fragmentary and inconclusive, but it is at the same time substantial enough to warrant illustration. For most feasts of the Baptist, and for commemorations of certain martyrs, the Byzantine rite prescribes as the first of its two Alleluia verses Psalm 91:13. Here the solo initium of the refrain may profitably be compared with its counterparts in such classical Roman Alleluias as "De profundis" (or "Confitebuntur caeli") and "Exsultate Deo" (or "Jubilate Deo"); equally instructive is a comparison of the verse with the Roman Alleluia verse "Justus ut palma," and if one makes this comparison, one will discover that just as the Psaltikon implies that the choirs are to sing the concluding word, πληθυνθήσεται, so the Graduale Romanum calls for choral performance of the corresponding word, "multiplicabitur."

Example 8

ἦχος δ´   Sinai 1280, f. 49

Αλ—λη ———— λου—ου ———— ου—ι—α

The example before us, brief as it is, gives a very fair idea of what the Byzantine Alleluia verse is like, not only in its general outlines, but also in the degree of its elaboration and in its declamation of the text. Melismatic development is restricted to the beginning of the verse and to the medial cadence. There is no singling out of significant words within a distinction, as sometimes happens in Western chant. Except at the end of the verse, there is no florid extension of unaccented final syllables. Text accent and musical accent stand in the closest possible relationship. Within a given mode, the Byzantine Alleluia verse knows only one form of final cadence, and this means that it knows only six such forms in all, for—as in Ambrosian chant—there are no F-mode Alleluias. As to the body of the verse, this is a centonate construction, and if one may consider all centonate melodies constructed from the same materials as variants of one another, then one may also reduce the 124 verses of the Byzantine Alleluia cycle to six basic types. And just as there are only six forms of final cadence and only six basic types of verse, so there are only six refrains, and the precentor must know them by heart, for most copies of the Psaltikon omit them entirely and no copy enters any one of them more than once.

Additional examples of the Byzantine Alleluia verse are transcribed by Wellesz in *The Music of the Byzantine Church* and in the second edition of his *History of Byzantine Music and Hymnography.* Wellesz has also touched, in his *Eastern Elements,* on the problem posed by the Alleluias with Greek text, formerly sung at the Lateran Basilica in Rome during the Pontifical Vespers of Easter week

and at certain Masses within the octave, including that for Dominica in Albis, a problem first broached by Hugo Gaisser in the *Rassegna gregoriana* for 1902. More recently Christian Thodberg has returned to the problem in *Der byzantinische Alleluiarion-zyklus* (1966), a searching analysis of the Alleluias of the Psaltikon to which is appended an exhaustive study of the Greek Alleluias sung at the Lateran, based on the several manuscripts of the so-called "Old Roman" tradition. Conceding that four of the Vesper Alleluias are mere adaptations of the Greek Psalter text to a Latin model melody, Thodberg concludes that the remaining three cannot be disposed of so simply; these are sung also or exclusively at Mass and their contacts with the corresponding Byzantine melodies, as transmitted by the Psaltikon, seem to him so numerous and so striking as to point unmistakably to common origin.

> When one compares them with one another directly, it appears impossible to explain the relation of the Western melodies to the Byzantine as due to a series of *coincidences.* Rightly understood, it is an overall agreement with respect not only to the general contours of the melodic line, but also to a number of its details. . . . On the strength of this we may in the end cautiously advance the hypothesis of the Western adoption of certain Byzantine Alleluia-verse melodies.

A tempting hypothesis, surely, but one that presents real difficulties. Considering the gap of five to six centuries that intervenes between the probable date of the presumed adoption of the melodies at the Lateran and the beginnings of the written tradition for them in East and West, considering also the poor quality of the sources on either side, difficulties to which Thodberg himself draws attention, it is only prudent to reserve judgment.

With the singing of the Alleluia, the solemn reading of the Gospel, and the chanting of a litany for the catechumens, the first part of the Divine Liturgy is at an end. After the chanting of a litany for the faithful, the service continues with the offertory, or cherubic hymn, and for this we return to the Asmatikon, where we find single settings for two such hymns—the ordinary one (Οἱ τὰ χερουβίμ), with its pseudo-Dionysian overtones, and the one substituted for it on Holy Saturday, in earlier times also at services for

the dedication of a church or for the anniversary of such a dedication (Σιγησάτω πᾶσα σάρξ).

The first of the two hymns is represented in the Asmatikon only by its first line and by its final Alleluia. Either this setting was regarded in its day as too well known to require copying or the intervening lines were sung by a soloist whose melody the Psaltikon has not preserved. As with the Trisagion, there is, of course, no "original" melody for this text—the singing of a cherubic hymn to accompany the solemn entrance of the clergy bearing the elements of the eucharistic sacrifice was made a rule as early as 574 under the Emperor Justin II, and the general view is that in so ruling the emperor was simply giving official sanction to what was already a well-established custom. With the fourteenth century and the appearance of the Koukouzelian "Orders of Service," new settings of the text begin to make their appearance, and in later sources it is not unusual to find whole sections devoted to them, the settings arranged in the order of the modal cycle. In the West, where in transliterated Greek or in Latin translation it became the usual offertory of the Missa graeca, the poem had already attained a certain currency as early as the tenth century. In the MS Paris, Bibl. Mazarine 384, it is translated as follows:

> *Qui cherubim mystice imitamur*
> *et vivificae trinitatis ter sanctum hymnum offerimus*
> *omnem nunc mundam deponamus solicitudinem*
> *sicuti regem omnium suscepturi*
> *cui ab angelicis invisibiliter ministratur ordinibus:*
> *Alleluia.*

In illustration, however, it has seemed preferable to present the second of the two hymns, not only because the setting found in the Asmatikon is complete, but also because as a setting of a text rarely called for it may be able to claim a certain degree of authenticity. It is far too long for reproduction here, but one can base an account of the whole on a transcription of its first two lines and of its final Alleluia. In our example, the division of the single lines into distinctions follows the characteristic punctuation of the sources. The beginning of the poem may be quoted in Gerald Moultrie's metrical translation:

Let all mortal flesh keep silence
And with fear and trembling stand.

Example 9

For the most part, the melody of our hymn remains within the narrow compass of the fifth G to d, rarely ascending in its later course to the high f and then only at significant words—the low D with which it begins is touched only once. The little four-note figure that concludes Distinction 1 also concludes many of those that follow, occurring ten times in all—in our example it is seen again over the final syllables of the words βροτεία and τρόμου. Still more frequent are the recurrences of the melisma first encountered over the word πᾶσα (Distinction 2); one will find it twice again in Distinction 5, once more in the final Alleluia, and in one form or another twenty times in the course of the melody as a whole. Invariably it is adapted to two syllables, and it is always adapted in the same way, the position of the second syllable being precisely fixed. Thus the essential material of which the melody is composed remains roughly the same from line to line, its several elements always recurring in roughly the same order; and the whole is perhaps best described as an elaborate, freely psalmodic treatment of the successive lines of the poem, its construction closely resembling that of the Roman tract.

In addition to the two hymns transmitted by the Asmatikon, there is still another—Νῦν αἱ δυνάμεις ("Now the celestial powers")—the ordinary offertory of the Liturgy of the Presanctified, documented as early as the year 615. For this the Koùkouzelian "Orders of Service" preserve a melody that they describe as "ancient"; its opening lines have been transcribed by Kenneth Levy in a contribution to the *Journal of the American Musicological Society* for 1963, and in this one will also find a partial transcription of another setting of Σιγησάτω πᾶσα σάρξ, as transmitted by the "Orders of Service," and an exhaustive discussion of the troparion Τοῦ δείπνου σου (the prototype of the Ambrosian ingressa or post-Evangelium "Coenae tuae mirabili"), a chant sung on Maundy Thursday both as koinonikon and as a substitute for the offertory.

In former times, in the great public churches of the empire, on days appointed for the commemoration of the several church councils, the acts of the councils were solemnly read at the Divine Liturgy, and at the commemorations of the councils of Chalcedon (451), Constantinople (680), and Nicaea (787) these acts incorporated the official text of the creed. Sometimes the text of the acts was provided with ekphonetic signs, and thus we have for the creed a sort of musical notation, however rudimentary; Gudrun Engberg has published this in the *Classica et Mediaevalia* for 1962 after the eleventh-century MS Oxford, Bodleian Library, Holkam 6. But in this form the creed was chanted only three times a year, not by the choirs and congregation or by the presiding dignitary, but by an appointed reader, and the chanting took place not after the offertory, but between the Trisagion and the prokeimenon. In its position after the offertory there is little reason to suppose that it has ever been sung; today it is simply recited by the choirs and congregation, and the probabilities are that this has always been the rule. Strangely enough, it is to Western manuscripts that we must turn for the earliest appearances of the Greek text of the creed with a genuinely musical notation.

The same is true also of the Greek text of the Sanctus. In the

West, melodies in Latin neumes with the text in transliterated Greek are found as early as the tenth and eleventh centuries in manuscripts from Aquitania, northern Italy, Germany, and Switzerland, while in the East our earliest important sources with musical notation for the Sanctus are the fourteenth-century copies of the Koukouzelian "Orders of Service," beginning with the year 1336. The Aquitanian and north Italian melodies are for all practical purposes one and the same, and the innumerable copies of the "Orders of Service" limit themselves to a single formula. Taking as his point of departure an earlier essay by Michel Huglo, published in 1950, Kenneth Levy has subjected the whole problem of the music for the Sanctus in East and West to a searching examination in volume V (1958–1963) of the *Annales musicologiques,* his cautiously stated conclusion being that the basic identity of the Eastern and Western melodies seems "reasonably certain." Levy's definitive study is abundantly illustrated and includes, in facsimile and transcription, the several melodies compared.

While the Asmatikon, in presenting the choral music of the Divine Liturgy, ignores the creed and Sanctus entirely, its provisions for the koinonikon, or communion antiphon, are the most lavish and varied of any that it makes. Our copies of the book arrange their melodies for it in two cycles: one in the order of the eight modes, with eight settings for each of the three texts most frequently used—those for Saturdays (Psalm 32:1), Sundays (Psalm 148:1), and the Liturgy of the Presanctified (Psalm 33:9); the other in the order of the calendar, with the koinonika for outstanding feasts, several of these in more than one setting—notably those for feasts of the Blessed Virgin (Psalm 115:4) and for commemorations of hierarchs (Psalm 111:6). Thus, while the koinonika limit themselves to twenty-six texts, as indicated in our earlier table, the number of distinct melodies is well in excess of twenty-six, varying however from one copy of the book to another. In this respect the koinonika differ from the prokeimena and allelouiaria, and they differ from them again in drawing, not only on the liturgical Psalter, but also on other books of the Old and New Testaments; there are even two nonscriptural texts—one for Maundy Thursday, the other for Easter Sunday—and these are without the Alleluia refrain with which all scriptural koinonika conclude. The koinonikon for Maundy Thursday has been published by Levy in the essay previously referred to in connection with the cherubic hymn, and it is there accompanied by a wealth of comparative material, including quotations from a number of other koinonika, some from the Asmatikon, some from the "Orders of Service," by a penetrating commentary, and by an analysis of the relations between the Byzantine melody and its paleo-Slavonic counterpart that has profoundly affected all later research in this area. Here a shorter illustration will serve the purpose, the koinonikon for Easter Sunday, chosen less to round out the modal cycle than because it provides in miniature an excellent summary of the characteristic procedures of the style. Its text has influenced that of the Ambrosian Transitorium "Corpus Christi accepimus," although the two melodies are wholly unrelated. A literal translation would read:

> *Corpus Christi accipite,*
> *fontem immortalem gustate.*

Example 10

Once again the division of the single lines into distinctions follows the characteristic punctuation of our source. The evident purpose of this seemingly eccentric and often inconsistent punctuation is to divide the melody into its component parts, and so divided it reveals itself as made up of shorter and longer formulas, two of which recur in the course of our example and most of which can be found over and over again in the asmatic repertory, sometimes at the same pitch, sometimes at the fifth above, associated not so much with particular modes as with particular arrangements of whole and half steps. And if one will compare Distinction 3 with the ending of Distinction 6, or Distinction 5 with Distinction 15, one will discover that each appearance of a melodic formula is provided with the same "asmatic letters" distributed in the same way. Certain ornamental groups and longer melismas the Asmatikon shares with the Sticherarion and Heirmologion, but its idiom, which makes little use of syllabic declamation and is infinitely richer in set formulas, is in the last analysis an idiom *sui generis.*

Additions to the asmatic collection of koinonika were still being made as late as the eleventh century, and early copies of the Typikon of Hagia Sophia actually enable us to follow the final stages of this development. Certain koinonika, including all of those that exist in more than one setting, must belong to an old layer, for both in the Patmos copy of the ninth to tenth century and in the Jerusalem copy, perhaps a century younger, a given koinonikon belonging to this group is sometimes described as ἀρχαῖον (ancient) to distinguish it from an alternate, described as νέον (new). But neither copy calls for all the koinonika of the collection, although the Jerusalem copy is in this respect more complete than the one from Patmos. The probabilities are that several of the koinonika for outstanding feasts are relatively late compositions. The Koukouzelian "Orders of Service" bring new settings of the established texts, and in time the traditional ones are forgotten. But even today the koinonikon is still sung in a highly florid style that recalls that of the Asmatikon, and, with the cherubic hymn, it remains the most prominent and most striking feature of the music for the Divine Liturgy.

Select Bibliography

Biezen, J. van. *The Middle-Byzantine Kanon-Notation of Manuscript H.* Bilthoven, 1968.

Brou, Louis. "Les chants en langue grecque dans les liturgies latines." *Sacris erudiri,* I (1948), 165–180; IV (1952), 226–138.

Christ, W., and Paranikas, M. *Anthologia graeca carminum christianorum.* Leipzig, 1871.

Conomos, D. E. *Byzantine Trisagia and Cheroubika of the Fourteenth and Fifteenth Centuries.* Salonica, 1975.

Di Salvo, Bartolomeo. "Asmatikòn." *Bollettino della Badia greca di Grottaferrata,* XVI (1962), 135–158.

Engberg, Gudrun. "Les Credos du Synodicon." *Classica et Mediaevalia,* XXIII (1962), 135–158.

Fleischer, Oskar. *Die spätgriechische Notenschrift.* Neumenstudien 3. Berlin, 1904.

Floros, Constantin. "Das Kontakion." *Deutsche Vierteljahrsschrift für Literaturwissenschaft und Geistesgeschichte,* XXXIV (1960), 84–106.

———— *Universale Neumenkunde.* 3 vols. Kassel, 1970.

Follieri, Enrica. *Initia hymnorum ecclesiae graecae.* 5 vols. Studi e testi 211–215 bis. Vatican City, 1960–66.

Gaisser, Hugo. "Brani greci nella liturgia latina." *Rassegna gregoriana,* I (1902), nos. 7–9.

Gastoué, Amédée. *Introduction à la paléographie musicale byzantine.* Paris, 1907.

Gerbert, Martin. *De cantu et musica sacra.* 2 vols. St. Blasien, 1774.

Haas, Max. *Byzantinische und slavische Notationen.* Paleographie der Musik, I, Faszikel 2. Cologne, 1972.

Handschin, Jacques. *Das Zeremonienwerk Kaiser Konstantins und die sangbare Dichtung.* Basel, 1942.

———— "Sur quelques tropaires grecs traduits en latin." *Annales musicologiques,* II (1954), 27–60.

Høeg, Carsten. "La théorie de la musique byzantine." *Revue des études grecques,* XXXV (1922), 321–334.

———— *La notation ekphonétique.* MMB, Subsidia 1, Fasc. 2. Copenhagen, 1935.

———— *The Hymns of the Hirmologium.* Pt. I. MMB, Transcripta 6. Copenhagen, 1952.

———— "Les rapports de la musique chrétienne et de la musique de l'antiquité classique." *Byzantion,* XXV–XXVII (1955–57), 383–412.

———— and Zuntz, Günther. *Prophetologium, Pars prima.* MMB, Lectionaria 1, Pars prima. Copenhagen, 1939–69.

Huglo, Michel. "La tradition occidentale des mélodies byzantines du Sanctus." *Der kultische Gesang der abendländischen Kirche.* Cologne, 1950, pp. 40–46.

———— "L'ancienne version latine de l'hymne acathiste." *Muséon,* LXIV (1951), 27–61.

———— "Les chants de la Missa greca de Saint-Denis." *Essays Presented to Egon Wellesz.* Oxford, 1966, pp. 74–83.

———— "Rélations musicales entre Byzance et l'Occident." *Proceedings of the Thirteenth International Congress of Byzantine Studies.* London, 1967, pp. 267–280.

Husmann, Heinrich. "Hymnus und Troparion." *Jahrbuch des staatlichen Instituts für Musikforschung* Berlin, 1971, pp. 7–86.

———— "Modulation und Transposition in den bi- und trimodalen Stichera." *Archiv für Musikwissenschaft,* XXVII (1970–71), 1–22.

———— "Die oktomodalen Stichera und die Entwicklung des byzantinischen Oktoechos." *Ibid.,* 304–325.

———— "Modalitätsprobleme des psaltischen Stils." *Ibid.,* XXVIII (1971–72), 44–72.

———— "Strophenbau und Kontrafakturtechnik der Stichera." *Ibid.,* XXIX (1972–73), 151–161, 213–234.

———— "Ein syrisches Sticherarion mit paläobyzantinischer Notation (Sinai Syr. 261)." *Hamburger Jahrbuch für Musikwissenschaft,* I (1975), 9–57.

Jammers, Ewald. *Musik in Byzanz, im päpstlichen Rom und im Frankenreich.* Abhandlungen der Heidelberger Akademie der Wissenschaften, Phil.-hist. Klasse, Jahrgang 1962, 1. Abhandlung. Heidelberg, 1962.

———— "Byzanz und die abendländische Musik." *Reallexikon der Byzantinistik,* Reihe A, I. Amsterdam, 1968, 169–227.

Kirchoff, Kilian. *Hymnen der Ostkirche.* Münster, 1960.

———— *Osterjubel der Ostkirche.* Münster, 1961.

_____ *Die Ostkirche betet.* 2 vols. Münster, 1962–63.

Levy, Kenneth. "The Byzantine Sanctus and Its Modal Tradition in East and West." *Annales musicologiques,* VI (1958–63), 7–67.

_____ "A Hymn for Thursday in Holy Week." *Journal of the American Musicological Society,* XVI (1963), 127–175.

Marzi, Giovanni. *Melodia e nomos nella musica bizantina.* Studi pubblicati dall'Istituto di filologia classica 8, Bologna, 1960.

Monumenta Musicae Byzantinae, Série principale. Copenhagen, 1933–75.

_____ 1. Sticherarium, ed. Carsten Høeg, H. J. W. Tillyard and Egon Wellesz [Vienna, Theol. gr. 181].

_____ 2. Hirmologium Athoum, ed. Carsten Høeg [Iviron 470].

_____ 3. Hirmologium Cryptense, ed. Lorenzo Tardo [Grottaferrata, E.γ.ii].

_____ 4. Contacarium Ashburnhamense, ed. Carsten Høeg [Florence, Bibl. Laurenziana, Ashb. 64].

_____ 5. Fragmenta Chiliandarica, ed. Roman Jakobson. 2 vols. [Chilandari 307 and 308].

_____ 6. Contacarium Palaeoslavicum Mosquense, ed. Arne Bugge [Moscow, Musée hist., 9].

_____ 7. Specimina notationum antiquiorum, ed. Oliver Strunk. Pars principalis and Pars suppletoria.

_____ 8. Hirmologium Sabbaiticum, ed. Jørgen Raasted. Pars principalis (2 vols.) and Pars suppletoria [Saba 83].

_____ 9. Triodium Athoum, ed. Enrica Follieri and Oliver Strunk. Pars principalis and Pars suppletoria [Vatopedi 1488].

Petrescu, J.-D. *Les idiomèles et le canon de l'office de Noël.* Paris, 1932.

_____ *Études de paléographie musicale byzantine.* Bucharest, 1965.

Pitra, J.-B. *L'hymnographie de l'église grecque.* Rome, 1867.

Raasted, Jørgen. *Intonation Formulas and Modal Signatures in Byzantine Musical Manuscripts.* MMB, Subsidia 7. Copenhagen, 1966.

Richter, Lukas. "Antike Überlieferungen in der byzantinischen Musiktheorie." *Deutsches Jahrbuch der Musikwissenschaft,* VI (1961), 75–115.

Schirò, Giuseppe. "Problemi heirmologici." *Proceedings of the Thirteenth International Congress of Byzantine Studies.* London, 1967.

Schlötterer, Reinhold. "Edition byzantinischer Musik." *Musikalische Edition im Wandel der Zeiten.* Kassel, 1971, pp. 28–49.

_____, Jammers, E., Schmid, H., and Waeltner, E. "Byzantinisches in der karolingischen Musik." *Berichte zum XI. Internationalen Byzantiner-Kongress.* Munich, 1958.

Tardo, Lorenzo. *L'antica melurgia bizantina.* Grottaferrata, 1938.

_____ *L'ottoeco nei mss. melurgici.* Grottaferrata, 1955.

Thibaut, J.-B. *Origine byzantine de la notation neumatique de l'église latine.* Bibliothèque musicologique 3. Paris, 1907.

———— *Monuments de la notation ekphonétique et hagiopolite de l'église grecque.* St. Petersburg, 1913.

Thodberg, Christian. *Der byzantinische Alleluiarionzyklus.* MMB, Subsidia 8. Copenhagen, 1966.

Tillyard, H. J. W. "The Problem of Byzantine Neumes." *Journal of Hellenic Studies,* XLI (1921), 29–49.

———— *Handbook of the Middle Byzantine Musical Notation.* MMB, Subsidia 1, Fasc. 1. Copenhagen, 1935; 2nd impression, 1970.

———— *The Hymns of the Sticherarium for November.* MMB, Transcripta 2. Copenhagen, 1938.

———— *The Hymns of the Octoechus.* MMB, Transcripta 3 and 5. Copenhagen, 1940 and 1949.

———— *Twenty Canons from the Trinity Hirmologium.* MMB, Transcripta 4. Boston, 1952.

———— "Byzantine Music about A.D. 1100." *The Musical Quarterly,* XXXIV (1953), 223–231.

———— *The Hymns of the Hirmologium, Part 3 ².* MMB, Transcripta 8. Copenhagen, 1956.

———— *The Hymns of the Pentecostarium.* MMB, Transcripta 7. Copenhagen, 1960.

Velimirović, Milos. *Byzantine Elements in Early Slavic Chant: The Hirmologium.* Main volume and Appendices. MMB, Subsidia 4. Copenhagen, 1960.

———— "Musique byzantine." *Encyclopédie des musiques sacrées,* II. Paris, 1969, 145–164.

———— "The Byzantine Heirmos and Heirmologion." *Gattungen der Musik in Einzeldarstellungen.* 1. Folge. Bern and Munich, 1973, pp. 192–244.

Verdeil, R. Palikarova. *La musique byzantine chez les bulgares et les Russes* MMB, Subsidia 3. Copenhagen, 1953.

Wellesz, Egon. "Die Struktur des serbischen Oktoëchos." *Zeitschrift für Musikwissenschaft,* II (1919–20), 140–148.

———— "Die Rhythmik der byzantinischen Neumen." *Ibid.,* II (1919–20), 617–638; III (1920–21), 321–336.

———— "Beiträge zur byzantinische Kirchenmusik." *Ibid.,* III (1920–21), 482–502.

———— "Die byzantinischen Lektionszeichen." *Ibid.,* XI (1928–29), 513–534.

———— "Studien zur Palaeographie der byzantinischen Musik. 1. Die prosodischen und ekphonetischen Zeichen." *Ibid.,* XII (1929–30), 385–397.

_____ "Studien zur byzantinischen Musik." *Ibid.*, XVI (1933–34), 213–228, 414–422.

_____ *Trésor de musique byzantine.* Paris, 1934.

_____ *Die Hymnen des Sticherarium für September.* MMB, Transcripta 1. Copenhagen, 1936.

_____ "Words and Music in Byzantine Liturgy." *The Musical Quarterly,* XXX (1947), 297–310.

_____ *Eastern Elements in Western Chant.* MMB, Subsidia 2. Boston, 1947; Copenhagen, 1967.

_____ *A History of Byzantine Music and Hymnography.* Oxford, 1949; 2nd ed., 1961.

_____ "Early Byzantine Neumes." *The Musical Quarterly,* XXXVIII (1952), 68–79.

_____ "Das Prooimion des Akathistos." *Die Musikforschung,* VI (1953), 193–206.

_____ "The 'Akathistos': A Study in Byzantine Hymnography." *Dumbarton Oaks Papers,* IX–X (1956), 141–174.

_____ *The Akathistos Hymn.* MMB, Transcripta 9. Copenhagen, 1957.

_____ *The Music of the Byzantine Church.* Anthology of Music, 15. Cologne, 1959.

_____ *Die Hymnen der Ostkirche.* Basilienses de Musica Orationes, 1. Basel, 1962.

_____ "Byzantine Music and Liturgy." *The Cambridge Medieval History,* IV, Part 2. Cambridge, 1967, 134–160.

Wellesz, Egon, and Velimirović, Miloš. *Studies in Eastern Chant.* 3 vols. London, 1966–73.

Westrup, Jack, ed. *Essays Presented to Egon Wellesz.* Oxford, 1966.

APPENDIX A

Index of Proper Names

APPENDIX B

Index of Places and Institutions

APPENDIX C

Index of Principal Manuscripts

APPENDIX D

Index of Principal Subjects